W9-BBO-012

Domestic Violence

SOURCEBOOK

Fifth Edition

Fifth Edition

Domestic Violence

SOURCEBOOK

Basic Consumer Health Information about Intimate Partner Abuse, Stalking, Sexual Harassment, and Human Trafficking, Including Facts about Risk Factors, Warning Signs, and Forms of Physical, Sexual, Mental, Emotional, and Financial Abuse in Women, Men, Adolescents, Immigrants, Elders, and Other Specific Populations

Along with Facts about Digital Dating Abuse and Cyberbullying, Victims and Abusers, Strategies for Preventing and Intervening in Abusive Situations, Interventions through Workplaces and Faith Communities, Tips Regarding Legal Protections, a Glossary of Related Terms, and a Directory of Resources for Further Information

OMNIGRAPHICS

615 Griswold, Ste. 901, Detroit, MI 48226

Bibliographic Note

Because this page cannot legibly accommodate all the copyright notices, the Bibliographic Note portion of the Preface constitutes an extension of the copyright notice.

* * *

Omnigraphics, Inc.

Editorial Services provided by Omnigraphics, Inc.,
a division of Relevant Information, Inc.

Keith Jones, *Managing Editor*

* * *

Copyright © 2016 Relevant Information, Inc.

ISBN 978-0-7808-1460-8
E-ISBN 978-0-7808-1459-2

Library of Congress Cataloging-in-Publication Data

Names: Omnigraphics, Inc., issuing body.

Title: Domestic violence sourcebook : basic consumer information about intimate partner abuse, stalking, sexual harassment, and human trafficking, including facts about risk factors, warning signs, and forms of physical, sexual, mental, emotional, and financial abuse in women, men, adolescents, recent immigrants, elders, and other specific populations; along with facts about victims and abusers, strategies for preventing and intervening in abusive situations, guidelines for managing emergencies and making safety plans, interventions through workplaces and faith communities, tips regarding legal protections, a glossary of related terms, and a directory of resources for further information.

Description: Fifth edition. | Detroit, MI : Omnigraphics, Inc., [2016] | Series: Health reference series | Includes bibliographical references and index.

Identifiers: LCCN 2015046612 (print) | LCCN 2015047904 (ebook) | ISBN 9780780814608 (hardcover : alk. paper) | ISBN 9780780814592 (ebook)

Subjects: LCSH: Family violence--United States. | Victims of family violence--Services for--United States. | Sexual abuse victims--Services for--United States.

Classification: LCC HV6626.2 .D685 2016 (print) | LCC HV6626.2 (ebook) | DDC 362.82/920973--dc23

LC record available at http://lccn.loc.gov/2015046612

Table of Contents

Part III: Abuse in Specific Populations

ix

Part IV: Preventing and Intervening in Domestic Violence

Part V: Emergency Management, Moving Out, and Moving On

Part VI: Additional Help and Information

Preface

About This Book

The scope of domestic violence in our society is staggering. Its victims include men and women and people of every age, race, ethnicity, religion, sexual orientation, and economic level. According to the National Coalition Against Domestic Violence (NCADV), an estimated 10 million people each year (and one in every three women and one in every four men during their lifetime) will experience physical violence in the hands of their intimate partners. One in seven women and one in eighteen men have been stalked, and one in six women has experienced an attempted or completed rape. Many of those caught in the cycle of domestic violence feel isolated and powerless and do not know the avenues of help available to them.

Domestic Violence Sourcebook, Fifth Edition offers information to victims of domestic violence and to those who care about them. It defines domestic abuse, describes the risk factors for abuse, and offers tips for recognizing abuse. It describes the different types of abuse, including rape, physical violence, emotional and verbal abuse, stalking, and human trafficking. Information about abuse in specific populations—including the lesbian, gay, bisexual, and transgender communities, immigrant communities, teen and elder populations, and within the military—is also included. In addition, the book discusses tips for building healthy relationships and intervening in abusive situations, and it offers detailed guidelines for managing emergency situations, protecting oneself before, during, and after a separation from an abuser, navigating the legal system, and preventing workplace violence. The book concludes with a glossary of related terms and directories of resources for additional help and information.

How to Use This Book

This book is divided into parts and chapters. Parts focus on broad areas of interest. Chapters are devoted to single topics within a part.

Part I: Facts about Domestic Violence, Stalking, and Sexual Harassment provides basic information about what domestic violence is, the prevalence of domestic violence, which characteristics and situations place victims at risk, and how victims, abusers, and those wanting to help can identify abuse. It also explains what stalking and sexual harassment are and what victims can do to increase their safety and end the abuse.

Part II: Intimate Partner Abuse describes the different types of intimate partner abuse and their physical, emotional, and socioeconomic effects. It also describes the effect domestic violence has on children exposed to it and discusses the co-occurrence of child abuse and intimate partner abuse.

Part III: Abuse in Specific Populations provides information about child abuse, teen dating violence, abuse of men, pregnant and disabled women, elder abuse, and abuse in the lesbian, gay, bisexual, and transgender population. It also describes the special issues involved when the abuse occurs within the military, or when the abuse occurs within the immigrant community. The part concludes with a discussion of human trafficking and the types of assistance available to its victims.

Part IV: Preventing and Intervening in Domestic Violence explains how to recognize and build healthy relationships. It discusses how parents, caretakers, friends, co-workers, faith communities, healthcare providers, and others can intervene in cases of abuse. It also describes measures employers can take to prevent violence in the workplace and how the legal system can help victims of domestic abuse.

Part V: Emergency Management, Moving Out, and Moving On discusses why victims stay with their abusers and details what victims will need to know if they decide to leave their abusive relationship and move on. It explains the steps involved in calling the police, preserving and collecting evidence, and documenting abuse. It describes the sources of help available to victims of domestic abuse and offers suggestions for safety planning, and safeguarding children. It also provides detailed information on Internet safety, identity protection, and how to navigate the legal system.

Part VI: Additional Help and Information includes a glossary of terms related to domestic violence and directories of resources offering additional help and support, including domestic violence hotlines, child abuse reporting numbers, and programs offering shelter for pets of domestic violence victims.

Bibliographic Note

This volume contains documents and excerpts from publications issued by the following U.S. and other government agencies: Administration of Aging (AOA); Bureau of Justice Statistics (BJS); Centers for Disease Control and Prevention (CDC); Central Intelligence Agency (CIA); Child Welfare Information Gateway; Community Oriented Policing Services (COPS); Federal Bureau of Investigation (FBI); Federal Trade Commission (FTC); Health Resources and Services Administration (HRSA); Military OneSource; National Criminal Justice Reference Service (NCJRS); The National Institute for Occupational Safety and Health (NIOSH); National Institute of Justice (NIJ); National Institute on Drug Abuse (NIDA); National Institute on Drug Abuse (NIDA); National Institutes of Health (NIH); National Responsible Fatherhood Clearinghouse; Occupational Health and Safety Administration (OSHA); Office of Equity, Diversity, and Inclusion (EDI); Office of Family Assistance (OFA); Office of Justice Programs (OJP); Office of Refugee Resettlement; Office on Women's Health (OWH); Social Security Administration (SSA); Substance Abuse and Mental Health Services Administration (SAMHSA); U.S. Agency for International Development; U.S. Army; U.S. Citizenship and Immigration Services (USCIS); U.S. Department of Commerce (DOC); U.S. Department of Health and Human Services (HHS); U.S. Department of Homeland Security (DHS); U.S. Department of Housing and Urban Development (HUD); U.S. Department of Justice (DOJ); U.S. Department of Veterans Affairs (VA); U.S. General Services Administration; U.S. Geological Survey (USGS); U.S. Government Publishing Office (GPO); U.S. Sentencing Commission (USSC); United States Agency for International Development (USAID); and Youth.gov.

It may also contain original material produced by Omnigraphics, Inc. and reviewed by medical consultants.

About the Health Reference Series

The *Health Reference Series* is designed to provide basic medical information for patients, families, caregivers, and the general public. Each volume takes a particular topic and provides comprehensive coverage. This is especially important for people who may be dealing with a newly diagnosed disease or a chronic disorder in themselves or in a family member. People looking for preventive guidance, information about disease warning signs, medical statistics, and risk factors for health problems will also find answers to their questions in the *Health Reference Series*. The *Series*, however, is not intended to serve as a tool for diagnosing illness, in prescribing treatments, or as a substitute for the physician/patient relationship. All people concerned about medical symptoms or the possibility of disease are encouraged to seek professional care from an appropriate health care provider.

A Note about Spelling and Style

Health Reference Series editors use *Stedman's Medical Dictionary* as an authority for questions related to the spelling of medical terms and the *Chicago Manual of Style* for questions related to grammatical structures, punctuation, and other editorial concerns. Consistent adherence is not always possible, however, because the individual volumes within the *Series* include many documents from a wide variety of different producers, and the editor's primary goal is to present material from each source as accurately as is possible. This sometimes means that information in different chapters or sections may follow other guidelines and alternate spelling authorities.

Medical Review

Omnigraphics contracts with a team of qualified, senior medical professionals who serve as medical consultants for the *Health Reference Series*. As necessary, medical consultants review reprinted and originally written material for currency and accuracy. Citations including the phrase, "Reviewed (month, year)" indicate material reviewed by this team. Medical consultation services are provided to the *Health Reference Series* editors by:

Dr. Vijayalakshmi, MBBS, DGO, MD
Dr. Senthil Selvan, MBBS, DCH, MD

Legal Review

Legal consultation services for *Domestic Violence Sourcebook, Fifth Edition* provided by: K. Karthikeyan, MA, BL

Our Advisory Board

We would like to thank the following board members for providing initial guidance on the development of this series:

* Dr. Lynda Baker, Associate Professor of Library and Information Science, Wayne State University, Detroit, MI

* Nancy Bulgarelli, William Beaumont Hospital Library, Royal Oak, MI

* Karen Imarisio, Bloomfield Township Public Library, Bloomfield Township, MI

* Karen Morgan, Mardigian Library, University of Michigan-Dearborn, Dearborn, MI

* Rosemary Orlando, St. Clair Shores Public Library, St. Clair Shores, MI

Health Reference Series *Update Policy*

The inaugural book in the *Health Reference Series* was the first edition of *Cancer Sourcebook* published in 1989. Since then, the *Series* has been enthusiastically received by librarians and in the medical community. In order to maintain the standard of providing high-quality health information for the layperson the editorial staff at Omnigraphics felt it was necessary to implement a policy of updating volumes when warranted.

Medical researchers have been making tremendous strides, and it is the purpose of the *Health Reference Series* to stay current with the most recent advances. Each decision to update a volume is made on an individual basis. Some of the considerations include how much new information is available and the feedback we receive from people who use the books. If there is a topic you would like to see added to the update list, or an area of medical concern you feel has not been adequately addressed, please write to:

Managing Editor
Health Reference Series
Omnigraphics, Inc.
615 Griswold, Ste. 901
Detroit, MI 48226

Part One

Facts about Domestic Violence, Stalking, and Sexual Harassment

Chapter 1

What Is Domestic Violence?

Chapter Contents

Section 1.1

Introduction to Domestic Violence

Text in this section is excerpted from "Understanding
Intimate Partner Violence," Centers for Disease Control and
Prevention (CDC), 2014; and text from "Domestic Violence,"
Department of Justice (DOJ), October 6, 2015.

Understanding Intimate Partner Violence

Intimate partner violence (IPV) occurs between two people in a
close relationship. The term "intimate partner" includes current and
former spouses and dating partners. IPV exists along a continuum
from a single episode of violence to ongoing battering. IPV includes
four types of behavior:

1. **Physical violence** is when a person hurts or tries to hurt a
   partner by hitting, kicking, or using another type of physical
   force.

2. **Sexual violence** is forcing a partner to take part in a sex act
   when the partner does not consent.

3. **Stalking** is a pattern of repeated, unwanted attention and
   contact by a partner that causes fear or concern for one's own
   safety or the safety of someone close to the victim.

4. **Psychological aggression** is the use of verbal and
   non-verbal communication with the intent to harm another
   person mentally or emotionally and/or exert control over
   another person.

Several types of IPV may occur together.

Why is IPV a public health problem?

IPV is a serious problem in the United States:

- On average, 24 people per minute are victims of rape, physical violence, or stalking by an intimate partner in the United States—
  more than 12 million women and men over the course of a year.

- Nearly 3 in 10 women and 1 in 10 men in the United States have experienced rape, physical violence, and/or stalking by a partner and report a related impact on their functioning.

- IPV resulted in 2,340 deaths in 2007—accounting for 14% of all homicides. Of these deaths, 70% were females and 30% were males.

- The medical care, mental health services, and lost productivity (e.g., time away from work) cost of IPV was an estimated $8.3 billion in 2003 for women alone.

These numbers underestimate the problem. Many victims do not report IPV to police, friends, or family. Victims may think others will not believe them or that the police cannot help.

How does IPV affect health?

IPV can affect health in many ways. The longer the violence goes on, the more serious the effects.

Many victims suffer physical injuries. Some are minor like cuts, scratches, bruises, and welts. Others are more serious and can cause death or disabilities. These include broken bones, internal bleeding, and head trauma.

Not all injuries are physical. IPV can also cause emotional harm. Victims may have trauma symptoms. This includes flashbacks, panic attacks, and trouble sleeping. Victims often have low self-esteem. They may have a hard time trusting others and being in relationships. The anger and stress that victims feel may lead to eating disorders and depression. Some victims even think about or commit suicide.

IPV is also linked to negative health outcomes, such as chronic pain, difficulty sleeping, activity limitations, and poor physical and mental health.

IPV is also linked to harmful health behaviors. Victims may try to cope with their trauma in unhealthy ways. This includes smoking, drinking, taking drugs, or having risky sex.

Who is at risk for IPV?

Several factors can increase the risk that someone will hurt his or her partner. However, having these risk factors does not always mean that IPV will occur.

Risk factors for perpetration (hurting a partner):

- Being violent or aggressive in the past

- Seeing or being a victim of violence as a child

- Using drugs or alcohol, especially drinking heavily

- Not having a job or other life events that cause stress

How can we prevent IPV?

The goal is to stop IPV before it begins. There is a lot to learn about how to prevent IPV. We do know that strategies that promote healthy behaviors in relationships are important. Programs that teach young people skills for dating can prevent violence. These programs can stop violence in dating relationships before it occurs.

We know less about how to prevent IPV in adults. However, some programs that teach healthy relationship skills seem to help stop violence before it ever starts.

Domestic violence can happen to anyone regardless of race, age, sexual orientation, religion, or gender. Domestic violence affects people of all socioeconomic backgrounds and education levels. Domestic violence occurs in both opposite-sex and same-sex relationships and can happen to intimate partners who are married, living together, or dating.

Domestic violence not only affects those who are abused, but also has a substantial effect on family members, friends, co-workers, other witnesses, and the community at large. Children, who grow up witnessing domestic violence, are among those seriously affected by this crime. Frequent exposure to violence in the home not only predisposes children to numerous social and physical problems, but also teaches them that violence is a normal way of life—therefore, increasing their risk of becoming society's next generation of victims and abusers.

Section 1.2

Are Coercion and Controlling Behaviors Linked to IPV?

Text in this section is excerpted from "Practical Implications of Current Intimate Partner Violence Research for Victim Advocates and Service Providers," National Criminal Justice Reference Service (NCJRS), December 2013.

It is commonly understood that power and control are "underlying factors" for IPV. Controlling behaviors by men have been associated with both higher likelihood of physical violence and sexual violence. Men who believe they have a right to control and discipline wives are more likely to beat them than those who do not share these beliefs. Other studies suggest that controlling behavior itself can be as, or more, threatening than physical and sexual violence.

A revealing New York study of 600 women, aged 15 to 24, who were patients at a reproductive health center, found two-thirds experienced one or more episodes of controlling behavior. Further, in almost half of the cases, the controlling behaviour overlapped with physical and sexual victimization. Researchers concluded that controlling behavior is a risk factor for physical and sexual intimate partner violence. The younger women, 15 to 18, those who had grown up with domestic violence, those who had been pregnant at least once, those that had suffered recent physical or sexual violence, and those who felt uncomfortable asking their partner to use a condom, were the most likely to experience the most controlling behavior by their partners.

The types of controlling behavior found in the male partner:

1. insisting on knowing the woman's location at all times (45.9 percent);

2. being angry if the woman spoke to another man (40.8 percent);

3. being suspicious of infidelity (40.5 percent);

4. attempting to keep the partner from seeing friends (26.5 percent);

5. ignoring or treating his partner indifferently (24.7 percent);

6. restricting contact with her family (6.3 percent); and

7. expecting his partner to ask permission before seeking health care (3.7 percent).

The study also found that young women experiencing these behaviors were more hesitant to answer questions about relationship violence—a fact that presents challenges for healthcare providers and others seeking to assist woman who are at most risk.

Section 1.3

Sexual Abuse and IPV

Text in this section is excerpted from "Practical Implications of Current Intimate Partner Violence Research for Victim Advocates and Service Providers," National Criminal Justice Reference Service (NCJRS), December 2013.

Are Sexual Abuse and Rape Part of IPV?

Sexual conduct that is illegal (e.g., rape, attempted rape, involuntary deviate sexual acts, sex trafficking) is a limited set of the full range of sexual abuse inflicted by intimate partners.

The spectrum of sexual acts that are abusive include: unwanted, non-consensual or coerced sex acts; forced or denial of contraception and abortion; sex after childbirth or during illness; unwanted intercourse during menstruation; sex during sleep; sexual humiliation and degradation; sexually proprietary behaviors (e.g., jealousy, nagging about sex and accusations of infidelity); "make up" sex following physical assault or perceived infidelity; virginity and vaginal inspections; commercial sexual exploitation of partners; infibulation and other mutilation; sex through trick, fraud or misrepresentation; sexual abuse by proxy or viewing/acting out pornography; exposure of children to sexual acts; economic support conditioned on sex; non-consensual sex with third parties, animals, or objects; and more.

Intimate partner sexual assaults often incorporate hurtful dimensions of degradation and humiliation.

There is limited research on "legal" acts of sexual abuse by batterers or its impact on victims. Much of the research on intimate partner sexual assault has focused solely on forced or involuntary sex that is actionable under state criminal statutes. Even the National Crime Victimization Survey (NCVS) and the National Violence Against Women Survey (NVAWS) ask few questions to elicit information beyond coercive sexual behavior and contain extremely low rates of intimate partner sexual assault.

Early research on sexual violence against wives, not just battered wives, suggested that between 10 and 14 percent of married women were raped by their husbands. The NVAWS estimates that 17 percent of women are raped at some time in their lives, but that percentage includes intimate as well as acquaintance and stranger rapes. Women are 86 percent of rape victims. Only 20 percent of women victims report their rape to the police.

Male sexual assault of intimate female partners is more prevalent than stranger and acquaintance sexual violence; 14 to 25 percent of women experience intimate partner sexual assaults. Another study of rural battered women found that half had been raped by their partners.

Between 43 and 55 percent of women experiencing physical assaults by intimate partner also experience sexual assaults by that partner. In turn, psychological and emotional abuse commonly co-occurs with physical and sexual violence. In a recent study of women victims of intimate partner violence who obtained protection orders, 25 to 30 percent reported that their abusers engaged in a wide range of sexual abuse, exploitation and assault. The protection order recipients who were sexually abused were also likely to be stalked. Those stalked were likely to be more severely sexually abused.

In a previous protection order study, 68 percent of the physically abused women also reported sexual assault. Of those sexually assaulted, 79 percent reported repeated forced sex. Few made complaints to police or plead the sexual assault in protection orders.

Battered women utilizing emergency shelter and domestic violence services indicate that between one-third and one-half have been sexually assaulted by their partners.

NISVS found a tremendous overlap of IPV rape, physical violence, and stalking. Over their lifetime, 12.5 percent of IPV women victims experienced rape, physical violence and stalking, 8.7 percent

9

experienced rape and physical violence, and only 4.4 percent experienced only rape.

Confirming the high rates of intimate partner sexual assault, a batterer intervention program study found that 53 percent of the men enrolled had sexually assaulted their partners. Most used emotional and physical coercion or threats to compel partners to engage in sex. Fully 33 percent of those who sexually assaulted their female partners did so when the women were asleep. The sexually violent men were also likely to engage in severe acts of physical violence that escalated over time. However, few men in the sample (8 percent) recognized that their acts constituted sexual abuse.

Some battered women suggest that the sexual abuse is the most insidious and traumatic of all the abuse suffered.

Chapter 2

Prevalence of Domestic Abuse

For the 10-year aggregate period 2003–12, domestic violence accounted for 21% of all violent victimizations (Figure 2.1). Domestic violence includes rape, sexual assault, robbery, and aggravated and simple assault committed by intimate partners, immediate family members, or other relatives. Intimate partner violence (15%) accounted for a greater percentage of all violent victimizations, compared to violence committed by immediate family members (4%) or other relatives (2%). Well-known or casual acquaintances accounted for 32% of all violent victimizations, and strangers accounted for 38%.

This report uses data from the National Crime Victimization Survey (NCVS) to describe the characteristics and patterns of domestic violence. Domestic violence includes victimizations committed by intimate partners (current or former spouses, boyfriends, or girlfriends), immediate family members (parents, children, or siblings), and other relatives. It details the number, percentage, and demographic characteristics of domestic violence victims, and describes victim and incident characteristics by the victim–offender relationship. Incident characteristics include the type of violence, the offender's use of a weapon, victim injury and medical treatment, and whether the incident was reported to police. The report focuses on domestic violence, but includes estimates of violence committed by acquaintances and strangers to provide comparisons.

Text in this chapter is excerpted from "Nonfatal Domestic Violence, 2003–2012," U.S. Department of Justice (DOJ), April 2014.

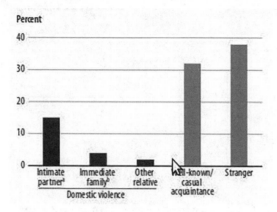

Percent

Figure 2.1. *Violent victimization, by victim-offender relationship, 2003–2012*

Highlights

In 2003–12:

- Domestic violence accounted for 21% of all violent crime.

- Intimate partner violence (15%) accounted for a greater percentage of all violent victimizations than violence committed by immediate family members (4%) or other relatives (2%).

- Current or former boyfriends or girlfriends committed most domestic violence.

- The majority of domestic violence was committed against females (76%) compared to males (24%).

- A similar percentage of violence by intimate partners and immediate family members was reported to police (56% each). An estimated 49% of violence by other relatives was reported to police.

- Most domestic violence (77%) occurred at or near the victim's home.

- Intimate partner violence resulted in injuries more often than violence perpetrated by immediate family members and other relatives.

- A weapon was involved in a larger percentage of violence committed by other relatives (26%) than intimate partners (19%) and immediate family members (19%).

Intimate partner violence accounted for 15% of all violent victimizations

In 2003–12, intimate partner violence accounted for 14.6% of all violent victimizations (Table 2.1.). Current or former boyfriends or girlfriends (7.8%) committed a greater percentage of all violent victimizations than spouses (4.7%) and ex-spouses (2.0%). Violence committed by immediate family members accounted for 4.3% of all violent victimizations, and other relatives accounted for 2.4%. The percentage of total violence perpetrated by other relatives (2.4%) was greater than the percentage by the victim's parents (1.2%), children (1.5%), or siblings (1.6%). These relationships were similar for serious violence and simple assault.

Domestic violence declined from 1994 to 2012

The rate of domestic violence declined 63%, from 13.5 victimizations per 1,000 persons age 12 or older in 1994 to 5.0 per 1,000 in 2012 (Table 2.2.). The overall pattern and size of the decline were similar to the decline in the overall violent crime rate. Total violence declined 67% from a rate of 79.8 per 1,000 to 26.1 per 1,000 (not shown).

From 1994 to 2012, violence committed by intimate partners declined at a faster rate than violent crime committed by immediate family members and other relatives. Violence committed by intimate partners declined 67%, from 9.8 per 1,000 persons age 12 or older in 1994 to 3.2 per 1,000 in 2012 (Figure 2.2). Violence committed by immediate family members declined 52% during the same period, from 2.7 to 1.3 per 1,000. Violence committed by other relatives decreased 49%, from 1.1 to 0.6 per 1,000.

Most of the decline in domestic violence occurred in the first half of the period from 1994 to 2002. Rates of violent crime committed by intimate partners and other relatives continued to decline from 2003 to 2012, while violent crime by immediate family members fluctuated between a rate of 0.9 per 1,000 and 1.3 per 1,000. From 2010 to 2012, violence perpetrated by intimate partners and other relatives remained relatively stable.

Serious domestic violence (rape, sexual assault, robbery, and aggravated assault) declined from 1994 to 2012. Serious intimate partner violence declined at a faster rate than serious violence committed by immediate family members and other relatives. Rates of serious intimate partner violence declined by over half, from 3.6 per 1,000 persons age 12 or older in 1994 to 1.0 per 1,000 in 2012 (Figure 2.3). During the same period, the rate of serious violence by immediate family

Table 2.1. Violent victimization, by type of crime and victim-offender relationship, 2003–2012

Victim–offender relationship	All violent crime		Serious violent crimes		Simple assault	
	Average annual number	Percent	Average annual number	Percent	Average annual number	Percent
Total	6,623,500	100.00%	2,194,070	100.00%	4,429,430	100.00%
Known	3,514,570	53.10%	1,072,520	48.90%	2,442,050	55.10%
Domestic	1,411,330	21.3	501220	22.8	910,110	20.5
Intimate partner	967,710	14.6	343,760	15.7	623,950	14.1
Spouse	314,330	4.7	116,520	5.3	197,810	4.5
Ex-spouse	134,690	2	29,330	1.3	105,350	2.4
Boy/girlfriend	518,700	7.8	197,910	9	320,790	7.2
Immediate family	284,670	4.3	98,520	4.5	186,150	4.2
Parent	80,890	1.2	31,400	1.4	49,480	1.1
Child	97,490	1.5	32,820	1.5	64,680	1.5
Sibling	106,290	1.6	34,300	1.6	71,990	1.6
Other relative	158,950	2.4	58,940	2.7	100,010	2.3
Well-known/casual acquaintance	2,103,240	31.8	571,300	26	1,531,940	34.6
Stranger	2,548,860	38.50%	929,450	42.40%	1,619,410	36.60%
Unknown	560,080	8.50%	192,100	8.80%	367,970	8.30%

Table 2.2. Percent of violent victimization, by victim–offender relationship and victim's sex, 2003–2012

Victim–offender relationship	Serious violent crime		Simple assault	
	Male	Female	Male	Female
Total	100.00%	100.00%	100.00%	100.00%
Known	34.30%	65.00%	43.50%	68.70%
Domestic	10	37	9.4	33.6
Intimate partner	5.8	26.6	4.5	25.3
Immediate family	2.7	6.5	3.2	5.4
Other relative	1.5	4	1.7	3
Well-known/casual acquaintance	24.3	28	34.1	35.1
Stranger	54.80%	28.60%	46.10%	25.40%
Average annual violent victimizations	1,151,980	1,042,090	2,382,070	2,047,370

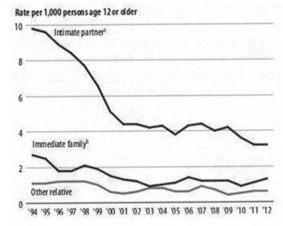

Figure 2.2. *Rate of domestic violence, by victim-offender relationship, 1993–2012*

members decreased from 0.7 to 0.3 per 1,000, and serious violence by other relatives decreased from 0.4 to 0.2 per 1,000. Similar to the pattern in overall domestic violence, most of the decline in these rates occurred from 1994 to 2002. Rates of serious intimate partner violence continued to decline from 2003 to 2012. During the same time period,

15

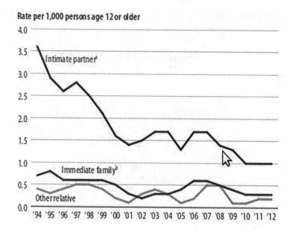

Figure 2.3. *Rate of serious domestic violence, by victim-offender relationship, 1993–2012*

serious violence by immediate family members fluctuated between 0.3 and 0.6 per 1,000, and serious violence perpetrated by other relatives varied between 0.1 and 0.5 per 1,000.

Rates of simple assault by intimate partners, immediate family members, and other relatives decreased from 1994 to 2012. The rate of simple assault by intimate partners declined from 6.2 to 2.2 per 1,000 (Figure 2.4). The rate of simple assault by immediate family members

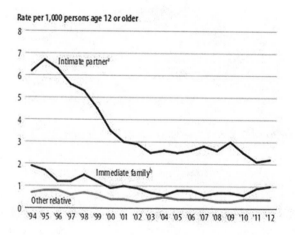

Figure 2.4. *Rate of simple assault domestic violence, by victim-offender relationship, 1993–2012*

decreased from 1.9 to 1.0 per 1,000, while the rate for other relatives declined from 0.7 to 0.4 per 1,000. As in overall domestic violence, the majority of the decline in these rates occurred from 1994 to 2002. Simple assaults by intimate partners remained relatively stable from 2003 to 2012, fluctuating from 2.1 per 1,000 to 3.0 per 1,000. Simple assaults perpetrated by immediate family members varied from a rate of 0.6 per 1,000 to 1.0 per 1,000, and the rate for other relatives fluctuated from 0.3 per 1,000 to 0.5 per 1,000 during the same time period.

Chapter 3

Risk Factors for Domestic Violence

Chapter Contents

Section 3.1

Why Does IPV Occur?

Text in this section is excerpted from "Practical Implications of
Current Intimate Partner Violence Research for Victim Advocates
and Service Providers," National Criminal Justice Reference
Service (NCJRS), December 2013.

Early in the Domestic Violence (DV) movement, four competing
theories about the causality of IPV gained the most traction among
scholars and activists: psychological impairment, anger management
problems, conflict resolution deficits, and male dominance over women
based in patriarchy and misogyny.

Over the ensuing decades, more than 20 theories emerged attempting to explain the reasons for IPV. Most envisioned offenders, especially repeat offenders, as antisocial, maladaptive, or otherwise psychopathic, a view continued to be implied in much media coverage of
DV murders and the like.

However, subsequent research has been unable to find empirical
evidence sufficient to support these explanations. For example, a
15-month follow-up analysis of 580 convicted DV offenders in four cities found that only "11 percent of repeat assaulters exhibited primary
psychopathic disorders," and more than half did not show indications
of secondary psychopathic disorders, a much broader classification.
The researchers noted that almost two-thirds (60 percent) of the batterers had "subclinical or low levels of personality dysfunction" and
possessed a multitude of personality types, with re-assaulters no more
likely to have a psychopathic disorder than others. Other researchers
have determined that only about 10 percent of IPV is due to mental
disorders.

If psychological theories cannot explain 90 percent of intimate partner abuse, then there must be alternative causal explanations. The
National Violence Against Women Survey (NVAWS) attempted to
develop predictive models of abusive behavior using logistic regression.
The strongest models found significant positive associations between
abuse and unmarried, cohabitating couples and abuse of the victim
as a child. A negative associated with IPV was found if the victim was

white. This model also found significant relationships between abuse and abuser jealousy, abuser isolation of the victim, and verbal abuse of the victim by the partner. The researchers suggest that these relationships offer empirical support to what another researcher refers to a "patriarchal terrorism." In their view, IPV is often "violence perpetrated against women by male partners as part of a systemic pattern of dominance and control."

Some posit that males operate in abuse-supporting peer groups that reinforce social norms allowing males to abuse females. These social supports do not operate in a social vacuum, but rather are bolstered by dominant social patriarchal patterns and coalesce with traditional perceptions of masculinity, privacy, sexual objectification of women, and heavy alcohol use.

As social science data becomes more accurate, researchers are better able to empirically verify (or reject) various theoretical causal assumptions. Evolving research, for example, questions the initial correlation between race and domestic violence by suggesting that social disorganization variables, not race, are associated with increased intimate partner violence. While previous indicators pointed to a higher incidence of intimate partner abusive behavior among African-Americans, researchers did not consider community contextual factors, i.e., limited informal and formal social controls that influence the collective efficacy of an area.

Researchers suggest that "area racial composition and violent crime rates can be explained by other structural correlates of race," including high unemployment, poverty, family fragmentation, economic hardship, and isolation from conventional society; all features that potentially reduce legitimate opportunity structures and weaken informal ties and social control, which are said to foster increased crime and violence. Using data from the National Survey of Families and Households and the 1990 U.S. Census, these researchers suggest that neighborhood disadvantage is responsible for much of the correlation between race and domestic violence, explaining that "the rate of intimate violence is highest in the most disadvantaged communities and lowest in the least disadvantaged communities."

Research utilizing results of California's massive health survey links neighborhood bar concentration with increased IPV emergency room visits. Researchers suggest that bars, likely frequented by men with and without their partners, may encourage heavy drinking linked to increased aggression. Like other such studies, this research goes beyond individual risk factors for IPV and looks at neighborhood, and environmental risk factors. The researchers note that using emergency room visits as their measure of IPV means they were finding much more serious IPV than that found in studies measuring IPV reported in police incident reports or arrests.

Research, thus, sheds important empirical light upon the race-IPV connection by suggesting that varying ecological factors are more powerful predictors.

It is important to note that "correlation" is not the same thing as "causation."

Section 3.2

Individual, Relational, Community, and Societal Risk Factors

Text in this section is excerpted from "Intimate Partner Violence: Risk and Protective Factors," Centers for Disease Control and Prevention (CDC), February 11, 2015.

Persons with certain risk factors are more likely to become victims or perpetrators of intimate partner violence (IPV). Those risk factors contribute to IPV but might not be direct causes. Not everyone who is identified as "at risk" becomes involved in violence.

Some risk factors for IPV victimization and perpetration are the same, while others are associated with one another. For example, childhood physical or sexual victimization is a risk factor for future IPV perpetration and victimization.

A combination of individual, relational, community, and societal factors contribute to the risk of becoming an IPV victim or perpetrator. Understanding these multilevel factors can help identify various opportunities for prevention.

Individual Risk Factors

- Low self-esteem

- Low income

- Low academic achievement

- Young age

- Aggressive or delinquent behavior as a youth
- Heavy alcohol and drug use
- Depression
- Anger and hostility
- Antisocial personality traits
- Borderline personality traits
- Prior history of being physically abusive
- Having few friends and being isolated from other people
- Unemployment
- Emotional dependence and insecurity
- Belief in strict gender roles (e.g., male dominance and aggression in relationships)
- Desire for power and control in relationships
- Perpetrating psychological aggression
- Being a victim of physical or psychological abuse (consistently one of the strongest predictors of perpetration)
- History of experiencing poor parenting as a child
- History of experiencing physical discipline as a child

Relationship Factors
- Marital conflict-fights, tension, and other struggles
- Marital instability-divorces or separations
- Dominance and control of the relationship by one partner over the other
- Economic stress
- Unhealthy family relationships and interactions

Community Factors
- Poverty and associated factors (e.g., overcrowding)
- Low social capital-lack of institutions, relationships, and norms that shape a community's social interactions

- Weak community sanctions against IPV (e.g., unwillingness of neighbors to intervene in situations where they witness violence)

Societal Factors

Traditional gender norms (e.g., women should stay at home, not enter workforce, and be submissive; men support the family and make the decisions)

Section 3.3

Power and Control Model

Text in this section is excerpted from "A Comprehensive Approach for Community-Based Programs to Address Intimate Partner Violence and Perinatal Depression," U.S. Department of Health and Human Services (HHS), January 2013.

There are five types of intimate partner violence as defined by the CDC:

1. Physical violence is the intentional use of physical force with the potential for causing death, disability, injury, or harm. Physical violence includes, but is not limited to: scratching; pushing; shoving; throwing; grabbing; biting; choking; shaking; slapping; punching; burning; use of a weapon; and use of restraints or one's body, size, or strength against another person.

2. Sexual violence encompasses three categories: 1) use of physical force to compel a person to engage in a sexual act against his or her will, whether or not the act is completed; 2) attempted or completed sex act involving a person who is unable to understand the nature or condition of the act, to decline participation, or to communicate unwillingness to engage in the sexual act, e.g., because of illness, disability, or the influence of alcohol or other drugs, or because of intimidation or pressure; and 3) abusive sexual contact.

3. Threats of physical or sexual violence include the use of words, gestures, or weapons to communicate the intent to cause death, disability, injury, or physical harm.

4. Psychological/emotional violence involves trauma to the victim caused by acts, threats of acts, or coercive tactics. Psychological/emotional abuse can include, but is not limited to, humiliating the victim, controlling what the victim can and cannot do, withholding information from the victim, deliberately doing something to make the victim feel diminished or embarrassed, isolating the victim from friends and family, and denying the victim access to money or other basic resources. It is considered psychological/ emotional violence when there has been prior physical or sexual violence or prior threat of physical or sexual violence.

5. Stalking is often included among the types of IPV. Stalking generally refers to harassing or threatening behavior that an individual engages in repeatedly, such as following a person, appearing at a person's home or place of business, making harassing phone calls, leaving written messages or objects, or vandalizing a person's property.

The following figure depicts multiple forms of abuse and violence that allow a perpetrator to establish and maintain power and control by creating an intimidating, threatening environment. The Power and Control Wheel in Dating Relationships, developed by the Kansas Coalition Against Sexual and Domestic Violence and adapted from the Power and Control Wheel developed by the Domestic Abuse Intervention Programs, Duluth, MN, illustrates how many different actions fit into a larger system of abuse and violence.

Figure 3.1. *Power and Control Model*

25

Section 3.4

Economic Stress and IPV

"Economic Stress and Domestic Violence,"
© 2016 Omnigraphics, Inc.
Reviewed January 2016.

Economic stress and domestic violence are intricately linked. Studies have found that the rate of domestic violence is three times higher among couples who report severe financial strain than among couples who report little or no financial strain. Stress related to economic factors can contribute to domestic violence in many ways. People who experience severe financial hardships are likely to feel anger, frustration, and a sense of inadequacy. Sometimes these feelings translate into aggression, control, and violence toward family members living in the household.

Although nothing excuses abusive behavior, in some cases it is related to a psychological need to exert dominance or control. Since cultural norms of masculinity define men as patriarchs, providers, and heads of the family unit, financial hardships and unemployment can undermine their sense of self-worth. Some men may respond to their perceived failure to measure up to cultural expectations by becoming violent and exerting power over their intimate partners or children. Research has shown that the risk of perpetrating domestic violence increased from 4.7 percent among couples where the male partner was consistently employed to 12.3 percent among couples where the male partner experienced multiple periods of unemployment.

The relationship between economic stress and domestic violence works both ways, however, as abuse can also create financial problems for families. Although abuse certainly occurs in middle-class and affluent families, studies have shown that the likelihood of domestic violence decreases as financial security increases. One study found that domestic violence rates were five times higher in American households with the lowest annual incomes than in those with the highest annual incomes. People who experience domestic violence are more likely to miss work and perform poorly on the job, which increases their risk of unemployment and economic insecurity. These financial hardships, in turn, can force domestic violence victims to remain in an abusive relationship.

Domestic Violence and Employment

One of the ways domestic violence impacts financial security is by affecting women's employment. Although women who are victims of domestic violence report the same desire to work as other women, their abusers may try to prevent them from obtaining paid employment. Some abusive partners—especially men who are unemployed—may view a female partner's decision to seek employment as a threat to their power or status. One study found that a woman's likelihood of being abused increased as her income rose relative to that of her partner.

Economic abuse is a form of domestic violence in which an abuser deliberately sabotages their intimate partner's efforts to find or keep a job. The tactics used in economic abuse may include destroying work clothes, damaging computers or other job-related equipment, interfering with child care arrangements, inflicting visible injuries, or stalking in the workplace. As a result of such efforts, women who experience domestic violence tend to have higher absenteeism and lower productivity rates than other female workers. These issues may result in job loss, which reduces the financial resources available for women to leave abusive relationships.

Poverty and Domestic Violence

The connection between economic stress and domestic violence can create a downward spiral that traps people in both abusive relationships and poverty. This cycle often perpetuates itself, as children who are raised in low-income households with domestic violence are much more likely to abuse others. Many families who live in impoverished circumstances only associate with others in their community who face similar economic situations, which reinforces the pattern by making domestic violence seem commonplace and socially accepted.

Domestic violence victims who live in poverty, therefore, often cannot count on family and friends to help them. Although many women who leave abusive relationships end up staying with family or friends, this resource may not be available to low-income women because their friends and family members may also face economic insecurity. As a result, an estimated one-third of domestic violence survivors end up homeless as a result of ending an abusive relationship.

Obtaining financial assistance from state and federal agencies can be difficult or even dangerous for survivors of domestic abuse. Many aid programs require applicants with children to help child support agencies locate and collect payments from the other parent. These requirements can put domestic violence survivors at risk by revealing their whereabouts to abusers. Although waivers are available in some cases, only a small fraction of eligible welfare applicants disclose the fact that they have experienced domestic violence. Some battered women do not report this information because they worry that child protective services agencies may remove the children from their custody.

Some steps that may help end the cycle of poverty and domestic violence include:

- Dismantling cultural norms that define masculinity as dominant and controlling;

- Promoting education and employment to help women be independent and resist economic abuse;

- Providing jobs and reliable forms of government assistance to reduce economic stress on poor and unemployed couples;

- Offering unemployment insurance to help domestic violence survivors who have to quit their jobs;

- Increasing the minimum wage to provide low-income women with resources to leave abusive relationships; and

- Supporting paid leave initiatives, which would allow survivors of domestic violence to take time off from work to seek medical care, find shelter, or obtain legal protection.

References

1. "Domestic Violence and Poverty." Get Domestic Violence Help, n.d.

2. Doyle, Sady. "The Poverty of Domestic Violence." *In These Times,* May 7, 2012.

3. Renzetti, Claire M., and Vivian M. Larkin. "Economic Stress and Domestic Violence." National Resource Center on Domestic Violence, 2011.

Section 3.5

Are Separated or Divorced Persons at Increased Risk for IPV?

Text in this section is excerpted from "Practical Implications of
Current Intimate Partner Violence Research for Victim Advocates
and Service Providers," National Criminal Justice Reference
Service (NCJRS), December 2013.

Rates of IPV for persons separated from intimate partners are higher than for divorced, married or never married persons. NCVS data reveal that approximately .042 percent of separated women and .013 percent of separated men were victims of IPV compared to .011 percent for divorced women and .003 percent for divorced men, .006 percent for women never married and .002 percent for men never married and .002 percent for married women and .001 percent for married men.

Similarly, an international review of IPV research found that divorced women are nine times more likely than married women to be physically assaulted by intimate partners, and separated women are at 30 times the risk.

Further, women victims of IPV may be at greater risk of sexual violence and rape after separation. In an exploratory rural study of battered women separated from their male partners, the rate of sexual assaults of women upon telling abusers of their intent to leave was 74 percent. At the time of trying to leave, it was 49 percent, and after leaving, it was 33 percent. Formerly married battered women were subjected to sexual assaults at a higher rate than formerly cohabiting battered women.

Although stalking often begins while the IPV perpetrator and victim are living together, not surprisingly, victims appear to be at elevated risk of stalking after separation and/or divorce.

Not all victims are at equal risk after they separate from or divorce their intimate abuser. One study found that in the two-year period after separation a third of abusers assaulted their victims, mostly often severely. The perpetrators most likely to assault their victims were those who had frequently threatened their partners with violence after separation, who were "sexually suspicious," and who had lived with their victims long before they first assaulted them. Yet, the same study found that for most women, separation proved protective against ongoing abuse. The relocation of the abuser to another city was a significant protective factor. Other research has found that separation may prevent or reduce the likelihood of physical and emotional abuse against women IPV victims.

While some argue that this research proves that marriage is the safest place for women to be, the comparatively lower rate of victimization for married couples may be a function of the fact that married couples tend to have less risk factors for IPV, including being older. In fact, research comparing women IPV victims under and over sixty years of age has found that for the older victims, marriage is the most unsafe marital status. These victims continue to suffer abuse well beyond age sixty.

Section 3.6

Domestic Violence in the Wake of Disasters

Text in this section is excerpted from "Disasters and Domestic Violence," U.S. Department of Veterans Affairs (VA), August 17, 2015.

Prevalence and Impact of Domestic Violence in the Wake of Disasters

Two questions require attention when considering the implications of domestic violence for post-disaster recovery.

The first question is whether domestic violence increases in prevalence after disasters. There are only minimal data that are relevant to this question. Mechanic et al. undertook the most comprehensive examination of intimate violence in the aftermath of a disaster after the 1993 Mid-western flood. A representative sample of 205 women who were either married or cohabiting with men and who were highly exposed to this disaster acknowledged considerable levels of domestic violence and abuse. Over the nine-month period after flood onset, 14% reported at least one act of physical aggression from their partners, 26% reported emotional abuse, 70% verbal abuse, and 86% partner anger. Whether these rates of physical aggression are greater than normal is not known because studies of domestic violence from previous years and under normal conditions have showed the existence of rates of violence as low as 1% and as high as 12%.

A few studies have produced evidence that supports the above. Police reports of domestic violence increased by 46% following the eruption of the Mt. St. Helens volcano. One year after Hurricane Hugo, marital stress was more prevalent among individuals who had been severely exposed to the hurricane (e.g., life threat, injury) than among individuals who had been less severely exposed or not exposed at all. Within six months after Hurricane Andrew, 22% of adult residents of the stricken area acknowledged having a new conflict with someone in their household. In a study of people directly exposed to the bombing of the Murrah Federal Building in Oklahoma City, 17% of non-injured persons and 42% of persons whose injuries required hospitalization reported troubled interpersonal relationships.

The second question is whether domestic violence, regardless of the reasons how or why it occurs, influences women's post-disaster recovery. An important finding from Mechanic et al.'s (2001) study was that the presence of domestic violence strongly influenced women's post-disaster mental health. Thirty-nine percent of women who experienced post-flood partner abuse developed post-flood PTSD compared to 17% of women who did not experience post-flood abuse. Fifty-seven percent of women who experienced post-flood partner abuse developed post-flood major depression compared to 28% of nonabused women. Similarly, Norris and Uhl found that as marital stress increased, so too did psychological symptoms such as depression and anxiety. Likewise, Norris et al. found that 6 and 30 months after Hurricane Andrew, new conflicts and other socially disruptive events were among the strongest predictors of psychological symptoms.

These findings take on additional significance when it is remembered that not only are women generally at greater risk than men for developing post-disaster psychological problems, but women who are married or cohabitating with men may be at even greater risk than single women. In contrast, married status is often a protective factor for men. It also has been found that the severity of married women's symptoms increases with the severity of their husbands' distress, even after similarities in their exposure have been taken into account.

In summary, although the research regarding the interplay of disaster and domestic violence is not extensive and little of it has been derived from studies of incidents of mass violence, the available evidence does suggest that services related to domestic violence should be integrated into other mental-health services for disaster-stricken families. Screening for women's safety may be especially important. Helping men find appropriate ways to manage/direct their anger will benefit them and their wives. It will also help their children, as children are highly sensitive to post-disaster conflict and irritability in the family.

Summary of Empirical Findings

- Although there is little conclusive evidence that domestic violence increases after major disasters, research suggests that its post-disaster prevalence may be substantial.

- In the most relevant study, 14% of women experienced at least one act of post-flood physical aggression and 26% reported post-flood emotional abuse over a 9-month period.

- One study reported a 46% increase in police reports of domestic violence after a disaster.

- Other studies show that substantial percentages of disaster victims experience marital stress, new conflicts, and troubled interpersonal relationships.

- There is more-conclusive evidence that domestic violence harms women's abilities to recover from disasters.

- In the most relevant study, 39% of abused women developed post-disaster PTSD compared to 17% of other women, and 57% of abused women developed post-disaster depression, compared to 28% of other women.

- Marital stress and conflicts are highly predictive of post-disaster symptoms.

- In light of the fact that, in general, married women are a high-risk group for developing post-disaster psychological problems, it seems advisable to integrate violence-related screenings and services into programs for women, men, and families.

Section 3.7

When and Which Abusers Are Likely to Reabuse?

Text in this section is excerpted from "Practical Implications of Current Intimate Partner Violence Research for Victim Advocates and Service Providers," National Criminal Justice Reference Service (NCJRS), December 2013.

When Are Abusers Likely to Reabuse?

Studies agree that for those abusers who reoffend, a majority do so relatively quickly. In states where no-contact orders are automatically imposed after an arrest for domestic violence, rearrests for order violations begin to occur immediately upon the defendant's release from the police station or court. For example, in both a Massachusetts misdemeanor arrest study and a Brooklyn, N.Y., felony arrest study, the majority of defendants rearrested for new abuse were arrested while their initial abuse cases were still pending in court. The arrest rate for violation of no-contact orders was 16 percent with a 14 percent arrest rate for new felony offenses.

Similarly, a little more than one-third of the domestic violence probationers in Rhode Island who were rearrested for domestic violence were rearrested within two months of being placed under probation supervision. More than half (60 percent) were arrested within six months.

A multistate study of abusers referred to batterer programs found that almost half of the men (44 percent) who reassaulted their partners did so within three months of batterer program intake, and two-thirds within six months. The men who reassaulted within the first three months were more likely to repeatedly reassault their partners than the men who committed the first reassault after the first three months. In the Bronx, similarly, reoffending happened early among those convicted for misdemeanor or domestic violence violations. Of those rearrested for domestic violence, approximately two-thirds reoffended within the first six months.

33

Which Abusers Are Likely to Reabuse?

The research consistently finds that basic actuarial information, readily available, provides as accurate a prediction of abuser risk to the victim as do more extensive and time-consuming investigations involving more sources, including clinical assessments. As a Bronx study on batterer treatment concluded, intensive individual assessments of attitudes or personality are not required to make reasonable judgments regarding abusers' risk of reabuse.

First, these factors include abuser gender. Males are more likely to reabuse than females. Second, younger defendants are more likely to reabuse and recidivate than older defendants. This has been found to be true in studies of arrested abusers and batterers in treatment programs as well as court-restrained abusers. Third, if the abuser has even one prior arrest on his criminal record for any crime (not just domestic violence), he is more likely to reabuse than if he has no prior arrest. A multistate study of more than 3,000 police arrests found that IPV offenders with a prior arrest record for any offense were more than seven times more likely to be rearrested than those without prior records.

The length of prior record is also predictive of reabuse as well as general recidivism. In looking at all restrained male abusers over two years, Massachusetts research documented that if the restrained abuser had just one prior arrest for any offense on his criminal record, his reabuse rate of the same victim rose from 15 to 25 percent; if he had five to six prior arrests, it rose to 50 percent. In the Rhode Island abuser probation study, abusers with one prior arrest for any crime were almost twice as likely to reabuse.

Related to the correlation between prior arrest history and reabuse, research also finds similar increased risk for reabuse if suspects are on warrants. In the Berkeley study, researchers documented that having a pending warrant at the time of an IPV incident for a prior nondomestic violence offense was a better predictor of reabuse than a prior domestic violence record alone.

Similarly, one large state-wide study found that if the suspect before the court for domestic violence was already on probation for anything else, or if another domestic violence case was also pending at the time of a subsequent arrest for domestic violence, that defendant was more likely to be arrested again for domestic violence within one year. In the one study that addressed this issue, suspects who were gone when police arrived were twice as likely to reabuse as those found on the scene by police.

Although research has generally failed to find a specific personality profile associated with risk for reabuse, a study of more than 800 middle-aged adults with borderline and antisocial personalities found that continued aggression was associated with the former, not the latter. This suggests that adults with borderline personalities may be less likely to see reductions in IPV as they age.

Chapter 4

Detecting Abuse

Chapter Contents

Section 4.1

Comparing Healthy and Abusive Relationships

Text in this section is excerpted from "Characteristics of Healthy & Unhealthy Relationships," Youth.gov, February 7, 2012. Reviewed January 2016.

Characteristics of Healthy and Unhealthy Relationships

Respect for both oneself and others is a key characteristic of healthy relationships. In contrast, in unhealthy relationships, one partner tries to exert control and power over the other physically, sexually, and/or emotionally.

Healthy Relationships

Healthy relationships share certain characteristics that teens should be taught to expect. They include:

- *Mutual respect.* Respect means that each person values who the other is and understands the other person's boundaries.

- *Trust.* Partners should place trust in each other and give each other the benefit of the doubt.

- *Honesty.* Honesty builds trust and strengthens the relationship.

- *Compromise.* In a dating relationship, each partner does not always get his or her way. Each should acknowledge different points of view and be willing to give and take.

- *Individuality.* Neither partner should have to compromise who he/she is, and his/her identity should not be based on a partner's. Each should continue seeing his or her friends and doing the things he/she loves. Each should be supportive of his/her partner wanting to pursue new hobbies or make new friends.

- *Good communication.* Each partner should speak honestly and openly to avoid miscommunication. If one person needs to sort out his or her feelings first, the other partner should respect those wishes and wait until he or she is ready to talk.

- *Anger control.* We all get angry, but how we express it can affect our relationships with others. Anger can be handled in healthy ways such as taking a deep breath, counting to ten, or talking it out.

- *Fighting fair.* Everyone argues at some point, but those who are fair, stick to the subject, and avoid insults are more likely to come up with a possible solution. Partners should take a short break away from each other if the discussion gets too heated.

- *Problem solving.* Dating partners can learn to solve problems and identify new solutions by breaking a problem into small parts or by talking through the situation.

- *Understanding.* Each partner should take time to understand what the other might be feeling.

- *Self-confidence.* When dating partners have confidence in themselves, it can help their relationships with others. It shows that they are calm and comfortable enough to allow others to express their opinions without forcing their own opinions on them.

- *Being a role model.* By embodying what respect means, partners can inspire each other, friends, and family to also behave in a respectful way.

- *Healthy sexual relationship.* Dating partners engage in a sexual relationship that both are comfortable with, and neither partner feels pressured or forced to engage in sexual activity that is outside his or her comfort zone or without consent.

Unhealthy Relationships

Unhealthy relationships are marked by characteristics such as disrespect and control. It is important for youth to be able to recognize signs of unhealthy relationships before they escalate. Some characteristics of unhealthy relationships include:

- *Control.* One dating partner makes all the decisions and tells the other what to do, what to wear, or who to spend time with. He or she is unreasonably jealous, and/or tries to isolate the other partner from his or her friends and family.

- *Hostility.* One dating partner picks a fight with or antagonizes the other dating partner. This may lead to one dating partner changing his or her behavior in order to avoid upsetting the other.

- *Dishonesty.* One dating partner lies to or keeps information from the other. One dating partner steals from the other.

- *Disrespect.* One dating partner makes fun of the opinions and interests of the other partner or destroys something that belongs to the partner.

- *Dependence.* One dating partner feels that he or she "cannot live without" the other. He or she may threaten to do something drastic if the relationship ends.

- *Intimidation.* One dating partner tries to control aspects of the other's life by making the other partner fearful or timid. One dating partner may attempt to keep his or her partner from friends and family or threaten violence or a break-up.

- *Physical violence.* One partner uses force to get his or her way (such as hitting, slapping, grabbing, or shoving).

- *Sexual violence.* One dating partner pressures or forces the other into sexual activity against his or her will or without consent.

It is important to educate youth about the value of respect and the characteristics of healthy and unhealthy relationships before they start to date. Youth may not be equipped with the necessary skills to develop and maintain healthy relationships, and may not know how to break up in an appropriate way when necessary. Maintaining open lines of communication may help them form healthy relationships and recognize the signs of unhealthy relationships, thus preventing the violence before it starts.

Section 4.2

Indicators of Domestic Violence

Text in this section is excerpted from "5 Signs That You May Be
in an Abusive Relationship," National Responsible Fatherhood
Clearinghouse (NRFC), November 5, 2015.

Five Signs That You May Be in an Abusive Relationship

Domestic Violence is a violation to a person at the core of their being. It
betrays love, destroys trust, inflicts irrevocable damage, and often leaves
a jaded perception of love in its wake. Many individuals that have been
harmed by an intimate partner feel afraid, embarrassed, blame themselves, and believe they are unable to reveal their pain to family members, friends, or others; even when they are in dire need of assistance.

It is important to evaluate relationships daily, and take inventory of
situations that may have given you pause. You might be experiencing
domestic violence if your partner:

1. Monitors your phone calls, emails, text messages, social
    media accounts; micromanages your time; make you account
    for every minute of your time (when you run errands, visit
    friends, commute to work);

2. Is overly critical; insulting; humiliates you (public or private);
    makes threats; blackmails you to expose private / sensitive
    personal information;

3. Acts insanely jealous; possessive; constantly accusing you
    of being unfaithful; smothers you/ 'clingy'; shows up unan-
    nounced (home, job, gym); stalks you; calls excessively;

4. Is hypersensitive; has unpredictable, radical mood changes;
    explosive temper; denies/minimizes the abuse/ blames you for
    the violent behavior (your fault); and

5. Threatens you with weapons; hit; kick; shove; slap; strangle;
    spit; or otherwise hurts you, your children, pets; cause visible
    injuries (bruises, cuts, burns); destroys /vandalize property
    (cell phone, car, home).

Your partner might offer reasonable explanations, apologize, promise to change, attend counseling, or make spiritual commitments; however, it is crucial to understand that domestic violence is cyclical, becoming more frequent and severe over time.

Despite many valiant efforts, victims cannot stop their partner's abusive behavior, and ultimatums don't make people change. Abuse isn't a couple's issue, but rather the choice of the abuser. Know your strength. Know your limitations.

Section 4.3

Self-Test for Women: Am I Being Abused?

Text in this section is excerpted from "Violence Against Women: Am I Being Abused?" Office on Women's Health (OWH), September 30, 2015.

It can be hard to know if you're being abused. You may think that your husband is allowed to make you have sex. That's not true. Forced sex is rape, no matter who does it. You may think that cruel or threatening words are not abuse. They are. And sometimes emotional abuse is a sign that a person will become physically violent.

Below is a list of possible signs of abuse. Some of these are illegal. All of them are wrong. You may be abused if your partner:

- Monitors what you're doing all the time

- Unfairly accuses you of being unfaithful all the time

- Prevents or discourages you from seeing friends or family

- Prevents or discourages you from going to work or school

- Gets very angry during and after drinking alcohol or using drugs

- Controls how you spend your money

- Controls your use of needed medicines

- Decides things for you that you should be allowed to decide (like what to wear or eat)

- Humiliates you in front of others
- Destroys your property or things that you care about
- Threatens to hurt you, the children, or pets
- Hurts you (by hitting, beating, pushing, shoving, punching, slapping, kicking, or biting)
- Uses (or threatens to use) a weapon against you
- Forces you to have sex against your will
- Controls your birth control or insists that you get pregnant
- Blames you for his or her violent outbursts
- Threatens to harm himself or herself when upset with you
- Says things like, "If I can't have you, then no one can."

If you think someone is abusing you, get help. Abuse can have serious physical and emotional effects. No one has the right to hurt you.

Chapter 5

Stalking

Chapter Contents

Section 5.1

Stalking: What It Is and What You Can Do about It

Text in this section is excerpted from "Violence against Women: Stalking," Office on Women's Health (OWH), September 30, 2015.

Stalking is contact (usually two or more times) from someone that makes you feel afraid or harassed.

Examples of stalking include:

- Following or spying on you
- Sending you unwanted emails or letters
- Calling you often
- Showing up at your house, school, or work
- Leaving you unwanted gifts

You can be stalked by a stranger, but most stalkers are people you know, like a boyfriend or ex-boyfriend. Sometimes, a current partner will stalk you by calling very often, texting constantly, or asking where you are all the time. These may be signs of an abusive relationship.

Stalking is a crime and can be dangerous. To learn more about the laws against stalking, contact the National Center for Victims of Crime helpline. Stalking can be very frightening, and can make you feel out of control, anxious, and depressed. It can affect your ability to sleep, eat, and work. If you are being stalked, get support from people who care about you.

If you think you're being stalked, consider these steps:

- File a complaint with the police. Make sure to tell them about all threats.
- If you are in immediate danger, find a safe place to go, like a police station, friend's house, domestic violence shelter, fire

station, or public area. If you can't get out of danger, but can get to a phone, call 911.

- Get a restraining order. A restraining order requires the stalker to stay away from you and not contact you. You can learn how to get a restraining order from a domestic violence shelter, the police, or an attorney in your area.

- Write down every incident. Include the time, date, and other important information.

- Keep evidence such as videotapes, voicemail messages, photos of property damage, and letters. Get names of witnesses.

- Contact support systems to help you, including domestic violence and rape crisis hotlines, domestic violence shelters, counseling services, and support groups. Keep these numbers handy in case you need them.

- Tell important people in your life about the stalking problem, including the police, your employer, family, friends, and neighbors.

- Carry a cellphone at all times so you can call for help.

- Consider changing your phone number (though some people leave their number active to collect evidence). You also can ask the phone company about call blocking and other safety features.

- Secure your home with alarms, locks, and motion-sensitive lights.

Cyberstalking

Cyberstalking is using the Internet, email, or other electronic communications to stalk someone. Examples of cyberstalking include:

- Sending unwanted, frightening, or obscene emails, text messages, or instant messages (IMs)

- Harassing or threatening someone in a chat room

- Posting improper messages on a message board

- Tracking your computer and Internet use

- Sending electronic viruses

- Pretending to be you in a chat room

If you are cyberstalked:

- Send the person a clear, written warning not to contact you again

- If the stalking continues, get help from the police. You also can contact a domestic violence shelter and the National Center for Victims of Crime Helpline for support and suggestions.

- Print out copies of evidence such as emails. Keep a record of the stalking and any contact with police.

- Consider blocking messages from the harasser

- Change your email address

- File a complaint with the person's Internet Service Provider (ISP)

- Never post online profiles or messages with details that could be used to identify or locate you (such as age, sex, address, work-place, phone number, school or places you hang out)

Section 5.2

Factors Contributing to Stalking

Text in this section is excerpted from "Stalking," Community Oriented Policing Services (COPS), July 2012.

Understanding the factors that contribute to stalking will help you frame your own local analysis questions, determine good effectiveness measures, recognize key intervention points, and select appropriate responses.

Stalking Behaviors

Stalking, by definition, is not a one-time act but a course of conduct. It may involve a mix of patently criminal acts and acts that, in isolation, would seem nonthreatening. It is the pattern and context of these criminal and noncriminal acts that constitute stalking.

Stalking often includes:

- Assaulting the victim

- Violating protective orders

- Sexually assaulting the victim

- Vandalizing the victim's property

- Burglarizing the victim's home or otherwise stealing from the victim

- Threatening the victim

- Killing the victim's pet(s)

Other common stalking behaviors include:

- Sending the victim cards or gifts

- Leaving telephone or e-mail messages for the victim

- Disclosing to the victim personal information the offender has uncovered about him or her

- Disseminating personal information about the victim to others

- Following the victim

- Visiting the victim at work

- Waiting outside the victim's home

- Sending the victim photographs taken of him or her without consent

- Monitoring the victim's Internet history and computer usage

- Using technology to gather images of or information about the victim

Types of Stalkers

While stalkers come from different backgrounds and have different personalities, researchers have developed several widely accepted typologies of them. It is important to emphasize that, while stalker typologies can be helpful, they are only general classifications. Whenever possible, a properly trained professional should conduct a threat assessment. Individual stalkers may not precisely fit any single category, and often exhibit characteristics associated with more than one category. However, the typology can alert investigators and victim advocates to certain general characteristics exhibited by similar stalkers, and help them with threat assessment and safety planning.

One widely accepted typology of stalkers is based on the stalker's underlying motives, and includes the following categories:

Simple obsessional. This is the most common type. The stalker is usually a male, and the victim an ex-spouse, ex-lover, or former boss. The stalking sometimes results from the stalker's feeling the victim has mistreated him or her. In intimate relationships, the stalking frequently begins before a breakup.

Love obsessional. The stalker is a stranger or casual acquaintance to the victim, but is obsessed and begins a campaign of harassment to make the victim aware of his or her existence. This type often stalks a celebrity or public figure, but can also stalk a noncelebrity.

Erotomania. The stalker falsely believes that the victim is in love with him or her, and that, but for some external obstacle or interference, they would be together. The victim may be rich or famous, or in a position of power (e.g., a movie star, employer, or political figure). In this situation, the stalker could also pose a great risk to those close to the victim (e.g., a spouse or lover perceived to be "in the way").

False victimization syndrome. This is extremely rare and involves someone who consciously or subconsciously wants to play the role of victim. He or she may make up a complex tale, claiming to be a stalking victim. In such cases, the would-be victim is sometimes the actual stalker, and the alleged offender is the real victim. Another typology used to classify stalkers identifies them by their relationship to the victim. This typology divides stalkers into two basic categories: intimate and nonintimate. The following is a brief description of these categories:

Intimate. A former relationship exists between the stalker and the victim. There is likely a history of abuse, such as domestic violence, by the stalker. The stalker often seeks to reestablish a relationship the victim has tried to end.

Nonintimate. The stalker has no interpersonal relationship with the victim. He or she may choose the victim after a brief encounter, or simply after observing the victim. The victim is often unable to identify the stalker when he or she first becomes aware of being stalked. This type is subdivided into two categories:

- **Organized.** The relationship between the stalker and the victim is characterized by one-way, anonymous communication from stalker to victim. The stalker is methodical and calculating, and the victim usually does not know the stalker's identity.

- **Delusional.** The relationship between the stalker and the victim is based solely on the stalker's psychological fixation on the victim. The stalker is delusional and falsely believes he or she has a relationship or other connection with the victim.

Again, stalkers often exhibit behaviors from more than one typology. The typologies are an overview, and you should never use them as a substitute for a thorough threat assessment.

Stalkers are, by their very nature, obsessive and dangerous.23 Regardless of typology, you should always consider stalkers capable of killing their victims. Anyone the stalker perceives as impeding his or her contact with the victim, including police, prosecutors, and advocates, is also at risk. Some stalkers seek union with their victims through murder-suicide. Any suicidal statements or gestures the stalker makes should serve as an indication that the stalker is a high-risk threat.

You should also examine the stalker's background for depression, psychiatric hospitalizations, and other indications that he or she may be suicidal.

Section 5.3

Security Tips for Stalking Victims

Text in this section is excerpted from "Interstate Stalking,"
U.S. Department of Justice (DOJ), April 20, 2015.

In 1996, Congress passed an anti-stalking law as part of the Violence Against Women Act (VAWA). Under this law, it is a federal felony to cross state lines to stalk or harass an individual if the conduct causes fear of serious bodily injury or death to the stalking victim or to the victim's immediate family members. It is a federal felony to stalk or harass on military or U.S. territorial lands, including Indian country (18 U.S.C. § 2261A). It is also a federal crime to cross state lines or enter or leave Indian country in violation of a qualifying Protection Order (18 U.S.C. § 2262).

There are also state laws dealing with the crime of stalking.

If You Are in Danger, Find a Safe Place to Go Such As:

- Police/Fire Department

- Homes of friends or relatives preferably unknown to the stalker

- Family crisis shelters

- Crowded public buildings or places

After You Are Safe, Notify Appropriate Police Agencies

- Give an accurate description of the stalker, his or her vehicle, address (if known) and a recent photograph if you have one.

- Notify security personnel in apartments and/or appropriate personnel at your work place, or children's school, and other places that are a part of your normal routine. Ask law enforcement about security measures they can initiate. Some agencies have alarms available for stalking victims or "panic button" alarms can be rented from private security agencies.

- As well as helping to protect you, by reporting a crime of stalking, police can keep an independent record of the incidents, which can assist them in developing a threat assessment of the stalker.

- Police reports may also help you get a protection order from a court or demonstrate that an existing order has been violated.

Stop All Contact with a Stalker—Now and for Good

Consult with a victim services provider about creating a personal safety plan and follow it.

If you believe the stalker truly poses a threat, consider obtaining a restraining order, but be aware that service of the order to the stalker may provoke a response.

Document Stalking Behavior

- It is important to keep a record of incidents which may support a criminal prosecution.

- Record dates, times of day and places of contact with the individual who is stalking you.

- Log any telephone calls and save answering machine messages.

- Save any correspondence from stalker, including the envelope.

- Document threats in detail.

- Provide names and addresses of witnesses to any incidents to law enforcement or a prosecutor.

Other Illegal Acts

If the stalker has assaulted you physically or sexually, has entered your home without permission, or has damaged or stolen your property, report it to police. They should also photograph injuries to your person or damage to your property. These are separate crimes which can be prosecuted.

Ways to Increase Your Home and Personal Safety

- Telling a stalker that you don't want to talk to him is still talking to him or her. Stop all contact.

- Treat any threat as legitimate and call police immediately. Install dead bolts. If you lose the key, change the locks.

- If possible, install outside lights activated by a motion detector.

- Maintain an unlisted phone number. If harassing calls persist, contact telephone company security and they can assist you with options to trace the origin of such calls.

- Use a telephone message machine to screen calls. This documents contact by a stalker, for police.

- Vary the routes you take and limit the time you spend walking.

- Keep children and pets indoors and always under supervision. If you have children in common, arrange through the court for the exchange of custody or visitation through a third party.

- Tell trusted relatives, friends, a landlord and neighbors about the situation.

- Provide family, friends, neighbors and your employer with a photo or description of the stalker and the car he or she drives.

- Advise your employer and co-workers of the problem and provide a picture of the stalker if available. If the stalker shows up at work, have someone contact the police, and avoid any personal contact.

- Don't park in secluded areas.

Section 5.4

Stalking Statistics

Text in this section is excerpted from "Prevalence and Characteristics of Sexual Violence, Stalking, and Intimate Partner Violence Victimization — National Intimate Partner and Sexual Violence Survey, United States, 2011," Centers for Disease Control and Prevention (CDC), September 5, 2014.

Stalking Victimization

In the United States, an estimated 15.2% of women (18.3 million women) have experienced stalking during their lifetimes that made them feel very fearful or made them believe that they or someone close to them would be harmed or killed (Table 6.1.). In addition, an estimated 4.2% of women (approximately 5.1 million women) were stalked in the 12 months before taking the survey.

Nationally, an estimated 5.7% of men (or nearly 6.5 million) have experienced stalking victimization during their lifetimes, while an estimated 2.1% of men (or 2.4 million) were stalked in the 12 months before taking the survey.

Prevalence of Stalking Victimization

An estimated 24.5% of American Indian/Alaska Native women experienced stalking during their lifetimes, and an estimated 22.4% of multiracial women were stalked during their lifetimes (Table 6.1.). An estimated 15.9% of non-Hispanic white women experienced stalking during their lifetimes, and the prevalence of stalking for Hispanic and non-Hispanic black women was an estimated 14.2% and 13.9%, respectively. The estimate for Asian or Pacific Islander women was not reported because the case count was too small to produce a reliable estimate.

An estimated 9.3% of multiracial men experienced stalking during their lifetimes, as did an estimated 9.1% of non-Hispanic black men, 8.2% of Hispanic men, and 4.7% of non-Hispanic white men. The estimates for the other racial/ethnic groups of men are not reported because case counts were too small to produce a reliable estimate.

Frequency of Stalking Acts among Stalking Victims

A variety of tactics were used to stalk victims during their lifetimes. An estimated 61.7% of female stalking victims were approached, such as at their home or work; over half (an estimated 55.3%) received unwanted messages, such as text and voice messages; an estimated 54.5% received unwanted telephone calls, including hang-ups (Table 6.2.). In addition, nearly half (an estimated 49.7%) of female stalking victims were watched, followed, or spied on with a listening device, camera, or global positioning system (GPS) device.

An estimated 58.2% of male stalking victims received unwanted telephone calls, and an estimated 56.7% received unwanted messages. An estimated 47.7% of male stalking victims were approached by their perpetrator, and an estimated 32.2% were watched, followed, or spied on with a listening or other device.

Characteristics of Stalking Perpetrators

Among persons who were victims of stalking during their lifetimes, the sex of the perpetrator varied somewhat by the sex of the victim. Among female stalking victims, an estimated 88.3% were stalked by only male perpetrators; an estimated 7.1% had only female perpetrators. Among male stalking victims, almost half (an estimated 48.0%) were stalked by only male perpetrators while a similar proportion (an estimated 44.6%) were stalked by only female perpetrators.

Both female and male victims often identified their stalkers as persons whom they knew or with whom they had an intimate relationship. Among female stalking victims, an estimated 60.8% were stalked by a current or former intimate partner, nearly one-quarter (an estimated 24.9%) were stalked by an acquaintance, an estimated 16.2% were stalked by a stranger, and an estimated 6.2% were stalked by a family member (Figure 6.1). Among male stalking victims, an estimated 43.5% were stalked by an intimate partner, an estimated 31.9% by an acquaintance, an estimated 20.0% by a stranger, and an estimated 9.9% by a family member.

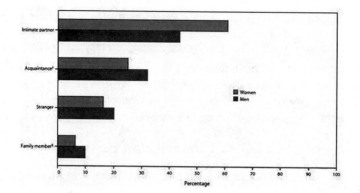

Figure 5.1. *Lifetime reports of stalking among female and male victims, by type of perpetrator*

The figure shows lifetime reports of stalking among female and male victims by type of perpetrator, using data from the National Intimate Partner and Sexual Violence Survey conducted in the United States in 2011. Four types of perpetrators are shown in order of prevalence: intimate partner, acquaintance (which includes friends, neighbors, family friends, first date, someone briefly known, and persons not known well), stranger, and family member (which includes immediate and extended family members).

Chapter 6

Sexual Harassment

Chapter Contents

Section 6.1

Sexual Harassment: What It Is

Text in this section is excerpted from "Manager Workplace Sexual
Harassment Prevention Toolkit: (Your Guide to Preventing and
Addressing Sexual Harassment in the Workplace)," Office of Equity,
Diversity, and Inclusion (EDI), September 25, 2014.

What is sexual harassment?

Unwelcome sexual advances, requests for sexual favours, and other
verbal or physical conduct of a sexual nature constitute sexual harassment when:

1. submission to such conduct is made either explicitly or implic-
    itly a term or condition of an individual's employment;

2. submission to or rejection of such conduct by an individual is
    used as the basis for employment decisions affecting such indi-
    vidual; or

such conduct has the purpose or effect of unreasonably interfering
with an individual's work performance or creating an intimidating,
hostile, or offensive working environment.

What are unwelcome sexual advances?

Unwelcome sexual advances constitute sexual harassment when
submission to such conduct is made either explicitly or implicitly as a
term or condition of an individual's employment.

What law(s) are violated by sexual harassment?

Sexual harassment is a form of sex discrimination that violates Title
VII of the Civil Rights Act of 1964. Title VII applies to employers with
15 or more employees, including state and local governments. It also
applies to employment agencies and to labor organizations, as well as
to the federal government.

Table 6.1. Examples of Sexual Harassment

Examples of Sexual Harassment	
Verbal:	**Visual:**
Sexual jokes	Staring
Whistling, kissing sounds, and smacking lips	Looking someone up and down
Repeatedly asking someone to make romantic plans, a date	Displaying images of a sexual nature
Sexual comments regarding someone's person	Winking, blowing kisses, licking lips
Written:	**Physical:**
Electronic forms of written communication such as e-mails, texts, electronic posts of a sexual nature	Touching oneself in a sexual manner while near another person
Hard copy forms of written communication such as letters and graffiti of a sexual nature	Blocking or crowding someone

Table 6.2. Key points

Victim	• The victim as well as the harasser may be a woman or a man. The victim does not have to be of the opposite sex.
	• The victim does not have to be the person harassed but could be anyone affected by the offensive conduct.
Harasser(s)	The harasser(s) can be the victim's supervisor, a supervisor in another area, a co-worker, an agent of the NIH, another NIH employee, or a non-employee who has a business relationship with the NIH.
Action(s)	• Unlawful sexual harassment may occur without economic injury to or discharge of the victim.
	• The harasser's conduct must be unwelcome

Section 6.2

Prevalence of Sexual Harassment

Text in this section is excerpted from "Preventing and
Addressing Workplace Harassment," U.S. Equal Employment
Opportunity Commission (EEOC), January 14, 2015.

Sexual Harassment Remains a Serious Problem for Women in the Workplace, Particularly for Women in Low-Wage Jobs and Traditionally Male-Dominated Jobs.

More than seventy-two million women work outside the home in the United States, comprising nearly half of workers in all occupations (47 percent). Women's paychecks are more critical to their families than ever—women today are the primary breadwinners in more than 41 percent of families with children. But for too many of these women, sexual harassment undermines their best efforts to provide for themselves and their families.

In federal fiscal year 2013, the combined total number of harassment charges filed with the EEOC and state and local Fair Employment Practices Agencies was over 30,000. More than 10,000 of these charges involved sexual harassment, and 82 percent were brought by women. But these charge statistics do not even begin to represent the extent of sexual harassment in the workplace. In a recent survey, 25 percent of women said that they have experienced sexual harassment at work, and yet 70 percent of women say they have never reported it. Whether suffering harassment from supervisors, co-workers, or third parties (such as customers), most victims of harassment are still suffering in silence.

Low-Wage Workers Face Particularly High Rates of Sexual Harassment.

Women comprise more than three-quarters of workers in the ten largest low-wage occupations (those that typically pay less than $10.10 an hour). Women working in the restaurant industry, particularly women who rely on tips to supplement a sub-minimum wage, are among the lowest-paid workers and experience sexual harassment at high rates. Women constitute 66 percent of the tipped occupations that receive a sub-minimum wage of $2.13 per hour that must be supplemented with tips—wages that leave many women working and living in poverty. And even though just seven percent of American women work in the restaurant industry, a review of EEOC charge data by the Restaurant Opportunities Center (ROC) United over an eleven-month period in 2011 found that nearly 37 percent of EEOC sexual harassment charges came from women in the restaurant industry.

A more recent ROC report further illuminates this problem. That report described harassment as simply "an accepted part of the culture" for women working in restaurants. The median wage for restaurant workers "hovers" around $9 an hour, which includes tips—and overall rates of harassment reported are high. Sixty percent of women and transgendered restaurant workers report that sexual harassment is an uncomfortable aspect of work life, over half of whom describe sexual harassment as occurring on at least a weekly basis. This harassment stems from management (according to 66 percent of restaurant workers), co-workers (according to 80 percent of restaurant workers), and customers (according to 78 percent of restaurant workers).

The culture of sexual harassment is exacerbated for women required by their employers to wear different, and more revealing, uniforms from their male co-workers, and three times as many women report feeling uncomfortable in their uniforms compared to men. Women responded, for example, that their uniforms included having to wear "corsets . . . pencil skirts or shorts, no pants," and high-heels at least one inch high, compared to their male coworkers who wore slacks, button-down shirts, and comfortable shoes. One woman bartender explained that she was instructed to appear as "date ready," that she had to "flaunt" her body, and deal with the results.

More than half of women surveyed by ROC reported that they believe that a wage structure that left them dependent on tips forced them to tolerate inappropriate behavior that made them nervous or uncomfortable. In fact, ROC reports that the very highest rates of sexual harassment for restaurant workers are experienced by women in tipped occupations, in states where the sub-minimum wage is $2.13 per hour.

Most restaurant workers who experience sexual harassment—in fact, a full majority—never report it, even though the harassment has a profound impact on their lives. According to ROC's findings:

Two-thirds of women workers felt they would face negative repercussions if they complained about or reported sexual harassment from management, and 46 percent felt there would be negative repercussions if they complained about or reported sexual harassment from co-workers. Seventy percent felt there would be negative repercussions if they complained about or reported sexual harassment from customers (nearly 63 percent of restaurant workers ignore sexually harassing behaviors from customers). A significant majority of women workers felt they would experience negative consequences, including financial loss, public humiliation, or job termination if they tried to report sexual harassment from management and customers.

Recent cases brought by employees in the retail industries further illustrate the types of harassment facing women working in low-paying jobs in stores—harassment that comes from customers, coworkers, and supervisors.

Sexual harassment is also a serious problem for women working in the hospitality industry, due in part to "the unusual hours and conditions of work, the interactions of persons in the delivery of service, and traditional personnel practices in the industry." Women who work as hotel employees report facing sexual harassment from co-workers, supervisors, and hotel guests.

And in agriculture jobs, women are underrepresented, comprising only 22 percent of the agriculture workforce, and they share a low hourly median wage with their male co-workers ($8.90). And women who work in agriculture are often migrant workers, and whole families and communities of farmworkers migrate, work, and live together during the work season. For migrant workers who are harassed, seeking justice can mean risking their livelihoods, putting their families at risk and potentially facing deportation.

Women in Higher Paid, Nontraditional Jobs Suffer High Rates of Sexual Harassment.

Although the pervasive nature of sexual harassment for women in low-wage jobs has been well documented, women in the better-paying jobs that are non-traditional for women also face high rates of sexual harassment, with few female co-workers to turn to help them address it.

Construction and extraction jobs are an important example. Those jobs typically offer women the opportunity to earn higher wages than in traditionally female occupations. The median hourly wage for construction and extraction occupations was $19.55 in 2013, which is roughly double the median hourly wage for female-dominated occupations like home health aides, maids, housekeepers, and child care workers.

Nonetheless, the number of women in construction and extraction has held steady for the past thirty years, not yet rising above 2.6 percent of the workforce. Women make up just 9.1 percent of construction workers, and 13.1 percent of miners. Most of the women in these industries have few or no female co-workers, and face extreme sexual harassment and denigration.

A study by the U.S. Department of Labor reported that 88 percent of women construction workers experience sexual harassment at work, more than three times the rate of women in the general workforce. In fact, according to the Occupational Safety and Health Administration, the mining industry features the highest rate of sexual harassment complaints per 100,000 employed women. In these industries, the harassment women may face intensifies the already high risks of physical injury, leaving some women afraid for their lives.

The problem of sexual harassment is exacerbated in environments where workers more generally are at risk for physical injury; reports of harassment facing women working in law enforcement and fire-fighting illustrates this point. Women account for 11.3 percent of sworn officers, 12.9 percent of sheriffs, and 16.1 percent of federal officers. In these industries, too, women face disproportionately high rates of gender-based harassment. "Anywhere from 60-70 percent of women officers experienced sexual/gender harassment." Women in law enforcement who have complained of harassment report that their departments stopped sending backup to assist them in violent situation; without this and other essential protection, women reported leaving the force entirely.

Women in fire fighting report facing similar perils resulting from sexual harassment on the job. According to census data, women account for only 3.7 percent of fire fighters. Shockingly, more than half of the nation's fire departments have never employed a woman fire fighter. Women fire fighters face sexual harassment at rates that are similar to construction and extraction workers. More than 84 percent of women fire fighters report experiencing gender discrimination in some form, including sexual harassment. If they complain of harassment, female fire fighters have reported facing comparably lethal retaliatory conduct as female police officers, such as male co-workers shutting off their water supplies.

Section 6.3

Understanding the Link between Childhood Bullying and Sexual Violence

Text in this section is excerpted from "Understanding the Link between Childhood Bullying and Sexual Violence," U.S. Department of Health and Human Services (HHS), March 19, 2013.

Most experts acknowledge that bullying is a serious problem that has negative consequences for both perpetrators and victims. However, we know very little about how bullying early in life affects future behaviors.

Several years ago, the Centers for Disease Control and Prevention began a partnership with researchers at the University of Illinois, Urbana-Champaign to better understand how bullying may lead to sexual violence. It's important to know whether youth who engage in bullying behavior are also at risk for sexually harassing their peers. This information can help us prevent sexual harassment from occurring in the first place.

- **Bullying:** Bullying is unwanted, aggressive behavior among school aged children that involves a real or perceived power imbalance.

- **Homophobic Teasing:** Negative attitudes and behaviors directed toward individuals who identify as or are perceived to be lesbian, gay, bisexual, or transgendered.

- **Sexual Harassment:** Includes comments, sexual rumor spreading, or groping.

For three years, researchers surveyed over 1,300 middle school youth yearly. The youth told them about their experiences with sexual harassment and bullying others as well as if they used phrases like "homo, gay, lesbo, fag or dyke" to tease other students.

This is what researchers found:

- 12% of females and 12% of males bullied others

- 34% of males and 20% of females teased a friend by calling him/her names like homo, gay, lesbo, fag or dyke (i.e., homophobic teasing)

- 34% of males and 28% of females made sexual comments to other students

- 5% of males and 7% of females spread a sexual rumor about another student

When researchers examined how these behaviors changed over the three years, they found that students who bullied others and teased others using homophobic slurs in 6th grade were more likely to tell us that they sexually harassed other students in 7th grade. This suggests that both bullying behaviors and homophobic teasing behaviors may be precursors to later sexual harassment behaviors, as the youth get older.

Section 6.4

Harassment in the Workplace

Text in this section is excerpted from "Prevention of Harassment in the Workplace," U.S. Department of Justice (DOJ), October 20, 2015.

Sexual harassment occurs when employment decisions affecting an employee, such as hiring, firing, promotions, awards, transfers or disciplinary actions, result from submission to or rejection of unwelcome sexual conduct. Sexual harassment can also be any activity which creates an intimidating, hostile, or offensive work environment for members of one sex, whether such activity is carried out by a supervisor or by a co-worker. This could include such workplace conduct as displaying "pinup" calendars or sexually demeaning pictures, telling sexually oriented jokes, making sexually offensive remarks, engaging in unwanted sexual teasing, subjecting another employee to pressure for dates, sexual advances, or unwelcome touching.

Action for Victims:

If you think you are being sexually harassed on the job:

- Know your rights.

- Tell the harasser that the behavior is unwelcome and must cease immediately.

- Report such behavior immediately to the supervisor, or a higher level official.

- Seek support from a friend or colleague.

- Keep a written record, documenting as precisely as possible what happened, when it took place, the names of witnesses, your response, and any other information that may be helpful later.

- Find out whether other employees have also been harassed and whether they could offer corroborating testimony.

- Seek advice on how to deal with the situation from your Office of Equal Employment Opportunity (EEO), the Office of Professional Responsibility, or the Office of the Inspector General.

- Learn about the EEO Complaint process.

- Discuss options with an EEO Counselor or your representative.

- File a complaint.

Action for Managers:

- Be sure that your own conduct sets an example, and is not such that you may be vulnerable to claims of sexual harassment.

- Take affirmative steps to ensure that your employees are not involved in harassment.

- Communicate this policy on harassment to all employees.

- Make it clear that claims of harassment will be investigated promptly and thoroughly and that appropriate discipline will follow.

- Assure employees that you will treat complaints seriously and fairly.

Part Two

Intimate Partner Abuse

Chapter 7

Types of Intimate Partner Abuse

Chapter Contents

Section 7.1

Primary Forms of Intimate Partner Abuse

Text in this section is excerpted from "Domestic Violence,"
U.S. Department of Justice (DOJ), October 6, 2015; and text from
"Intimate Partner Violence: Definitions," Centers for Disease
Control and Prevention (CDC), June 19, 2015.

Intimate partner violence (IPV) is a serious, preventable public health problem that affects millions of Americans. The term "intimate partner violence" describes physical violence, sexual violence, stalking and psychological aggression (including coercive acts) by a current or former intimate partner.

An intimate partner is a person with whom one has a close personal relationship that can be characterized by the following:

- Emotional connectedness

- Regular contact

- Ongoing physical contact and sexual behavior

- Identity as a couple

- Familiarity and knowledge about each other's lives

The relationship need not involve all of these dimensions. Examples of intimate partners include current or former spouses, boyfriends or girlfriends, dating partners, or sexual partners. IPV can occur between heterosexual or same-sex couples and does not require sexual intimacy.

IPV can vary in frequency and severity. It occurs on a continuum, ranging from one episode that might or might not have lasting impact to chronic and severe episodes over a period of years.

What Is Domestic Violence?

We define domestic violence as a pattern of abusive behavior in any relationship that is used by one partner to gain or maintain power and control over another intimate partner. Domestic violence can be physical, sexual, emotional, economic, or psychological actions or threats of actions that influence another person. This includes any behaviors that intimidate, manipulate, humiliate, isolate, frighten, terrorize, coerce, threaten, blame, hurt, injure, or wound someone.

Physical Abuse: Hitting, slapping, shoving, grabbing, pinching, biting, hair pulling, etc. are types of physical abuse. This type of abuse also includes denying a partner medical care or forcing alcohol and/or drug use upon him or her.

Sexual Abuse: Coercing or attempting to coerce any sexual contact or behavior without consent. Sexual abuse includes, but is certainly not limited to, marital rape, attacks on sexual parts of the body, forcing sex after physical violence has occurred, or treating one in a sexually demeaning manner.

Emotional Abuse: Undermining an individual's sense of self-worth and/or self-esteem is abusive. This may include, but is not limited to constant criticism, diminishing one's abilities, name-calling, or damaging one's relationship with his or her children.

Economic Abuse: Is defined as making or attempting to make an individual financially dependent by maintaining total control over financial resources, withholding one's access to money, or forbidding one's attendance at school or employment.

Psychological Abuse: Elements of psychological abuse include – but are not limited to – causing fear by intimidation; threatening physical harm to self, partner, children, or partner's family or friends; destruction of pets and property; and forcing isolation from family, friends, or school and/or work.

Domestic violence can happen to anyone regardless of race, age, sexual orientation, religion, or gender. Domestic violence affects people of all socioeconomic backgrounds and education levels. Domestic violence occurs in both opposite-sex and same-sex relationships and can happen to intimate partners who are married, living together, or dating.

Domestic violence not only affects those who are abused, but also has a substantial effect on family members, friends, co-workers, other witnesses, and the community at large. Children, who grow up witnessing domestic violence, are among those seriously affected by this crime. Frequent exposure to violence in the home not only predisposes children to numerous social and physical problems, but also teaches them that violence is a normal way of life – therefore, increasing their risk of becoming society's next generation of victims and abusers.

Section 7.2

Physical Abuse

Physical abuse is any deliberate use of bodily force that causes pain, injury, or trauma to another person. Some examples of actions that are considered physical abuse include punching, hitting, slapping, smacking, kicking, scratching, biting, pinching, shaking, choking, burning, pulling hair, throwing objects, and forcing someone to swallow a harmful substance. Physical abuse can be perpetrated by anyone, including parents, siblings, other relatives, boyfriends, girlfriends, babysitters, other caregivers, and classmates.

In the case of parents and caregivers, corporal punishment or physical discipline that is applied to children in an excessive or inappropriate manner can be abusive. The risk of child abuse is highest among parents who are immature, lack parenting skills, do not understand developmentally appropriate behavior, and were not exposed to positive parental role models in their own childhood. Other factors related to physical abuse include financial stress or other crises in the home environment, and drug or alcohol addiction.

Warning Signs and Negative Effects

The warning signs of physical abuse may be physical, emotional, or behavioral. Some of the possible physical indicators include bruises, cuts, abrasions, fractures, sprains, dislocations, burns, missing teeth, traumatic hair loss, internal injuries, and bleeding from body orifices. Since many types of physical injuries can result from accidents or participation in sports, it may be difficult to tell whether warning signs indicate abuse. Certain types of bruises are rarely accidental, however, including bilateral bruising on the arms, wrap-around bruising on the wrists, and bilateral bruising on the inner thighs.

In determining whether specific injuries are the result of physical abuse, it may be helpful to watch for patterns of similar injuries over time. Additional warning signs include injuries that are unexplained,

explained in an implausible manner, or explained differently by various family members. Physical abuse may also be suspected if medical treatment is delayed or sought from several different practitioners to prevent any one doctor from noticing a pattern.

The emotional and behavioral signs of physical abuse vary widely, depending on the person. Some victims of physical abuse react by becoming angry, aggressive, or violent, while others respond by becoming extremely quiet, passive, and withdrawn. It is common for people who experience physical abuse to feel frightened, worried, sad, depressed, worthless, lonely, isolated, angry, frustrated, numb, or desperate. Victims may also have trouble sleeping, concentrating on tasks, or eating normally. They may consider running away from home or harming themselves. Although many people who are physically abused feel guilty and worry that they may have done something to deserve the mistreatment, it is important to understand that physical abuse is never the victim's fault.

Some of the effects of physical abuse may continue over the long term. Studies show that people who are physically abused as children are more likely to behave aggressively as teenagers and adults. In fact, up to one-third of children who experience physical abuse become abusers in adulthood. Abused children also face a much greater risk of substance abuse, depression, post-traumatic stress disorder, and suicide.

Sources of Help and Support

When physical abuse occurs regularly over a long time, the victim may begin to see it as a normal part of life. Some people who experience physical abuse may be confused because they still have feelings of love or affection for the person who is hurting them. If the abuser is a parent or caregiver, the victim may worry that stopping the abuse would mean being alone or being placed in foster care. No matter what the circumstances, however, physical abuse is always wrong, and there are many sources available to help make it stop.

The first step in stopping physical abuse is confiding in a trusted person. It is important to feel comfortable and safe with the person chosen, whether it is a parent, family member, neighbor, religious leader, teacher, counselor, school nurse, or coach. Since talking about physical abuse can be difficult, it may be helpful to start by putting the information in writing. There are also websites and hotlines available to provide resources and support for people trying to stop physical abuse.

Telling someone about physical abuse not only helps the victim, but it can also protect other people from being abused in the future. People in certain professions—including teachers, social workers, doctors, therapists, and day-care providers—who notice signs of child abuse are required by law to report it to law enforcement or child protective services agencies.

References

1. Dubowitz, H. and D. DePanfilis. "What Is Physical Abuse?" *Handbook for Child Protection Practice*. Thousand Oaks, CA: Sage, 2000.

2. "Physical Abuse." ChildLine, n.d.

Section 7.3

Sexual Abuse

Text in this section is excerpted from "Violence Against Women, Sexual Assault and Abuse," Office on Women's Health (OWH), September 30, 2015.

What are rape and sexual assault?

Rape is sex you don't agree to, including forcing a body part or an object into your vagina, rectum (bottom), or mouth. In the United States, almost one in five women has been raped during her lifetime.

Sexual assault or abuse is any type of sexual activity that a person does not agree to, including:

- Rape or attempted rape

- Touching your body or making you touch someone else's

- Incest or sexual contact with a child

- Someone watching or photographing you in sexual situations

- Someone exposing his or her body to you

Sometimes, sexual violence is committed by a stranger. Most often, though, it is committed by someone you know, including a date or an intimate partner like a husband, ex-husband, or boyfriend. Sexual violence is always wrong, and a person who is sexually abused does not ever "cause" the attack.

Keep in mind that there are times when a person is not able to agree to sex, such as if they are drunk or have been drugged with a date rape drug, or if they are underage.

Women who are sexually abused may suffer serious health problems, such as sexually transmitted infections, stomach problems, and ongoing pain. They also are at risk for emotional problems, like depression, anxiety, and post-traumatic stress disorder. If you or someone you know has been sexually abused, it is important to get help as soon as possible.

Getting help for sexual assault

Take steps right away if you have been assaulted:

- Get away from the attacker and find a safe place as fast as you can. Call 911.

- Call someone you trust or a hotline, such as the free National Sexual Assault Hotline at 800-656-HOPE (4673).

- Protect any evidence. Do not clean any part of your body or comb your hair. Do not change clothes. Try not to touch anything at the crime scene.

- Go to your nearest hospital emergency room right away. You need to be examined and treated for injuries you may not even know you have. Ask to be screened for sexually transmitted infections (STIs) and for emergency contraception to help prevent pregnancy. The hospital also can collect evidence like hairs, saliva, semen, or clothing fiber that the attacker may have left behind.

- Discuss filing a police report. If you're not sure whether you want to file a report, ask hospital staff if they can collect evidence without filing a report. It is best to collect evidence as soon as possible.

After a sexual assault, you may need a lot of emotional support. Every woman responds differently, but reactions can include feeling terribly shocked, confused, and afraid. Some women experience denial or feeling emotionally numb. Whatever your experience, reach out to people who care about you and get help from a mental health professional. The hospital usually can put you in touch with a counselor or support group. Even if a long time has passed since you were abused, you still can get help.

If someone you know has been abused or assaulted you can help by listening and offering comfort. If the person wants, you also can go along to the police station, the hospital, or counseling sessions. Make sure the person knows the abuse is not his or her fault, and that it is natural to feel angry and ashamed.

Staying safe from sexual assault

Steps you can take to reduce your chances of being sexually assaulted include:

- Making sure you don't drink too much alcohol, so you can keep yourself safe

- Parking in well-lit areas

- Not leaving a social event with someone you just met

- Keeping your car and home doors locked

- Having your key ready as you approach your door

One important way to stay safe at clubs and parties is to learn more about date rape drugs. These are drugs that have no smell or taste that can be slipped into drinks. They are used to make it hard for a person to fight off a rape or to remember what happened.

Another important way to avoid sexual abuse is to leave a relationship that is becoming unhealthy. Remember, no one has a right to pressure you into doing sexual things you do not want to do.

Section 7.4

Emotional Abuse

Text in this section is excerpted from "Violence against Women:
Emotional Abuse," U.S. Department of Health and Human
Services (HHS), September 30, 2015; and text from "Verbal/Emotional
Abuse," Office on Women's Health (OWH), October 31, 2013.

Verbal and emotional abuse can be hard to spot because there aren't physical signs. Emotional abuse happens when someone constantly yells at you or uses words to hurt you. Eventually, your self-esteem is damaged. Verbal and emotional abusers can be parents or other family members, a boyfriend, a girlfriend, a teacher, or anyone who makes you feel badly about yourself.

Someone who is an emotional abuser will use mean names, put-downs, insults, sexual harassment, or other ways to gain power over the other person.

You may feel like if you're not being hurt physically, you are not being abused. But attempts to scare, isolate, or control you also are abuse. They can affect your physical and emotional well-being. And they often are a sign that physical abuse will follow.

You may be experiencing emotional abuse if someone:

- Monitors what you're doing all the time
- Unfairly accuses you of being unfaithful all the time
- Prevents or discourages you from seeing friends or family
- Tries to stop you from going to work or school
- Gets angry in a way that is frightening to you
- Controls how you spend your money
- Humiliates you in front of others
- Threatens to hurt you or people you care about
- Threatens to harm himself or herself when upset with you

- Says things like, "If I can't have you then no one can."

- Decides things for you that you should decide (like what to wear or eat)

Section 7.5

Verbal Abuse

"Verbal Abuse," © 2016 Omnigraphics, Inc.
Reviewed January 2016.

Verbal abuse is the use of words, body language, and actions to insult, humiliate, and control another person. Verbal abuse makes victims doubt their abilities, viewpoints, and choices, and thus destroys their self-esteem. In this way, it enables abusers to gain power in the relationship and manipulate their victims' thoughts, feelings, and behavior. Although verbal abuse of intimate partners and children may occur under the guise of love, it is a form of bullying that generates confusion, anxiety, and fear in its victims.

When people think about verbal abuse, they may picture yelling and screaming. Although loud, angry shouting can certainly constitute verbal abuse, it can also include quiet comments and subtle looks, gestures, and body language. Even giving someone the "silent treatment," or refusing to acknowledge their need to communicate, can translate to verbal abuse. All forms of verbal abuse create confusion in the victim, so that he or she begins to believe the accusations and assertions made by the abuser. In addition, verbal abusers often deflect accountability for their words and actions onto their victims, making them believe that they are responsible for problems in the relationship.

Verbal abuse may be perpetrated by a partner, parent, friend, boss, or co-worker. It can occur in the home, in the workplace, in an educational setting, or on the street. Although it does not leave visible bruises or scars, verbal abuse can be just as harmful to victims and as devastating to families as physical abuse. In fact, verbal abuse is a necessary component of physically abusive relationships. Without verbal abuse to degrade and coerce the victim into self-doubt, the victim could simply leave the relationship following an episode of physical violence. In fact, physical violence sometimes occurs when the abuser feels that verbal abuse is no longer sufficient to control the victim.

Effects of Verbal Abuse

Among the common effects of verbal abuse are fear, anxiety, and confusion. Victims often feel as if they must remain vigilant at all times, watching for clues of impending abuse and "walking on egg-shells" to keep the abuser happy. When the victim receives kindness or love from the abuser, they may feel as if the positive attention is short-lived and cannot be trusted.

Verbal abuse works by planting seeds of self-doubt, so that victims come to believe that something is wrong with them on a basic level. They may relive experiences and analyze their own actions to see where they made mistakes that may have precipitated the abuse. Many victims of verbal abuse have low self-confidence, doubt their own judgment, lose their spontaneity, and have difficulty making decisions.

Studies show that people who experience verbal abuse are more prone to psychological problems like depression, post-traumatic stress disorder (PTSD), sleep and eating disorders, substance abuse, self-mutilation, and suicide. Victims of verbal abuse may also develop physical health problems related to stress, such as chronic pain, migraines, stammering, indigestion, ulcers, and heart disease.

Children who are verbally abused tend to internalize the criticism they receive from their abuser. For instance, a child who is repeatedly told he or she is naughty or stupid is likely to grow up believing it and behaving accordingly. Studies show that children who are verbally abused face a higher risk of developing social problems, including physical aggression, delinquency, and substance abuse. These risks occur regardless of the children's age, gender, or economic status.

Dealing with Verbal Abuse

Victims of verbal abuse often find it difficult to leave the abusive relationship. In addition to problems related to self-doubt, they may have complicated feelings of love for an abuser who is an intimate partner or family member, or they may feel trapped by financial need. As a result, it is important for people to learn to recognize and respond to verbal abuse. Some suggestions aimed at helping to prevent or stop verbal abuse include:

- Establish personal boundaries on acceptable behavior from other people and enforce them. Setting boundaries helps people recognize verbal abuse and take steps to protect themselves from emotional harm. It is also an effective tactic to avoid becoming entangled in abusive relationships.

- Address verbal abuse in real time as it occurs. People who recognize verbal abuse as an attempt to manipulate their emotions or control their behavior are empowered to call attention to what the abuser is doing. Perhaps the easiest response to verbal abuse is to say "Stop it" or "I will not let you talk to me that way."

- Replace unhealthy negative emotions such as anger, anxiety, and self-doubt with healthy negative emotions like sadness, disappointment, and frustration. While negative feelings are appropriate in response to verbal abuse, unhealthy ones can lead to counterproductive behaviors, while healthy ones can lead to positive actions.

- Get help and support. Victims of verbal abuse who tell a trusted person about it are more likely to remain clear-headed and emotionally strong when abuse occurs.

- Take positive steps to build self-esteem and self-worth, such as pursuing education, volunteerism, exercise, hobbies, or employment.

References

1. Bierma, Paige. "Verbal Abuse and Depression." Health Day, 2016.

2. Holly, Kellie. "What Is Verbal Abuse?" Healthy Place, July 30, 2012.

Section 7.6

Economic Abuse

Text in this section is excerpted from "Practical Implications
of Current Intimate Partner Violence Research for Victim
Advocates and Service Providers," National Criminal Justice
Reference Service (NCJRS), December 2013.

Economic abuse by an intimate partner includes controlling a victim's ability to acquire, use, manage, maintain, and dispose of economic resources. Virtually all perpetrators of IPV impose various tactics of economic abuse on their partners. A shelter study, for example, found that 99 percent of female victims indicated that they were subjected to one or more forms of economic abuse.

Tactics of economic abuse include, but are not limited to: prevention and disruption of education or employment, interference with transportation, failure to provide childcare, compromise of housing, deprivation of food and medicine, interruption of sleep, destruction of work clothes and/or job-related manuals, disposal of assets, theft of income, denial of library or Internet access, commercial sexual exploitation, and limitation of communications with economic support networks.

Many women victims of IPV suffer significant material deprivation as a consequence of economic abuse. Most low-income victims seeking domestic violence services report that the material hardships they faced were caused by abusive partners. In one study, three quarters of battered women stated that the abuser was "very much or completely" responsible for the economic hardships they experienced.

Economic abuse can also affect victims in higher income families as well. Perpetrators can limit victim access to assets, e.g., by refusing to include victims as co-owners of real estate, vehicles or businesses, by denying access to cash, checking accounts, savings or investments, by confiscating victim earnings, by depriving access to insurance, by creating debt, or by theft or conversion of assets. Without assets victims cannot achieve financial stability or escape from poverty.

Economic abuse also includes interference in victim participation in education or training programs. Economic abuse involves prohibition or restraint from participation in employment and interruption or termination of employment. Much of the early research on economic abuse related to employment derived from the experiences of victims who were recipients of public welfare. In these studies, perpetrators discouraged, prevented or interfered with victim work significantly; from 16 percent to 59 percent of the victims reported this type of economic abuse. Working victims advised that 35 percent to 56 percent were harassed by abusers at their places of employment; 55 percent to 85 percent reported tardiness, leaving early, or missing work completely as a result of abuse; 44 to 60 percent stated they were reprimanded at work for behaviors stemming from their abuse; and 24 to 52 percent reported loss of employment as a result of the economic abuse of intimate partners. Job interference occurs before, during and after work hours.

Victims stalked by intimate partners are likely to be harassed at the workplace by their partners who engage in work disruption, create attendance and performance problems, and precipitate job loss. Women victims are at 5 times the risk of intimate partner assault at the workplace as are men. Victims have higher levels of job instability than non-abused women. Even when employers institute programs to mitigate abuser interference, victim fear and concerns about safety may be so profound that these services only succeed in short-term retention of employment. The effects of abuser interference in victim employment are complicated, and vary, based on the primacy of this form of economic abuse in the array of perpetrator tactics, the job itself, and the personal circumstances of the victim.

Chapter 8

When Abuse Turns Deadly

Chapter Contents

Section 8.1

Prevalence of Intimate Partner Homicide

Text in this section is excerpted from "Serious Intimate Partner
Violence Against Females Declined 72 Percent from 1994 to 2011,"
Bureau of Justice Statistics (BJS), November 21, 2013.

From 1994 to 2011, the rate of serious intimate partner violence,
such as rape, sexual assault, robbery or aggravated assault, declined
72 percent for females, the Justice Department's Bureau of Justice
Statistics (BJS) announced today. During the same time, the percentage of female intimate partner victims who were physically attacked,
attacked with a weapon, injured or required medical treatment
remained relatively stable.

Nonfatal intimate partner violence includes serious violence and
simple assault committed by an offender who is the victim's current or
former spouse, boyfriend or girlfriend. The severity of intimate partner violence is measured by the type of violent crime, type of physical
attack, whether the victim was threatened before the attack, presence
of a weapon, victim injury and medical treatment. Estimates of nonfatal violence are based on data from the National Crime Victimization
Survey, which collects self-reported information from victims of crime.

During the most recent 10-year period (2002–11), the offender physically attacked the victim in more than two-thirds of intimate partner
victimizations against females (67 percent). In about half of female
victimizations (52 percent), the intimate partner threatened to harm
the victim prior to the physical attack. In addition, about 5 percent
of female victims were hit by an object their intimate partner held or
threw at them, 36 percent were grabbed, held, tripped, jumped on or
pushed, and 8 percent suffered sexual violence.

In 2011, 18 percent of intimate partner victimizations against
females involved a weapon, similar to the percentage observed in 1994.
In 2002–11, about 4 percent of nonfatal female intimate partner victims were shot at, stabbed or hit with a weapon. About half of intimate
partner victimizations against females resulted in physical injury, with
13 percent suffering serious physical injury such as gun shot or knife
wounds, internal injuries, unconsciousness or broken bones.

Between 2002 and 2011, about 18 percent of female intimate partner victimizations resulted in medical treatment for victim injuries.

In addition to estimates for nonfatal female victimizations, the report includes for comparison the number of homicides committed by intimates, estimates of nonfatal male intimate partner violence and non-intimate partner violence.

Estimates of male intimate partner violence include—

- From 1994 to 2011, the rate of serious violence (rape, sexual assault, robbery and aggravated assault) committed by an intimate partner declined 64 percent for males.

- During the most recent 10-year period (2002–11), nonfatal serious violence accounted for more than a third of intimate partner violence against males (39 percent).

- Aggravated assault (22 percent) accounted for the largest percentage of serious intimate partner violence against males, followed by robbery (16 percent). Rape or sexual assault (1 percent) accounted for the smallest percentage of intimate violence experienced by males.

- Sixty-five percent of male victims of intimate partner violence were physically attacked by the offender, and in almost a third of male victimizations (31 percent) the intimate partner threatened to harm the victim before the physical attack.

- A weapon was present in 27 percent of male intimate partner victimizations, and about 8 percent of males victimized by an intimate partner were shot at, stabbed or hit with a weapon.

Of the 3,032 homicides involving female victims in 2010 (the most recent year), 39 percent were committed by an intimate, 37 percent by a non-intimate and 24 percent by an offender with an unknown relationship to the victim. Among the 10,878 homicide incidents involving male victims in 2010, three percent were committed by an intimate, 48 percent by a non-intimate and 50 percent by an offender with an unknown relationship to the victim.

Section 8.2

Intimate Partner Strangulation

Text in this section is excerpted from "Hearing on the
Implementation of the Violence Against Women Reauthorization Act
of 2013," U.S. Sentencing Commission (USSC), February 13, 2014.

Law enforcement is only recently learning what survivors of non-fatal strangulation have known for years: "Many domestic violence offenders and rapists do not strangle their partners to kill them; they strangle them to let them know they can kill them – any time they wish." There are clear reasons why strangulation assaults, particularly in an intimate partner relationship, should be a separate felony offense and taken extremely seriously at sentencing:

- Strangulation is more common than was once realized. Recent studies have shown that 34 percent of abused pregnant women reported being "choked." In another study, 47 percent of female domestic violence victims reported being "choked."

- Victims of multiple non-fatal strangulations "who had experienced more than one strangulation attack, on separate occasions, by the same abuser, reported neck and throat injuries, neurologic disorders and psychological disorders with increased frequency."

- Almost half of all domestic violence homicide victims have experienced at least one episode of strangulation prior to a lethal or near-lethal violent incident. Victims of one episode of strangulation are over six times more likely to be a victim of attempted homicide by the same partner, and are over seven times more likely of becoming a homicide victim at the hands of the same partner.

- Even given the lethal and predictive nature of these assaults, the largest non-fatal strangulation case study ever conducted ("the San Diego Study") found that most cases lacked physical evidence or visible injury of strangulation – only 15 percent of the victims had a photograph of sufficient quality to be used in court as physical evidence of strangulation, and no symptoms were documented or reported in 67 percent of the cases.

- The San Diego Study found major signs and symptoms of strangulation that corroborated the assaults, but often only minor visible external injury.

- Loss of consciousness can occur within 5–10 seconds, and death within 4–5 minutes. The seriousness of the internal injuries, even with no external injuries, may take a few hours to be appreciated, and death can occur days later.

- Because most strangulation victims do not have visible external injuries, strangulation cases are frequently minimized by law enforcement, medical advocacy, mental health professionals, and courts.

- Even in fatal strangulation cases, there is often no evident external injury (confirming the findings regarding the seriousness of non-fatal, no-visible-injury strangulation assaults).

- Non-fatal strangulation assaults may not fit the elements of other serious assaults due to the lack of visible injury. Studies are confirming that an offender can strangle someone nearly to death with no visible injury, resulting in professionals viewing such an offense as a minor misdemeanor or as no provable crime at all.

- Experts across the medical profession now agree that manual or ligature strangulation is "lethal force" and is one of the best predictors of a future homicide in domestic violence cases.

Section 8.3

Firearms and Domestic Violence

"Firearms and Domestic Violence,"
© 2016 Omnigraphics, Inc.
Reviewed January 2016.

When domestic violence occurs in households where firearms are present, the violence is much more likely to be deadly. Research has shown that the presence of a gun in the household increases the risk of homicide by 500 percent for women in domestic violence situations. Firearms also frequently play a role in nonlethal domestic violence incidents. A survey of female domestic violence survivors in California shelters found that the abuser had used a gun to threaten or harm the victim in 64 percent of households that contained firearms.

Congress has attempted to address the link between firearms and domestic violence deaths by passing laws aimed at restricting the purchase and possession of guns by perpetrators of domestic violence. One such law, known as the Lautenberg Amendment, prohibits firearms sales to people who have been convicted of misdemeanor domestic violence offenses involving the use of physical force or the threatened use of a deadly weapon. It also covers people who are subject to domestic violence personal protection orders. Under federal law, the offender must be a spouse (current or former), parent, or guardian of the victim; share a child in common with the victim; or have lived with the victim as an intimate partner.

Over 109,000 people were denied the purchase of a firearm from 1998 to 2014 because records showed that they had been convicted of a misdemeanor crime of domestic violence. More than 46,000 people who were subject to domestic violence protection orders had their gun-purchase applications denied during that same period. Research also suggests that the law served as a deterrent to prevent other people involved in domestic violence cases from applying to purchase firearms.

Preventing Gun Violence

Critics contend, however, that the federal laws concerning firearms and domestic violence have significant limitations. For instance, federal law does not protect people in certain types of relationships, such as people who are dating but do not live together or have a child together. Yet dating relationships carry a high risk of domestic violence. Data from 2008 showed that people who were currently dating made up nearly half of all homicide victims involving intimate partner abuse. In addition, federal law does not prohibit gun purchases by people convicted of domestic violence against family members other than spouses or children. Therefore, parents and siblings who are victims of domestic abuse are not protected.

Another shortcoming mentioned by critics is that the federal prohibitions on firearm possession by domestic abusers fail to ensure that abusers relinquish any guns that they already own. As a result, many people who are subject to protective orders or who have been convicted on domestic violence charges continue to possess firearms in violation of the law. Studies have shown that perpetrators who continued to possess firearms after they were prohibited from doing so were more likely to attempt homicide or threaten their partners with guns than those who had relinquished their firearms.

Critics also point out that laws prohibiting domestic violence perpetrators from possessing firearms cannot be effective without requiring a federal criminal background check prior to the sale of any gun. Sales by unlicensed, private sellers are not subject to federal background checks, however, and many states do not report comprehensive information about domestic violence convictions and protection orders to federal databases. As a result, many domestic abusers are able to obtain guns in violation of the law. Studies show that they often use these guns against their intimate partners. In states that require a background check before every handgun sale, 38 percent fewer women are shot to death in domestic violence incidents.

Although many gun-control proposals are controversial, policies that aim to protect victims of domestic violence receive widespread public support. A 2013 poll found that over 80 percent of the people surveyed, including 75 percent of people who owned guns, supported laws prohibiting people who violate a domestic violence restraining order from owning firearms for ten years. The poll also indicated that more than 72 percent of both gun owners and non-gun owners supported laws prohibiting people who are convicted of domestic violence from owning firearms for ten years.

References

1. "Domestic Violence and Firearms Policy Summary." Law Center to Prevent Gun Violence, May 11, 2014.

2. Sugarmann, Josh. "For Women, Gun Violence Often Linked to Domestic Violence." Huffington Post, January 10, 2014.

Section 8.4

Can Police Accurately Assess the Risk of Victims for Lethality?

Text in this section is excerpted from "Practical Implications
of Current Intimate Partner Violence Research for Victim
Advocates and Service Providers," National Criminal Justice
Reference Service (NCJRS), December 2013.

Several risk assessment tools have been devised for use by police officers in assessing the risk of recidivism of intimate partner violence (IPV) perpetrators. None measure the risk for lethality. The Ontario Domestic Assault Risk Assessment (ODARA) tool, an actuarial assessment tool used by many police agencies in Canada and the United States, is an instrument containing 13 yes or no questions that rank IPV perpetrators on risk for future domestic assault by men against wives, former spouses, common law partners and teen dating violence victims. A high score on the ODARA indicates that an offender is likely to commit more assaults, commit them sooner, and cause more injury. The ODARA includes a victim's assessment of recidivism risk as one of the factors in the tool completed by police. Research on the ODARA demonstrates the validity, reliability and generalizability of the tool.

The Lethality Assessment Protocol (LAP), based on extensive review of domestic violence homicides, was crafted by the Maryland domestic violence (DV) coalition and law enforcement. The LAP is a "multi-pronged intervention program that consists of a research-based lethality screening tool, an accompanying referral protocol that provides direction for the screener based on the results of the screening process, and follow-up contact."

The LAP tool consists of 11 questions designed to elicit information from victims when law enforcement officers respond to IPV incidents; LAP enables officers to quickly assess risk for highly dangerous/lethal recidivism. If the victim answers yes to any of the first three questions, they are deemed to be in "high-danger."

1. Has he ever used a weapon against you or threatened you with a weapon?

2. Has he threatened to kill you or your children?

3. Do you think he might try to kill you? Another eight questions follow. Even in the absence of any positive answers to the first three, positive answers to four of the remaining questions, triggers a conclusion that victims are in "high danger" of lethal assault.

4. Does he have a gun or can he get one easily?

5. Has he ever tried to choke you?

6. Is he violently or constantly jealous or does he control most of your daily activities?

7. Have you left him or separated after living together or being married?

8. Is he unemployed?

9. Has he ever tried to kill himself?

10. Do you have a child that he knows is not his?

11. Does he follow or spy on you or leave threatening messages?

If the victim's responses fall into the "high danger" category, law enforcement immediately connect the victim with a local DV advocate in order to apprise her of the advocacy, legal options and services available. After this preliminary phone consultation, an advocate from the DV program reaches out for a second connection with the victim. While there is no research on the effectiveness of the LAP Protocol, the Kansas City Star reports that there has been a 300 percent increase in victims seeking the services of DV programs since LAP was instituted in 2009, and in Maryland, of the victims identified as "high danger" in a five-year period, 59 percent spoke on the phone to a hotline worker and 19 percent sought additional DV program assistance.

The LAP tool is a refinement of the "Danger Assessment" instrument (DA) previously used and validated in clinical and shelter settings.

There are other risk and lethality scales utilized by law enforcement that are also based on victim input. The DV MOSAIC, developed by de Becker, has been found to be the best scale for predicting subsequent stalking and threats.

Section 8.5

How Many IPV Victims Attempt / Complete Suicide?

Text in this section is excerpted from "Practical Implications
of Current Intimate Partner Violence Research for Victim
Advocates and Service Providers," National Criminal Justice
Reference Service (NCJRS), December 2013.

The Centers for Disease Control (CDC) is building a National
Violent Death Reporting System. As of July 2011, 18 states were
participating. In that year, these states reported 573 intimate partner homicides, 386 of which were females. During that same year,
these states reported 2,909 "intimate partner problem" suicides, 439
of which were females. In other words, five times as many people
died as a result of "intimate partner problem" suicides as intimate
partner homicides.

While the National Violent Death Reporting System does not define
"intimate partner problem" as IPV, research suggests a link between
IPV specifically and victim suicide. The Washington State Domestic
Violence Fatality Review has concluded that far more women died of
intimate partner-related suicides than homicides. A study of women
admitted to a large Connecticut hospital revealed that 20 percent of
battered women had made multiple suicide attempts compared to eight
percent of non-battered women.A recent study of mostly poor African
American abused women admitted to a large urban public hospital in
the South found that 32 percent had attempted suicide in the past,
34 percent once, 19 percent twice, 16.3 percent three times, and 31.4
percent four or more times.

Data from the 2003-2007 National Violent Death Reporting System of
women who died in the perinatal period – while pregnant or up to a year
after birth – found 94 suicides and 139 homicides, or two suicides and
nearly three homicides for every 100,000 live births. More than 54 percent of the suicides and 45 percent of the homicides of women involved
IPV. Older White women were at greatest risk of suicide. Younger Black
women, 24 years and younger, were most at risk for homicide.

Unraveling all of the factors associated with suicide is not easy. A sample of 611 women living in an urban area, half of whom were HIV-positive, found that thoughts of suicide were most prevalent among infected women who also were victims of intimate partner violence. However, HIV-negative women who were abused were also at significantly elevated risk for depression, anxiety, and thoughts of suicide. Another comparative study of women seeking medical treatment in four community-based primary care, internal medicine practices found those who had suffered abuse were more likely to have attempted suicide, but, significantly, did not have more hospitalizations for psychiatric disorders.

Researchers, completing a World Health Association study in Pakistan on violence against women were struck by the strong association found between domestic violence (DV) and suicidal thoughts among wives. In cases of physical and sexual violence, they found the risk of suicidal thoughts was elevated four times compared to those not exposed to this violence. In cases of psychological violence, measured as insults, intimidation, threats, and humiliation, it was elevated five times.

Extensive research suggests that separation and divorce may be risk markers for suicide and suicide attempts, just as they are risk markers for lethal IPV.

A study of African American patients in an urban public hospital in the South suggests, not surprisingly, that victims who had better positive coping skills for dealing with their abuse were less likely to attempt suicides than those without these skills. If battered women had good problem-solving skills, strong social supports, and operated from a stance of greater empowerment, they were less likely to attempt suicide than their peers who accommodated abuser demands and felt themselves helpless to solve problems.

Women are much less likely than men to complete suicides in general. According to the Violent Death Reporting System, women were most likely to use poison (40.8 percent) and firearms (31.9 percent) in their suicide attempts. The most common method used by male suicide decedents was a firearm (56.0 percent) followed by hanging/strangulation/suffocation (24.4 percent). The method of suicide attempt may account for the greater completion rate for male suicides over female suicides.

Chapter 9

Physical Effects of Domestic Violence

Chapter Contents

Section 9.1

Types of Domestic Violence Injuries

"Types of Domestic Violence Injuries,"
© 2016 Omnigraphics, Inc.
Reviewed January 2016.

Certain types and patterns of physical injuries are more commonly caused by domestic violence assaults than by accidents, participation in sports, or other means. Examples include some types of bruises and scrapes on the head, face, neck, arms, or abdomen; injuries to the genitals or rectum; broken or loose teeth; and ruptured eardrums. Being aware of these types of injuries and watching for suspicious patterns can help identify and protect people who are experiencing physical abuse.

Most of the physical injuries associated with domestic violence are caused by blunt force trauma. This type of trauma can occur when a moving object (such as a fist, foot, or weapon) strikes the body, or when a moving body strikes a fixed object (such as a wall, floor, or table). Injuries can also result from actions such as grabbing, choking, pinching, and biting. All of these sources of injury leave physical signs that may raise suspicions of domestic violence.

Types of Injuries

Bruises are among the most common types of injuries found in survivors of domestic violence. Although bruises can have many accidental causes, certain locations and distributions of bruises may raise concerns about physical abuse. Bruising occurs when physical trauma causes blood to leak out of small blood vessels and pool in surrounding tissues. This blood shows through the surface of the skin as discoloration and swelling. The size, shape, and color of bruises vary, so their appearance cannot be reliably used to determine the date of an injury or the degree of force involved. Bruises in the following locations, however, are often caused by domestic violence:

- Tiny "pinpoint" bruises, or petechiae, around the eyes or mouth may result from choking or strangulation attempts.

- Finger-shaped bruises on the throat, face, arms, or thighs are often caused by forceful grabbing, holding, or pinching.

- Counter-pressure bruises on the spine or hipbones often result from forceful restraint on the ground or against a wall.

- Black eyes are often caused by a punch to the face or a skull fracture.

Abrasions are injuries affecting the top layers of the skin that are typically caused by scraping, rubbing, or crushing. They appear red in color and may bleed or ooze slightly. Abrasions can provide medical professionals with valuable clues about physical abuse because they always occur at the site of impact, and they sometimes indicate the direction of impact or retain an imprint of the causative object. For instance, an abrasion from a kick may retain an imprint of the tread of a shoe.

Lacerations occur when the skin and other soft body tissues are torn, split, stretched, or compressed as a result of blunt force trauma. Lacerations differ from cuts, which are caused by impacts with sharp objects rather than blunt objects or surfaces. Laceration wounds tend to be irregular and jagged. Lacerations to the lips and mouth from being smashed against the teeth are often caused by domestic violence. Although the rate of healing depends on many factors, doctors can sometimes estimate the date of injury by examining a laceration.

Some other injuries that are considered characteristic of domestic violence include cigarette burns, rope burns, bite marks, and welts that retain an imprint of a hand or an object used as a weapon.

Patterns of Injury

The location and distribution of physical injuries on the body can also provide indications of domestic violence. Certain patterns of injury are commonly found in cases of physical abuse, including:

- Frequent injuries to the head and neck, which are the location of 50 percent of domestic violence injuries.

- Injuries distributed among the body parts covered by a bathing suit—such as the breasts, buttocks, and genitals—which are usually hidden under clothing.

- Bilateral injuries affecting both sides of the body, and especially the arms and legs.

- Defensive injuries to the palms, forearms, feet, back, or buttocks from trying to block punches or protect against an attack.

- Bruises or other injuries in various stages of healing, or evidence of both old and new injuries, which may suggest repeated or ongoing abuse.

- Unexplained injuries or injuries that do not fit the stated cause.

- Untreated injuries, or injuries for which the victim has delayed seeking medical attention.

References

1. Dryden-Edwards, Roxanne. "Domestic Violence Signs and Symptoms." eMedicineHealth, 2016.

2. "Injuries Associated with Assault and Abuse." Forensics Talk, September 2006.

Section 9.2

Medical Consequences of Domestic Violence

Text in this section is excerpted from "Intimate Partner Violence: Consequences," Centers for Disease Control and Prevention (CDC), March 3, 2015.

Consequences

Approximately, 27.3% of women and 11.5% of men in the United States have experienced contact sexual violence, physical violence, or stalking by an intimate partner and reported at least one measured impact related to these or other forms of violence in that relationship. In general, victims of repeated violence over time experience more serious consequences than victims of one-time incidents. The following list describes some, but not all, of the consequences of intimate partner violence (IPV).

Physical

Nearly 1 in 4 women (22.3%) and 1 in 7 men (14.0%) aged 18 and older in the United States have been the victim of severe physical violence by an intimate partner in their lifetime. Nearly, 14% of women

(13.4%) and 3.54% of men have been injured as a result of IPV that included contact sexual violence, physical violence, or stalking by an intimate partner in their lifetime. In 2010, 241 males and 1095 females were murdered by an intimate partner.

Apart from deaths and injuries, physical violence by an intimate partner is associated with a number of adverse health outcomes. Several health conditions associated with intimate partner violence may be a direct result of the physical violence (for example, bruises, knife wounds, broken bones, traumatic brain injury, back or pelvic pain, headaches). Other conditions are the result of the impact of intimate partner violence on the cardiovascular, gastrointestinal, endocrine and immune systems through chronic stress or other mechanisms.

Examples of health conditions associated with IPV include:

- Asthma
- Bladder and kidney infections
- Circulatory conditions
- Cardiovascular disease
- Fibromyalgia
- Irritable bowel syndrome
- Chronic pain syndromes
- Central nervous system disorders
- Gastrointestinal disorders
- Joint disease
- Migraines and headaches

Children might become injured during IPV incidents between their parents. A large overlap exists between IPV and child maltreatment.

Reproductive

- Gynecological disorders
- Pelvic inflammatory disease
- Sexual dysfunction
- Sexually transmitted infections, including HIV/AIDS

- Delayed prenatal care

- Preterm delivery

- Pregnancy difficulties like low birth weight babies and perinatal deaths

- Unintended pregnancy

Psychological

Physical violence is typically accompanied by emotional or psychological abuse. IPV–whether sexual, physical, or psychological–can lead to various psychological consequences for victims.

- Anxiety

- Depression

- Symptoms of post-traumatic stress disorder (PTSD)

- Antisocial behavior

- Suicidal behavior in females

- Low self-esteem

- Inability to trust others, especially in intimate relationships

- Fear of intimacy

- Emotional detachment

- Sleep disturbances

- Flashbacks

- Replaying assault in the mind

Social

Victi.ms of IPV sometimes face the following social consequences:

- Restricted access to services

- Strained relationships with health providers and employers

- Isolation from social networks

- Homelessness

Health Behaviors

Women with a history of IPV are more likely to display behaviors that present further health risks (e.g., substance abuse, alcoholism, suicide attempts) than women without a history of IPV.

IPV is associated with a variety of negative health behaviors. Studies show that the more severe the violence, the stronger its relationship to negative health behaviors by victims.

- Engaging in high-risk sexual behavior
  - Unprotected sex
  - Decreased condom use
  - Early sexual initiation
  - Choosing unhealthy sexual partners
  - Multiple sex partners
  - Trading sex for food, money or other items
- Using harmful substances
  - Smoking cigarettes
  - Drinking alcohol
  - Drinking alcohol and driving
  - Illicit drug use
- Unhealthy diet-related behaviors
  - Fasting
  - Vomiting
  - Abusing diet pills
  - Overeating
- Overuse of health services

Section 9.3

Domestic Abuse and Traumatic Brain Injury

"Domestic Violence and Traumatic Brain Injury,"
© 2016 Omnigraphics, Inc.
Reviewed January 2016.

Traumatic brain injury (TBI) is a type of damage to the brain that results from an external physical force being applied to the head. TBI may occur when the head strikes a stationary object, such as the ground or a wall, or when the head is struck by a hard object, such as a baseball bat. TBI can also result from forceful shaking of the head, which causes the brain to move around within the skull, or from penetration of the skull by a foreign object, such as a bullet or a knife. Brain injury may also occur from the deprivation of oxygen through choking or near drowning.

Although media attention has raised awareness of the risk of TBI among athletes and military veterans, little consideration has been given to the prevalence of TBI among women who are survivors of domestic violence. Yet research has shown that 90 percent of all injuries from domestic violence occur to the face, head, or neck. One study found that 30 percent of women who sought emergency medical treatment for domestic violence injuries had lost consciousness at least once, and 67 percent showed symptoms of TBI. Another study found that 75 percent of the battered women in three domestic violence shelters reported receiving a brain injury from an intimate partner, while 50 percent had sustained multiple brain injuries.

Many of the common acts of physical aggression that are used by perpetrators of domestic violence can cause brain injuries, including beating someone on the head with fists or other objects, pushing someone down stairs or into a solid object, shaking someone strenuously, choking or holding someone underwater, and shooting or stabbing someone in the face or head. Victims of domestic violence may not realize that they have sustained a brain injury, especially if they do not seek or receive medical treatment. But a history of TBI leads to a substantially greater risk of sustaining further brain injuries, and repeated brain injuries are known to have a cumulative effect.

Effects of TBI

TBI affects people differently, so the symptoms may vary depending on the individual. There are some initial symptoms that are fairly common, however, including a brief loss of consciousness, dizziness, headaches, loss of short-term memory, slower processing of information, fatigue, and sensitivity to light and sound. With repeated injuries or lack of medical treatment, people with TBI may experience increasing levels of physical, cognitive, and functional disabilities. Some of the most common problems include:

- weakness, clumsiness, and motor control difficulties
- communication difficulties, including slurring of speech and problems with word finding
- issues involving balance, vision, and hearing
- difficulty concentrating or paying attention, along with increased distractibility
- issues with problem solving and task completion
- difficulty with long-term goal setting, prioritizing, planning, and organization
- increased tension, anxiety, and irritability
- impulsiveness and lapses in judgment
- increased risk of depression and substance abuse.

Survivors of domestic violence may experience a wide range of challenges related to TBI. Slower reaction time and inattentiveness, for instance, may increase the risk that physical abuse will result in further brain injuries. Abusive partners may also try to use the symptoms of a brain injury as tools to manipulate and control their victims. For instance, they may take advantage of short-term memory loss to make victims doubt their memories and perceptions of past abuse.

Survivors with TBI may also find it more difficult assess situations, make plans for their own safety, leave an abusive partner, and live independently or in a domestic violence shelter. They may also have trouble accessing support services, remembering appointments, and navigating the criminal justice system. Testifying in child custody or criminal court proceedings requires survivors to remember details of abuse and communicate them clearly and sequentially. Yet these abilities may be compromised in individuals with TBI, which may reduce their credibility in court and negatively affect their outcomes. Domestic violence survivors with TBI may also experience problems caring for children or maintaining employment.

Supporting Survivors with TBI

Advocates and service providers for survivors of domestic violence must be aware of the high risk of TBI among their clients. Shelters and counseling facilities should put screening procedures in place to identify people with TBI, train staff to address their special needs and challenges, and implement organizational policies to better support them. Some additional tips for helping domestic violence survivors with TBI include:

- Treat people as individuals. Strive to understand and accommodate their unique challenges and strengths, provide positive and respectful feedback, and empower them to make necessary changes in their lives.

- Be aware that an abuse survivor may have TBI even in the absence of a formal diagnosis. If TBI has been diagnosed, however, do not assume that the individual has cognitive or functional disabilities.

- Recognize that behavioral concerns and noncompliance with shelter rules may be linked to an underlying TBI. Provide accommodations as needed—such as a planner to help a person with memory deficits remember communal responsibilities—to enable abuse survivors to adapt to the shelter environment.

- Keep in mind that recovery from a brain injury takes time and does not necessarily happen in a linear or sequential manner. As a result, people's needs may change frequently.

- Adapt safety planning to make it more appropriate for people living with TBI. Many safety planning discussions require domestic violence survivors to envision hypothetical circumstances or remember long lists of actions to be executed in a crisis. But these discussions can be challenging for people with TBI who struggle with abstract thought or memory problems. To make the discussions more productive, experts recommend minimizing outside distractions, holding shorter meetings more frequently, focusing on a single topic at each meeting, making action items simple and concrete, and concluding by summarizing the information and checking for understanding.

- Educate others about TBI and its intersection with domestic violence.

References

1. "The Intersection of Brain Injury and Domestic Violence." New York State Coalition Against Domestic Violence, n.d.

2. "Traumatic Brain Injury and Domestic Violence Facts." Alabama Department of Rehabilitation Services, 2012.

Section 9.4

Domestic Violence and HIV Risk

Text in this section is excerpted from "Intersection of Intimate Partner Violence and HIV in Women," Centers for Disease Control and Prevention (CDC), February 2014.

What We Know about IPV and HIV in Women

- Intimate partner violence (IPV) includes physical violence, sexual violence, threats of physical or sexual violence, stalking and psychological aggression (including coercive tactics) by a current or former intimate partner.

- Findings from the 2010 National Intimate Partner and Sexual Violence Survey (NISVS) indicate that 35.6% of women in the United States have experienced rape, physical violence, or stalking by an intimate partner in their lifetime, and 5.9% or 6.9 million women experienced these forms of violence in the year prior to the survey.

- In addition, 1 in 5 women have experienced an attempted, completed, or alcohol-drug facilitated rape (defined as a physically forced or threatened vaginal, oral, and/or anal penetration) in their lifetime, mostly by a current or former partner.

- Approximately 80% of female victims of rape experienced their first rape before the age of 25.

- Nearly 1 in 2 women have experienced other forms of sexual violence in their lifetime (e.g., sexual coercion, unwanted sexual contact).

- Over 1.1 million people in the United States are estimated to be living with HIV and nearly 1 in 5 is unaware of their infection.

- Approximately 50,000 Americans become infected with HIV each year.

- Women and adolescent girls accounted for 20% of new HIV infections in the United States in 2010 and represented approximately 21% of HIV diagnoses among adults and adolescents in 2011.

- African Americans bear the greatest burden of HIV among women; Hispanic women are disproportionately affected. Of new infections in 2010, 64% occurred in blacks, 18% were in whites, and 15% were in Hispanics/Latinas. The rate of new infections among black women was 20 times that of white women, and over 4 times the rate among Hispanic/Latina women.

- The most common methods of HIV transmission among women are high-risk heterosexual contact (87% for black women, 86% for Hispanic women) and injection drug use.

Mechanisms

Exposure to IPV can increase women's risk for human immunodeficiency virus (HIV) infection through:

- forced sex with an infected partner
- limited or compromised negotiation of safer sex practices
- increased sexual risk-taking behaviors

Links between IPV and HIV

The association between violence against women and risk for HIV infection has been the focus of a growing number of studies. Findings from these studies indicate:

- Women and men who report a history of IPV victimization are more likely than those who do not to report behaviors known to increase the risk for HIV, including injection drug use, treatment for a sexually transmitted infection (STI), giving or receiving money or drugs for sex, and anal sex without a condom in the past year. This is true even when other factors such as demographic characteristics, other unhealthy behaviors (smoking, heavy drinking, high body mass index) and negative health conditions (e.g., stroke, disability, and asthma) are similar.

- HIV-positive women in the United States experience IPV at rates that are higher than for the general population. Across a number of studies, the rate of IPV among HIV-positive women (55%) was double the national rate, and the rates of childhood sexual abuse (39%) and childhood physical abuse (42%) were more than double the national rate.

- Rates of violence victimization among HIV-positive women are comparable to those for HIV-negative women drawn from similar populations and with similar levels of HIV risk behaviors. However, HIV-positive women may experience abuse that is more frequent and more severe.

- Women in relationships with violence have four times the risk for contracting STIs, including HIV, than women in relationships without violence.

- Fear of violence can influence whether some women get tested for HIV. However, in one U.S. study, fear of partner notification and partner violence were not statistically associated with women's decisions to get or not get an HIV test.

- Sexual abuse in childhood and forced sexual initiation in adolescence are associated with increased HIV risk-taking behaviors, including sex with multiple partners, sex with unfamiliar partners, sex with older partners, alcohol-related risky sex, anal sex, and low rates of condom use as well as HIV infection, in adult women.

Studies of HIV-Positive Women

Several studies have examined the relationship between violence and the timing of becoming infected with HIV or disclosing HIV status. These studies suggest that IPV can be both a risk factor for HIV, and a consequence of HIV.

- A history of victimization is a significant risk factor for unprotected sex for both HIV-positive women and men. HIV-positive women and gay/bisexual men reporting a history of violence per-petration are also more likely to report engaging in unprotected sex, particularly when drugs were used in conjunction with sex.

- HIV serostatus disclosure may be an initiating or contributing factor for partner violence. In U.S. samples, 0.5–4% of HIV-pos-itive women report experiencing violence following HIV serosta-tus disclosure. Violence perceived to be triggered by HIV disclo-sure was as high in years following diagnosis as in the initial year of diagnosis.

- Relationship violence and trauma history can compromise the health and prevention practices of women living with HIV. Recently abused women have more than 4 times the rate of antiretroviral therapy failure, and of not practicing safe sex, as women who have not experienced abuse recently.

Studies of Women with a History of Abuse

- Forced sex occurs in approximately 40 to 45 percent of physically violent intimate relationships and increases a woman's risk for STIs by 2 to 10 times that of physical abuse alone.

- Women who had ever experienced forced sex were more likely to report HIV risk behaviors but less likely to have been tested for HIV despite greater perceived likelihood of having HIV than non-abused women.

- Women who had been physically abused as adults were only one-fifth as likely to report consistent condom use after two safer sex counseling sessions as women who had not been abused.

- Women who had experienced both physical and sexual violence, compared to women who reported physical violence alone, were more likely to have had a recent STI (14% vs. 4%), to have had an STI during the relationship (43% vs. 20%), to use alcohol as a coping behavior (72% vs. 47%), and to have been threatened when negotiating condom use (35% vs. 10%).

- Women who experience IPV or sexual violence are at greater risk for a range of adverse health consequences, including increased prevalence of stress, depression, and chronic anxiety than their non-abused counterparts. A recent national study found that women who experienced rape or stalking by any perpetrator or physical violence by an intimate partner in their lifetime were more likely than women who did not experience these forms of violence to report having asthma, diabetes, and irritable bowel syndrome, and both women and men who experienced these forms of violence were more likely to report frequent headaches, chronic pain, difficulty sleeping, activity limitations, poor physical health, and poor mental health than women and men who did not experience these forms of violence.

- Significant associations have also been found between IPV and altered red blood cell and decreased T-cell function and relationships between stress, depression, and other psychosocial factors with disease progression have been found in HIV infected persons.

- Women with HIV have nearly six times the national rate of post-traumatic stress disorder. Chronic depression has been associated with greater decline in CD4 cell count in women living with HIV, and HIV-positive women with chronic depression are more than twice as likely to die than HIV-positive women with limited or no depression, even when other health and social factors are similar.

Chapter 10

Emotional and Socioeconomic Effects of Domestic Violence

Chapter Contents

Section 10.1

The Impact of Intimate Partner Violence on Victim Mental Health

Text in this section is excerpted from "Practical Implications of
Current Intimate Partner Violence Research for Victim Advocates
and Service Providers," National Criminal Justice Reference Service,
Office of Justice Programs (NCJRS), December 2013; and text from
"Sexual Violence: Consequences," Centers for Disease Control and
Prevention (CDC), February 19, 2015.

It is widely agreed that intimate partner violence (IPV) can create serious and long-lasting psychological and emotional injuries for
many victims, although not all victims are equally affected. Many
symptoms, such as depression, may resolve when social support and
safety increases for victims. For other women, however, being abused
over a period of time may result in significant mental distress. For
example, in a study with a large sample of randomly selected women,
48 percent of those who had been battered reported they had needed
help with mental health issues in the past 12 months.

National Intimate Partner and Sexual Violence Survey (NISVS) asked
IPV victims to rate their mental health. Both female and male victims
reported higher rates of "poor" mental health than non-victims, although
3.4 percent of female victims reported "poor" mental health compared to
2.7 percent of male victims. Compared to non-victims, female victims were
three times more likely to report poor mental health and male victims
were only a little more than twice as like to report poor mental health.

Victims may suffer low self-esteem, depression, hopelessness, anger,
distrust, and anxiety. IPV victims are more likely to suffer from depression than the general population. Many may contemplate or attempt
suicide. An analysis of 16 published longitudinal studies involving
more than 36,000 participants found IPV increased the likelihood of
suicide attempts as well as doubling depression among women. The
study also found the reverse, depressed women were more likely to
experience IPV. Men who experienced IPV also experienced increased
depression but no increase in suicide attempts and the depressed men
were no more likely to experience IPV.

Studies consistently reveal that a large proportion of battered women suffer from posttraumatic stress disorder (PTSD). A meta-analysis across multiple samples of battered women, including those in settings other than domestic violence agencies (e.g., hospital emergency rooms, psychiatric settings), found a weighted mean prevalence of 48 percent for depression and 64 percent for PTSD. Studies have found that half of the women who experienced PTSD remained symptomatic even after they had been out of a violent relationship for 6 to 9 years.

Studies find that women victims of IPV can suffer the same PTSD symptoms as any other trauma survivor. They may become overly sensitive to situations that bring up the traumatic event causing a cognitive bias and developing physiological symptoms such as a racing pulse or cold sweats that can impair their self-efficacy and coping strategies. In short, the study found that the women survivors were at increased risk for a cycle of self-defeating behaviors due to bias.

One of the largest health surveys, conducted in 2009, for almost 50,000 households across California found that women were more than twice as likely as men to have been IPV victims. More than half of adult IPV victims experienced recent symptoms of serious psychological distress such as anxiety and depression. Both male and female IPV victims were three times more likely than non-victims to report acute psychological distress in the past year. They were also far more likely to seek mental health care.

Although women were more than twice as likely as men to have been IPV victims, both male and female IPV victims were more likely than non-victims to report serious psychological distress during the past year. One in three of IPV victims reported they needed help for a mental, emotional, or substance abuse problem. As a result, IPV victims were 2.5 times (23.9 percent) more likely than non-victims (9.5 percent) to report seeing their primary care physician, a psychiatrist, a social worker, or a counselor in the past year.

NISVS found 22.3 percent of IPV victimized women reported PTSD symptoms over their lifetime as did 4.7 percent of IPV victimized men. A significant correlate of PTSD is that many sufferers may self-medicate to reduce symptoms of arousal, to block out intrusive thoughts, to calm themselves, or to create numbness. Binge drinking is also associated with IPV victimization. The large California survey, for example, found that more than half of the victims subjected to recent violence reported engaging in binge drinking over the prior year, significantly higher rates than non-victims.

A study conducted in Israel compared battered women with other women who had also suffered traumatic events, but not from intimate partners. The battered women exhibited significantly higher levels of psychiatric symptoms and risk for suicide than the control group; 51.6 percent of the battered women suffered from PTSD. The findings emphasize the toll and severity of IPV trauma, even compared to other trauma experienced.

Sexual violence can have harmful and lasting consequences for victims, families, and communities. The following list describes some of those consequences.

Physical Consequences

- More than 32,000 pregnancies result from rape every year with the highest rates of rape-induced pregnancy reported by women in abusive relationships

- Some long-term consequences of sexual violence include:

    - Chronic pain

    - Gastrointestinal disorders

    - Gynecological complications

    - Migraines and other frequent headaches

    - Sexually transmitted infections

    - Cervical cancer

    - Genital injuries

Psychological Consequences

Victims of sexual violence face both immediate and chronic psychological consequences.

Immediate psychological consequences include the following:

- Shock

- Denial

- Fear

- Confusion

- Anxiety

- Withdrawal

- Shame or guilt

- Nervousness
- Distrust of others
- Symptoms of post-traumatic stress disorder
  - Emotional detachment
  - Sleep disturbances
  - Flashbacks
  - Mental replay of assault

Chronic psychological consequences include the following:

- Depression
- Generalized anxiety
- Attempted or completed suicide
- Post-traumatic stress disorder
- Diminished interest/avoidance of sex
- Low self-esteem/self-blame

Social

Sexual violence also has social impacts on its victims, such as the following:

- Strained relationships with family, friends, and intimate partners
- Less emotional support from friends and family
- Less frequent contact with friends and relatives
- Lower likelihood of marriage
- Isolation or ostracism from family or community

Health Risk Behaviors

Sexual violence victimization is associated with several health risk behaviors.

Some researchers view the following health behaviors as both consequences of sexual violence and factors that increase a person's vulnerability to being victimized again in the future.

- Engaging in high-risk sexual behavior
  - Unprotected sex
  - Early sexual initiation
  - Choosing unhealthy sexual partners
  - Having multiple sex partners
  - Trading sex for food, money or other items
- Using harmful substances
  - Smoking cigarettes
  - Drinking alcohol
  - Drinking alcohol and driving
  - Taking drugs
- Unhealthy diet-related behaviors
  - Fasting
  - Vomiting
  - Abusing diet pills
  - Overeating
- Delinquency and criminal behavior
- Failure to engage in healthy behaviors, such as motor vehicle seat belt use

Section 10.2

Domestic Violence and Homelessness

Text in this section is excerpted from "Domestic Violence,"
U.S. Interagency Council on Homelessness (USICH), 2013.

Domestic violence creates vulnerability to homelessness for women and children, particularly those with limited economic resources.

Among women with children currently experiencing homelessness, more than 80 percent have previously experienced domestic violence. Domestic violence often includes exertion of financial and psychological control, leaving survivors with poor credit, limited networks of support, and few resources. Many survivors must leave their homes to escape violence but may not have access to safe housing and needed services.

Growing numbers of programs that serve survivors of domestic violence are providing short- or medium-term housing assistance to help families move to safe housing. Domestic violence advocates and social services providers are an essential part of a coordinated strategy to prevent and end homelessness. Emergency shelters often serve as the first stop for survivors of domestic violence to escape the immediate danger of abuse, but stays are often limited to 90 days to maintain beds for those in immediate danger.

Chapter 11

Children and Exposure to Domestic Violence

Chapter Contents

Section 11.1

Effects of Domestic Violence on Children

Text in this section is excerpted from "Domestic Violence
and the Child Welfare System," U.S. Department of Health
and Human Services (HHS), October 2014; and text from
"Child Maltreatment: Consequences," Centers for Disease
Control and Prevention (CDC), January 14, 2014.

Children who have been exposed to domestic violence are more
likely than their peers to experience a wide range of difficulties, and
the potential effects vary by age and developmental stage. The challenges faced by children and youth exposed to domestic violence generally fall into three categories:

- **Behavioral, social, and emotional problems.** Children in
  families experiencing domestic violence are more likely than
  other children to exhibit signs of depression and anxiety; higher
  levels of anger and/or disobedience; fear and withdrawal; poor
  peer, sibling, and social relationships; and low self-esteem.

- **Cognitive and attitudinal problems.** Children exposed to
  domestic violence are more likely than their peers to experience
  difficulties in school and with concentration and task completion; core lower on assessments of verbal, motor, and cognitive
  skills; lack conflict resolution skills; and possess limited problem
  solving skills. Children exposed to domestic violence also are
  more likely to exhibit pro-violence attitudes.

- **Long-term problems.** In addition to higher rates of delinquency and substance use, exposure to domestic violence is also
  one of several adverse childhood experiences (ACEs) that have
  been shown be risk factors for many of the most common causes
  of death in the United States, including alcohol abuse, drug
  abuse, smoking, obesity, and more.

Additional factors that influence the impact of domestic violence
on children include:

- **Nature of the violence.** Children who witness frequent and
  severe forms of violence or fail to observe their caretakers

resolving conflict may undergo more distress than children who witness fewer incidences of physical violence and experience positive interactions between their caregivers.

- **Age of the child.** Younger children appear to exhibit higher levels of emotional and psychological distress than older children. Children ages 5 and younger may experience developmental regression—the loss of acquired skills—or disruptions in eating or sleeping habits. Adolescents may exhibit impulsive and/or reckless behavior, such as substance use or running away. Age-related differences can result from older children's more fully developed cognitive abilities, which help them to better understand the violence and select various coping strategies to alleviate upsetting symptoms. Additionally, because very young children are more likely to have closer physical proximity to and stronger emotional dependence on their mothers (often the victims of domestic violence), they may be more susceptible to and exhibit enhanced trauma symptoms.

- **Elapsed time since exposure.** Children often have heightened levels of anxiety and fear immediately after a violent event. Fewer observable effects are seen in children as time passes after the violent event.

- **Gender.** In general, boys exhibit more externalized behaviors (e.g., aggression and acting out), while girls exhibit more internalized behaviors (e.g., withdrawal and depression).

- **Presence of child physical or sexual abuse.** Children who witness domestic violence and are physically or sexually abused are at higher risk for emotional and psychological maladjustment than children who witness violence and are not abused.

Child maltreatment affects children's health now and later, and costs our country as much as other high profile public health problems. Neglect, physical abuse, custodial interference and sexual abuse are types of child maltreatment that can lead to poor physical and mental health well into adulthood. The physical, psychological, behavioral, and economic consequences of child maltreatment are explained below:

Prevalence: about 14% of Children Suffer Abuse

- An estimated 681,000 children were confirmed by Child Protective Services as being victims of maltreatment in 2011.

- A cross-sectional, U.S. national telephone survey of the child maltreatment experiences of 4,503 children and youth aged 1 month to 17 years in 2011 found that 13.8% experienced child maltreatment in the last year (included neglect, physical abuse, emotional abuse, custodial interference, or sexual abuse by a known adult).

Physical

- In 2011, approximately 1,570 children died from abuse and neglect across the country—a rate of 2.10 deaths per 100,000 children.

- Maltreatment during infancy or early childhood can cause important regions of the brain to form and function improperly with long-term consequences on cognitive, language, and socio-emotional development, and mental health. For example, the stress of chronic abuse may cause a "hyperarousal" response in certain areas of the brain, which may result in hyperactivity and sleep disturbances.

- Children may experience severe or fatal head trauma as a result of abuse. Nonfatal consequences of abusive head trauma include varying degrees of visual impairment (e.g., blindness), motor impairment (e.g., cerebral palsy) and cognitive impairments.

- Children who experience maltreatment are also at increased risk for adverse health effects and certain chronic diseases as adults, including heart disease, cancer, chronic lung disease, liver disease, obesity, high blood pressure, high cholesterol, and high levels of C-reactive protein.

Psychological

- In one long-term study, as many as 80 percent of young adults who had been abused met the diagnostic criteria for at least one psychiatric disorder at age 21. These young adults exhibited many problems, including depression, anxiety, eating disorders, and suicide attempts.

- In addition to physical and developmental problems, the stress of chronic abuse may result in anxiety and may make victims more vulnerable to problems such as post-traumatic stress disorder, conduct disorder, and learning, attention, and memory difficulties.

Behavioral

- Children who experience maltreatment are at increased risk for smoking, alcoholism, and drug abuse as adults, as well as engaging in high-risk sexual behaviors.

- Those with a history of child abuse and neglect are 1.5 times more likely to use illicit drugs, especially marijuana, in middle adulthood.

- Studies have found abused and neglected children to be at least 25 percent more likely to experience problems such as delinquency, teen pregnancy, and low academic achievement. Similarly, a longitudinal study found that physically abused children were at greater risk of being arrested as juveniles. This same study also found that abused youth were less likely to have graduated from high school and more likely to have been a teen parent. A National Institute of Justice study indicated that being abused or neglected as a child increased the likelihood of arrest as a juvenile by 59 percent. Abuse and neglect also increased the likelihood of adult criminal behavior by 28 percent and violent crime by 30 percent.

- Early child maltreatment can have a negative effect on the ability of both men and women to establish and maintain healthy intimate relationships in adulthood.

Economic

- The total lifetime economic burden resulting from new cases of fatal and nonfatal child maltreatment in the United States in 2008 is approximately $124 billion in 2010 dollars. This economic burden rivals the cost of other high profile public health problems, such as stroke and type 2 diabetes.

- The estimated average lifetime cost per victim of nonfatal child maltreatment is $210,012 (in 2010 dollars) including:

  - childhood health care costs

  - adult medical costs

  - productivity losses

- child welfare costs

- criminal justice costs

- special education costs

- The estimated average lifetime cost per death is $1,272,900, including medical costs and productivity losses.

- Research suggests the benefits of effective prevention likely outweigh the costs of child maltreatment.

Most of the studies examining the consequences of child maltreatment have used a retrospective approach. This requires conducting studies to determine if any association exists between a history of childhood abuse and/or neglect and current health conditions in adults. Fewer research projects have employed a more rigorous longitudinal approach. This type of research strategy identifies children who are at risk or who have already been maltreated and follows them for a long period of time, sometimes decades, to see what conditions develop.

Despite these findings, not all children exposed to domestic violence will experience negative effects. Children's risk levels and reactions to domestic violence exist on a continuum; some children demonstrate enormous resiliency, while others show signs of significant maladaptive adjustment.

Protective factors such as social competence, intelligence, high self-esteem, and a supportive relationship with an adult (especially a non-abusive parent) can help protect children from the adverse effects of exposure to domestic violence. It's important for domestic violence, child welfare, and other child-serving professionals to understand the impact of trauma on child development and how to minimize its effects without causing additional trauma.

Section 11.2

Child Abuse and IPV: How Prevalent Is Co-Occurrence?

Text in this section is excerpted from "Child Abuse
and Intimate Partner Violence," National Institute of
Justice (NIJ), March 11, 2011. Reviewed January 2016.

Child maltreatment and domestic violence often co-occur. The
National Survey of Child and Adolescent Well-Being (NSCAW) is a
nationally recognized probability study of more than 5,000 children
ages 0 to 14 who have been abused or maltreated. An NIJ-funded
supplemental survey to NSCAW, called the Family Violence Services
Study (FVSS), examined the services provided to children and families
who face abuse and maltreatment.

The FVSS found the following:

- Of families involved in child welfare investigations for child maltreatment, 29 percent had abused children within the past year.
Approximately 45 percent of children in these families had experienced maltreatment over the course of their lifetime.

- Only 15 percent of child abuse cases reported by mothers were
identified by child welfare staff.

- Child welfare and domestic violence organizations have few tools
available to assess the co-occurrence of domestic violence and
child maltreatment and have difficulty coordinating to identify
best practices for service.

In response to the low rates of service provision, FVSS researchers developed 19 recommendations for helping child welfare agencies
assess child maltreatment cases and coordinate response.

Evaluating a Program to Reduce Child Maltreatment and Intimate Partner Violence

In 1999, the National Council of Juvenile and Family Court Judges
published Effective Intervention in Domestic Violence and Child

Maltreatment Cases: Guidelines for Policy and Practice, more commonly known as "the Greenbook" because of its green cover. A roadmap for collaboration, the Greenbook presents guidelines designed to "eliminate or decrease the risks that battered mothers, caseworkers, and judges must take on behalf of children."

NIJ and three agencies under the U.S. Department of Health and Human Services conducted an evaluation of a 5-year demonstration project called the Greenbook Initiative. The Greenbook Initiative provides a framework for helping families that are experiencing both child maltreatment and domestic or intimate partner violence. A collaborative approach among child welfare agencies, courts, and other parties can enhance family safety and well-being by responding to the entire family rather than an isolated victim.

At six demonstration sites, child welfare agencies, domestic violence service providers and dependency courts worked together to implement guidelines found in the Greenbook. The demonstration sites agreed to establish collaborative structures and develop policies and procedures to enhance the safety and well-being of battered women and their children. The 5-year evaluation showed that collaboration and cross-training between child welfare agencies, domestic violence service providers and dependency courts resulted in some positive changes in practice, collaboration and relationship building. The extent and types of changes varied across the sites and sustaining new practices proved difficult.

Section 11.3

Domestic Abuse and Childhood Obesity

"Domestic Abuse and Childhood Obesity,"
© 2016 Omnigraphics, Inc.
Reviewed January 2016.

Of the many negative impacts of domestic violence on children, one of the most surprising is that it can damage their DNA—the basic genetic code contained in cells that makes each person unique. A 2014 study found that children who were exposed to domestic violence, suicide, or the incarceration of a family member showed evidence of chromosomal damage.

Specifically, children who had experienced or witnessed domestic violence had significantly shorter telomeres than children raised in more stable family environments. Telomeres are caps that protect the ends of chromosomes from deterioration when cells replicate. In this way, telomeres help preserve the genetic information stored in chromosomes. A small amount of telomeric DNA is lost as part of the normal process of cell division, so telomeres gradually become shorter as people age. When the extent of telomere shortening reaches a certain limit, the cell is programmed to stop dividing or die. As a result, scientists consider telomere length to be a biological indicator of a person's general health and projected lifespan.

The rate at which telomeres shorten is influenced by many factors, including certain elements of the person's lifestyle. Lifestyle factors such as smoking, obesity, unhealthy eating habits, lack of exercise, and exposure to environmental pollution can increase the rate of telomere shortening. Another factor that can accelerate the process of telomere shortening is stress, which may explain why children who are exposed to domestic violence tend to have shorter telomeres than their peers.

The study showed that the children who had the greatest exposure to traumatic family situations had the shortest telomeres, even after controlling for age, socioeconomic status, and other factors. The impact of domestic violence was more pronounced in girls than in boys. The researchers found that girls who were exposed to family trauma had the shortest telomeres, and thus the most genetic damage.

Shorter telomeres have been linked to a higher risk for early onset of age-associated health problems, including heart disease, obesity, diabetes, cognitive decline, mental illness, and premature death. Research has also shown, however, that improving diet, exercise, and other lifestyle factors has the potential to reduce the rate of telomere shortening, which may delay the onset of age-related diseases and prolong lifespan. This finding suggests that interventions aimed at stopping domestic violence and promoting stable home environments can help children live longer, healthier lives.

References

1. Brannon, Keith. "Domestic Violence Scars Kids' DNA." *Futurity*, June 16, 2014.

2. Griffiths, Sarah. "Domestic Violence Can 'Scar' a Child's DNA." *Daily Mail*, June 18, 2014.

Part Three

Abuse in Specific Populations

Chapter 12

Child Abuse

Chapter Contents

Section 12.1

Types of Child Abuse

Text in this section is excerpted from "What Is Child Abuse and
Neglect?" Child Welfare Information Gateway, July 2013, and
text from "Child Maltreatment: Definitions," Centers for Disease
Control and Prevention (CDC), August 21, 2015; and text from "Child
Maltreatment: Prevention Strategies," Centers for Disease Control
and Prevention (CDC), February 9, 2015.

What Are the Major Types of Child Abuse and Neglect?

Within the minimum standards set by Child Abuse Prevention and
Treatment Act (CAPTA), each State is responsible for providing its own
definitions of child abuse and neglect. Most States recognize the four
major types of maltreatment: physical abuse, neglect, sexual abuse, and
emotional abuse. Signs and symptoms for each type of maltreatment
are listed below. Additionally, many States identify abandonment and
parental substance abuse as abuse or neglect. While these types of maltreatment may be found separately, they often occur in combination.

Physical abuse is nonaccidental physical injury (ranging from
minor bruises to severe fractures or death) as a result of punching,
beating, kicking, biting, shaking, throwing, stabbing, choking, hitting (with a hand, stick, strap, or other object), burning, or otherwise
harming a child, that is inflicted by a parent, caregiver, or other
person who has responsibility for the child. Such injury is considered
abuse regardless of whether the caregiver intended to hurt the child.
Physical discipline, such as spanking or paddling, is not considered
abuse as long as it is reasonable and causes no bodily injury to the
child.

Neglect is the failure of a parent, guardian, or other caregiver to
provide for a child's basic needs. Neglect may be:

- Physical (e.g., failure to provide necessary food or shelter, or lack
  of appropriate supervision)

- Medical (e.g., failure to provide necessary medical or mental
  health treatment)

- Educational (e.g., failure to educate a child or attend to special education needs)

- Emotional (e.g., inattention to a child's emotional needs, failure to provide psychological care, or permitting the child to use alcohol or other drugs)

Sometimes cultural values, the standards of care in the community, and poverty may contribute to maltreatment, indicating the family is in need of information or assistance. When a family fails to use information and resources, and the child's health or safety is at risk, then child welfare intervention may be required. In addition, many States provide an exception to the definition of neglect for parents who choose not to seek medical care for their children due to religious beliefs.

Sexual abuse includes activities by a parent or caregiver such as fondling a child's genitals, penetration, incest, rape, sodomy, indecent exposure, and exploitation through prostitution or the production of pornographic materials.

Sexual abuse is defined by CAPTA as "the employment, use, persuasion, inducement, enticement, or coercion of any child to engage in, or assist any other person to engage in, any sexually explicit conduct or simulation of such conduct for the purpose of producing a visual depiction of such conduct; or the rape, and in cases of caretaker or inter-familial relationships, statutory rape, molestation, prostitution, or other form of sexual exploitation of children, or incest with children."

Emotional abuse (or psychological abuse) is a pattern of behavior that impairs a child's emotional development or sense of self-worth. This may include constant criticism, threats, or rejection, as well as withholding love, support, or guidance. Emotional abuse is often difficult to prove, and therefore, child protective services may not be able to intervene without evidence of harm or mental injury to the child. Emotional abuse is almost always present when other types of maltreatment are identified.

Abandonment is now defined in many States as a form of neglect. In general, a child is considered to be abandoned when the parent's identity or whereabouts are unknown, the child has been left alone in circumstances where the child suffers serious harm, or the parent has failed to maintain contact with the child or provide reasonable support for a specified period of time. Some States have enacted laws—often called safe haven laws—that provide safe places for parents to relinquish newborn infants.

Substance abuse is an element of the definition of child abuse or neglect in many States. Circumstances that are considered abuse or neglect in some States include the following:

- Prenatal exposure of a child to harm due to the mother's use of an illegal drug or other substance

- Manufacture of methamphetamine in the presence of a child

- Selling, distributing, or giving illegal drugs or alcohol to a child

- Use of a controlled substance by a caregiver that impairs the caregiver's ability to adequately care for the child

Child Maltreatment

Child maltreatment is any act or series of acts of commission or omission by a parent or other caregiver (e.g., clergy, coach, teacher) that results in harm, potential for harm, or threat of harm to a child.

Acts of Commission (Child Abuse)

Words or overt actions that cause harm, potential harm, or threat of harm

Acts of commission are deliberate and intentional; however, harm to a child might not be the intended consequence. Intention only applies to caregiver acts—not the consequences of those acts. For example, a caregiver might intend to hit a child as punishment (i.e., hitting the child is not accidental or unintentional), but not intend to cause the child to have a concussion. The following types of maltreatment involve acts of commission:

- Physical abuse

- Sexual abuse

- Psychological abuse

Acts of Omission (Child Neglect)

Failure to provide needs or to protect from harm or potential harm

Acts of omission are the failure to provide for a child's basic physical, emotional, or educational needs or to protect a child from harm or potential harm. Like acts of commission, harm to a child might not be the intended consequence. The following types of maltreatment involve acts of omission:

- Physical neglect

- Emotional neglect

- Medical and dental neglect

- Educational neglect

- Inadequate supervision

- Exposure to violent environments

Section 12.2

Recognizing Child Abuse and Neglect

Text in this section is excerpted from "What Is Child Abuse and Neglect? " Child Welfare Information Gateway, July 2013.

In addition to working to prevent a child from experiencing abuse or neglect, it is important to recognize high-risk situations and the signs and symptoms of maltreatment. If you do suspect a child is being harmed, reporting your suspicions may protect him or her and get help for the family. Any concerned person can report suspicions of child abuse or neglect. Reporting your concerns is not making an accusation; rather, it is a request for an investigation and assessment to determine if help is needed.

Some people (typically certain types of professionals, such as teachers or physicians) are required by State law to make a report of child maltreatment under specific circumstances—these are called mandatory reporters. Some States require all adults to report suspicions of child abuse or neglect.

The following signs may signal the presence of child abuse or neglect.

The Child:

- Shows sudden changes in behavior or school performance

- Has not received help for physical or medical problems brought to the parents' attention
- Has learning problems (or difficulty concentrating) that cannot be attributed to specific physical or psychological causes
- Is always watchful, as though preparing for something bad to happen
- Lacks adult supervision
- Is overly compliant, passive, or withdrawn
- Comes to school or other activities early, stays late, and does not want to go home
- Is reluctant to be around a particular person
- Discloses maltreatment

The Parent:

- Denies the existence of—or blames the child for—the child's problems in school or at home
- Asks teachers or other caregivers to use harsh physical discipline if the child misbehaves
- Sees the child as entirely bad, worthless, or burdensome
- Demands a level of physical or academic performance the child cannot achieve
- Looks primarily to the child for care, attention, and satisfaction of the parent's emotional needs
- Shows little concern for the child

The Parent and Child:

- Rarely touch or look at each other
- Consider their relationship entirely negative
- State that they do not like each other

The above list may not be all the signs of abuse or neglect. It is important to pay attention to other behaviors that may seem unusual or concerning.

Signs of Physical Abuse

Consider the possibility of physical abuse when the **child**:

- Has unexplained burns, bites, bruises, broken bones, or black eyes
- Has fading bruises or other marks noticeable after an absence from school
- Seems frightened of the parents and protests or cries when it is time to go home
- Shrinks at the approach of adults
- Reports injury by a parent or another adult caregiver
- Abuses animals or pets

Consider the possibility of physical abuse when the **parent or other adult caregiver:**

- Offers conflicting, unconvincing, or no explanation for the child's injury, or provides an explanation that is not consistent with the injury
- Describes the child as "evil" or in some other very negative way
- Uses harsh physical discipline with the child
- Has a history of abuse as a child
- Has a history of abusing animals or pets

Signs of Neglect

Consider the possibility of neglect when the **child**:

- Is frequently absent from school
- Begs or steals food or money
- Lacks needed medical or dental care, immunizations, or glasses
- Is consistently dirty and has severe body odor
- Lacks sufficient clothing for the weather
- Abuses alcohol or other drugs
- States that there is no one at home to provide care

Consider the possibility of neglect when the **parent or other adult caregiver**:

- Appears to be indifferent to the child

- Seems apathetic or depressed
- Behaves irrationally or in a bizarre manner
- Is abusing alcohol or other drugs

Signs of Sexual Abuse

Consider the possibility of sexual abuse when the **child:**

- Has difficulty walking or sitting
- Suddenly refuses to change for gym or to participate in physical activities
- Reports nightmares or bedwetting
- Experiences a sudden change in appetite
- Demonstrates bizarre, sophisticated, or unusual sexual knowledge or behavior
- Becomes pregnant or contracts a venereal disease, particularly if under age 14
- Runs away
- Reports sexual abuse by a parent or another adult caregiver
- Attaches very quickly to strangers or new adults in their environment

Consider the possibility of sexual abuse when the **parent or other adult caregiver:**

- Is unduly protective of the child or severely limits the child's contact with other children, especially of the opposite sex
- Is secretive and isolated
- Is jealous or controlling with family members

Signs of Emotional Maltreatment

Consider the possibility of emotional maltreatment when the child:

- Shows extremes in behavior, such as overly compliant or demanding behavior, extreme passivity, or aggression
- Is either inappropriately adult (parenting other children, for example) or inappropriately infantile (frequently rocking or head-banging, for example)

- Is delayed in physical or emotional development

- Has attempted suicide

- Reports a lack of attachment to the parent

Consider the possibility of emotional maltreatment when the **parent or other adult caregiver:**

- Constantly blames, belittles, or berates the child

- Is unconcerned about the child and refuses to consider offers of help for the child's problems

- Overtly rejects the child

Section 12.3

Preventing Child Abuse and Neglect

Text in this section is excerpted from "Preventing Child Abuse and Neglect," Child Welfare Information Gateway, July 2013.

Prevention Strategies

Child abuse and maltreatment is a serious problem that can have lasting harmful effects on its victims. The goal for child maltreatment prevention is clear—to stop child abuse and neglect from happening in the first place. Child abuse is a complex problem rooted in unhealthy relationships and environments. Safe, stable, and nurturing relationships and environments for all children and families can prevent child abuse. However, the solutions are as complex as the problem.

Increasing factors that protect children can reduce the occurrence of abuse. Preventing child maltreatment means influencing individual behaviors, relationships among families and neighbors, community involvement, and the culture of a society. Prevention strategies include effective programs that focus on attitude change and on modifying policies and societal norms to create safe, stable, and nurturing environments. We need to implement effective prevention strategies to stop child abuse and neglect before it happens and to foster commitment to social change

Many State, local, and Tribal governments sponsor prevention activities and provide a variety of prevention services. Some prevention efforts are intended for everyone, such as public service announcements (PSAs) aimed at raising awareness about child maltreatment within the general population. Others are specifically targeted for individuals and families who may be at greater risk for child abuse or neglect.

Prevention requires a continuum of strategies at the individual, relationship, community, and societal levels. Another key to success is providing prevention services that are evidence based or evidence informed. This means that rather than relying on assumptions about what works, research has been conducted to demonstrate that a particular service actually improves outcomes for children and families. This helps service providers feel confident in what they are doing, and it can help justify a program's continued funding when resources are scarce.

Prevent Child Abuse America's 50 chapters nationwide sponsor a number of evidence based, State-specific programs to help individuals and communities prevent child maltreatment.

State children's trust and prevention funds collectively distribute more than $100 million in funding each year to support a diverse array of evidence-based and innovative state wide and community based prevention strategies.

Prevention programs are more effective when they involve parents as partners in all aspects of program planning, implementation, and evaluation. Parents are more likely to make lasting changes when they are empowered to identify solutions that make sense for them.

Common activities of prevention programs include:

- Public awareness campaigns, such as PSAs, posters, and brochures that promote healthy parenting, child safety, and how to report suspected maltreatment.

- Skills-based curricula that teach children safety and protection skills, such as programs that focus on preventing sexual abuse

- Parent education programs to help parents develop positive parenting skills and decrease behaviors associated with child abuse and neglect

- Home visiting programs that provide support and assistance to expecting and new mothers in their homes

- Parent mentor or leadership programs that provide role models and support to families in crisis

- Parent support groups, where parents work together to strengthen their families and build social networks of services to meet the specific needs of the people who live in surrounding neighborhoods

- Respite and crisis care programs, which offer temporary relief to caregivers in stressful situations by providing short-term care for their children

- Family resource centers, which work with community members to develop a variety of services to meet the specific needs of the people who live in surrounding neighborhoods

The FRIENDS National Resource Center for Community-Based Child Abuse Prevention, a service of the Children's Bureau, works closely with Circle of Parents® to foster parent leadership, education, and involvement.

Stop it Now! is a national organization focused on preventing sexual abuse and offers information, supports, and resources for prevention. Some of its materials aimed at parents include prevention tip sheets, abuse warning signs tip sheets, and archives of its publication PARENTtalk. PARENTtalk was published from 1998 to 2007 and was written by and for parents and caregivers of youth with sexual behavior problems.

Protective Factors

Prevention programs have long focused on reducing particular risk factors, or conditions that research shows are associated with child abuse and neglect. Increasingly, prevention services are also recognizing the importance of promoting protective factors, circumstances in families and communities that increase the health and well-being of children and families. These factors help parents who might otherwise be at risk of abusing or neglecting their children to find resources, supports, or coping strategies that allow them to parent effectively, even under stress.

The following six protective factors have been linked to a lower incidence of child abuse and neglect:

- **Nurturing and attachment.** When parents and children have strong, warm feelings for one another, children develop trust that their parents will provide what they need to thrive.

- **Knowledge of parenting and of child and youth development.** Parents who understand how children grow and develop and know the typical developmental milestones can provide an environment where children can live up to their potential.

- **Parental resilience.** Parents who are emotionally resilient have a positive attitude, creatively problem solve, effectively address challenges, and are less likely to direct anger and frustration at their children.

- **Social connections**. Trusted and caring family friends provide emotional support to parents by offering encouragement and assistance in facing the daily challenges of raising a family.

- **Concrete supports for parents.** Parents need basic resources such as food, clothing, housing, transportation, and access to essential services that address family-specific needs (such as child care, health care, and mental health services) to ensure the health and well-being of their children.

- **Social and emotional competence**. Children with the ability to positively interact with others, self-regulate their behaviors, and communicate their feelings have relationships that are more positive with family, friends, and peers. Children without these competencies may be at greater risk for abuse.

Section 12.4

The Risk and Prevention of Maltreatment of Children with Disabilities

Text in this section is excerpted from "The Risk and Prevention of Maltreatment of Children with Disabilities," Child Welfare Information Gateway, March 2012. Reviewed January 2016.

Child abuse and neglect can affect any child, but children with disabilities are at greater risk of maltreatment than children without disabilities.

The Scope of the Problem

Estimates vary greatly regarding the number of children with disabilities in the general population, depending in part on how disability is defined. According to the U.S. Census Bureau, nearly 4 percent of children have a disability (2009).

In 2009, there were 9.3 unique victims of child maltreatment per 1,000 children in the population (U.S. Department of Health and Human Services, 2010). Because States are not required to submit data on the disability status of abused or neglected children, variation in the way States define and collect these data makes it difficult to accurately estimate the rates of maltreatment among children with disabilities.

Risk Factors

While no single factor places a child at risk for abuse or neglect, the interaction of factors seems to increase risk. Some common factors that increase risk of maltreatment for all children, regardless of disability status, include:

- Parent's experience of maltreatment as a child
- Parent's negative attitude toward the child or lack of knowledge of child development
- Parental substance abuse, depression, anxiety, or antisocial behavior
- Single-parent households
- Poverty or unemployment
- Social isolation or lack of support
- Family violence or violence in the community

In addition, there are a number of risk factors related to society, families and parents, children, and nonfamilial caregivers that place children with disabilities at risk for abuse or neglect.

Societal Risk Factors

Many researchers believe societal attitudes and limited knowledge regarding children with disabilities place them at greater risk for abuse or neglect. Described below are some societal risk factors for maltreatment among this population:

- When children with disabilities are separated from their peers, it makes them seem "different" and unworthy of the same social or educational opportunities.

- By devaluing the contributions of children with disabilities to society, it becomes more acceptable to treat them poorly or use violence.

- The belief that caregivers would never harm children with disabilities results in lack of attention to the problem.

- When children with disabilities are viewed as asexual, it may lead caregivers to deny them sex education that could help prevent abuse.

- By believing some children with disabilities do not feel pain, unnecessarily harmful therapies may be used.

- Children with disabilities who internalize the above societal attitudes may feel shame or feel less worthy of being treated respectfully.

- A lack of training impacts the ability of social workers, teachers, and other professionals to identify and report suspected maltreatment of children with disabilities.

Family or Parental Risk Factors

One of the most frequently cited family or parental risk factors for the maltreatment of children with disabilities is the increased stress of caring for a child with special needs and coping with challenging behaviors. The following risk factors summarize issues related to the family's reaction to the child with a disability and the parent's knowledge and skills to care for the child:

- The family views the child as "different," sees the disability as an embarrassment, or mourns the loss of a "normal" child.

- The parent lacks the skills, resources, or supports to respond to the child's special needs and provide adequate care or supervision.

- The parent is unaware his or her child with disabilities is at greater risk of maltreatment and may be unprepared to identify and protect the child from risky situations.

- The parent of a child who exhibits challenging behaviors may be more likely to exert unnecessary control or use physical punishment.

- The parent of a child with disabilities who is unresponsive, unaffectionate, or exhibits behavior problems may have difficulty forming a strong attachment with the child; frequent hospitalizations may also weaken the parent-child attachment.

- The cost of ongoing treatment or care for a child with disabilities may put a financial strain on the family or affect parental job stability.

Child-Related Risk Factors

There are numerous risk factors for maltreatment that address characteristics of the child with a disability; most of them relate to the way individuals respond to or care for children with disabilities. Although children are not responsible for being victims of maltreatment, the following factors place them at greater risk:

- Boys with disabilities or children with disabilities who are in preschool or younger are more likely than children without disabilities to be abused.

- Children who exhibit challenging behaviors or have intensive needs may overwhelm caregivers.

- Children with disabilities who rely on caregivers for their daily needs may not know when behavior is inappropriate or may have been taught to obey caregivers' demands.

- Emotional dependence on caregivers may prevent children from attempting to stop the abuse or neglect because they fear losing the relationship.

- The nature of some children's disability may prevent them defending themselves, escaping from the abusive situation, or reporting the abuse; this may cause potential perpetrators to believe they can "get away with it."

Risk Factors for Institutional and Nonfamilial Maltreatment

Although maltreatment is most often perpetrated by family members, children with disabilities are also at risk when they being are cared for by others. Listed below are risk factors for children with disabilities in institutions or being cared for by nonfamilial caregivers:

- An abusive subculture that allows for extreme power and control inequities between caregivers and children

- Dehumanization and detachment from the children

- Clustering vulnerable children with others who might harm them and tolerating inappropriate behavior among children

- Isolating children or allowing little to no outside contact

- Lack of procedures for reporting abuse or monitoring investigations of abuse

Promising Practices

The following section highlights program examples, collaborative responses, and various prevention methods that may help you, families, caregivers, educators, and others avert the risk or occurrence of maltreatment. Additionally, this section points to common signs of abuse or neglect, resources, and training specific to addressing maltreatment of children with disabilities.

Prevention

Considering the increased risks faced by children with disabilities, efforts to prevent maltreatment should be coordinated and multifaceted. Prevention may be aimed at the general public or targeted specifically to families at risk of child maltreatment or involved with the child welfare system. Approaches may be parallel, in which separate programs are implemented for children with disabilities, or integrated, in which the needs of children with disabilities are accommodated in programs serving all children.

This section looks at prevention at the societal or community level, followed by family-focused and child-focused prevention efforts and prevention of nonfamilial maltreatment.

Societal and Community-Level Prevention

One of the first steps in prevention is raising awareness of the problem. Heightened awareness can lead to more funding for research and better programming to prevent and combat the problem. The following strategies can help change societal attitudes about children with disabilities:

- **Help others see children with disabilities as valued and unique individuals.** Counteract negative attitudes by discussing the strengths of children with disabilities and their families and the unique perspectives they bring to their communities.

- **Promote inclusion of children with disabilities into everyday life.** Identify and address physical and social accessibility for children with disabilities and their families (e.g., access to public buildings and parks, equal opportunities to participate in sports or social events).

- **Develop leadership skills in parents and family members of children with disabilities.** They can be powerful advocates for promoting the safety of their children and all children in the community.

- **Share responsibility for the well-being of children with disabilities.** Publish a "report card" on the well-being of the community's children and families, including children with disabilities and their families.

- **Encourage workplaces and local businesses to establish family-friendly policies**, including specialized supports for families of children with disabilities.

Family-Focused Prevention

Because parents and other primary caregivers spend the most time with their children, prevention programs often focus on services to families. Services can either be offered to all families that have children with disabilities or to families considered to be at risk of maltreating their children. Parents of children involved with the child welfare system can also benefit from prevention programs, particularly to reduce the risk of repeat maltreatment. Families of children with mild and severe impairments should be included in programs, since research shows children with mild impairments are sometimes at greater risk of maltreatment.

Below are strategies for supporting families of children with disabilities to reduce the risk of abuse or neglect:

- **Increase parent knowledge of child development and issues specific to the child's disability.** Connect the family to appropriate treatment services and a disability professional who can support the family in providing proper care and adapting parenting skills to the child's unique needs.

- **Strengthen parent-child interactions** by teaching parents communication techniques and equipping them with alternative communication devices, if needed. Supporting positive interactions can reduce frustration and improve attachment.

- **Offer a home visiting program** in which professional or paraprofessional staff visit families to provide in-home services. The visitor can develop a relationship with the family in order to assess their strengths and needs, improve positive parenting strategies, and connect them to needed support.

- **Organize parent support groups** where parents can share their experiences in a supportive group setting. Parents can trade information on resources, problem-solve issues related to their child's disability, and create informal support networks.

- **Coordinate respite care** to provide parents with short-term child care services. Whether it is planned or offered during times of crisis, taking a break from the demands of caring for a child with disabilities can help parents reduce stress and the risk of abuse or neglect.

- **Prevent repeat maltreatment** by working with the family to address attitudes toward physical punishment and identify alternative behavioral management strategies. Reduce family stressors by providing financial, child care, and other concrete supports.

Overall, research shows that using a strengths-based approach to working with children and families is an effective child abuse prevention strategy. Rather than focusing solely on the family's needs and risk factors for maltreatment, recent prevention resource guides from the Children's Bureau encourage professionals to promote protective factors that strengthen families so they can better care for their children.

Child-Focused Prevention

In the past, the mistaken belief that children with disabilities are not vulnerable to abuse or neglect and do not need information about it has kept some parents and professionals from communicating openly with children on the subject. Most researchers now agree that teaching children with disabilities about the risks of abuse and neglect as well as ways to communicate with others can help reduce maltreatment among this population of children. Summarized below are some prevention strategies when working with children with disabilities:

- **Help children protect themselves.** Hold regular trainings to share information about abuse and neglect and talk about feelings children may experience if abuse is attempted. Help children understand how to identify it, respond to it, and tell others.

- **Teach children about their, and others', bodies and sexuality.** Review the proper names for body parts and functions. Explain the difference between appropriate and inappropriate social or sexual behavior.

- **Reduce children's social isolation.** Ensure children with disabilities are included and feel welcome at all activities. Support them as they form and strengthen relationships with peers and trusted adults.

- **Maximize children's communication skills and tools.** Practice communication skills with them. Model healthy relationships and positive interactions with other children and adults.

- **Involve parents in their children's education.** Inform them when their children learn about abuse or sexuality; offer them the same training materials. Provide strategies for parents to reinforce the lessons at home.

- **Ensure prevention programs are inclusive and appropriate to children's ability levels, culture, and gender.** Remember that some children may need to be trained more frequently in order to retain the information.

Prevention of Nonfamilial Maltreatment

To prevent the abuse or neglect of children with disabilities in institutional settings, managers and workers may consider implementing the following strategies:

- **Carefully screen job applicants** for experience working with children with disabilities and for prior reports of maltreatment.

- **Train staff** in positive behavior management techniques that limit the use of restraint or seclusion.

- **Maintain effective staff/child ratios** and set realistic expectations for staff responsibilities.

- **Provide strong supervision and support** that emphasizes a culture of child protection and relationship-building between staff and children.

- **Establish procedures and staff training** on how to identify and report suspected maltreatment.

- **Ensure an open environment** that welcomes families and allows for unannounced checks by external reviewers.

Families can also take the following actions to help prevent abuse or neglect by other caregivers of their children:

- **Ensure caregiver knowledge of the child's special needs** and strategies for managing behaviors.

- **Be familiar with the child's caregivers;** know their caregiving techniques and routines.

- **Maintain an open relationship** in which concerns can be addressed.

- **Discuss abuse awareness with caregivers;** help them locate training opportunities.

- **Inform caregivers the child has been trained** in abuse prevention techniques.

Section 12.5

Child Sexual Abuse

Text in this section is excerpted from "Child Sexual Abuse,"
U.S. Department of Veterans Affairs (VA), September 2, 2015.

What Is Child Sexual Abuse?

Child sexual abuse includes a wide range of sexual behaviors that take place between a child and an older person. These behaviors are meant to arouse the older person in a sexual way. In general, no thought is given to what effect the behavior may have on the child. For the most part, the abuser does not care about the reactions or choices of the child.

Child sexual abuse often involves body contact. This could include sexual kissing, touching, and oral, anal, or vaginal sex. Not all sexual abuse involves body contact, though. Showing private parts ("flashing"), forcing children to watch pornography, verbal pressure for sex, and exploiting children as prostitutes or for pornography can be sexual abuse as well. Researchers estimate that in our country about one out of six boys and one out of four girls are sexually abused.

Under the child sexual abuse laws, the abuser must be older than the victim in most cases. Some states require the abuser to be at least five years older.

Who Commits Child Sexual Abuse?

- Most often, sexual abusers know the child they abuse, but are not family. For example, the abuser might be a friend of the family, babysitter, or neighbor. About 6 out of 10 abusers fall into that group.

- About 3 out of 10 of those who sexually abuse children are family members of the child. This includes fathers, uncles, or cousins.

- The abuser is a stranger in only about 1 out of 10 child sexual abuse cases.

- Abusers are men in most cases, whether the victim is a boy or a girl.

- Women are the abusers in about 14% of cases reported against boys and about 6% of cases reported against girls.

- Child pornographers and other abusers who are strangers may make contact with children using the Internet.

What Are the Effects of Childhood Sexual Abuse?

It is not always easy to tell whether a child has been sexually abused. Sexual abuse often occurs in secret, and there is not always physical proof of the abuse. For these reasons, child sexual abuse can be hard to detect.

Some child sexual abuse survivors may show symptoms of PTSD. They may behave in a nervous, upset way. Survivors may have bad dreams. They may act out aspects of the abuse in their play. They might show other fears and worries. Young children may lose skills they once learned and act younger than they are. For example, an abused child might start wetting the bed or sucking his or her thumb. Some sexual abuse survivors show out-of-place sexual behaviors that are not expected in a child. They may act seductive or they may not maintain safe limits with others. Children, especially boys, might "act out" with behavior problems. This could include being cruel to others and running away. Other children "act in" by becoming depressed. They may withdraw from friends or family. Older children or teens might try to hurt or even kill themselves.

Sexual abuse can be very confusing for children. For a child, it often involves being used or hurt by a trusted adult. The child might learn that the only way to get attention or love is to give something sexual or give up their self-respect. Some children believe the abuse is their fault somehow. They may think the abuser chose them because they must have wanted it or because there is something wrong with them. If the abuser was of the same sex, children (and parents) might wonder if that means they are "gay."

Almost every child sexual abuse victim describes the abuse as negative. Most children know it is wrong. They usually have feelings of fear, shock, anger, and disgust. A small number of abused children might not realize it is wrong, though. These children tend to be very young or have mental delays. Also some victims might enjoy the attention, closeness, or physical contact with the abuser. This is more likely if these basic needs are not met by a caregiver. All told, these reactions make the abuse very hard and confusing for children.

If childhood sexual abuse is not treated, long-term symptoms can go on through adulthood. These may include:

- PTSD and anxiety.

- Depression and thoughts of suicide.

- Sexual anxiety and disorders, including having too many or unsafe sexual partners.

- Difficulty setting safe limits with others (e.g., saying no to people) and relationship problems.

- Poor body image and low self-esteem.

- Unhealthy behaviors, such as alcohol, drugs, self-harm, or eating problems. These behaviors are often used to try to hide painful emotions related to the abuse.

If you were sexually abused as a child and have some of these symptoms, it is important for you to get help.

What Can Caregivers Do to Help Keep Children Safe?

Although caregivers cannot protect their children 100% of the time, it is important to get to know the people that come around your child. Most importantly, provide a safe, caring setting so children feel able to talk to you about sexual abuse.

Other tips to keep your children safe include:

- Talk to others who know the people with whom your child comes in contact.

- Talk to your children about the difference between safe touching and unsafe touching.

- Tell the child that if someone tries to touch his or her body in their private areas or do things that make the child feel unsafe, he should say NO to the person. He needs to tell you or a trusted adult about it right away.

- Let children know that their bodies are private and that they have the right not to allow others to touch their bodies in an unsafe way.

- Let them know that they do not have to do EVERYTHING the babysitter, family member, or group leader tells them to do.

- Alert your children that abusers may use the Internet. Watch over your child on the Internet.

What Should You Do If You Think Your Child Has Been Sexually Abused?

If a child says she or he has been abused, try to stay calm. Reassure the child that what happened is not her fault, that you believe her, that you are proud of her for telling you (or another person), and that you are there to keep her safe. Take your child to a mental health and medical professional right away. Many cities have child advocacy centers where a child and her family can get help. These centers interview children and family members in a sensitive, warm place. They can help you report the abuse to legal authorities. They can help you find a medical examiner and therapist skilled in child sexual abuse.

Children can recover from sexual abuse and go on to live good lives. The best predictor of recovery is support and love from their main caregiver. As a caregiver, you might also consider getting help for yourself. It is often very hard to accept that a child has been sexually abused. You will not be supporting your child, though, if you respond in certain unhelpful ways. For example, you will not be able to provide support if you are overwhelmed with your own emotions. Don't downplay the abuse ("it wasn't that bad"), but also try not to have extreme fears related to the abuse ("my child will never be safe again"). It will not help children if you force them to talk, or if you blame the child. Getting therapy for yourself can help you deal with your own feelings about the abuse. Then you might be better able to provide support to your child.

Section 12.6

Long-Term Consequences of Child Abuse and Neglect

Text in this section is excerpted from "Long-Term Consequences of Child Abuse and Neglect," Child Welfare Information Gateway, July 2013.

The impact of child abuse and neglect is often discussed in terms of physical, psychological, behavioral, and societal consequences. In reality, however, it is impossible to separate the types of impacts. Physical consequences, such as damage to a child's growing brain, can have psychological implications, such as cognitive delays or emotional difficulties. Psychological problems often manifest as high-risk behaviors. Depression and anxiety, for example, may make a person more likely to smoke, abuse alcohol or drugs, or overeat. High-risk behaviors, in turn, can lead to long-term physical health problems, such as sexually transmitted diseases, cancer, and obesity. Not all children who have been abused or neglected will experience long-term consequences, but they may have an increased susceptibility.

Factors Affecting the Consequences of Child Abuse and Neglect

Individual outcomes vary widely and are affected by a combination of factors, including:

- The child's age and developmental status when the abuse or neglect occurred

- The type of maltreatment (physical abuse, neglect, sexual abuse, etc.)

- The frequency, duration, and severity of the maltreatment

- The relationship between the child and the perpetrator

Researchers also have begun to explore why, given similar conditions, some children experience long-term consequences of abuse and neglect while others emerge relatively unscathed. The ability to cope, and even thrive, following a negative experience is often referred to as "resilience." It is important to note that resilience is not an inherent trait in children but results from a mixture of both risk and protective factors that cause a child's positive or negative reaction to adverse experiences. A number of protective and promotive factors—individually, within a family, or within a community—may contribute to an abused or neglected child's resilience. These include positive attachment, self-esteem, intelligence, emotion regulation, humor, and independence.

Physical Health Consequences

The immediate physical effects of abuse or neglect can be relatively minor (bruises or cuts) or severe (broken bones, hemorrhage, or even death). In some cases, the physical effects are temporary; however, the pain and suffering they cause a child should not be discounted.

Child abuse and neglect can have a multitude of long-term effects on physical health. NSCAW researchers found that, at some point during the 3 years following a maltreatment investigation, 28 percent of children had a chronic health condition. Below are some outcomes other researchers have identified:

Abusive head trauma. Abusive head trauma, an inflicted injury to the head and its contents caused by shaking and blunt impact, is the most common cause of traumatic death for infants. The injuries may not be immediately noticeable and may include bleeding in the eye or brain and damage to the spinal cord and neck. Significant brain development takes place during infancy, and this important development is compromised in maltreated children. One in every four victims of shaken baby syndrome dies, and nearly all victims experience serious health consequences.

Impaired brain development. Child abuse and neglect have been shown to cause important regions of the brain to fail to form or grow properly, resulting in impaired development. These alterations in brain maturation have long-term consequences for cognitive, language, and academic abilities and are connected with mental health disorders. Disrupted neurodevelopment as a result of maltreatment can cause children to adopt a persistent fear state as well as attributes that are normally helpful during threatening moments but counterproductive in the absence of threats, such as hypervigilance, anxiety, and behavior impulsivity.

Poor physical health. Several studies have shown a relationship between various forms of child maltreatment and poor health. Adults who experienced abuse or neglect during childhood are more likely to suffer from cardiovascular disease, lung and liver disease, hypertension, diabetes, asthma, and obesity. Specific physical health conditions are also connected to maltreatment type. One study showed that children who experienced neglect were at increased risk for diabetes and poorer lung functioning, while physical abuse was shown to increase the risk for diabetes and malnutrition. Additionally, child maltreatment has been shown to increase adolescent obesity. A longitudinal study found that children who experienced neglect had body mass indexes that grew at significantly faster rates compared to children who had not experienced neglect.

Psychological Consequences

The immediate emotional effects of abuse and neglect—isolation, fear, and an inability to trust—can translate into lifelong psychological consequences, including low self-esteem, depression, and relationship difficulties. Researchers have identified links between child abuse and neglect and the following:

Difficulties during infancy. Of children entering foster care in 2010, 16 percent were younger than 1 year. When infants and young children enter out-of-home care due to abuse or neglect, the trauma of a primary caregiver change negatively affects their attachments.

Nearly half of infants in foster care who have experienced maltreatment exhibit some form of cognitive delay and have lower IQ scores, language difficulties, and neonatal challenges compared to children who have not been abused or neglected.

Poor mental and emotional health. Experiencing childhood trauma and adversity, such as physical or sexual abuse, is a risk factor for borderline personality disorder, depression, anxiety, and other psychiatric disorders. One study using ACE data found that roughly 54 percent of cases of depression and 58 percent of suicide attempts in women were connected to adverse childhood experiences. Child maltreatment also negatively impacts the development of emotion regulation, which often persists into adolescence or adulthood.

Cognitive difficulties. NSCAW researchers found that children with substantiated reports of maltreatment were at risk for severe developmental and cognitive problems, including grade repetition. In its final report on the second NSCAW study (NSCAW II), more than 10 percent of school-aged children and youth showed some risk of cognitive problems or low academic achievement, 43 percent had emotional or behavioral problems, and 13 percent had both.

Social difficulties. Children who experience neglect are more likely to develop antisocial traits as they grow up. Parental neglect is associated with borderline personality disorders, attachment issues or affectionate behaviors with unknown/little-known people, inappropriate modeling of adult behavior, and aggression.

Behavioral Consequences

Not all victims of child abuse and neglect will experience behavioral consequences. However, behavioral problems appear to be more likely among this group. According to NSCAW, more than half of youth reported for maltreatment are at risk for an emotional or behavioral problem. Child abuse and neglect appear to make the following more likely:

Difficulties during adolescence. NSCAW data show that more than half of youth with reports of maltreatment are at risk of grade repetition, substance abuse, delinquency, truancy, or pregnancy. Other studies suggest that abused or neglected children are more likely to engage in sexual risk-taking as they reach adolescence, thereby increasing their chances of contracting a sexually transmitted disease.

Victims of child sexual abuse also are at a higher risk for rape in adulthood, and the rate of risk increases according to the severity of the child sexual abuse experience(s).

Juvenile delinquency and adult criminality. Several studies have documented the correlation between child abuse and future juvenile delinquency. Children who have experienced abuse are nine times more likely to become involved in criminal activities.

Alcohol and other drug abuse. Research consistently reflects an increased likelihood that children who have experienced abuse or neglect will smoke cigarettes, abuse alcohol, or take illicit drugs during their lifetime. In fact, male children with an ACE Score of 6 or more (having six or more adverse childhood experiences) had an increased likelihood—of more than 4,000 percent—to use intravenous drugs later in life.

Abusive behavior. Abusive parents often have experienced abuse during their own childhoods. Data from the Longitudinal Study of Adolescent Health showed that girls who experienced childhood physical abuse were 1–7 percent more likely to become perpetrators of youth violence and 8–10 percent more likely to be perpetrators of interpersonal violence (IPV). Boys who experienced childhood sexual violence were 3–12 percent more likely to commit youth violence and 1–17 percent more likely to commit IPV.

Societal Consequences

While child abuse and neglect usually occur within the family, the impact does not end there. Society as a whole pays a price for child abuse and neglect, in terms of both direct and indirect costs.

Direct costs. The lifetime cost of child maltreatment and related fatalities in 1 year totals $124 billion, according to a study funded by the CDC. Child maltreatment is more costly on an annual basis than the two leading health concerns, stroke and type 2 diabetes. On the other hand, programs that prevent maltreatment have shown to be cost effective. The U.S. Triple P System Trial, funded by the CDC, has a benefit/cost ratio of $47 in benefits to society for every $1 in program costs.

Indirect costs. Indirect costs represent the long-term economic consequences to society because of child abuse and neglect.

These include costs associated with increased use of our health-care system, juvenile and adult criminal activity, mental illness, substance abuse, and domestic violence. Prevent Child Abuse America estimates that child abuse and neglect prevention strategies can save taxpayers $104 billion each year. According to the Schuyler Center for Analysis and Advocacy (2011), every $1 spent on home visiting yields a $5.70 return on investment in New York, including reduced confirmed reports of abuse, reduced family enrollment in Temporary Assistance for Needy Families, decreased visits to emergency rooms, decreased arrest rates for mothers, and increased monthly earnings. One study found that all eight categories of adverse childhood experiences were associated with an increased likelihood of employment problems, financial problems, and absenteeism. The authors assert that these long-term costs—to the workforce and to society—are preventable.

Prevention Practice and Strategies

To break the cycle of maltreatment and reduce the likelihood of long-term consequences, communities across the country must continue to develop and implement strategies that prevent abuse or neglect from happening. While experts agree that the causes of child abuse and neglect are complex, it is possible to develop prevention initiatives that address known risk factors.

Trauma-Informed Practice

While the priority is to prevent child abuse and neglect from occurring, it is equally important to respond to those children and adults who have experienced abuse and neglect. Over the past 30 years, researchers and practitioners have developed a better understanding of the effects of trauma. More has been done in the way of developing supports to address these effects, build resiliency, and, hopefully, prevent further trauma. Trauma-informed practice refers to the services and programs specifically designed to address and respond to the impact of traumatic stress. The importance of this approach has become especially evident in the child welfare system, as a majority of children and families involved with child welfare have experienced some form of past trauma. When human service systems recognize and respond to the impact of trauma and use this knowledge to adapt policies and practices, children, youth, and families benefit.

Section 12.7

Child Maltreatment Statistics

Text in this section is excerpted from "Child Abuse and Neglect
Fatalities 2013: Statistics and Interventions," Child Welfare
Information Gateway, April 2015.

Despite the efforts of the child protection system, child maltreatment fatalities remain a serious problem. Although the untimely
deaths of children due to illness and accidents are closely monitored,
deaths that result from physical assault or severe neglect can be more
difficult to track. The circumstances surrounding a child's death, its
investigation, and communication across all the disciplines involved
complicate data collection.

How Many Children Die Each Year from Child Abuse or Neglect?

According to data from the National Child Abuse and Neglect Data
System (NCANDS), 50 States reported a total of 1,484 fatalities. Based
on these data, **a nationally estimated 1,520 children died from
abuse and neglect in 2013**. This translates to a rate of 2.04 children
per 100,000 children in the general population and an average of four
children dying every day from abuse or neglect. This rate decreased
slightly from FFY 2012 and showed a 12.7 percent decrease from 2009.
NCANDS defines "child fatality" as the death of a child caused by an
injury resulting from abuse or neglect or where abuse or neglect was
a contributing factor.

The number and rate of fatalities have fluctuated during the past
5 years. The national estimate is influenced by which States report
data as well as by the U.S. Census Bureau's child population estimates.
Some States that reported an increase in child fatalities between 2010
and 2012 attributed it to improvements in reporting after the passage
of the Child and Family Services Improvement and Innovation Act.

Most data on child fatalities come from State child welfare agencies.
However, States may also draw on other data sources, including health
departments, vital statistics departments, medical examiners' offices,

law enforcement, and fatality review teams. This coordination of data collection contributes to better estimates.

Many researchers and practitioners believe that child fatalities due to abuse and neglect are still underreported. One report on national child abuse and neglect deaths in the United States estimates that approximately 50 percent of deaths reported as "unintentional injury deaths" are reclassified after further investigation by medical and forensic experts as deaths due to maltreatment. It is often more difficult to establish whether a fatality was caused by neglect than it is to establish a physical abuse fatality. The different agencies that come into contact with a case of a possible child neglect fatality may have differing definitions of what constitutes neglect, and these definitions may be influenced by the laws, regulations, and standards of each agency.

Issues affecting the accuracy and consistency of child fatality data include:

- Variation among reporting requirements and definitions of child abuse and neglect and other terms

- Variation in death investigation systems and training

- Variation in State child fatality review and reporting processes

- The length of time (up to a year in some cases) it may take to establish abuse or neglect as the cause of death

- Inaccurate determination of the manner and cause of death, resulting in the miscoding of death certificates; this includes deaths labeled as accidents, sudden infant death syndrome (SIDS), or "manner undetermined" that would have been attributed to abuse or neglect if more comprehensive investigations had been conducted

- Limited coding options for child deaths, especially those due to neglect or negligence, when using the International Classification of Diseases to code death certificates

- The ease with which the circumstances surrounding many child maltreatment deaths can be concealed or rendered unclear

- Lack of coordination or cooperation among different agencies and jurisdictions

A report by the U.S. Government Accountability Office that assessed NCANDS data, surveys and interviews with State child welfare administrators and practitioners, and site visit reports to three States suggests that facilitating the sharing of information and increased cooperation among Federal, State, and local agencies would provide a more accurate count of maltreatment deaths. A study of child fatalities in three States found that combining at least two data sources resulted in the identification of more than 90 percent of child fatalities ascertained as due to child maltreatment.

What Groups of Children Are Most Vulnerable?

Research indicates that very young children (ages 4 and younger) are the most frequent victims of child fatalities. NCANDS data for 2013 demonstrated that children younger than 1 year accounted for 46.5 percent of fatalities; children younger than 3 years accounted for almost three-fourths (73.9 percent) of fatalities. These children are the most vulnerable for many reasons, including their dependency, small size, and inability to defend themselves.

How Do These Deaths Occur?

Fatal child abuse may involve repeated abuse over a period of time (e.g., battered child syndrome), or it may involve a single, impulsive incident (e.g., drowning, suffocating, or shaking a baby). In cases of fatal neglect, the child's death results not from anything the caregiver does, but from a caregiver's failure to act. The neglect may be chronic (e.g., extended malnourishment) or acute (e.g., an infant who drowns after being left unsupervised in the bathtub).

In 2013, 71.4 percent of children who died from child maltreatment suffered neglect either alone or in combination with another maltreatment type, and 46.8 percent suffered physical abuse either alone or in combination with other maltreatment. Medical neglect either alone or in combination was reported in 8.6 percent of fatalities.

Who Are the Perpetrators?

No matter how the fatal abuse occurs, one fact of great concern is that the perpetrators are, by definition, individuals responsible for the care and supervision of their victims. In 2013, parents, acting alone or with another parent, were responsible for 78.9 percent of child abuse or neglect fatalities. More than one-quarter (27.7 percent) were perpetrated by the mother acting alone, 12.4 percent were perpetrated by the father acting alone, and 24.6 percent were perpetrated by the mother and father acting together. Nonparents (including kin and child care providers, among others) were responsible for 17.0 percent of child fatalities, and child fatalities with unknown perpetrator relationship data accounted for 4.2 percent of the total.

There is no single profile of a perpetrator of fatal child abuse, although certain characteristics reappear in many studies. Frequently, the perpetrator is a young adult in his or her mid-20s, without a high school diploma, living at or below the poverty level, depressed, and who may have difficulty coping with stressful situations. Fathers and mothers' boyfriends are most often the perpetrators in abuse deaths; mothers are more often at fault in neglect fatalities.

How Do Communities Respond to Child Fatalities?

The response to the problem of child abuse and neglect fatalities is often hampered by inconsistencies, including:

- Underreporting of the number of children who die each year as a result of abuse and neglect

- Lack of consistent standards for child autopsies or death investigations

- The varying roles of Child Protective Services (CPS) agencies in investigation in different jurisdictions

- Uncoordinated, non-multidisciplinary investigations

- Medical examiners or elected coroners who do not have specific child abuse and neglect training

To address some of these inconsistencies, multidisciplinary and multiagency child fatality review teams have emerged to provide a coordinated approach to understanding child deaths, including deaths caused by religion-based medical neglect. Federal legislation further supported the development of these teams in an amendment to the 1992 reauthorization of the Child Abuse Prevention and Treatment Act (CAPTA), which required States to include information on child death review (CDR) in their program plans. Many States received initial funding for these teams through the Children's Justice Act, from grants awarded by the Administration on Children, Youth and Families in the U.S. Department of Health and Human Services (HHS).

Child fatality review teams, which exist at a State, local, or State/local level in the District of Columbia and in every State,[31] are composed of prosecutors, coroners or medical examiners, law enforcement personnel, CPS workers, public health-care providers, and others. Child fatality review teams respond to the issue of child deaths through improved interagency communication, identification of gaps in community child protection systems, and the acquisition of comprehensive data that can guide agency policy and practice as well as prevention efforts.

The teams review cases of child deaths and facilitate appropriate follow-up. Follow-up may include ensuring that services are provided for surviving family members, providing information to assist in the prosecution of perpetrators, and developing recommendations to improve child protection and community support systems.

Recent data show that 49 States have a case-reporting tool for CDR; however, there had been little consistency among the types of information compiled. This contributed to gaps in the understanding of infant and child mortality as a national problem. In response, the National Center for the Review and Prevention of Child Deaths, in cooperation with 30 State CDR leaders and advocates, developed a web-based CDR Case Reporting System for State and local teams to use to collect data and analyze and report on their findings.

As of February 2015, 43 States were using the standardized system, and 3 more were considering adopting the system.42 As more States use the system and the numbers of reviews entered into it increase, a more representative and accurate view of how and why children die from abuse and neglect will emerge (Palusci & Covington, 2013). The ultimate goal is to use the data to advocate for actions to prevent child deaths and to keep children healthy, safe, and protected.

Since its 1996 reauthorization, CAPTA has required States that receive CAPTA funding to set up citizen review panels. These panels of volunteers conduct reviews of CPS agencies in their States, including policies and procedures related to child fatalities and investigations. As of December 2013, 17 State CDR boards serve additional roles as the citizen review panels for child fatalities.

How Can These Fatalities Be Prevented?

When addressing the issue of child maltreatment, and especially child fatalities, prevention is a recurring theme. The prevention strategies and initiatives discussed below offer a variety of approaches.

Child fatality review teams. Well-designed, properly organized child fatality review teams appear to offer hope for defining the underlying nature and scope of fatalities due to child abuse and neglect. The child fatality review process helps identify risk factors that may assist prevention professionals, such as those engaged in home visiting and parenting education, to prevent future deaths. In addition, teams are demonstrating effectiveness in translating review findings into action by partnering with child welfare and other child health and safety groups. In some States, review team annual reports have led to State legislation, policy changes, or prevention programs. Findings associated with these reviews have identified decreases in child fatalities.

Data collection and analysis. Some States have begun to integrate other data with CPS data to help identify high-risk families and provide prevention services before maltreatment happens. Integrating data from birth certificates, emergency room visits, and other social services sectors with CPS data and then analyzing those data for trends in risk may also help child welfare professionals make better-informed decisions about prevention. Users of the CDR Case Reporting System can record their recommendations for prevention efforts. Examples of recommendations include improved multiagency coordination policies for death investigations; improvements in CPS intake, referral, and case-management procedures; intensive home visiting; worker training; and improved judicial practices.

A public health approach. A number of experts have championed a public health approach to addressing child maltreatment fatalities, which focuses on improving the health and well-being of individuals and communities before child maltreatment happens. Specifically, a public health approach involves defining the problem, identifying risk and protective factors, understanding consequences, and developing prevention strategies (Covington, 2013). And, true to its name, a public health approach involves the entire community in preventing child maltreatment and ensuring that parents have the support and services they need before abuse and neglect can occur.

Improved training. Several recent articles have noted the need for better training for child welfare workers in identifying potentially fatal situations. Current child welfare training curricula do not always address child maltreatment fatalities; in fact, a recent study of preservice child welfare training curricula in 20 States found that only 10 States even mentioned child maltreatment fatalities, and only 1 State included a full section on the topic. Given the complex nature of child maltreatment, training needs to go beyond the use of tools and assessments to include good critical thinking and decision-making skills.

Federal initiatives. The federal government has a long history of promoting prevention. The first National Child Abuse Prevention Week, declared by Congress in 1982, was replaced the following year with the first National Child Abuse Prevention Month. Other activities followed, including a 1991 initiative by Louis W. Sullivan, M.D., the Secretary of HHS, designed to raise awareness and promote coordination of prevention and treatment. In 2003, the Office on Child Abuse and Neglect, within the Children's Bureau, Administration for Children and Families, HHS, launched a child abuse prevention initiative that included an opportunity for individuals and organizations across the country to work together. This ongoing initiative also includes the publication of an annual resource guide.

Increasingly, this effort focuses on promoting protective factors that enhance the capacity of parents, caregivers, and communities to protect, nurture, and promote the healthy development of children.

Chapter 13

Teen Dating Violence

Chapter Contents

Section 13.1

What Is Teen Dating Violence?

This section includes excerpts from "Violence Against Women:
Dating Violence," Office on Women's Health (OWH), September 30,
2015; text from "Understanding Teen Dating Violence," Centers for
Disease Control and Prevention (CDC), Feb 27, 2014; and text from
"Mandatory Reporting and Keeping Youth Safe," U.S. Department of
Health and Human Services (HHS), May 3, 2013.

In the United States, teens and young women experience the highest rates of relationship violence. In fact, 1 in 10 female high-schoolers say they have been physically abused by a dating partner in the past year.

If you haven't dated much, it can be hard to know when a relationship is unhealthy. Some signs of teen dating abuse include:

- Constantly texting or sending instant messages (IMs) to monitor you

- Insisting on getting serious very quickly

- Acting very jealous or bossy

- Pressuring you to do sexual things

- Posting sexual photos of you online without permission

- Threatening to hurt you or themselves if you break up

- Blaming you for the abuse

Teenage girls in physically abusive relationships are much more likely than other girls to become pregnant. Abuse can get worse during pregnancy, and it can harm the baby growing inside you. Never get pregnant hoping that it will stop the abuse. You can ask your doctor about types of birth control that your partner doesn't have to know you are using.

If you are under 18, your partner could get arrested for having sex with you, even if you agreed to have sex. Laws covering this are different in each state. You can learn more about the law in your state.

Leaving an Abusive Dating Relationship

If you think you are in an abusive relationship, learn more about getting help. See a doctor or nurse to take care of any physical problems. And reach out for support for your emotional pain. Friends, family, and mental health professionals all can help. If you're in immediate danger, dial 911.

If you are thinking about ending an abusive dating relationship, keep some tips in mind:

- Create a safety plan, like where you can go if you are in danger.

- Make sure you have a working cellphone handy in case you need to call for help.

- Create a secret code with people you trust. That way, if you are with your partner, you can get help without having to say you need help.

- If you're breaking up with someone you see at your high school or college, you can get help from a guidance counselor, advisor, teacher, school nurse, dean's office, or principal. You also might be able to change your class schedules or even transfer to another school.

- If you have a job, talk to someone you trust at work. Your human resources department or employee assistance program (EAP) may be able to help.

- Try to avoid walking or riding alone.

- Be smart about technology. Don't share your passwords. Don't post your schedule on Facebook, and keep your settings private.

Staying Safe When Meeting Someone New

If you are meeting someone you don't know or don't know well, you can take steps to stay safe. Try to:

- Meet your date in a public place

- Tell a friend or family member your date's name and where you are going

- Avoid parties where a lot of alcohol may be served
- Make sure you have a way to get home if you need to leave
- Have a cellphone handy in case you need to call for help

Why is Dating Violence a Public Health Problem?

Dating violence is a widespread issue that had serious long-term and short-term effects. Many teens do not report it because they are afraid to tell friends and family.

- Among adult victims of rape, physical violence, and/ or stalking by an intimate partner, 22% of women and 15% of men first experienced some form of partner violence between 11 and 17 years of age.
- Approximately 9% of high school students report being hit, slapped, or physically hurt on purpose by a boyfriend or girl-friend in the 12 months before surveyed.

How Does Dating Violence Affect Health?

Dating violence can have a negative effect on health throughout life. Youth who are victims are more likely to experience symptoms of depression and anxiety, engage in unhealthy behaviors, like using tobacco, drugs, and alcohol, or exhibit antisocial behaviors and think about suicide. Youth who are victims of dating violence in high school are at higher risk for victimization during college.

Myths and Facts about Teen Dating Violence

Myth: It is only maltreatment if it is violent
Fact: Neglect, emotional abuse, sexual coercion, and statutory rape often occur without physical violence or leaving marks.

Myth: The most common form of maltreatment suffered by youth at home is sexual abuse.
Fact: The most common form of abuse is neglect, followed by physical abuse, *then* sexual abuse. Most children who are maltreated experience more than one type of abuse and more than one abuse event.

Myth: Most abuse is carried out by men, especially fathers.
Fact: Maltreatment is more likely to be carried out by mothers, not fathers.

Myth: Child maltreatment only happens in lower-income or rural families.

Fact: Child maltreatment happens across all socioeconomic groups, and it happens in urban and rural environments.

Myth: Dating violence is always males hurting their girlfriends.

Fact: Females can be perpetrators to their male partners, and dating violence occurs in same-sex relationships.

Myth: Youth usually tell someone that they are being abused or thinking about suicide.

Fact: Most youth do not tell. Shame or fear that others will blame the victim or will not believe reports of abuse prevent many from speaking out. Most youth do not tell an adult about suicidal thoughts or plans; some youth will tell their peers.

Section 13.2

Types of Teen Dating Violence and Consequences

This section includes excerpts from "Dating Matters: Understanding Teen Dating Violence Prevention Training," Centers for Disease Control and Prevention (CDC), July 22, 2015.

Types of Teen Dating Violence

- **Physical** – When a partner is physically attacked such as pinched, hit, shoved, or kicked.

- **Emotional/Psychological** – Threatening a partner or harming his or her sense of self-worth. Examples include name-calling, coercion, shaming, bullying, embarrassing on purpose, or keeping him/her away from friends and family. This form of teen dating violence can happen in person or online, such as through email or social media.

- **Sexual** – Forcing a partner to engage in a sex act when he or she does not or cannot consent. Sexual violence is not just rape.

It includes forcing any type of sexual act, including touching or kissing. People can force others into sexual contact by using physical force, or by using words—such as threats or pressure. Some forms of sexual violence do not involve physical contact and include acts like exposing sexual body parts to someone else.

Consequences for Victims of Teen Dating Violence

- Increased absenteeism
- Problems in non-dating relationships
- Decline in well-being
- Failure to participate in school activities
- Poor academic performance
- Thoughts of suicide
- Fear
- Depression and/or anxiety
- Drug, alcohol, and tobacco use
- Injury Delinquent behavior
- Experiencing violence in subsequent relationships

Consequences of Engaging in Teen Dating Violence

- Loss of friend's respect
- Poor academic performance
- Alienation from friends and family
- Physical and health problems
- Juvenile or criminal record/confinement
- Loneliness Expulsion from school
- Loss of job

Warning Signs for Teen Dating Violence

- Problems at school
- Consistent school attendance problems
- A noticeable drop in grades

- A sudden request for class schedule changes
- A noticeable weight change
- Changes in behavior
- Passive or quieter than usual
- Drop in self-confidence
- Isolation from social group
- Regular bruising or other injuries
- Alcohol or drug use
- One teen seems to be controlling the other

Physically – one person's arm is always firmly around the other person

Socially – one person monopolizes the other person's time

Electronically – one person is repeated calling, texting, e-mailing, messaging online, etc.

Warning Signs for Engaging in Teen Dating Violence

- Insists on walking a dating partner to class
- Threatens to hurt others
- Threatens to hurt self if dating partner breaks up with him/her
- Insults a dating partner in public or private
- Damages or destroys a dating partner's personal belongings
- Attempts to control what a dating partner wears

Section 13.3

Teen Dating Violence: Risk Factors

This section includes excerpts from "Risk and Protective Factors,
Psychosocial Health Behaviors and Teen Dating Violence," National
Institute of Justice (NIJ), January 6, 2015.

Demographic, Individual, Relational, and Cultural Factors

One important goal of research on teen dating violence is to understand which youth are more vulnerable to experiencing violence in their relationships. Identifying youth at risk for violence increases the likelihood of early intervention and prevention. Researchers seek to identify the risk factors indicating an increased likelihood for dating violence and the protective factors that buffer against dating violence. Risk factors and protective factors can be found across multiple contexts or domains, including factors specific to an individual, peer group or social group, relationship, or community/environment. Multiple risk factors and protective factors may be at play within a relationship. Researchers have begun to focus on identifying which risk factors and protective factors most strongly relate to teen dating violence.

In an NIJ-funded study of 5,647 teens (51.8 percent female, 74.6 percent Caucasian) from 10 middle schools and high schools (representing grades 7 to 12) throughout New York, New Jersey and Pennsylvania, researchers identified several factors related to increased risk for dating violence. The researchers focused especially on cyber abuse but found that the following factors related to multiple forms of abuse:

- Gender: Female teens reported more cyber, psychological and sexual violence, while male teens reported more physical dating violence.

- Sexual activity: Teens who had been involved in sexual activity were more likely to experience cyber, physical, psychological and sexual dating abuse.

- Delinquency: The more delinquent activities that teens engaged in, the more likely they were to experience cyber, physical, psychological and sexual dating abuse.

Another NIJ-funded study examined multiple risk factors among 223 at-risk, low-income teens in central Virginia. The study first examined potential risk factors that each partner could bring to a relationship. These factors could be grouped into four broad categories:

1. Precarious sexual history

2. Risky family background

3. Poor self-regulation skills

4. Risky social environment

When examined together, risk factors that could be changed (e.g., having delinquent peers) related more strongly to dating violence than risk factors that could not be changed (e.g., exposure to maltreatment in childhood).

The study also examined certain relationship-specific factors that might be associated with increased violence within the relationship:

- In relationships involving high levels of delinquent behaviors by both partners, higher levels of violence were exhibited.

- The older the teens' romantic partners were, the more likely the teens were to experience dating violence and engage in risky sexual behaviors. This finding was explained in part by the fact that the larger the age gap was between teens and their older partners, the more likely both partners were to engage in delinquent behaviors during the relationship.

An NIJ-funded longitudinal study of 1,162 students in the Midwest examined factors that led teens to engage in bullying, sexual harassment and dating violence while in middle and high school.

The researchers found that youths who bullied other students while in middle school were more likely to engage in more serious forms of interpersonal aggression connected with dating and romantic relationships as they grew older. But the connection between bullying others in middle school and perpetrating teen dating violence in high school was not direct. Instead, bullying behavior in middle school predicted bullying behavior in high school, which, in turn, was linked to perpetrating teen dating violence.

In middle school, aggression toward a sibling was a predictor of bullying behavior for both girls and boys. For girls, family conflict and having delinquent friends were also predictors of bullying behavior. For boys, family conflict was not a predictor of bullying behavior, but both having delinquent friends and self-reported delinquency were predictors.

Among high school students, researchers found direct links between those who bullied and those who perpetrated teen dating violence. Female teens who bullied others were likely to perpetrate sexual, verbal and physical dating violence. Male teens who bullied others were likely to perpetrate verbal and physical dating violence.

NIJ-funded research also has examined factors related to victimization among a national sample of 1,525 Latino teens. Results revealed that being a victim of one type of violence might place teens at risk for other forms of violence. Many victims of dating violence also were victims of crime or of peer/sibling violence. In addition, even after accounting for the fact that young people were often victims of multiple forms of violence, dating violence, in particular, was associated with delinquency.

- Violent delinquency was associated with greater psychological and physical dating violence.

- Nonviolent delinquency, specifically property and drug delinquency, was associated with greater psychological dating violence.

This study also identified two factors that might help to protect against dating violence among Latino teens:

- Cultural orientation: Teens who were more oriented toward their Latino culture were less likely to experience physical or psychological dating violence.

- Social support: Teens who reported greater social support were less likely to experience stalking or psychological, physical or sexual dating violence.

Overall, findings from NIJ-funded studies suggest a need to screen for teen dating violence and provide intervention programming among youth who have experienced other forms of violence or who have engaged in delinquent behaviors.

Risk Factors for the Perpetration of Youth Violence

Research on youth violence has increased our understanding of factors that make some populations more vulnerable to victimization and perpetration. Risk factors increase the likelihood that a young person will become violent. However, risk factors are not direct causes of youth violence; instead, risk factors contribute to youth violence.

Research associates the following risk factors with perpetration of youth violence:

Individual Risk Factors

- History of violent victimization
- Attention deficits, hyperactivity or learning disorders
- History of early aggressive behavior
- Involvement with drugs, alcohol or tobacco
- Low IQ
- Poor behavioral control
- Deficits in social cognitive or information-processing abilities
- High emotional distress
- History of treatment for emotional problems
- Antisocial beliefs and attitudes
- Exposure to violence and conflict in the family

Family Risk Factors

- Authoritarian childrearing attitudes
- Harsh, lax or inconsistent disciplinary practices
- Low parental involvement
- Low emotional attachment to parents or caregivers
- Low parental education and income
- Parental substance abuse or criminality
- Poor family functioning
- Poor monitoring and supervision of children

Peer and Social Risk Factors

- Association with delinquent peers
- Involvement in gangs

- Social rejection by peers
- Lack of involvement in conventional activities
- Poor academic performance
- Low commitment to school and school failure

Community Risk Factors

- Diminished economic opportunities
- High concentrations of poor residents
- High level of transiency
- High level of family disruption
- Low levels of community participation
- Socially disorganized neighborhoods

Psychosocial Health Behaviors

Teen dating violence has been associated with negative psychosocial health behaviors, but we cannot say definitively that teen dating violence causes negative health outcomes. Much of the research is correlational. Nevertheless, research can determine whether youth who experience dating violence are also at risk for negative psychosocial health behaviors. Knowing what types of health behaviors are associated with teen dating violence can help service providers better recognize and adequately respond to the needs of teens who experience dating violence.

The NIJ-funded study of dating violence among 5,647 teens from middle schools and high schools (representing grades 7 to 12) throughout New York, New Jersey and Pennsylvania identified two psychosocial health behaviors associated with teen dating violence:

- Depression: Teens who reported more cyber, psychological, physical and sexual dating violence reported more frequent feelings of depression.

- Anger/hostility: Teens who reported more cyber, psychological and physical dating violence reported more frequent feelings of anger or hostility.

Similar findings emerged from a national study of relationships among 1,525 Latino teens. Researchers controlled for a total count of the number of different types of victimization that the participants experienced, including conventional crime and peer/sibling victimization. After controlling for total victimization, dating violence remained associated with depression and hostility:

- Experiencing sexual dating violence was associated with clinical levels of depression.

- Experiencing psychological dating violence was associated with greater hostility.

Section 13.4

How Peers Can Affect Risk and Protective Factors

Text in this section is excerpted from "Teen Dating Violence:
How Peers Can Affect Risk and Protective Factors," National
Institute of Justice (NIJ), November 2014.

Compared to childhood, adolescence is a period marked by significant changes in the nature and importance of interpersonal relationships. Relationships with friends become more autonomous and central to personal well-being and, for the first time, many youth become involved in romantic relationships. Although the initiation of romantic relationships is a positive and healthy experience for many youth, it is a source of violence and abuse for others. Approximately 9 percent of high school students report being hit, slapped or physically hurt on purpose by their boyfriend or girlfriend in the past year. Teen dating violence rates appear to be even higher among certain populations, such as youth who have a history of exposure to violence.

Recognizing the large number of youth who experience dating violence, policymakers at the federal and state levels have worked to raise awareness of dating violence, prevent violence from occurring, and offer more protection and services to victims. In response to this increased focus on teen dating violence, research has begun to flourish. Since 2008, the National Institute of Justice (NIJ) has provided close to $15 million in funding for basic, applied and policy-level

179

research on dating violence. These projects have led to increased knowledge about risk and protective factors and psychosocial health behaviors associated with teen dating violence, and to the development and evaluation of dating violence prevention programs targeting diverse samples of youth. Research has also examined adolescents' knowledge of and barriers to using protection orders against violent partners.

Peer Roles in Teen Dating Violence

Peer roles are best understood within a multisystemic framework. That is, when teens begin dating, each partner enters into the relationship with his or her own set of perceptions, attitudes and behaviors shaped, in part, by the broader social "contexts," or environments, in which they live. Teens interact with peers in many different social contexts, for example, schools, social clubs, sports teams, neighborhood parks or community centers. Each social context can promote attitudes and behaviors that encourage or discourage dating violence. For example, teens' and their peers' perceptions of whether violence is acceptable within romantic relationships might depend on the level of violence they witness at school or in their neighborhood.

Thus, when considering how peers might shape dating experiences, it is important to consider not only the context of teens' close peer group but also the larger school and community contexts in which teens and their peers interact.

Teens' peers have the potential to considerably shape their dating experiences. Teens spend most of their days in school with peers and, in their free time, spend proportionally more time with peers than with parents or any other adults. The desire to fit in and be liked by peers heightens in adolescence, and teens begin to rely on peers as a primary source of support and guidance. In addition, peer groups often set norms and offer social rewards for dating; for example, youth who date are often perceived as more socially accepted or popular than youth who do not date. As such, peers are likely to have a significant impact on teens' decisions about whether to date, whom to date, and when to break up with romantic partners. Furthermore, the experiences that teens witness or perceive their peers to have within romantic relationships might shape teens' perceptions of what is normal or acceptable in their own romantic relationships.

It is critical to consider the very public nature of teens' romantic relationships. Teen couples often interact in the presence of peers at school or in other social settings where other teens and adults are present, such as a mall, a movie theatre, or at home. Because of this, interactions that occur in public, or that happen in private but are shared with peers, might quickly become public knowledge to the larger peer network. Even when teens are not physically together, they are often still interacting by cell phone, text messages, social media sites, online video games and other electronic outlets that allow them to disseminate information quickly and widely.

As a result, when relationships become violent or unhealthy in other ways, teens are at risk for experiencing embarrassment, being publicly ridiculed, or developing negative reputations among their peers. These concerns are very real to teens; they have to contend with their image among close friends and the larger peer network on a daily basis.

Of particular interest to service providers is that the presence of peers might instigate, elevate or reduce the likelihood of teen dating violence, depending on the situation. For example, if a girl hits a boy in front of his friends, the boy might feel pressure to "save face" and hit her in return. On the other hand, if peers are present when a couple is arguing, the peers might help defuse the situation and prevent the argument from escalating to violence — or peers who witness or hear about violence occurring also might seek help from an adult.

Clearly, teens' orientation toward peers and the significant amount of time spent with them affords numerous opportunities for peers to impact teens' behaviors and decisions within romantic relationships.

Findings emerging from NIJ-funded research on peer roles in teen dating violence can be viewed in terms of three overarching questions:

1. Do risky peer contexts increase the likelihood that teens will experience dating violence?

2. What roles do peers play in seeking help after teens experience violence?

3. Can group interventions or those focused on social contexts reduce the risk for teen dating violence?

1 Do risky peer contexts increase the likelihood that teens will experience dating violence?

Research consistently shows the tendency for dating violence to overlap with peer victimization, suggesting that youth who are victims or perpetrators of peer violence tend to be the same youth at risk for experiencing violence within romantic relationships. As such, researchers have begun to identify risky or antisocial characteristics of teens' broader peer social environments that increase the risk for dating violence.

Peer violence and dating violence tend to co-occur.

Two studies using community-based samples directly examined the links between dating violence and peer violence, including the associations between bullying among peers and dating violence.

One study of 1,162 teens attending high school in Illinois revealed concurrent links between youth who bully and youth who perpetrate teen dating violence, suggesting an overlap in teens who victimize peers and those who victimize dating partners. Specifically, female teens who bullied others were also likely to perpetrate sexual harassment and sexual, verbal and physical dating violence. Similarly, male teens who bullied others were also likely to perpetrate sexual harassment, physical dating violence and verbal dating violence.

A survey of 5,647 teens across three northeastern states focused more specifically on the co-occurrence of cyberbullying and teen dating violence. Results revealed significant overlaps in who perpetrated cyberbullying and cyberdating violence — 26 percent of teens who perpetrated cyberbullying also perpetrated cyberdating violence, compared with only 7 percent of teens who did not perpetrate cyberbullying. Overlap also existed in victimization experiences. Teens who experienced cyberbullying by peers were more than three times as likely to experience cyberdating violence, compared with those who did not experience cyberbullying (38 percent versus 13 percent, respectively).

Furthermore, a national study of 1,525 Latino teens revealed links between victimization by dating partners and a wide range of other forms of victimization. About 71 percent of dating violence victims experienced peer/sibling violence, sexual victimization, stalking, conventional crime or another form of victimization in the prior year. Dating violence and peer/sibling violence were the two most common forms of victimization to co-occur. About 57 percent of teen victims of dating violence were also victims of peer/sibling violence.

The consistency with which peer violence and teen dating violence have been found to co-occur illustrates that teens who struggle with establishing healthy peer relationships also have difficulties in romantic relationships. Although we know little about the details of how this occurs, these findings are in line with theories that suggest that outcomes in one relationship tend to be shaped by experiences, beliefs and attitudes learned in other relationships.

Youth in risky, antisocial environments are at significant risk for teen dating violence.

Practitioners often must provide services to teens who have multiple risk factors for dating violence and thus would benefit by knowing which risk factors are most important to address in situations where time and resources might be limited. One study simultaneously examined multiple risk factors, including social context, within a sample of low-income teens who were receiving community-based services allocated to at-risk populations. Among the 223 youth in that study, there were 11 known risk factors for dating violence, divided into four categories: risky social environment, risky sexual history, risky family background and poor ability to self-regulate. Risky social environment represented a combination of teens' ratings of peer delinquency, exposure to peer dating abuse, negative neighborhood quality and attitudes toward relationship abuse.

When the four categories of risk factors were examined simultaneously, risky social environment was the strongest correlate of physical and emotional dating violence victimization and perpetration within a romantic relationship. Teens from risky family backgrounds were also more likely to experience and perpetrate emotional and physical dating violence. However, this finding was partly explained by the fact that the more high-risk the teens' family backgrounds were, the more likely they were to become involved in risky social contexts, such as having delinquent peers or witnessing dating violence among their peers.

Studies consistently show that teens who engage in delinquent behaviors are at risk for experiencing and perpetrating dating violence. Indeed, teens' own participation in delinquent behaviors is a likely indicator that they are embedded within a risky social environment. The vast majority of adolescent delinquency is committed in groups of peers, and teens' and their peers' levels of delinquency tend to be similarly aligned. Moreover, teens who engage in delinquency are also likely to choose delinquent romantic partners, creating risky romantic relationship contexts that are, in turn, associated with higher levels of dating violence and other health-risk behaviors.

Findings from NIJ-funded studies contribute to a growing body of literature suggesting that a diverse set of peer attributes are linked to whether teens experience or perpetrate dating violence, including close peers' and the broader peer group's behaviors, attitudes and guidance; teens' social standing among the broader peer group; and the quality of relationships with close peers. Moreover, peer risk factors tend to be more strongly associated with dating violence perpetration and victimization in adolescence than with family risk factors.

2 What roles do peers play in help-seeking after teens experience violence?

Teen dating violence has been associated with negative psychosocial health outcomes, including delinquency, hostility and depression. Once teens experience violence in one relationship, they are at significant risk for experiencing violence in another relationship. Thus, it is important that teens who experience dating violence seek help soon after, so they can receive services to protect against the potential psychosocial impacts of violence and reduce the likelihood of future violence.

Peers also can have a significant impact on how teens respond to dating violence. Studies have identified two ways in which peers play a role in the aftermath of dating violence: (1) Peers often serve as first responders to dating violence, and (2) peers can hinder or encourage legal help-seeking in the form of a protection order.

Peers as first responders to dating violence.

It is difficult to determine how many teens seek help after violence occurs because researchers often ask different questions about help-seeking and dating abuse. For example, some researchers examine the percentage of teens who sought help after experiencing certain forms of serious physical or sexual abuse, whereas others examine help-seeking among teens who experienced any form of dating violence. Regardless, one clear message has emerged: *Many teens do not seek help from anyone after violence has occurred, and those who do seek help most frequently turn to a friend.*

In a study of 2,173 teens who reported being the victim of cyber, physical, psychological or sexual dating abuse, only 8.6 percent reported seeking help from at least one person; more females (11 percent) sought help than males (5.7 percent). Very few teens — only 4.1 percent of females and 2 percent of males — sought help after they experienced dating abuse for the first time. Among the teens who did seek help, more than three-quarters (77.2 percent) turned to a friend for help and 48.5 percent turned to parents. Less than 10 percent sought help from other service providers, such as a teacher or police officer. For those who did seek help, both males (69.2 percent) and females (82 percent) were most likely to seek help from friends.

Somewhat higher rates were reported in another study that asked only about help-seeking after experiencing physical, sexual or stalking dating violence in the past year. Of the roughly 90 Latino teens who had experienced such violence, about 63 percent sought help afterward (60 percent of males and 69 percent of females). Compared with psychological or cyber forms of abuse, it is possible that teens are more likely to recognize physical, sexual and stalking dating violence as abuse and thus seek help. Nonetheless, few teens (15.6 percent) sought help from formal sources such as school, social services or legal professionals. Instead, male and female teens were most likely to turn to friends for help (43.6 percent and 41.4 percent, respectively).

These findings add to the growing evidence that peers tend to be the most frequent first responders to teen dating violence among male and female teens, teens of varying racial and ethnic backgrounds, and teens who experience different forms of dating violence.

Peers play a role in teens' help-seeking.

A recent exploratory study examined teens' use of protection orders, also called civil orders of protection or restraining orders. In July 2008, New York state law was modified to give teens access to protection orders without parental consent and without having a child in common with their partner. The study examined all petitions filed by dating violence victims age 18 and younger throughout 2009 and 2010 — a 2-year period shortly after the law took effect. The study found that the orders were not being used widely; victims filed only 1,200 petitions during the 2-year period. To better understand potential barriers to obtaining protection orders, the researchers conducted focus groups and interviewed teens who were potentially at risk for dating violence or had begun the process of filing for a protection order.

These conversations revealed that many youth were hesitant to obtain protection orders because they were afraid of escalating violence, were reluctant to end the relationship, or felt overwhelmed with other responsibilities. Another common barrier to seeking a protection order was how family and friends would feel about it. For example, teens were concerned about being viewed as a "snitch" or as responsible for the violence. Some teens felt ashamed to admit their victimization to others, as shown in the following examples:

"I feel like you'd get talked about at school. 'Cause, like, I feel like we live in a small town, so everyone would know and figure out, and they'd talk about you."

"Your friends whatever, like, might look at you a different way ... they see it as you went to the police and you couldn't handle it — that's really not for guys."

Teens also were concerned that protection orders place victims at risk for retaliation by the abusive partners' peer network and might lead to social isolation resulting from losing mutual friends after the breakup. For example, one teen's decision to end the relationship and seek a protective order led to the dissolution of nearly her entire peer network: "It's like I don't have anybody." Another teen stated, *"[His] friends target you. When I was with him he got some other girls, and they were all, like, gang members ... and now there's, like, a whole group of girls after me and, like, I don't feel safe at all."*

On the other hand, teens' social networks can also be a source of motivation to seek legal protection. Teens reported that moral support from their friends and family is what helped them make it through the process of obtaining a protection order. Teens who had obtained a protection order recommended making peer support networks available for those who are considering taking legal action against an abusive partner.

Although research on protection orders in abusive teen relationships is nascent, preliminary work illustrates that teens' decisions to bring legal action against an abusive partner are shaped by more than the abusiveness of the relationship and guidance from caring adults. Teens also weigh the potential benefits of the protection order against the potential negative consequences such legal action might have on their image and social well-being among peers.

3 Can group interventions or those focused on social contexts reduce the risk for teen dating violence?

Researchers, practitioners, and policymakers are invested in identifying and implementing interventions that decrease the likelihood of dating violence among teen partners. Growing evidence supports the finding that teens tend to weigh the perceptions of peers when making decisions about romantic relationships. Such knowledge raises the question of whether interventions conducted on a group level — that is, among groups of peers within a school or other social setting — would be effective at reducing the risk for teen dating violence. Practically speaking, interventions in schools and other community-based peer settings are worthwhile because they offer opportunities to reach large numbers of teens in the environments where they spend a significant amount of their time.

Most of the effective teen dating violence interventions identified to date have been school-based programs. The majority of these programs take a universal preventive approach — where all students in a school receive the intervention — and have been developed for implementation among high school students. Yet, many youth have already started dating and have experienced dating violence before high school. As such, the new generation of teen dating violence prevention programs is beginning to focus on middle school youth, which will increase the likelihood of reaching teens before they begin dating or when they first start to date. *Start Strong: Building Healthy Teen Relationships* and *Dating Matters* are two examples of comprehensive, multicomponent teen dating violence prevention initiatives implemented with middle school-aged youth and their families across the United States.

Between 2005 and 2011, NIJ funded the development and evaluation of Shifting Boundaries, one of the first teen dating violence intervention programs designed for middle school students. Shifting Boundaries was developed and tested in an early study in Cleveland, Ohio, and then modified and re-evaluated in 117 sixth- and seventh-grade classes (30 public middle schools) in New York City. Schools and classrooms were randomly assigned to (1) a classroom intervention with both a personal interaction and a law and justice curriculum, including discussions on relational boundaries, laws and legal penalties; or (2) a school building intervention that consisted of building-based restraining orders, a display of posters about the reporting of dating violence and harassment, and monitoring of violence "hot spots"; (3) a combined classroom and building intervention; or (4) a control group. Compared with teens in the control group, teens who received the school building intervention seemed to benefit in many ways, regardless of whether they had the classroom intervention. Specifically, 6 months after the intervention, teens who received the school building intervention showed significant reductions in sexual and other victimization by dating partners compared with teens in the control group. At that time, teens were presented with example cases of dating violence and asked if they would intervene. Teens who received only the school building intervention were significantly more likely than teens in the control group to report that they would intervene if they witnessed dating violence.

Community-based interventions can also reduce dating violence risk among high-risk youth. Youth who have been exposed to known risk factors might need specialized intervention that aligns with their pattern of risk. Moreover, high-risk youth might be less likely to participate fully in school-based interventions, compared with lower-risk teens. For example, they might miss more days of school or be less engaged in learning opportunities. One study developed and evaluated two community-based group interventions to prevent dating violence victimization of teen girls involved in the child welfare system.

Specifically, it compared the incidence of dating violence among female teens who did not receive an intervention with female teens who completed either (1) a social learning/feminist group intervention focused on gendered attitudes, beliefs about relationships, and relational skills, or (2) a risk detection/ executive-functioning group intervention focused on noticing contextual danger cues, regulating emotions and knowing how to respond in difficult situations. Teens who received one of the group treatment interventions were two to five times less likely to report being sexually or physically victimized by romantic partners over the course of the study, compared with teens who did not participate in one of the group interventions.

Additional research is needed to determine exactly why the Shifting Boundaries building-wide intervention and the community-based social learning/feminist and risk detection/executive-functioning group interventions reduced the likelihood of dating violence among teens. The interventions are similar in that they use structured peer contexts—school-based and group interventions — to deliver programming.

In addition, they focus on improving teens' knowledge, attitudes and norms regarding dating violence, and they aim to teach teens how to recognize and respond to violence that occurs between youth. The findings regarding Shifting Boundaries are consistent with other research that shows positive school environments — including positive norms, values and expectations — are associated with lower levels of student aggression and bullying behaviors.

Implications and Key Future Research Questions

Findings across numerous studies document many links between teens' experiences with peers and the likelihood that they will be victims of dating violence, seek help if violence occurs, and access services and legal protections. Given the importance of peers during adolescence, it is critical to identify important areas for future research. Practitioners and policymakers need the best possible evidence regarding peers and peer contexts to identify teens who are at risk for dating violence. Only through strategically smart research and evaluation can the researchers learn how to prevent and intervene in violent teen romantic relationships and how to promote positive outcomes in romantic relationships. Here are some key future research questions:

1 Can we focus on risky peer networks to identify teens at risk for dating violence?

Teens who experience or perpetrate dating violence tend to also be in broader peer networks that involve multiple other forms of risky health behaviors, such as bullying, delinquency and substance use. Thus, one way to identify youth who are at risk for dating violence is to screen for dating violence risk factors among broader peer networks that involve teens known to be involved in other forms of risky behavior. For example, screening among teens enrolled in treatment programs through the juvenile justice system might reveal large numbers of teens who have experienced dating violence. Similarly, if a high school is known to have a high rate of bullying victimization, the students might also be at high risk for dating violence.

Given the overlap of different forms of violence perpetration and victimization, screenings among high-risk peer networks could focus on risk behaviors overall rather than risk for one specific behavior. If we can identify the peer networks most at risk by virtue of the promotion of norms, attitudes and behaviors that are associated with violence, then we can target the most intensive prevention and intervention efforts at the highest risk groups of teens and potentially offer group-level wraparound services to reduce a broad range of risky behaviors. Of course, this is dependent on the existence of effective, accessible and well-implemented prevention and intervention programming for high-risk groups. It also is important to consider how best to define the boundaries of peer networks in targeting screening efforts. For example, peer networks located in specific settings such as treatment programs or detention facilities may be easier to define than those located in broader contexts such as schools, where there are multiple peer networks.

2 What is the best way to use peers and peer contexts as an avenue for preventing dating violence?

Given the importance of peer relationships in adolescence and the mounting evidence that peers can shape the quality of each other's dating experiences, peers and peer contexts seem to be an appropriate target for prevention and intervention programming. In fact, a number of dating violence interventions have been widely implemented across the United States to encourage teens — who are often bystanders or the first to learn when dating violence occurs — to intervene. Other interventions are aimed at modifying peer norms about violence, particularly gender-based norms. Based on early examinations of peer- and norm-based interventions, four major questions have emerged that merit future attention by researchers and practitioners:

1. When will teens intervene in a violent relationship?

2. Why should gender be considered when designing and evaluating intervention programs?

3. What role do the norms, behaviors and reputations of the teens in the group play in understanding the effectiveness of the intervention?

4. How should technology be used to help prevent dating violence and other types of interpersonal violence?

5. How can we promote positive peer relationships as a precursor to positive romantic relationships?

1 When will teens intervene in a violent relationship?

Despite the fact that significant research resources have been dedicated to understanding peer bystander interventions, very little is known about the conditions under which adolescent peers will actually intervene in violent relationships. One study revealed that most high school teens offered nurturing responses when their friends confided in them about being victims of dating violence. However, the more severe the dating violence, the more likely teens were to "respond" with avoidance, possibly illustrating an unwillingness or uncertainty about how to offer help in serious cases of violence.

There are many reasons why teens might be hesitant to intervene in their friends' relationships. For example, they might not know how to intervene, they might not recognize when intervention is warranted, they might not want to betray the confidentiality of the friend who confided in them, or they might fear retaliation from the abuser or from the friend of the abuser.

Often, researchers study teens' intentions to intervene if they witness violence; for instance, they may give teens an example of a dating violence situation and ask whether they would intervene. Research shows that programs can increase teens' intentions to intervene if they are bystanders to dating violence or bullying. However, intentions do not always predict behavior, and more research is needed to determine what types of bystander programs increase teens' likelihood of actually intervening. A recent evaluation of the Coaching Boys into Men dating violence prevention program suggests that when high school athletic coaches encouraged bystander intervention in cross-gender violence, male athletes reported higher levels of intervening in abusive or harassing behaviors —such as making rude comments about a girl's body or physically hurting a girl — by their peers. Similarly, evidence suggests that bystander programs can encourage teens to intervene in situations of sexual assault or harassment on college campuses.

Nonetheless, it is important to consider how perceptions of romantic relationships as private and "the couple's business" might prevent teens from seeking help or intervening in violence that occurs within romantic (as opposed to casual) relationships, particularly if teens learn about but do not witness the violence. Moreover, there are many different ways teens could intervene in violent relationships; they could, for example, directly confront the abuser, tell a trusted adult, encourage their friend to tell a trusted adult, or provide a direct referral to services. More research is needed to determine the safest and most effective ways youth can intervene, the ways they feel most comfortable intervening, and the best way for service providers to offer teens different methods for intervening.

2 How should gender be considered when designing and evaluating intervention programs?

The researchers know, based on preliminary work on peer- and norm-based interventions, that gender should be considered when designing and evaluating intervention programs. Some interventions — such as Men Can Stop Rape and Coaching Boys into Men — are gender-specific, designed for male teens, and others are designed to help female teens recognize danger signs. However, a limitation of many of these programs is that they tend to focus on preventing male teens' abusive behaviors and victimization among female teens. It is well-documented that both male and female teens perpetrate dating violence. Moreover, although some evidence suggests that female teens might experience more severe types of abuse compared with male teens, dating violence has been associated with negative social and health outcomes for both male and female teens. Thus, the development and evaluation of peer- and norm-based programs that target female-perpetrated dating violence is warranted. For example, these programs might target peer norms about the acceptability of female violence toward males — that, for example, "it's okay for girls to hit boys" or "if a boy gets slapped, he deserved it."

Some programs have shown more positive effects with teens of a particular gender. For example, "Fourth R: Skills for Youth Relationships" includes individual- and school-level components designed to prevent dating violence and promote healthy relationships. Among ninth-graders, the program showed significant effects on reducing perpetration of physical dating violence among males but not among females. Research on other programs that aim to modify attitudes about dating violence has revealed mixed findings, with some producing stronger effects among female teens and others producing stronger effects among male teens. On the one hand, differences in the efficacy of programs for male versus female teens might imply a need for more gender-specific programming — for example, programs that target norms and perspectives known to promote dating violence for each gender. Alternatively, the focus on gender-based norms, sexuality and masculinity in many existing intervention programs might be preventing the development of programming that is equally effective at reducing male- and female-perpetrated violence. Gender-neutral programming focused on components of healthy relationships (for both boys and girls) might produce positive effects for both genders. It is also possible that programs need both gender-neutral and gender-specific components. Future research examining the role of gender in teens' responsiveness to intervention is warranted.

3 What role do the norms, behaviors and reputations of teens in the group play in understanding the effectiveness of the intervention?

In designing peer-based interventions, it is important to consider how the norms, behaviors and reputations of the teens that compose the group might impact the effectiveness of the intervention. Some evidence suggests that teens' perceptions of the attitudes and behaviors of others in their peer group are more strongly related to teens' aggressive behaviors than peers' true attitudes and behaviors. In addition, when teens are aggregated into groups, deviancy training occurs such that, over time, the more deviant teens in the group appear to influence those who are less deviant, particularly at-risk teens. As a result, some peer-based interventions have resulted in increases in violent and delinquent behaviors. Little is known about the contexts in which deviancy training might occur within peer-based teen dating violence prevention and intervention programs. Such research is especially relevant because growing evidence suggests that teens who are involved in delinquent behaviors are at high risk for experiencing and perpetrating dating violence. Future research is needed to identify whether interventions can effectively target the highest risk peer groups, without enhancing the risk for dating violence, through the aggregation of peers who might perpetuate unhealthy dating attitudes and behaviors.

4 How should technology be used to help prevent dating violence and other types of interpersonal violence?

There is significant potential for using technology and electronic peer networks to prevent dating violence and promote positive interpersonal relationships. We already know a great deal about the ways that teens use technology to bully one another and perpetrate dating violence. However, we know little about how we can use technology to prevent dating violence or other types of interpersonal violence. For example, the messages teens post to online social networking sites that reach wide audiences (such as Facebook and Twitter) can convey their perceptions of what is normal or acceptable in romantic relationships. As such, efforts to shape the quality of messages that youth post or share among their friends could reach a significant number of youth. Similarly, peers could be trained to recognize and respond appropriately when adolescents post help-seeking or threatening types of messages.

5 How can we promote positive peer relationships as a precursor to positive romantic relationships?

It is important to keep in mind that preventing violent relationships is simply one component of the broader goal of promoting healthy, prosocial relationships. Although romantic relationships are marked by some unique characteristics — such as intense emotions, gender norms, and sexual behaviors — teens already have a great deal of experience in close interpersonal relationships before they begin dating. There is growing consensus among researchers that early interpersonal relationships with family and friends set the stage for the quality of later relationships with romantic partners.

In fact, among teens who have experienced poor relationships with parents, positive relationships with peers have been shown to buffer teens against a range of risky behaviors, including risky sexual behaviors and poor romantic relationship qualities. Programs that help develop healthy peer relationships should begin early in adolescence, when youth are first learning to establish more autonomous and meaningful peer relationships. Youth can learn and practice with peers many of the positive qualities that are important in healthy romantic relationships, including respect, equality, supportiveness, warmth and autonomy. For example, initiatives such as *Start Strong* and *Dating Matters* are broadly focused on building healthy relationships starting early in adolescence, and they aim to reduce risk and promote positive relationships in the long term. Continued research is needed to determine the longitudinal effects of these initiatives on the quality of peer and romantic relationships, particularly as teens make the transition from adolescence into adulthood.

Conclusion

Romantic relationships can seem very personal in nature because they involve the behaviors, thoughts and actions of two people who commit to one another romantically. Events that occur within relationships tend to be perceived as "the couple's business." Yet, there is growing evidence that romantic relationship experiences are shaped both by experiences as a couple and by the unique experiences each partner brings to the relationship. Teens place significant value on their relationships with peers while also beginning to translate the skills they have learned in close peer relationships into new relationships with romantic partners. As such, programs and policies aimed at preventing teen dating violence or promoting healthy teen relationships more broadly are likely to be most effective if they take into consideration the potential ways in which peers and peer contexts shape teens' experiences within close relationships.

Section 13.5

Safety Planning for Teens

Text in this section is excerpted from "Staying Safe in Relations,"
U.S. Department of Health and Human Services (HHS), May 2013.

Staying Safe in Relations

A new relationship can be an adventure. But for both adults
and teens, it's important to be aware of how relationships can take
unexpected turns. Whether you're new to romantic relationships and
dating for the first time, or making new friends online or in person,
caution is needed. What seems like a promising relationship can sometimes become an abusive one.

Threats to one's safety can appear in a number of ways. Relationship violence can take the form of physical, sexual, or emotional abuse.
While females are more at risk for violence, both genders can be subject to abuse. Threats can be online, such as when "cyberbullying"
occurs via social media or messaging. Sex offenders can find and take
advantage of young people on the Internet. Abuse usually involves one
person trying to manipulate and harm another.

Safe Dating for Teens

Dating relationships can be a fun and exciting part of life. They can
also be confusing, especially if dating is new to a teen.

Here are some tips for parents.

- Before your teen starts dating, help him or her set guidelines
  for acceptable and unacceptable behavior by dating partner. If
  it's your teen's first date with someone, suggest they go out with
  another couple or in a group.

- Remind teens to stay true to themselves and not be pressured by
  a date to do something they don't want to do.

- Discuss with your teen some of the warning signs of potential
  abusers. An example would be when someone starts taking

control or acting obsessively or aggressively—including on the phone or by text.

- Get your teen's agreement to a curfew time for specific activities. Should they need to miss a curfew, require that they call home immediately.

- Talk with your teen about how to resolve conflicts peacefully.

- Finally, encourage your child to share their experiences and concerns with you. Without judging, educate your teen on how healthy relationships should work. The advice can last a lifetime!

Developing a Personal Safety Plan

When a relationship becomes abusive, it's often hard to escape. Concerns about family safety, living arrangements, finances and related issues often make the decision to leave difficult. And yet, tolerating abuse is the worst possible thing to do. Abuse always gets worse if it is not stopped.

Advantages of Planning

It can be hard to admit the seriousness of a relationship problem. But it's always better to be prepared should abuse worsen. With a plan in place, you'll be better able to follow established steps toward safety. The following are some suggested safety plan elements.

- Plan in advance how you and your loved ones will get to a safe place quickly if violence occurs.

- Practice getting out of your home safely. Identify which doors, windows, elevator, or stairwell to use.

- Identify trusted neighbors you can tell about potential violence. Ask them to call the police if they hear a disturbance at your home.

- Devise a code word to use with your children, family and friends when you need the police.

- Prepare an "emergency kit." Leave money, an extra set of keys, copies of important documents, important phone numbers, and extra clothes and medicines in a safe place or with someone you trust.

- Ask that person to let you and your children stay with him or her—on a moment's notice—in an emergency.

- Keep local crisis hotline numbers in your wallet or purse so you can get help and advice at any time.

- Develop a safety plan with your children for when you are not with them.

- Inform your child's school or day care about who has permission to pick up your child.

- If you have pets, make arrangements for them to be cared for in a safe place.

Section 13.6

Teen Dating Violence Statistics

Text in this section is excerpted from "Prevalence of Teen Dating Violence," National Institute of Justice (NIJ), October 29, 2014.

Prevalence of Teen Dating Violence

Estimates of teen dating violence prevalence vary widely, because studies define and measure violence differently over different periods of time for different populations. In this section, find estimates on prevalence from:

- Nationally representative surveys

- Study of middle and high schools in New York, New Jersey, and Pennsylvania

- Longitudinal study of students in the midwest

- Study of dating violence among Latino adolescents

Nationally Representative Surveys

Youth Risk Behavior Survey, a nationally representative annual survey of youth in grades 9 to 12, found that, of those students who dated someone in the last 12 months, approximately one in 10 reported being a victim of physical violence from a romantic partner during that year.

The National Longitudinal Study of Adolescent Health, analyzing a nationally representative sample of adolescents in grades 7 to 12 who were then followed over time, showed that approximately 30 percent of people ages 12 to 21 in heterosexual relationships reported experiencing psychological abuse in the past 18 months; 20 percent of youth in same-sex relationships reported experiencing the same type of abuse.

About 10 percent of students in the Youth Risk Behavior Study who had dated someone in the last 12 months reported that they had been kissed, touched or physically forced to have sexual intercourse against their will by a dating partner during that year.

To date, there are no nationally representative data on perpetration of dating violence.

Study of Middle and High Schools in New York, New Jersey and Pennsylvania

One NIJ-funded study examined the prevalence of dating violence among 5,647 teens (51.8 percent female, 74.6 percent Caucasian) from 10 middle schools and high schools (representing grades 7-12) throughout New York, New Jersey and Pennsylvania. Findings indicated that within the past year:

- 18.0 percent of respondents reported experiencing cyber dating abuse (e.g., "my partner used my social networking account without permission" or "my partner sent texts/emails to engage in sexual acts I did not want").

- 20.7 percent experienced physical dating violence (e.g., reporting that a partner "pushed" or "kicked" the respondent).

- 32.6 percent experienced psychological dating abuse (e.g., "my partner threatened to hurt me" or "my partner would not let me do things with other people").

- 9.0 percent experienced sexual coercion (e.g., "my partner pressured me to have sex when [he or she] knew I didn't want to").

The study also specifically examined dating violence rates among teens who had dated within the past year (66 percent of total teens; n=3,745). The following percentages of dating teens reported experiencing forms of abuse:

- Cyber dating abuse: 26.3 percent

- Physical dating violence: 29.9 percent
- Psychological dating abuse: 47.2 percent
- Sexual coercion: 13.0 percent

Longitudinal Study of Students in the Midwest

An NIJ-funded longitudinal study of 1,162 students in the Midwest examined the prevalence of several kinds of abuse that male and female middle and high school students experienced and perpetrated in teen dating relationships.

Physical violence. About one-third of girls and boys (35 percent and 36 percent, respectively) reported experiencing physical violence in a teen dating relationship. More girls reported perpetrating physical dating violence than boys (34 percent vs. 17 percent).

Verbal emotional abuse. Verbal emotional abuse was the most common form of abuse in teen dating relationships for both girls and boys: 73 percent of girls and 66 percent of boys reported experiencing at least one instance of verbal abuse in a dating relationship in high school. In addition, 64 percent of girls and 45 percent of boys reported perpetrating verbal emotional abuse toward a dating partner.

Sexual coercion. Nearly one in four girls and one in seven boys reported being victims of sexual coercion in a teen dating relationship.

Study of Dating Violence among Latino Adolescents

NIJ-funded research has also examined the prevalence of dating violence among a national sample of Latino adolescents. Phone interviews were conducted with 1,525 Latino teens, ranging in age from 12 to 18, most of whom (76.1 percent) were born in the United States. Respondents reported experiencing the following within the past year:

- At least one form of dating violence: 19.5 percent
- Psychological dating violence: 14.8 percent
- Physical dating violence: 6.6 percent
- Sexual dating violence: 5.6 percent
- Stalking: 1.0 percent

Chapter 14

Date Rape

What Are Rape and Sexual Assault?

Rape is sex you don't agree to, including forcing a body part or an object into your vagina, rectum (bottom) or mouth. In the United States, almost one in five women has been raped during her lifetime.

Sexual assault or abuse is any type of sexual activity that a person does not agree to, including:

- Rape or attempted rape
- Touching your body or making you touch someone else's
- Incest or sexual contact with a child
- Someone watching or photographing you in sexual situations
- Someone exposing his or her body to you

Sometimes, sexual violence is committed by a stranger. Most often, though, it is committed by someone you know, including a date or an intimate partner like a husband, ex-husband, or boyfriend. Sexual violence is always wrong, and a person who is sexually abused does not ever "cause" the attack.

Keep in mind that there are times when a person is not able to agree to sex, such as if they are drunk or have been drugged with a date rape drug, or if they are underage.

Text in this chapter is excerpted from "Violence Against Women," Office on Women's Health (OWH), September 30, 2015; and from "What Are Date Rape Drugs and How Do You Avoid Them?" National Institute on Drug Abuse (NIDA), March 16, 2015.

Women who are sexually abused may suffer serious health problems, such as sexually transmitted infections, stomach problems, and ongoing pain. They also are at risk for emotional problems, like depression, anxiety, and post-traumatic stress disorder. If you or someone you know has been sexually abused, it is important to get help as soon as possible.

What Are Date Rape Drugs and How Do You Avoid Them?

You may have been warned that sometimes people secretly slip drugs into other people's drinks to take advantage of them sexually. These drugs are called "date rape drugs."

Date rape, also known as "drug-facilitated sexual assault," is any type of sexual activity that a person does not agree to. It may come from someone you know, may have just met, and/or thought you could trust.

Date rape drugs can make people become physically weak or pass out. This is why people who want to rape someone use them, because they leave individuals unable to protect themselves.

Many of these drugs have no color, smell, or taste, and people often do not know that they've taken anything. Many times people (usually girls or women, but not always) who have been drugged are unable to remember what happened to them.

The Dangerous Three

The three most common date rape drugs are Rohypnol® (flunitrazepam), GHB (gamma hydroxybutryic acid), and ketamine.

Rohypnol (also known as roofies, forget-me-pill, R-2) is a type of prescription pill known as a benzodiazepine—it's chemically similar to drugs such as Valium or Xanax, but unlike these drugs, it is not approved for medical use in this country.

- It has no taste or smell and is sometimes colorless when dissolved in a drink.

- People who take it can feel very sleepy and confused and forget what happens after its effects kick in.

- It can also cause weakness, trouble breathing, and make it difficult for those who have taken it to move their body.

The effects of Rohypnol can be felt within 30 minutes of being drugged and can last for several hours.

GHB (also known as cherry meth, scoop, goop) is a type of drug that acts as a central nervous system depressant and is prescribed for the treatment of narcolepsy (a sleep disorder).

- It can cause people to throw up, slow their heart rate, and make it hard to breathe.

- At high doses, it can result in a coma or death.

- It is a tasteless, odorless drug that can be a powder or liquid. It's colorless when dissolved in a drink.

- Mixing it with alcohol makes these effects worse.

- GHB can take effect in 15 to 30 minutes, and the effects may last for 3 to 6 hours.

Ketamine (also known as cat valium, k-hole, purple) is a dissociative anesthetic, so called because it distorts perceptions of sight and sound and produces feelings of detachment from the environment and self. It also reduces pain and overall feeling. Like other anesthetic drugs, it is used during surgical procedures in both humans and animals.

- It is a tasteless, odorless drug that can be a powder or liquid.

- It can cause hallucinations and make people feel totally out of it.

- It can also increase heartbeat, raise blood pressure, and cause nausea.

- The effects of ketamine may last for 30 to 60 minutes.

To prevent misuse of Rohypnol, the manufacturer recently changed the pill to look like an oblong olive green tablet with a speckled blue core. When dissolved in light-colored drinks, the new pills dye the liquid blue and alert people that their drink has been tampered with. Unfortunately, generic versions of Rohypnol may not contain the blue dye.

All Drugs Lower Your Defenses

It's important to remember that all drugs affect how well your mind and body operate. In fact, alcohol is linked to far more date rapes than the drugs we've mentioned here. And nearly all drugs of abuse make people vulnerable to being taken advantage of by impairing judgment, reducing reaction time, and clouding a person's thinking.

And as disgusting as it is, when you don't have your wits about you, someone may take that as an opportunity to push themselves on you.

So What Can You Do to Avoid Date Rape Drugs?

If you are at a party where people are drinking alcohol, you should be aware that there could be predators hoping to make you drunk or vulnerable. No matter what you are drinking, even if it's sodas or juice, people can slip drugs in your drinks—so pour all drinks yourself and never leave them unattended (even if you have to take them into the bathroom with you).

Also, be sure to stick with your friends—there's safety in numbers.

But even if you leave your drink or leave your friends behind, know this for certain: if you are drugged and taken advantage of, it's **not** your fault.

Chapter 15

Digital Dating Abuse

Chapter Contents

Section 15.1

Texting and Sexting

Text in this section is excerpted from "Building a Prevention
Framework to Address Teen 'Sexting' Behaviors," National Criminal
Justice Reference Service (NCJRS), October 30, 2013.

Emergence and Framing of the "Teen Sexting Problem"

Concern over teen sexting behaviors is a fairly recent phenomenon.
While discussions of the legal and policy issues surrounding "self produced child pornography" appeared in the legal literature as early as
2007 (Leary, 2010), national attention to the issue–and media adoption of the "sexting" label, accelerated following the December 2008
release of survey results by the National Campaign to Prevent Teen
and Unplanned Pregnancy (NCPTUP). The NCPTUP survey, which
received widespread media coverage throughout 2009, indicated that
approximately 26% of teens reported having sent a nude/semi nude
picture/video of himself or herself to someone. These findings, along
with concurrent national news stories such as the July 2008 suicide of
an Ohio teen following the dissemination of compromising pictures she
had sent to a former boyfriend, and the child pornography prosecution
of six teenagers in Pennsylvania, prompted a surge in sexting related
stories and commentary on television, newspaper editorial pages, talk
radio, blogs, and Internet message boards.

In 2009, amidst growing media attention, some began to question
the significance and extent of the "sexting problem." Some commen-
tators asserted that survey data collected via Internet surveys or
cell phone interviews may have overestimated the magnitude of
the behavior by "self-selecting" technology focused youth. Others
claimed that the media's response to the NCPTUP survey results
was misguided, and that alternative assessments had failed to identify sexting as a wide spread practice (Berton, 2009). In evaluating
political responses to the issue, still other suggested that concerns
over sexting were largely driven by generalized adult alarm over the
changing modes and norms of teen sexual expression in the information age.

Research on Teen Sexting

This initial discourse about teen sexting was based on speculation and limited data. Recent years, however, have produced expanded empirical investigation of the phenomenon, leading to greater understanding of the scope, dynamics, and correlates of teen sexting behavior. In 2009, additional survey generated data concerning the incidence, prevalence, and correlates of teen sexting behavior was released by several organizations, including the Pew Research Center (2009), Cox Communications (2009) and MTV in conjunction with the Associated Press (2009).

Throughout 2010-2012, several studies began to emerge in peer reviewed research journals, including an analysis of sexting cases coming to the attention of law enforcement and several surveys assessing the prevalence and/or correlates of sexting behavior among teens and young adults.

Lack of a Uniform Definition. The "sexting" label has been applied to a broad range of behaviors and contexts, as evidenced by the variety of definitions across the numerous studies. Behaviors include those related to creation, receipt, sending, and/or sharing; descriptors include a range of qualifiers such as "inappropriate," "sexually suggestive," "nude," and "semi-nude"; and media referenced include various permutations of text messages, photos, and videos. Based on their analysis of approximately 500 sexting cases that had come to the attention of law enforcement, Wolak and colleagues proposed a typology the distinguished cases as either "aggravated" or "experimental." "Aggravated" cases that either involved adults, had an explicit intent to harm, or were considered to result from substantial recklessness. "Experimental" cases, a majority of the 500 cases in their sample, encompassed a wide range of circumstances consistent with developmentally expectable (although often irresponsible) adolescent behaviors.

Although the Wolak et al. Study focused on a narrow sample consisting of cases sufficiently severe to warrant police involvement, the diversity of motivational circumstances associated with sexting behaviors has been further supported by the survey literature. For example:

- In the 2009 Pew study, teens highlighted scenarios that included exchange of sexually suggestive text messages, images sent as part of "joking around," images sent in the context of flirting and courtship, and messages/images involving clear harassment or intent to embarrass or harm.

- The NCPTUP survey reported that among those that had sent/posted suggestive messages or nude/semi-nude pictures/videos most did so "to be fun/flirtatious," "as a 'sexy' present for a boyfriend/girlfriend," or "in response to one that was sent to" them (NCPTUP, 2008).

- In the Mitchell et al. study, the appearance in/creation of "nude or nearly nude images" was twice as likely to be attributed to a romantic relationship than as a "prank/joke" (Mitchell et al., 2012).

- Englander found the most common motivation for sexting among a majority (66%) of her respondents was "because a date or boyfriend/girlfriend wanted the picture" (Englander, 2012); Although Temple et al. did not specifically ask their surveyed teens as to the senders/recipients of naked pictures, they concurred that sexting appears to occur within the context of dating.

These and similar findings suggest that interpretation of any sexting prevalence figures must carefully account for the manner in which the behaviors are framed in the context of media reports, policy discourse, and research studies.

Methodological Variation. Beyond variation in operational definition, comparison of "sexting" prevalence estimates must also account for differences in survey participant samples and procedures. Approximately one third of the studies that we reviewed had nationally representative samples, while the remainder varied from sampling a single high school/college to sampling across three different states.

Many of the surveys we reviewed included non-minor teens and/or young adults within their samples, while others have over sampled minor youth at the older end of the age spectrum (i.e., 16–17 years old)—a factor that could explain higher overall rates. Of note, the Mitchell et. al. study (which generally provides the lowest observed rates) surveyed those as young as 10 years old, while the NCPTUP study (showing much higher rates) surveyed those up to 26 years old.

Additionally, surveys have been administered through a variety of means, including Internet, phone, and school-based surveys. Approximately half of the studies reviewed utilized school based surveys, two were telephone based, and the remaining were online/computer based surveys. Each of these approaches has unique methodological advantages and limitations. While one approach is not necessarily superior to another, differences in the response biases associated with each approach might help to explain variability in results across survey studies.

Prevalence and Incidence Estimates

Given definitional ambiguities and methodological variations such as those noted above, it is not surprising that estimates of teen engagement in "sexting behaviors" have varied considerably. Here, the researchers briefly summarize the prevalence research to date, and attempt to contextualize the findings. To do so, we include separate assessments of the prevalence statistics for four sets of activities commonly associated with sexting:

- Creating/producing and sending images of oneself,
- Receiving such images,
- Being asked to send such images, and
- Forwarding/sharing these images with others.

Creating/producing and sending images of oneself. As noted earlier, the 2009 NCPTUP survey reported that 20% of teens indicated having sent or posted nude or partially nude images of themselves via Internet or cellphone. Studies from school based samples confined to specific jurisdictions have produced both higher and lower estimates. One survey of 948 Texas high school students suggested that 28% had engaged in the behavior (Temple et al., 2012) while another school based study in Utah placed the figure at 18% (Strassberg, McKinnon, Sustaíta, & Rullo, 2012). Neither of these studies found statistically significant differences between boys and girls engaging in the behavior, although within both samples the rates for boys were slightly higher.

Studies using national samples have generally produced significantly lower estimates. The Pew study from 2009, based on a phone sample of 800 youth, indicated that just 4% of teens ages 12 to 17 reported sending nude or partially nude sexually suggestive pictures. Mitchell and colleagues, in a study of 1,560 youth Internet users ages 10 to 17, estimated that 2.5% of teens had appeared in and/or created an image, 1.8% had self-produced an image, and 1.3% indicated that they had appeared in or created "images showing breasts, genitals, or someone's bottom. In reconciling these results with those of the school based studies, it should be noted that the

Texas and Utah high school surveys primarily consisted of youth age 15 and older whereas the two national surveys included younger youth.

Receiving images. Youth have reported being two to four times more likely to have received sexual images than to have created, produced and/or sent such images. The Pew study reported 15% receiving such an image (compared to 4% who had reported creating and sending); the Cox Communication survey reported that 17% had received sexts (vs. 9% creating/sending); and the study by Mitchell and colleagues indicated that 7.1% reported receiving a sexual image (5.9% with nudity), compared to the 2.5% who reported creating or appearing in such an image (1.8% with nudity). The high school survey in Utah reported figures that were substantially higher, indicating that nearly 50% of boys and 31% of girls had been receivers (compared to 18% who had reported sending such images). As noted above, these higher figures may be partially associated by variations in the sampling frame, including those associated with the age of the respondents.

Being asked to send images. Among the surveys that have evaluated teen sexting behavior, few have queried youth about their experiences of being asked to send an image of themselves. These experiences, however, may represent salient dimensions of the dynamics of sexting, particularly related to subtly coercive gender dynamics. This experience seems to be far more common among girls than boys. The study by Temple and colleagues, evaluating the experiences of Texas high school students, suggested that 68% of girls and 42% of boys had been asked to send a sexting image—a statistically significant difference. Further, 27% of girls reported being bothered by receiving such a request, compared to only 3% of boys. Beyond gender effects, the study also found that Hispanic and African American youth were more likely than white youth to send an image upon receiving a request.

Forwarding and sharing images. Although initial image creation/production may be thought of as the most troubling within the spectrum of sexting behaviors, the activity of forwarding or sharing images with youth other than those to whom the sender intended may be viewed as the least socially condoned and potentially the most harmful. Whereas sending and receiving activity may often occur within the confines of one on one relationships, forwarding and sharing implicitly involves one or more third parties, and may occur without the consent or knowledge of the image's original sender. The Utah high school study indicated that 27% of boys and 21% of girls have forwarded pictures to others. While such sharing of images might be done for benign reasons (e.g., when youth are bored or want to appear "cool"), sharing images also suggests a nexus between sexting and bullying behavior, and also raises potential legal issues related to distribution of illegal pornographic material. In terms of reported prevalence, forwarding behavior seems to occupy a middle ground between creation, production, sending and receiving.

Correlates and Risk Factors

While much media and policy discourse tends to focus on the overall incidence and prevalence of sexting behaviors, focusing on such aggregate data may obscure important sources of variation in these behaviors across the teen population. Notably, data have shown that the probability and nature of sexting involvement varies considerably among teens, and is associated with a range of demographic and psychosocial characteristics. Understanding sexting in relation to these characteristics is vital to generating effective prevention and intervention strategies.

Age. Not surprisingly, studies have established a positive correlation between age and various forms of sexting experience, with older teens more likely to have engaged in these behaviors than younger teens. While it is likely that sexting activity increases with age, these results should be cautiously interpreted for two main reasons. First, surveys have generally framed questions in terms of lifetime prevalence (e.g., "Have you ever...?"), rather than specific time periods (e.g., "During the past month/year, have you...?"). Accordingly, it is also not surprising that the cumulative experiences of older teens yield higher numbers than those for younger teens. Although differences of sexting rates by age are significant enough to warrant attention, more research is needed to establish the rates of sexting behaviors by youth age. Second, the motivational and behavioral dynamics for sexting behaviors among younger teens seem to differ significantly from those observed within older teen samples. This issue is addressed in relation to the researchers interview data that is presented in the next section.

Gender differences. Comparisons of sexting behaviors by youth gender have yielded inconsistent results. Examining rates of creating/

producing and sending images, some studies have shown significantly higher proportions of girls engaging in the behavior while others have shown no significant gender differences. There is more consistent research indicating that gender differences exist regarding underlying motivations, social conditions, and attitudes toward the behavior. For example, the study by Temple and colleagues found that girls were significantly more likely than boys to have been asked to send an image of themselves, and moreover, that they were nine times more likely to be solicited by such a request. According to the NCPTUP survey, teen girls are almost three times more likely than teen boys to cite pressure from the opposite sex as the reason for sending or posting sexy messages or sexually suggestive content. In a 2012 study conducted by Englander, girls were found to be about twice as likely as boys to be "pressured" into sexting. Hence, while the overall rates of engaging in certain types of sexting behavior may ultimately be similar for boys and girls, it is reasonable to assume that the dynamics of these behaviors are substantially different across genders. This theme is explored in the presentation of the researcher's interview data in the results section.

Risky behaviors. Prior to the emergence of sexting as a distinct issue of concern, a substantial body of literature examining technology facilitated risky teen behaviors suggested a strong association between "online" risks and behaviors and "offline" risks and behaviors. Consistent with these findings, research conducted to date has indicated that youth who engage in sexting behaviors are more likely to be sexually active. Findings also suggest that youth engaged in sexting behaviors are more likely to endorse symptoms of depression, suicidality, substance abuse, and general mental health problems.

A survey of teens in several school districts in a Midwestern state found positive associations between reported sexting and sexually risky behaviors (i.e., unprotected sex, anal intercourse), mental health symptoms, such as depression and suicidality, substance use and abuse, and academic difficulties (Dake, et al., 2012). These findings are consistent with other survey research with teens and young adults that has identified correlations between sexting and mental health symptoms and between sexting and general sexual activity. Several studies have shown a relationship between sexting and rates of sexual activity and sexually risky behaviors, particularly among girls. Additionally, a study of California teens found that knowing someone who had engaged in sexting behaviors was strongly associated with the individual's own behavior, consistent with broader public health research demonstrating that behavior among adolescents is strongly tied to perceptions of peer norms.

Section 15.2

Technology Use and Digital Dating Abuse among Teens

Text in this section is excerpted from "Technology, Teen Dating Violence and Abuse, and Bullying," National Criminal Justice Reference Service (NCJRS), August 2013.

Youth Technology Use

Youths' daily activities and social worlds revolve around new media practices such as using cell phones, engaging in instant messaging, watching and creating online videos, and connecting to social networking websites. Youth spend more time with technology than any other activity besides sleeping. While technology use can be positive and create educational opportunities, increase access to useful information, and increase convenience in other areas (e.g., on-line shopping), it also poses many risks to youth from peers and adult predators. The primary focus in this study is the ways in which youth interact with peers and dating partners via technology, including through cell phones and social media.

Based on data from a nationally representative sample of 799 youth, most youth ages 12–17 have cell phones (77 percent). More youth text by cell phone than talk by cell phone, but those that most frequently text, also talk most frequently. Three-quarters of all teens text, with two-thirds reporting they do so every day. The median number of texts sent by 12- to 17-year-old teens per day is 60. Older girls text the most, with a median of 100 texts per day, compared to only 50 for older boys.

For teens in a dating relationship, contact between partners via cell phones happens at all hours of the day and night. Between 10 p.m. to midnight, almost one in three teens report having communicated with their partner by cell phone or texting 10 or more times. Between midnight and 5 a.m., 17 percent of teens report having communicated with their partner by texting 10 or more times per hour. In terms of chatting on cell phones, about a quarter of youth say they talk daily to friends, which is fewer than was reported in 2009 (38 percent). Notably, only 14 percent say they talk with friends on landlines daily, and 31 percent say they never talk to friends on a landline.

Being online is a source of risk and opportunity for youth. There has been much research about the benefits of Internet use, as well as the risks that are posed to youth perpetrated both by adults and peers. Ninety-five percent of youth ages 12–17 are online. Overall, Internet use does not vary much by region—91 percent of rural teens, 87 percent of urban teens, and 93 percent of suburban teens use the Internet. But, daily Internet use does vary by region—40 percent of urban teens and 39 percent of suburban teens use the Internet several times per day, compared to 25 percent of rural teens. However, growing access to broadband Internet may increase teen media use in rural areas: over 75 percent of families with children recently reported having broadband Internet access at home, up from 50 percent in 2004. This has important implications for rural teen media use because 40 percent of teens who have broadband access at home report using the Internet multiple times a day (compared to 21 percent of teens who live in households with a dial-up connection).

In addition, wireless access impacts teens' Internet use, since more than 25 percent of teens report using their cell phone to go online. The most recent estimates show that 23 percent of youth ages 12–17 have a smartphone, with no differences in phone ownership by race/ethnicity or income. In addition, 16 percent of youth report having used a tablet to go online in the 30 days before they were asked about such use.

Social networking is key to teen's media use: 80 percent of youth ages 12–17 report using social networking sites (e.g., Facebook, Myspace), up from 73 percent just two years before, and many report using such sites daily. Among online teens, older teens (ages 14 to 17) are more likely to use social networking sites than younger teens ages 12 and 13; and in fact, some social networking sites prohibit accounts for those under 14. Though most youth use social networking sites, youth from lower income families (under $30,000) are more likely to use such sites than teens in wealthier households (80 percent vs. 70 percent.

The majority of youth who use social media (69 percent) report that other youth are mostly kind to one another on social networking sites. However, and notably for the purposes of this study, another 20 percent of youth who use social media say that their peers are mostly unkind to others via this technology. Further, 88 percent of youth reported having observed other teens being mean or cruel on social networking sites, and 12 percent said they observed this behavior frequently. Fifteen percent reported that they were the victim of cruelty through social media in the 12 months prior to being surveyed. Further, 25 percent of teens on social media reported having an experience resulting in a face-to-face confrontation with someone, 13 percent reported concern about having to go to school the next day, and 8 percent reported having actually had physical altercations with someone because of something that occurred on a social network site.

All this suggests that youth use technology frequently and it plays an important role in how they interact with other youth and dating partners. The next section examines the literature on teen dating violence and abuse and on bullying, and how technology plays a role in these two types of interpersonal violence.

Cyber Abuse within Teen Dating Violence

Little is known about the extent to which teens experience teen dating violence via technology (cyber abuse), but a few studies have examined this issue. Draucker and Martsolf (2010) conducted a qualitative study with 56 participants to examine the role of electronic communications in dating violence and abuse. Their study highlights the myriad ways that youth can use technology to abuse their partners. Specifically, they found eight ways in which partners used electronic communications, the last six of which were related to violence, abuse, or controlling behaviors: (1) establishing a relationship; (2) nonaggressive communication; (3) arguing; (4) monitoring the whereabouts of a partner or controlling their activities; (5) emotional aggression toward a partner; (6) seeking help during a violent episode; (7) distancing a partner's access to self by not responding to calls, texts, and other contacts via technology; and (8) reestablishing contact after a violent episode. Poignant qualitative narrative from this study provided examples of cyber abuse, such as a male hacking into his partner's Facebook account, reading all of the messages she had ever received or posted, and then talking through these with her. Another example involved one partner creating a hate website about their former partner and allowing others to post to it with similarly nasty insults.

There have been a few studies assessing the prevalence of cyber abuse in teen dating relationships. For middle school youth, nearly a third of students (31 percent) reported being a victim of electronic dating aggression (RTI International, 2012). In another study conducted in 2006, 615 teens age 13 to 18 from around the country participated in a study conducted by Teen Research Unlimited, commissioned by Liz Claiborne, Inc. The findings showed that youth are both victims and perpetrators of abuse through technological devices; however, the details of the findings were only released regarding victimization experiences. More specifically, 25 percent of youth reported having been called names, harassed, or put down by their partner via cell phone and texting; 22 percent reported having been asked by cell phone or the Internet to do something sexual they did not want to do; 19 percent reported that their partner used a cell phone or the Internet to spread rumors about them; 18 percent reported that their partners used a social networking site to harass them or put them down; 11 percent reported that their partner shared private or embarrassing pictures or videos of them; 17 percent reported that they were made to feel afraid of what their partner might do if they did not respond to their partner's cell phone call, e-mail, instant message, or text message; and 10 percent reported being physically threatened by their partner through an e-mail, instant message, or text message.

Section 15.3

Cyberbullying

Text in this section is excerpted from "Cyberbullying,"
Office on Women's Health (OWH), April 15, 2014.

What is Cyberbullying?

Cyberbullying is hurting someone again and again using a computer, a cellphone, or another kind of electronic technology. Examples of cyberbullying include the following:

- Texting or emailing insults or nasty rumors about someone

- Posting mean comments about someone on Facebook, Twitter, and other social media sites
- Threatening someone through email or other technology
- Tricking someone into sharing embarrassing information
- Forwarding private text messages to hurt or embarrass someone
- Posting embarrassing photos or videos of someone
- Pretending to be someone else online to get that person in trouble or embarrass her
- Creating a website to make fun of someone

Some teens think it's easier to get away with bullying online than in person. Also, girls may be more likely to cyberbully than boys. Keep in mind that it's pretty easy to find out who has been cyberbullying. In fact, cyberbullies can get in a lot of trouble with their schools, and possibly even with the police.

Cyberbullying hurts. It can be easier to type something really mean than to say it to a person. But being cyberbullied can sometimes feel even worse than other kinds of bullying. That's because cyberbullying can come at you anytime, anywhere and can reach a lot of people.

Being cyberbullied can make you feel angry, afraid, helpless, and terribly sad. Also, teens who are cyberbullied are more likely than other teens to have problems such as using drugs, skipping school, and even getting sick.

If you are being cyberbullied, talk to an adult you trust. An adult can help you figure out how to handle the problem, and can offer you support.

If you are cyberbullying, it's time to stop. You are not only hurting someone else, you could hurt yourself. You can lose friends and get in trouble with your school or even with the police. If you can't seem to stop yourself from cyberbullying, get help from an adult you trust.

You may hurt someone online without really meaning to do it. It may seem funny to vote for the ugliest kid in school, for example, but try to think about how that person feels. And if you get a message that makes you mad, go away and come back before writing something you may regret. Nearly half of teenage cellphone users say they regretted a text message they sent. Remember, nothing is really secret or private on the Internet, and things you post online can stay there forever.

How to prevent cyberbullying?

Here are some tips that may help protect you from being cyberbullied:

- Don't give out your passwords or personal information. Even your friends could wind up giving your passwords to someone who shouldn't have them.

- Use the privacy options on social networking sites like Facebook, Instagram, and Tumblr that let you choose who can see what you post.

- Don't befriend people online if you don't know them, even if you have friends in common.

- Be careful about what you write or what images you send or post because nothing is really private on the Internet.

- If you are using a site like Facebook on a computer in the library, log out before you walk away. If you don't log out, the next person who uses the computer could get into your account.

If you are cyberbullied

If you are cyberbullied, you can get help. Here are some important tips:

- If someone bullies you, don't respond. Bullies are looking for a reaction, and you may be able to stop the bullying if you ignore or block the person.

- Save any evidence of cyberbullying, print it out, and show it to a trusted adult.

- Use options that let you block email, cellphone, and text messages from a cyberbully. You can also stop a person from seeing your Facebook information. If you need help, ask an adult, your cellphone company, or the website where you want to block someone.

- If you are being cyberbullied, ask if your school can get involved.

- Report bullying to your Internet service provider, phone company, email provider, or the website where it happened. Sites like Twitter, YouTube, and Instagram have online forms for reporting.

- Report cyberbullying to police if it involves threats of violence or pornography. Stopbullying.gov has more information on cyberbullying and the law.

Sometimes, teens don't want to tell their parents that they are being cyberbullied because they are afraid their parents will take away their phone or computer. If you have this concern, tell your parents, and work with them to figure out a solution. The most important thing is for you to be safe.

Section 15.4

Chatting with Kids about Being Online

Text in this section is excerpted from "Chatting with Kids about Being Online," Office of Justice Programs (OJP), January 2014.

Talking to Your Kids

The best way to protect your kids online? Talk to them. While kids value the opinions of their peers, most tend to rely on their parents for help on the issues that matter most.

Start early.

Young kids see their parents using all kinds of devices — and also might be playing games or watching shows on them. As soon as your child starts using a phone, mobile device, or computer, it's time to talk to them about online behavior and safety.

Initiate conversations.

Even if your kids are comfortable approaching you, don't wait for them to start the conversation. Use everyday opportunities to talk to your kids about being online. For example, news stories about cyberbullying or texting while driving can spur a conversation with kids about their experiences and your expectations.

Communicate your expectations.

Be honest about your expectations and how they apply in an online context. Communicating your values clearly can help your kids make smarter and more thoughtful decisions when they face tricky situations. For instance, be specific about what's off-limits — and what you consider to be unacceptable behavior.

Be patient and supportive.

Resist the urge to rush through these conversations with your kids. Most kids need to hear information repeated, in small doses, for it to sink in. If you keep talking with your kids, your patience and persistence will pay off in the long run.

Work hard to keep the lines of communication open, even if you learn your kid has done something online that you find inappropriate.

Listening and taking their feelings into account helps keep conversations afloat. You may not have all the answers, and being honest about that can go a long way.

Communicating at Different Ages

Young Kids

Supervision is important.

When very young children start using mobile devices or a computer, they should be supervised closely by a parent or caregiver. If little kids aren't supervised online, they may stumble onto content that could scare or confuse them.

When you're comfortable that your young children are ready to explore on their own, it's still important to stay in close touch. You may want to restrict access to sites or apps that you've visited and know to be appropriate—at least in terms of their educational or entertainment value.

Consider parental controls.

If you're concerned about what your kids see online, consider tools with these features:

- **Filtering and blocking**. These tools limit access to certain sites, words, or images. Some products decide what's filtered; others leave that to parents. Some filters apply to websites; others to email and chat.

- **Blocking outgoing content**. This software prevents kids from sharing personal information online or via email.

- **Limiting time**. This software allows you to limit your kid's time online and set the time of day they can access the Internet.

- **Browsers for kids**. These browsers filter words or images you don't want your kids to see.

- **Kid-oriented search engines**. These perform limited searches or filter search results for sites and material appropriate for kids.

- **Monitoring tools.** Software that alerts parents to online activity without blocking access. Some tools record the addresses of websites a child has visited; others provide a warning message when a kid visits certain sites. Monitoring tools can be used with or without a kid's knowledge.

Tweens

Tweens need to feel "independent" but not alone as they start exploring on their own. Many 8- to 12-year-olds are adept at finding information online, but they still need guidance to help them understand which sources are trustworthy.

Think about limits.

Consider setting limits on how long and how often they can be online—whether on computers, phones, or other mobile devices. For younger tweens, parental controls can be effective. However, many middle school kids have the technical know-how to get around those controls.

Teens

Teens are forming their own values and beginning to take on the values of their peers. Many are eager to experience more independence from their parents. However, they need to learn how to exercise judgment about being safe online and act in accordance with their family ethic.

Teens have more Internet access through mobile devices—as well as more time to themselves—so it isn't realistic for you to try to be in the same room when they're online. They need to know that you and other family members can ask them about what they're doing online.

What Can You Do?

Talk about credibility.

It's important to emphasize the concept of credibility. Even the most tech-savvy kids need to understand that:

- not everything they see on the Internet is true
- people online may not be who they appear to be or say they are
- information or images they share can be seen far and wide
- once something is posted online, it's nearly impossible to "take it back"

Talk about manners.

Because they don't see facial expressions, body language, and other visual cues, teens and tweens may feel free to do or say things online that they wouldn't offline. Remind them that real people with real feelings are behind profiles, screen names, and avatars.

Talk about expectations.

When you talk to your kids, set reasonable expectations. Anticipate how you will react if you find out that they've done something online you don't approve of.

If your child confides in you about something scary or inappropriate they've encountered online, try to work together to prevent it from happening again.

Socializing Online

Kids share pictures, videos, thoughts, plans, and their whereabouts with friends, family, and sometimes, the world at large. Socializing online can help kids connect with others, but it's important to help your child learn how to navigate these spaces safely.

Oversharing

Some pitfalls that come with online socializing are sharing too much information, or posting pictures, videos, or words that can damage a reputation or hurt someone's feelings. Applying real-world judgment and sense can help minimize those downsides.

What Can You Do?

Remind your kids that online actions have consequences.

The words kids write and the images they post have consequences offline.

- **Kids should post only what they're comfortable with others seeing**. Parts of your children's profiles may be seen by a broader audience than you — or they — are comfortable with, even if they use privacy settings. Encourage your kids to think about the language they use online, and to think before posting pictures and videos, or altering photos posted by someone else. Employers, college admissions officers, coaches, teachers, and the police may view these posts.

- **Remind kids that once they post it, they can't take it back**. Even if they delete the information from a site, they have little control over older versions that may be saved on other people's devices and may circulate online. And a message that's supposed to disappear from a friend's phone? There's software that lets them keep it.

Tell kids to limit what they share.

- **Help your kids understand what information should stay private**. Tell them why it's important to keep some things — about themselves, family members, and friends — to themselves. Information like their Social Security number, street address, phone number, and family financial information is private and should stay that way.

- **Talk to your teens about avoiding sex talk online**. Teens who don't talk about sex with strangers online are less likely to come in contact with predators. In fact, researchers have found that predators usually don't pose as children or teens, and most teens who are contacted by adults they don't know find it creepy. Teens should not hesitate to ignore or block them, and trust their gut when something feels wrong.

- **Send group messages with care.** Suggest that your kids think about who needs to see their message before sending to multiple people.

Limit access to your kids' profiles.

- **Use privacy settings.** Many social networking sites, chat, and video accounts have adjustable privacy settings, so you and your kids can restrict who has access to kids' profiles. Talk to your kids about the importance of these settings, and your expectations for who should be allowed to view their profile.

- **Review your child's friends list.** Suggest that your kids limit online "friends" to people they actually know. Ask about who they're talking to online.

Cyberbullying

Cyberbullying is bullying or harassment that happens online. It can happen in an email, a text message, an online game, or on a social networking site. It might involve rumors or images posted on someone's profile or circulated for others to see.

What Can You Do?

Help prevent cyberbullying.

- **Talk to your kids about bullying.** Tell your kids that they can't hide behind the words they type and the images they post or send. Bullying is a lose-lose situation: Hurtful messages make the target feel bad, and they make the sender look bad. Often they can bring scorn from peers and punishment from authorities.

- **Tell your kids to talk to you about bullying, too.** Ask your kids to let you know if an online message or image makes them feel threatened or hurt.

- **Recognize the signs of a cyberbully.** Cyberbullying often involves mean-spirited comments. Check out your kid's social networking pages from time to time to see what you find. Could your kid be the bully? Look for signs of bullying behavior, such as creating mean images of another kid.

- **Help stop cyberbullying.** Most kids don't bully, and there's no reason for anyone to put up with it. If your kids see cyberbullying happening to someone else, encourage them to try to stop it by telling the bully to stop, and by not engaging or forwarding anything. One way to help stop bullying online is to report it to the site or network where you see it.

What to do about a cyberbully.

- **Don't react to the bully**. If your child is targeted by a cyber-bully, keep a cool head. Remind your child that most people realize bullying is wrong. Tell your child not to respond in kind. Instead, encourage your kid to work with you to save the evidence and talk to you about it. If the bullying persists, share the record with school officials or local law enforcement.

- **Protect your child's profile**. If your child finds a profile that was created or altered without their permission, contact the site to have it taken down.

- **Block or delete the bully**. Delete the bully from friends lists or block their user name, email address, and phone number.

Using Mobile Devices

What age is appropriate for a kid to have a phone or a mobile device? That's something for you and your family to decide. Consider your kid's age, personality, maturity, and your family's circumstances.

What Can You Do?

Phones, Features, and Options

Decide on the right options and features.

Your wireless company and mobile phone should give you some choices for privacy settings and child safety controls. Most carriers allow parents to turn off features like web access, texting, or downloading. Some cell phones are made especially for children. They're designed to be easy to use, and have features like limited Internet access, minute management, number privacy, and emergency buttons.

Get smart about smartphones.

Many phones offer web access and mobile apps. If your children are going to use a phone and you're concerned about what they might find online, choose a phone with limited Internet access or turn on web filtering.

Get familiar with location-based services.

Many mobile phones have GPS technology installed. Kids with these phones can pinpoint where their friends are — and be pinpointed by their friends. Tell your kids to limit these features so they're not broadcasting their location to the world. Explain that there can be downsides to letting anyone and everyone know where they are. In addition, some carriers offer GPS services that let parents map their kid's location.

Password-protect phones.

A password, numeric code, gesture, or fingerprint can lock a phone from intruders. Not only can this prevent "pocket-dialing," but it also can help keep information and photos from falling into the wrong hands.

Develop Rules

Explain what you expect.

Talk to your kids about when and where it's appropriate to use their phones and other mobile devices. You also may want to establish rules for responsible use. Do you allow calls, texting, or playing games on apps at the dinner table? Do you have rules about cell phone use at night? Should they give you their phones while they're doing homework, or when they're supposed to be sleeping?

Set an example.

It's illegal to drive while texting or talking on the phone without a hands-free device in most states, but it's dangerous everywhere. Set an example for your kids, and talk to them about the dangers and consequences of distracted driving.

Mobile sharing and Networking

Socializing and sharing on-the-go can foster creativity and fun, but could cause problems related to personal reputation and safety.

Use care when sharing photos and videos.

Most mobile phones have camera and video capability, making it easy for teens to capture and share every moment. Encourage kids to get permission from the photographer or the person in the shot before posting videos or photos. It's easier to be smart upfront about what media they share than to do damage control later.

Use good judgment with social networking from a mobile device.

The filters you've installed on your home computer won't limit what kids can do on a mobile device. Talk to your teens about using good sense when they're social networking from their phones, too.

Mobile Apps

What should I know about apps?

Apps might:

- collect and share personal information
- let your kids spend real money — even if the app is free
- include ads
- link to social media

But the apps might not tell you they're doing it.

What Can You Do?

Here's what you and your kids can do to learn about an app before you download it:

- look at screen shots
- read the description, content rating, and user reviews
- do some research on the developer, including outside reviews from sources you respect
- check what information the app collects

Can I restrict how my kids use apps?

Before you pass the phone or tablet to your kids, take a look at the settings. You may be able to:

- **restrict content** to what's right for your kid's age
- **set a password** so apps can't be downloaded without it, and kids can't buy stuff without it
- **turn off Wi-Fi and data services** or put the phone in airplane mode so it can't connect to the Internet.

The best way to keep up with kids' apps is to try them out yourself, and talk to your kids about your rules for buying and using apps.

Texting

Encourage manners.

If your kids are texting, encourage them to respect others. Texting shorthand can lead to misunderstandings. Tell them to think about how a text message might be read and understood before they send it.

Safeguard privacy.

Remind your kids to:

- ignore texts from people they don't know

- learn how to block numbers from their cell phone

- avoid posting their cell phone number online

- never provide personal or financial information in response to a text

Recognize text message spam.

Help your kids recognize text message spam and explain the consequences:

- it often uses the promise of free gifts — or asks you to verify account information — to get you to reveal personal information

- it can lead to unwanted charges on your cell phone bill

- it can slow cell phone performance

What Can You Do?

Review your cell phone bill for unauthorized charges, and report them to your carrier. Tell your kids:

- **to delete messages that ask for personal information**— even if there's a promise of a free gift. Legitimate companies don't ask for information like account numbers or passwords by email or text.

- **not to reply to — or click on — links in the message**. Links can install malware and take you to spoof sites that look real, but that exist to steal your information.

Sexting

Sending or forwarding sexually explicit photos, videos, or messages from a mobile device is known as "sexting." Tell your kids not to do it. In addition to risking their reputation and their friendships, they could be breaking the law if they create, forward, or even save this kind of message. Teens may be less likely to make a bad choice if they know the consequences.

Making Computer Security a Habit

The security of your computer, phone, and other mobile devices can affect the safety of your online experience — and that of your kids. Malware could allow someone to steal your family's personal or financial information. Malware is software that can:

- install viruses

- monitor or control your computer use

- send unwanted pop-up ads

- redirect your device to websites you're not looking for

- record your keystrokes

What Can You Do?

- **Use security software and keep it updated**. Well-known companies offer plenty of free options. Set the software to update automatically.

- **Keep your operating system and web browser up-to-date**. Hackers take advantage of software that doesn't have the latest security updates. You also can customize the built-in security and privacy settings in your operating system or browser. Check the Tools or Options menus to explore your choices. While you're at it, keep your apps updated, too.

Teaching kids Computer security

Talk to your kids about how they can help protect their devices and your family's personal information.

Create strong passwords, and keep them private.

The longer the password, the harder it is to crack. Date of birth, login name, or common words are not safe passwords. Ask your kids to be creative and come up with different passwords for different accounts.

It may be tempting to re-use the same password, but if it's stolen, hackers can use it to access other accounts. Kids also can protect their passwords by not sharing them with anyone, including their friends.

*Don't provide personal or financial information unless the website is
secure.*

If you or your kids send messages, share photos, use social networks, or bank online, you're sending personal information over the
Internet. Teach your kids: if the URL doesn't start with https, don't
enter any personal information. That "s" stands for secure. It means
the information you're sending is encrypted and protected.

Watch out for "free" stuff.

Free games, apps, music, and other downloads can hide malware.
Don't download anything unless you trust the source. Teach your kids
how to recognize reputable sources.

Be cautious about P2P file-sharing. Some kids share music,
games, or software online. Peer-to-peer (P2P) file-sharing allows people
to share these kinds of files through an informal network of computers
running the same software.

Sometimes spyware, malware, or pornography can be hidden in a
shared file. If your kids download copyrighted material, you could be
subject to legal action. It's important to talk to your kids about the
security and other risks involved with file-sharing.

- **Install file-sharing software properly.** Check the default
  settings so that nothing private is shared. By default, almost
  all P2P file-sharing applications will share files in your "Downloads" or "Shared" folders. If you save personal files in shared
  folders, other P2P users may access files you don't mean to share
  — including private documents like your tax returns or other
  financial documents.

- **Use security software to scan files.** Before your kids open or
  play any downloaded file, use security software to scan it. Make
  sure the security software is up-to-date and running.

Using Public Wi-Fi Securely

Many public places — like coffee shops, libraries, and airports —
offer Wi-Fi hotspots. These hotspots can be convenient, but they're
often not secure. That could make it easy for someone else to access
your family's online accounts or steal your personal information —
including private documents, photos, and passwords.

What Can You Do?

Use secure Wi-Fi networks.

Secure networks use encryption, which protects the information you send online by scrambling it so others can't access it. You can be sure that a network is secure only if you're asked to provide a **WPA** or **WPA2** password.

Tell your kids if they're not asked for a password, they shouldn't use that network to sign in to accounts or send any personal information. And don't assume that a Wi-Fi hotspot uses encryption: most of them don't.

Use secure websites (https:/ /).

A secure site will encrypt your information while you are signed in to it — even if the network doesn't. How will your kids know if a site is secure? Tell them to look for https in the web address of every page they visit — not just when they log in. The "s" stands for secure.

Don't stay permanently signed in to accounts.

Recommend that your kids log out when they've finished using a site.

Phishing Scams

Phishing is when scam artists send texts, emails, or pop-up messages to get people to share their personal and financial information. Scammers use this information to access your accounts, steal your identity, and commit fraud.

What Can You Do?

Here's how you and your kids can avoid getting tricked by scam artists.

- **Don't reply to texts, emails, or pop-up messages that ask for personal or financial information**, and don't click on any links in the message.

- **Be cautious about opening any attachments** or downloading any files from emails you receive, regardless of who sent

231

them. Unexpected files may contain viruses that your friends or family members didn't know were there.

- **Get your kids involved**, so they can develop their scam "antennas" and careful Internet habits. Look for teachable moments — if you get a phishing message, show it to your kids to help them understand that things aren't always what they seem.

How to report phishing scams.

Forward phishing emails to **spam@uce.gov**. They will be added to a database that law enforcement agencies use to pursue investigations. If you or your kids were tricked by a phishing scam, file a complaint at **ftc.gov/complaint**.

Protecting Your Child's Privacy

As a parent, you have control over the personal information companies collect online from your kids under 13. The Children's Online Privacy Protection Act (COPPA) gives you tools to do that.

The Federal Trade Commission enforces the COPPA Rule. If a site or service is covered by COPPA, it has to get your consent before collecting personal information from your child and it has to honor your choices about how that information is used.

The COPPA Rule was put in place to protect kids' personal information on websites and online services — including apps — that are directed to children under 13. The Rule also applies to a general audience site that knows it's collecting personal information from kids that age.

COPPA requires those sites and services to notify parents directly and get their approval before they collect, use, or disclose a child's personal information.

Section 15.5

Some Statistics on Electronic Aggression

Text in this section is excerpted from "Electronic Media and Youth
Violence: A CDC Issue Brief for Educators and Caregivers," Centers
for Disease Control and Prevention (CDC), January 9, 2014.

Overview

Technology and adolescents seem destined for each other; both are
young, fast paced, and ever changing. In previous generations teens
readily embraced new technologies, such as record players, TVs, cas-
sette players, computers, and VCRs, but the past two decades have
witnessed a virtual explosion in new technology, including cell phones,
iPods, MP-3s, DVDs, and PDAs (personal digital assistants). This new
technology has been eagerly embraced by adolescents and has led to an
expanded vocabulary, including instant messaging ("IMing"), blogging,
and text messaging.

New technology has many social and educational benefits, but
caregivers and educators have expressed concern about the dangers
young people can be exposed to through these technologies. To respond
to this concern, some states and school districts have, for example,
established policies about the use of cell phones on school grounds and
developed policies to block access to certain websites on school computers. Many teachers and caregivers have taken action individually by
spot-checking websites used by young people, such as MySpace. This
section focuses on the phenomena of *electronic aggression:* any kind
of aggression perpetrated through technology—any type of harassment or bullying (teasing, telling lies, making fun of someone, making
rude or mean comments, spreading rumors, or making threatening or
aggressive comments) that occurs through email, a chat room, instant
messaging, a website (including blogs), or text messaging.

Caregivers, educators, and other adults who work with young
people know that children and adolescents spend a lot of time using
electronic media (blogs, instant messaging, chat rooms, email, text
messaging). What is not known is exactly how and how often they
use different types of technology. Could use of technology increase

233

the likelihood that a young person is the victim of aggression? If the answer is yes, what should caregivers and educators do to help young people protect themselves? To help answer these questions, the Centers for Disease Control and Prevention, Division of Adolescent and School Health and Division of Violence Prevention, held an expert panel on September 20-21, 2006, in Atlanta, Georgia, entitled "Electronic Media and Youth Violence."

The information presented in this section is based upon what is currently known; we still have a lot to learn about electronic aggression. The research findings described here need to be repeated and validated by other researchers and the possible action steps for educators, educational policy makers, and caregivers need to be evaluated for effectiveness.

How Common Is Electronic Aggression?

Because electronic aggression is fairly new, limited information is available, and those researching the topic have asked different questions about it. Thus, information cannot be readily compared or combined across studies, which limits our ability to make definitive conclusions about the prevalence and impact of electronic aggression.

What we know about electronic aggression is based upon a few studies that measure similar but not exactly the same behaviors. For example, in their studies, some of the panelists use a narrow definition of electronic aggression (e.g., aggression perpetrated through email or instant messaging), while others use a broader definition (e.g., aggression perpetrated through email, instant messaging, on a website, or through text messaging).

In addition to different definitions, in their research the panelists also asked young people to report about their experiences over different time periods (e.g., over the past several months, since the beginning of school, in the past year), and surveyed youth of different ages (e.g., 6th-8th-graders, 10-15-year-olds, 10-17-year-olds). As a result, the most accurate way to describe the information we have is to give ranges that include the findings from all of the studies.

We know that most youth (65-91%) report little or no involvement in electronic aggression. However, 9% to 35% of young people say they have been the victim of electronic aggression. As with face-to-face bullying, estimates of electronic aggression perpetration are lower than victimization, ranging from 4% to 21%. In some cases, the higher end of the range (e.g., 21% and 35%) reflects studies that asked about electronic aggression over a longer time period (e.g., a year as opposed to 2 months). In other cases, the higher percentages reflect studies that defined electronic aggression more broadly (e.g., spreading rumors, telling lies, or making threats as opposed to just telling lies).

When we look at data across all of the panelists' studies, the percentage of young people who report being electronic aggression victims has a fairly wide range (9-35%). However, if we look at victimization over a similar time frame, such as "monthly or more often" or "at least once in the past 2 months," the range is much narrower, from 8% to 11%.

Similarly, although the percentage of young people who admit they perpetrate electronic aggression varies considerably across studies (4-21%), the range narrows if we look at similar time periods. Approximately 4% of surveyed youth report behaving aggressively electronically "monthly or more often" or "at least once in the past 2 months."

Chapter 16

Understanding School Violence

School Violence

School violence is youth violence that occurs on school property, on the way to or from school or school-sponsored events, or during a school-sponsored event. A young person can be a victim, a perpetrator, or a witness of school violence. School violence may also involve or impact adults. Youth violence includes various behaviors. Some violent acts—such as bullying, pushing, and shoving—can cause more emotional harm than physical harm. Other forms of violence, such as gang violence and assault (with or without weapons), can lead to serious injury or even death.

Why Is School Violence a Public Health Problem?

School associated violent deaths are rare.

- 11 homicides of school-age youth ages 5 to 18 years occurred at school during the 2010-2011 school year.

- Of all youth homicides, less than 1% occur at school, and this percentage has been relatively stable for the past decade.

Text in this section is excerpted from "Understanding School Violence," Centers for Disease Control and Prevention (CDC), 2015.

In 2012, there were about 749,200 nonfatal violent victimizations at school among students 12 to 18 years of age.

Approximately 9% of teachers report that they have been threatened with injury by a student from their school; 5% of school teachers reported that they had been physically attacked by a student from their school.

In 2011, 18% of students ages 12–18 reported that gangs were present at their school during the school year.

In a 2013 nationally representative sample of youth in grades 9-12:

- 8.1% reported being in a physical fight on school property in the 12 months before the survey.

- 7.1% reported that they did not go to school on one or more days in the 30 days before the survey because they felt unsafe at school or on their way to or from school.

- 5.2% reported carrying a weapon (gun, knife or club) on school property on one or more days in the 30 days before the survey.

- 6.9% reported being threatened or injured with a weapon on school property one or more times in the 12 months before the survey.

- 19.6% reported being bullied on school property and 14.8% reported being bullied electronically during the 12 months before the survey.

How Does School Violence Affect Health?

Deaths resulting from school violence are only part of the problem. Many young people experience nonfatal injuries. Some of these injuries are relatively minor and include cuts, bruises, and broken bones. Other injuries, like gunshot wounds and head trauma, are more serious and can lead to permanent disability.

Not all injuries are visible. Exposure to youth violence and school violence can lead to a wide array of negative health behaviors and outcomes, including alcohol and drug use and suicide. Depression, anxiety, and many other psychological problems, including fear, can result from school violence.

Who Is at Risk for School Violence?

A number of factors can increase the risk of a youth engaging in violence at school. However, the presence of these factors does not always mean that a young person will become an offender.

Risk factors for school and youth violence include:

- Prior history of violence
- Drug, alcohol, or tobacco use
- Association with delinquent peers
- Poor family functioning
- Poor grades in school
- Poverty in the community

How Can We Prevent School Violence?

The goal is to stop school violence from happening in the first place. Several prevention strategies have been identified.

- Universal, school-based prevention programs can significantly lower rates of aggression and violent behavior. These programs are delivered to all students in a school or grade level. They teach about various topics and develop skills, such as emotional self-awareness and control, positive social skills, problem solving, conflict resolution, and teamwork.

- Parent-and family-based programs can improve family relations and lower the risk for violence by children especially when the programs are started early. These programs provide parents with education about child development and teach skills to communicate and solve problems in nonviolent ways.

- Street outreach programs can significantly reduce youth violence. These programs connect trained staff with at-risk youth to conduct conflict mediation, make service referrals, and change beliefs about the acceptability of violence.

How Does CDC Approach Prevention?

CDC uses a four-step approach to address public health problems like school violence:

Step 1: Define the problem

Before we can prevent school violence, we need to know how big the problem is, where it is, and who it affects. CDC learns about a problem by gathering and studying data. These data are critical because they help us know where prevention is most needed.

Step 2: Identify risk and protective factors

It is not enough to know that school violence affects certain students in certain areas. We also need to know why. CDC conducts and supports research to answer this question. We can then develop programs to reduce or get rid of risk factors and to increase protective factors.

Step 3: Develop and test prevention strategies

Using information gathered in research, CDC develops and evaluates strategies to prevent school violence.

Step 4: Ensure widespread adoption

In this final step, CDC shares the best prevention strategies. CDC may also provide funding or technical help so communities can adopt these strategies.

What Does CDC Do to Prevent School Violence?

The CDC leads many activities that help us to understand and effectively prevent school violence. Some of these activities include:

- **Youth Risk Behavior Surveillance System (YRBSS)** The YRBSS monitors health-risk behaviors among youth, including physical fighting, bullying, weapon carrying, and suicide. Data are collected every two years and provide nationally representative information about youth in grades 9-12.

- **School-Associated Violent Death Study.** CDC leads a collaboration with the Departments of Education and Justice to monitor school-associated violent deaths at the national level.

- **School Health Policies and Practices Study (SHPPS).** The SHPPS is a national survey that assesses policies and practices at the state, district, school, and classroom levels. Eight elements of school health are assessed, including approaches to keep a school environment safe and to prevent violence.

- **Health Curriculum Analysis Tool (HECAT).** The HECAT contains guidance, appraisal tools, and resources to help schools conduct an analysis of health education curricula based on the National Health Education Standards and CDC's Characteristics of an Effective Health Education Curriculum. The results can help schools select or develop curricula to address a number of topics, including violence prevention.

- **School Health Index (SHI).** The SHI is a self-assessment and planning tool that schools can use to improve their health and safety policies and programs. Five topics are covered, including violence.

- **National Centers for Youth Violence Prevention (YVPC).** Through collaborations between researchers and local organizations (including the local health department), the YVPCs work with high-risk communities to carry out and evaluate a multifaceted, science-based approach for reducing youth violence.

- **Guide to Community Preventive Services.** The Community Guide is a resource for systematic reviews of research and recommendations about what works to improve public health. Examination of youth violence prevention strategies have included firearm laws, therapeutic foster care, universal school-based violence prevention programs, and transfer of juveniles to adult courts.

- **Striving To Reduce Youth Violence Everywhere (STRYVE).** CDC's national STRYVE initiative provides information, training, and tools to help increase public health leadership in preventing youth violence, promote the widespread use of evidence-based prevention strategies, and reduce national rates of youth violence.

Chapter 17

Abuse in Pregnancy

Chapter Contents

Section 17.1

Domestic Violence during Pregnancy: Prevalence and Consequences

Text in this section is excerpted from "Practical Implications of Current Intimate Partner Violence Research for Victim Advocates and Service Providers," National Criminal Justice Reference Service (NCJRS), January 9, 2013.

What Are the Special Risks of IPV against Pregnant Women?

Domestic violence significantly increases the risk of pregnancy trauma and placental abruption which account for more than ten percent of perinatal deaths. If women suffer domestic violence during the prenatal period, they are 30 times at risk for clinical pregnancy trauma and 5 times higher risk for experiencing placental abruption compared with women who did not report domestic violence.

Researchers looked at medical records for more than 2,873 diverse women who gave birth in 2000 to 2002 in Syracuse, New York. They found that 3.7 percent reported domestic violence during the prenatal period. Even after controlling for other risk factors and social demographic variables associated with pregnancy trauma and placental abruption, IPV was found to be an independent and significant risk for pregnancy trauma and placental abruption.

IPV during pregnancy is associated with additional adverse pregnancy outcomes, including preterm birth and having a low birth weight baby, as well as increased risk of cesarean delivery, uterine rupture, hemorrhage and antenatal hospitalization. It is also linked with higher rates of maternal morbidity, including low weight gain, anemia, kidney infections, and first- and second-trimester bleeding. IPV is also a cause of depression and other psychological problems. Women who are abused during pregnancy are more likely to delay entry into prenatal care.

In fact, despite the expenditure of billions of dollars on health care in the United States, the US ranks 27th out of 33 developed countries for life expectancy at birth because a significant cause of infant mortality is complications related to pre-term birth and/or low birth rate outcomes linked to IPV.

What Is the Relationship Between Abuse during Pregnancy and Post-Partum Depression?

Studies in Los Angeles, Brazil, Australia, and the United Kingdom have all documented a significant association between intimate partner violence and post-natal depression. They first looked at 210 low income Latina women from two clinics in Los Angeles, finding that those who endured violence at the hands of a partner during or within a year of pregnancy were more than five times (5.4) more likely to suffer postpartum depression than women who had not experienced such violence. In fact, intimate partner violence turned out to be a much stronger prenatal predictor of postpartum depression than even prenatal depression, generally considered the most significant predictor. In addition, the intimate partner violence had a stronger effect on postpartum depression than prior episodes of trauma from either partners or non-partners.

The Brazilian study found the association between intimate partner violence and postnatal depression, but also found that intimate-partner psychological violence during pregnancy was strongly associated with the development of postnatal depression, independent of accompanying physical or sexual abuse. The study involved 1,045 pregnant Brazilian women. It also found that psychological violence was the most common form of intimate partner violence in the study.

The Australian study found that 40 percent of first-time mothers reporting depression post-partum also reported IPV. The risk of post-partum depression was found to be three times higher for women suffering emotional abuse and four times higher for those suffering physical abuse. Most of the reports of depression occurred more than six months after delivery.

The UK research assessed 13,617 women and found that those who suffered emotional or physical abuse during pregnancy were 2.5 times more likely to have depressive symptoms when their child was eight weeks old (25 percent) compared to those who had not (10 percent). The study also found that while seven percent of the women reported emotional and/or physical violence at 18 weeks gestation, at 33 months after the child was born, rates increased to 14 percent of the women experiencing domestic violence. Almost three-quarters of women who experienced antenatal domestic violence pregnancy also experienced post-natal violence.

Is There a Link between Abortions and IPV?

Numerous studies here and abroad link abortions with domestic violence. The link ranges from 20 percent in Canada for physical abuse and 27 percent for sexual abuse, to 33 percent in New Zealand, and 35.1 percent in England.

Research in the United States found that of the women having abortions in North Carolina up to 31.4 percent had experienced physical or sexual abuse at some time in their lives and, of these, more than half had witnessed domestic violence as children. Almost 22 percent had experienced abuse over the past year.

A more recent study of 986 women seeking abortions in Iowa found nearly 14 percent had experienced intimate partner violence in the previous 12 months. Interestingly, however, the abuse was mostly (74 percent) not by the current partner. One researcher surmised that the women may seek an abortion after leaving an abusive relationship for fear of the former partner harming the child, especially when the former partner is the biological father.

A study in Quebec compared women seeking abortions with those who did not. It found significant differences in demographics between pregnant women experiencing IPV and those not. Those seeking abortions were younger, single or in a relationship "that was in difficulty or breaking down," less educated, had lower incomes, had a prior abortion, and their pregnancies were more likely unplanned. They were also significantly at greater risk for being victims of abuse, including abuse over their lifetime, as well as physical, psychological, and sexual abuse in the past year.

The risk of physical and or sexual IPV in the past year was almost four times higher for the women seeking an abortion than those continuing their pregnancies. Although women with planned pregnancies were less likely to seek abortions, the majority of women with planned pregnancies seeking abortions had suffered abuse. Researchers concluded the IPV victims changed their minds and sought abortions so as "not to bring a child into the world under conditions of violence."

Section 17.2

Stress of Domestic Violence Can Be Passed to Unborn Children

Text in this section is excerpted from "Practical Implications of
Current Intimate Partner Violence Research for Victim Advocates
and Service Providers," National Criminal Justice Reference
Service (NCJRS), January 9, 2013.

Can Prenatal Exposure to IPV Adversely Affect the Health of the Child?

Prenatal exposure to maternal stress caused by IPV can have lifelong implications for the child, including behavioral problems and
even mental illness. A recent small study of 25 children, teens and
their mothers found that children, even teenage children, whose mothers had been abuse victims during pregnancy, had altered expression
of a gene linked to stress response and behavioral problems. The
research suggests that the genetic alteration associated with their
mother's abuse while pregnant could impair their ability to cope with
stress and the altered gene expression in the womb can persist into
adulthood.

Another study looked at the specific behavior of children of women
who had experienced antenatal violence. It documented the children
were more likely to have behavioural problems. The behavioral problems of these children, recorded at 42 months of age, included hyperactivity, emotion, and conduct problems. Antenatal violence was more
commonly reported in the mothers of children with behavioral problems at 42 months (11 percent) compared with mothers with children
with no problems (7 percent).

Further, a large study of more than 5 million pregnant women in
California over a 10-year period (1991-2002) found an association
between IPV assaults and low birth weight babies. Infants born to
women who were hospitalized for injuries received from an assault
during their pregnancies weighed, on average, one-third pound less
than did infants born to women who were not hospitalized. Assaults
in the first trimester were associated with the largest decrease in

birth weight. Low birth weight babies have an increased risk of death or of developing several health and developmental disorders, including greater risk for sudden infant death syndrome (SIDS), breathing problems, cerebral palsy, heart disorders and learning disabilities.

Chapter 18

Intimate Partner Violence against Women with Disabilities

Are Women with Disabilities at Increased Risk for IPV?

Criminal justice-based surveys and health-based surveys produce different estimates about the prevalence of IPV experienced by women with disabilities compared with women without disabilities. The national, multi-state crime surveys conducted by the U.S. Department of Justice suggest that people with disabilities are at no greater risk of IPV than those without, although people with disabilities are at elevated risk of sexual assault.

The NCVS identified six types of disabilities: sensory, physical, cognitive functioning, self-care, go-outside-the-home, and employment. It defines "disabilities" as a long-lasting (six months or more) sensory, physical, mental, or emotional condition that makes it difficult for a person to perform daily living activities." Women with disabilities are more likely than men with disabilities to be victims of IPV (16 percent vs. 5 percent).

Text in this chapter is excerpted from "Practical Implications of Current Intimate Partner Violence Research for Victim Advocates and Service Providers," National Criminal Justice Reference Service (NCJRS), January 9, 2013.

The NCVS also found that the risk of IPV for women with and without a disability is basically equivalent (27.3 percent vs. 24.1 percent), and the risk for IPV was comparable for persons with and without disabilities (13 percent vs. 14 percent). Women with disabilities are more likely than men with disabilities to be victims of IPV (16 percent vs. 5 percent). However, the NCVS found that persons with a disability have an age-adjusted rate of rape or sexual assault that is more than twice the rate for persons without a disability.

Yet, in 2000, the NVAWS reported that there is "no empirical evidence that having a disability increases one's risk of intimate partner violence."

On the other hand, the 2006 Behavioral Risk Factor Surveillance System Survey (BRFSS), conducted across seven states, confirmed that women with a disability are more likely to experience IPV than those without a disability. The survey reached 23,154 female respondents of whom 6,309 had a disability. Researchers found that women with a disability were significantly more likely to report experiencing some form of IPV in their lifetime, when compared with women without a disability (37.3 percent vs. 20.6 percent). Women with a disability were more likely to report ever being threatened with violence (28.5 percent vs. 15.4 percent without a disability) and hit, slapped, pushed, kicked or physically hurt (30.6 percent vs. 15.7 percent without a disability) by an intimate partner. Similarly, women with a disability were more likely to report ever experiencing unwanted sex by an intimate partner than those without a disability (19.7 percent vs. 8.2 percent).

Other analysis of the 2006 BRFSS data documented that the health problems of women IPV victims with disabilities were greater than those of women with disabilities that did not experience IPV. Women with disabilities who experienced IPV were found to be 35 percent less likely to report their health as good to excellent and 58 percent more likely to report an unmet health care need owing to costs than their disabled counterparts not experiencing IPV.

Data from the General Social Survey of Statistics Canada (GSS), 1999, confirms many other studies in finding that there is no statistical difference in violence inflicted on women with disabilities by their intimate partners as compared to women without disabilities, but only in a one year retrospective. When examining the five years prior to the survey, the prevalence of violence inflicted by intimate partners of women with disabilities was significantly higher and the violence more severe than the IPV against women without disabilities.

Similarly, a meta-analysis of 26 prior studies that included some 21,500 people with a range of physical and mental disabilities from seven countries (Australia, Canada, New Zealand, Taiwan, the United Kingdom, United States, and South Africa) found that disabled adults are 1.5 times more likely to be a victim of intimate partner violence, sexual assault or other physical violence than those without a disability. Those with mental illness are nearly four times more likely to be victimized. About three percent of people with physical, mental, emotional or other health problems that restrict activities experienced violence within the past 12 months. About six percent of people with intellectual disabilities were victimized in the past year, while 25 percent of people with mental illnesses were abused. While the studies aggregated all types of violent victimization against victims, three of the studies included, covering 574 individuals with mental illness, found the risks of intimate partner violence at nearly 40 percent.

According to the prime researcher, "Lifetime exposure to violence, and the proportions of individuals with disability who are directly threatened with violence or otherwise live in fear of becoming a victim, are likely to be substantially higher than the prime researcher's estimate." There are several reasons cited in the social science literature for the paucity of research on and undercounting of IPV against women with disabilities.

One important reason for possible undercounting is that the tactics of abuse measured in most survey research do not include additional, and perhaps more salient, tactics of abuse utilized by intimate partners against women with disabilities. Women with disabilities may not be fully included because of the misconception that women with disabilities are asexual and not engaged in intimate relationships. Women with disabilities are devalued, "roleless" and marginalized in multiple, complex ways.

Are Women Who Are Deaf at Increased Risk for IPV?

There is a dearth of research on the prevalence of IPV against women who are deaf or hard of hearing. Most figures are anecdotal, and estimate that IPV victimization rates are close to equivalent between deaf and hearing women. A domestic violence program specifically serving deaf women estimates that 25 percent of deaf women are victims of IPV annually. A recent study of deaf college women between the ages of 18 and 25 who had been in a dating or intimate relationship the year prior to the study found that twice as many deaf undergraduate women were victimized by a dating or intimate partner as were hearing women students. Although the average number of physical assaults and sexual coercion victimizations of deaf and hearing students was comparable, deaf women reported significantly higher rates of psychological aggression.

Chapter 19

Abuse of Men

Chapter Contents

Section 19.1

About Domestic Violence against Men

Text in this section is excerpted from "5 Signs That You
May Be in an Abusive Relationship," Office of Family
Assistance (OFA), November 5, 2015.

Some Signs That You May Be in an Abusive Relationship

Domestic Violence is a violation to a person at the core of their
being. It betrays love, destroys trust, inflicts irrevocable damage, and
often leaves a jaded perception of love in its wake. Many individuals
that have been harmed by an intimate partner feel afraid, embarrassed, blame themselves, and believe they are unable to reveal their
pain to family members, friends, or others; even when they are in dire
need of assistance.

Contrary to the very perilous myth, domestic violence is not gender based. According to the National Coalition Against Domestic
Violence (NCADV), 1 in 4 men have been victims of some form of
physical violence by an intimate partner. Due to society's general
apathetic response when it comes to the abuse of men (despite the
severity), domestic violence is often dismissed when men seek assistance from law enforcement and social services agencies. Men are
threatened, physically, emotionally, verbally, psychologically abused,
and in many instances seriously injured by the person that bears
their last name; the one they have vowed to love, promised to protect, provide for, and never harm; by the person they share a child/
children with.

Domestic violence is an incredibly dangerous crime, and behaviors
can be very difficult to detect; especially for victims. It can be as subtle
as an unkind word or as blatant as a slap across the face. Insecurities
are masked, and what appears in the beginning stages as attentive,
generous, and concerned; becomes possessive, extremely jealous, and
controlling.

It is important to evaluate relationships daily, and take inventory
of situations that may have given you pause.

You might be experiencing domestic violence if your partner:

1. Monitors your phone calls, emails, text messages, social media accounts; micromanages your time; make you account for every minute of your time (when you run errands, visit friends, commute to work);

2. Is overly critical; insulting; humiliates you (public or private); makes threats; blackmails you to expose private / sensitive personal information;

3. Acts insanely jealous; possessive; constantly accusing you of being unfaithful; smothers you/ 'clingy'; shows up unannounced (home, job, gym); stalks you; calls excessively;

4. Is hypersensitive; has unpredictable, radical mood changes; explosive temper; denies/minimizes the abuse/ blames you for the violent behavior (your fault); and

5. Threatens you with weapons; hit; kick; shove; slap; strangle; spit; or otherwise hurts you, your children, pets; cause visible injuries (bruises, cuts, burns); destroys /vandalize property (cell phone, car, home).

Your partner might offer reasonable explanations, apologize, promise to change, attend counseling, or make spiritual commitments; however, it is crucial to understand that domestic violence is cyclical, becoming more frequent and severe over time.

Despite many valiant efforts, victims cannot stop their partner's abusive behavior, and ultimatums don't make people change. Abuse isn't a couple's issue, but rather the choice of the abuser. Know your strength. Know your limitations.

Section 19.2

Sexual Assault of Men

Text in this section is excerpted from "Men and Sexual Trauma," U.S. Department of Veterans Affairs (VA), September 2, 2015.

Men and Sexual Trauma

At least 10% of men in our country have suffered from trauma as a result of sexual assault. Like women, men who experience sexual assault may suffer from depression, PTSD, and other emotional problems as a result. However, because men and women have different life experiences due to their different gender roles, emotional symptoms following trauma can look different in men than they do in women.

Who Are the Perpetrators of Male Sexual Assault?

- Those who sexually assault men or boys differ in a number of ways from those who assault only females.

- Boys are more likely than girls to be sexually abused by strangers or by authority figures in organizations such as schools, the church, or athletics programs.

- Those who sexually assault males usually choose young men and male adolescents (the average age is 17 years old) as their victims and are more likely to assault many victims, compared to those who sexually assault females.

- Perpetrators often assault young males in isolated areas where help is not readily available. For instance, a perpetrator who assaults males may pick up a teenage hitchhiker on a remote road or find some other way to isolate his intended victim.

- As is true about those who assault and sexually abuse women and girls, most perpetrators of males are men. Specifically, men are perpetrators in about 86% of male victimization cases.

- Despite popular belief that only gay men would sexually assault men or boys, most male perpetrators identify themselves as heterosexuals and often have consensual sexual relationships with women.

What Are Some Symptoms Related to Sexual Trauma in Boys and Men?

Particularly when the assailant is a woman, the impact of sexual assault upon men may be downplayed by professionals and the public. However, men who have early sexual experiences with adults report problems in various areas at a much higher rate than those who do not.

Emotional Disorders

Men and boys who have been sexually assaulted are more likely to suffer from PTSD, anxiety disorders, and depression than those who have never been abused sexually.

Substance Abuse

Men who have been sexually assaulted have a high incidence of alcohol and drug use. For example, the probability for alcohol problems in adulthood is about 80% for men who have experienced sexual abuse, as compared to 11% for men who have never been sexually abused.

Encopresis

One study revealed that a percentage of boys who suffer from encopresis (bowel incontinence) had been sexually abused.

Risk-Taking Behavior

Exposure to sexual trauma can lead to risk-taking behavior during adolescence, such as running away and other delinquent behaviors. Having been sexually assaulted also makes boys more likely to engage in behaviors that put them at risk for contracting HIV (such as having sex without using condoms).

How Does Male Gender Socialization Affect the Recognition of Male Sexual Assault?

- Men who have not dealt with the symptoms of their sexual assault may experience confusion about their sexuality and role as men (their gender role). This confusion occurs for many reasons. The traditional gender role for men in our society dictates that males be strong, self-reliant, and in control. Our society often does not recognize that men and boys can also be victims. Boys and men may be taught that being victimized implies that they are weak and, thus, not a man.

- Furthermore, when the perpetrator of a sexual assault is a man, feelings of shame, stigmatization, and negative reactions from others may also result from the social taboos.

- When the perpetrator of a sexual assault is a woman, some people do not take the assault seriously, and men may feel as though they are unheard and unrecognized as victims.

- Parents often know very little about male sexual assault and may harm their male children who are sexually abused by downplaying or denying the experience.

What Impact Does Gender Socialization Have upon Men Who Have Been Sexually Assaulted?

Because of their experience of sexual assault, some men attempt to prove their masculinity by becoming hyper-masculine. For example, some men deal with their experience of sexual assault by having multiple female sexual partners or engaging in dangerous "macho" behaviors to prove their masculinity. Parents of boys who have been sexually abused may inadvertently encourage this process.

Men who acknowledge their assault may have to struggle with feeling ignored and invalidated by others who do not recognize that men can also be victimized.

Because of ignorance and myths about sexual abuse, men sometimes fear that the sexual assault by another man will cause them to become gay. This belief is false. Sexual assault does not cause someone to have a particular sexual orientation.

Because of these various gender-related issues, men are more likely than women to feel ashamed of the assault, to not talk about it, and to not seek help from professionals.

Are Men Who Were Sexually Assaulted as Children More Likely to Become Child Molesters?

Another myth that male victims of sexual assault face is the assumption that they will become abusers themselves. For instance, they may have heard that survivors of sexual abuse tend to repeat the cycle of abuse by abusing children themselves. Some research has shown that men who were sexually abused by men during their childhood have a greater number of sexual thoughts and fantasies about sexual contact with male children and adolescents. However, it is important to know that **most male victims of child sexual abuse do not become sex offenders**.

Furthermore, many male perpetrators do not have a history of child sexual abuse. Rather, sexual offenders more often grew up in families where they suffered from several other forms of abuse, such as physical and emotional. Men who assault others also have difficulty with empathy, and thus put their own needs above the needs of their victims.

Is There Help for Men Who Have Been Sexually Assaulted?

It is important for men who have been sexually assaulted to understand the connection between sexual assault and hyper-masculine, aggressive, and self-destructive behavior. Through therapy, men often learn to resist myths about what a "real man" is and adopt a more realistic model for safe and rewarding living.

It is important for men who have been sexually assaulted and who are confused about their sexual orientation to confront misleading societal ideas about sexual assault and homosexuality.

Men who have been assaulted often feel stigmatized, which can be the most damaging aspect of the assault. It is important for men to discuss the assault with a caring and unbiased support person, whether that person is a friend, clergyman, or clinician. However, it is vital that this person be knowledgeable about sexual assault and men.

A local rape crisis center may be able to refer men to mental-health practitioners who are well-informed about the needs of male sexual assault victims.

Summary

There is a bias in our culture against viewing the sexual assault of boys and men as prevalent and abusive. Because of this bias, there is a belief that boys and men do not experience abuse and do not suffer from the same negative impact that girls and women do. However, research shows that at least 10% of boys and men are sexually assaulted and that boys and men can suffer profoundly from the experience. Because so few people have information about male sexual assault, men often suffer from a sense of being different, which can make it more difficult for men to seek help. If you are a man who has been assaulted and you suffer from any of these difficulties, please seek help from a mental-health professional who has expertise working with men who have been sexually assaulted.

Chapter 20

Elder Abuse

Chapter Contents

Section 20.1

Causes and Characteristics of Elder Abuse

Text in this section is excerpted from "Causes and Characteristics of
Elder Abuse," National Institute of Justice (NIJ), January 7, 2013.

Understanding the Causes of Elder Abuse

Because concern for elder abuse as a criminal issue is a fairly recent
development, there are gaps in our knowledge about the extent and
causes of such abuse.

The majority of research on elder mistreatment has focused on victims; the motivations of abusers and the relationship between abuses
and victims have received little attention. This produces an incomplete
picture of the dynamics fueling elder abuse. Also, the field of research
has relied heavily on the caregiver stress model, which holds that elder
abuse can be attributed to the stress associated with providing care
and assistance to frail, highly dependent elderly people. However, this
model does not fit all situations and types of elder abuse.

The field lacks an adequate guiding theory to explain the range
of causes behind elder abuse and promote systematic data collection.

Researchers have adapted a number of existing theories of interpersonal violence to supplement the study of elder abuse and have
proposed a range of explanations:

- Abusers have learned from the behavior of others around them
  that violence is a way to solve problems or obtain a desired
  outcome.

- Abusers feel they don't receive enough benefit or recognition
  from their relationship with the elderly person, so they resort to
  violence in an effort to obtain their "fair share."

- A combination of background and current factors, such as recent
  conflicts and a family history of "solving" problems through violence, influences the relationship.

- Abusers use a pattern of coercive tactics to gain and maintain
  power and control in a relationship.

- Many factors in elder abuse arise through individual, relationship, community and societal influences.

- Elder abuse can be attributed to both the victim's and the abuser's social and biomedical characteristics, the nature of their relationship, and power dynamics, within their shared environment of family and friends.

A more robust response to elder abuse will need to be guided by theory that accounts for both the victim and the abuser, including their cognitive functioning, the types of abuse, the domestic setting, and the nature of their relationship.

Case Characteristics of Elder Abuse in Domestic Settings

Elder abuse cases tend to be multidimensional. Improving our understanding of the complexity of elder abuse cases can help researchers both develop and evaluate theory-based explanations for abuse. Recent research has shed some light on case characteristics common to different types of elder abuse.

Physical abuse. Contrary to common belief, many elderly victims of physical abuse are high functioning. The abuser is typically a family member, often the adult offspring of the victim. The abuser may be a long-term dependent of the victim because of health or financial issues and may take out resentment for this dependence on the elderly victim. These victims are generally aware that they are being mistreated, but their sense of parental or family obligation makes them reluctant to cut off the abuser.

Neglect. In cases of elder neglect, the victim may be physically frail or cognitively vulnerable. The caregiver does not take adequate care of the victim, who may acknowledge his or her own shortcomings as a parent and conclude that the tables are being turned — and that he or she deserves no better.

Financial exploitation. Victims of financial exploitation often lack someone with whom they can discuss and monitor financial issues. They may have an emerging, unrecognized cognitive impairment; worry about a future loss of independence; and be overly trusting of a caregiver capable of theft, fraud and misuse of assets.

Hybrid cases. Cases where financial exploitation is combined with physical abuse or neglect typically involve financially dependent family members, particularly adult offspring, who have been cared for by the elderly person. As the elderly person declines in health and becomes more socially isolated, he or she relies more on the abuser for care, resulting in a mutual dependency. Such hybrid cases are unique in many ways and tend to have worse outcomes for victims than other kinds of elder abuse, perhaps because the abuse is accompanied by the stress of financial loss.

Section 20.2

Identifying Elder Abuse

Text in this section is excerpted from "Identifying Elder Abuse,"
National Institute of Justice (NIJ), May 6, 2013.

Bruising in the Geriatric Population

Documenting normal bruising patterns in this population is the first step toward differentiating accidental from suspicious bruising. An NIJ-funded study found that:

- Accidental bruises occur in a predictable pattern.

- Most accidental large bruises are on the extremities.

- The initial color and appearance of bruises changes over time and is less predictable than previously thought.

- Individuals who are on medications known to make bruising more severe and those with compromised functional ability are more likely to have multiple bruises.

The second step in differentiating accidental from suspicious bruising is to document bruises in elderly individuals who are confirmed victims of elder mistreatment. A follow-up study funded by NIJ found that:

- Sixty percent of examined bruises were inflicted, 14 percent were accidental and 26 percent were of unknown causes. Most participants from the study of non-abused elders (71 percent) could not identify the cause of any of their bruises.

- A majority of abused elders (56 percent) had a large bruise (>5 cm), which is much higher than the percent of non-abused elders from the previous study with a large bruise (7 percent).

- Abused older adults were more likely than non-abused elders to have bruises on the head, neck or torso.

Determining Abuse as a Cause of Elder Death

NIJ funded research examining the decision-making processes medical examiners and coroners use when investigating suspicious deaths.

One study found that medical examiners can rarely differentiate symptoms of illness from signs of abuse in elderly decedents. As a result, signs of abuse commonly recognized in younger decedents are missed in elders, and abuse is rarely seen as a cause of death. These findings call for additional research on both the decision-making practices of medical examiners and the forensic markers of elder mistreatment. They also highlight the need for medical examiners to receive additional training on this issue.

Another study documented practices that 46 of the 58 California coroner/medical examiner (CME) agencies use to decide whether to investigate an elder's death. This study confirmed that CME offices do not assume jurisdiction over many elder deaths that experts in the field of elder mistreatment thought should be investigated because of signs of potential abuse or neglect.

In a subsequent phase of the project, the researchers worked with a Multidisciplinary Advisory Board to develop the Elder Suspicious Death Field Screen (ESDFS) and conducted a pilot study in three California CME agencies. Researchers expected to receive several thousand ESDFS forms during the six-month pilot study. Two of the agencies discontinued use of the ESDFS during the study, however, and in the end, only 115 ESDFS forms were completed. An expert panel reviewed 55 of the completed forms. The panel believed that two-thirds of the cases they reviewed should have received a higher level of investigation then was undertaken. In particular, the expert panel agreed that in many of the "waived" cases, someone should have viewed the entire body. Post-pilot-test interviews revealed that agencies' resistance to using the ESDFS was related to: (1) high workload and burnout; (2) a lack of integration between the ESDFS and current automated systems or redundancy with current screening items; and (3) investigators who saw no benefit to using the ESDFS.

In a separate study, researchers examined implementation of the Arkansas law giving county medical examiners the authority to investigate deaths occurring in long-term care facilities (LCF). They conducted focus group interviews with medical examiners, coroners and geriatricians from 27 states to determine their involvement in investigations into the deaths of LCF residents. Although the researchers' findings suggest that the Arkansas law had a positive impact on attention to elder mistreatment and the quality of care of LCF residents in Pulaski county, whether care has improved state-wide is not clear because of differences in implementation.

The second phase of this study concluded in 2007. The resulting data indicate that the Arkansas Long-Term Care Reporting law, which mandated that all deaths that occur in nursing homes in Arkansas be investigated officially, has not made a difference in quality of care in the state. The project also revealed additional factors associated with higher level of mistreatment suspicion, including family dissatisfaction with care; minority race; tube feeding; the presence of a severe pressure sore or recent ostomy.

Potential Markers for Elder Mistreatment

Researchers in Arkansas identified specific characteristics within four categories of markers that investigators can look for to determine whether elder mistreatment is occurring or has occurred.

This study is ongoing; the researchers hope to:

- Determine whether the Arkansas Long-Term Care Reporting law has actually made a difference in quality of care.

- Further elucidate markers.

- Development of an adaptive investigative model for coroners and medical examiners.

Better Tools to Assess Psychological and Financial Abuse

NIJ-funded researchers have developed and tested two measurement tools that give the field better ways to assess financial and psychological abuse of elders:

- Older Adults Psychological Abuse Measure, which has 31 items.

- Older Adults Financial Exploitation Measure, which has 30 items.

The researchers used concept mapping to develop measurements of abuse. They tested the tools on 226 clients of adult protective services with substantiated cases of abuse.

Adult Protective Services in six sites in Illinois are using the two new measures along with assessment tools to measure physical and sexual abuse and neglect. They are doing so as part of an NIJ-funded followup project designed to pilot test a prototype for an electronic Elder Abuse Decision Support System— a computer-based application of the developed measures to help practitioners identify abuse.

Section 20.3

Elder Abuse: Risk and Protective Factors

Text in this section is excerpted from "Elder Abuse: Risk and Protective Factors," Centers for Disease Control and Prevention (CDC), January 14, 2014.

Risk Factors

A combination of individual, relational, community, and societal factors contribute to the risk of becoming a perpetrator of elder abuse. They are contributing factors and may or may not be direct causes.

Understanding these factors can help identify various opportunities for prevention.

Risk Factors for Perpetration

Individual Level

- Current diagnosis of mental illness

- Current abuse of alcohol

- High levels of hostility

- Poor or inadequate preparation or training for care giving responsibilities

- Assumption of caregiving responsibilities at an early age
- Inadequate coping skills
- Exposure to abuse as a child

Relationship Level

- High financial and emotional dependence upon a vulnerable elder
- Past experience of disruptive behavior
- Lack of social support
- Lack of formal support

Community Level

- Formal services, such as respite care for those providing care to elders, are limited, inaccessible, or unavailable

Societal Level

A culture where:

- there is high tolerance and acceptance of aggressive behavior;
- health care personnel, guardians, and other agents are given greater freedom in routine care provision and decision making;
- family members are expected to care for elders without seeking help from others;
- persons are encouraged to endure suffering or remain silent regarding their pains; or
- there are negative beliefs about aging and elders.

In addition to the above factors, there are also specific characteristics of institutional settings that may increase the risk for perpetration of vulnerable elders in these settings, including: unsympathetic or negative attitudes toward residents, chronic staffing problems, lack of administrative oversight, staff burnout, and stressful working conditions.

Protective Factors

Protective factors reduce risk for perpetrating abuse and neglect. Protective factors have not been studied as extensively or rigorously as risk factors. However, identifying and understanding protective factors are equally as important as researching risk factors.

Several potential protective factors are identified below. Research is needed to determine whether these factors do indeed buffer elders from abuse.

Protective Factors for Perpetration

Relationship Level

- Having numerous, strong relationships with people of varying social status

Community Level

- Coordination of resources and services among community agencies and organizations that serve the elderly population and their caregivers.
- Higher levels of community cohesion and a strong sense of community or community identity
- Higher levels of community functionality and greater collective efficacy

Factors within institutional settings that may be protective include: effective monitoring systems in place; solid institutional policies and procedures regarding patient care; regular training on elder abuse and neglect for employees; education about and clear guidance on how durable power of attorney is to be used; and regular visits by family members, volunteers, and social workers.

Section 20.4

Financial Exploitation of the Elderly

This section includes excerpts from "Financial Exploitation of
the Elderly," National Institute of Justice (NIJ), May 12, 2015;
and text from "Sexual Abuse of the Elderly," National Institute of
Justice (NIJ), April 16, 2014.

Incidence of Financial Exploitation

The U.S. has no national reporting mechanism to track the financial exploitation of elders, but in a 1998 study by the National Center
on Elder Abuse, financial abuse accounted for about 12 percent of all
elder abuse reported nationally in 1993 and 1994 and 30 percent of
substantiated elder abuse reported submitted to adult protective services in 1996, after reports of self-neglect were excluded.

A 2000 survey by the National Association of Adult Protective Services Administrators conducted for the National Center on Elder Abuse
found that financial exploitation comprised 13 percent of the mistreatment allegations investigated. Many experts in the field, however,
believe that the level of elder exploitation may well exceed what has
been reported to authorities and documented by researchers.

One NIJ-funded study of 2,000 community-residing elderly individuals in Arizona and Florida found that 5.6 percent reported being
victims of financial mistreatment. The most common types of financial
mistreatment were having someone steal or spend their money, sell
or take their property, or forge their signature. The risk of financial
mistreatment was higher for individuals who engaged in fewer social
or other activities outside of the home (e.g., participating in social
activities away from home, getting together with people who do not
live in the home, going to the movies), had low self-control, were male
and identified as a racial minority.

Characteristics of Financial Exploitation

NIJ-funded researchers examined two sets of data to determine
some of the differences between cases where an elderly person was

the victim of financial exploitation and those where he or she was the victim of both financial exploitation and neglect or physical abuse, a combination referred to as hybrid financial exploitation.

The researchers, who studied 54 cases in depth — 38 were financial exploitation alone, and 16 were hybrid financial exploitation — found that the characteristics and dynamics of the two types of cases vary depending on the type of exploitation involved. The data revealed several differences between the two types of cases.

The researchers identified two types of independence: physical and financial. Physically independent elders were able to care for themselves, could drive, and were cognitively intact and physically healthy. Financially independent elders had the financial assets to cover their needs and often owned their homes. Elderly victims who were physically and financially independent were more likely to experience pure financial exploitation.

Elderly victims experiencing hybrid financial exploitation tended to be financially independent but physically dependent. They had significant health problems, were unable to drive and were to some degree dependent on others for assistance.

Victims of hybrid financial exploitation were more likely than victims of pure financial exploitation to have:

- Been victimized by a relative.

- Experienced abuse multiple times over a longer period of time (123 months vs. 32 months for victims of financial exploitation alone without neglect or abuse).

- Suffered a negative health consequence, financial loss, a disruption in social relationships, or some combination of these as a consequence of their victimization.

Based on the larger dataset of all reported cases in Virginia, the researchers identified a number of characteristics of the 472 victims of financial exploitation. These victims:

- **Were independent.** Independent elders were 66 percent more likely to experience pure financial exploitation (without accompanying neglect or abuse) than the victims who were dependent.

- **Were not experiencing dementia or confusion.** Elders who were not experiencing dementia or confusion were 29 percent more likely to experience pure financial exploitation than the victims who were experiencing dementia or confusion.

- **Had abusers who were not overburdened in providing social support.** Elders with abusers who perceived that they had reliable social support were 88 percent more likely to experience pure financial exploitation compared to victims with abusers with overburdened social support.

The researchers also found that the 162 victims of hybrid financial exploitation were 81 percent more likely to experience hybrid exploitation when the abuser did not provide financial support to the victim, but the victim did provide financial support to the perpetrator.

Financial Exploitation of the Elderly in a Consumer Context

An NIJ-funded study sought to determine the nature and extent of consumer fraud victimization and to identify risk and protective factors for fraud victimization among elderly residents of Arizona and Florida.

Researchers found that nearly 60 percent of the 2,000 survey participants were targeted by at least one fraud attempt during the prior year. Approximately 14 percent of the study participants were fraud victims within the past year. The most common types of fraud were phony magazine subscriptions, prize scams, donations to nonexistent charities and retrieval of personal financial information under false pretenses.

Factors that consistently increase an elderly individual's likelihood of being targeted and experiencing financial fraud victimization include remote purchasing, low self-control and telemarketing purchases.

Respondents who purchased something in response to a telemarketing call from a company with whom they had not previously done business during the previous year increased their risk of becoming a fraud target by more than 200 percent and their risk of financial fraud victimization by more than 600 percent compared with those who had not made such purchases.

The study also sought to determine the extent to which residents were aware of and used their state-based fraud prevention programs. Overall, most participants were not familiar with their state-based programs.

Section 20.5

Prevalence of Elder Abuse

Text in this section is excerpted from "Extent of Elder Abuse Victimization," National Institute of Justice (NIJ), May 12, 2015.

Elder Abuse Victimization

The full extent of elder abuse is uncertain. There are few reliable national measures of elder abuse. This is partially because there is no uniform reporting system for elder abuse in the United States. Additionally, the available national incidence and prevalence data from administrative records are unreliable because states have different definitions of elder and different reporting mechanisms.

An NIJ-funded, nationally representative study of more than 7,000 community-residing elders found that approximately one in 10 elders reported experiencing at least one form of elder mistreatment in the past year.

Other large-scale studies of elder abuse have been undertaken, but the data used in many of those studies make it difficult to confidently draw conclusions about the national picture of elder abuse.

The Extent of Elder Abuse Among Community-Residing Elders

The NIJ-funded National Elder Mistreatment Study examined the prevalence of elder mistreatment and victimization among 7,000 elders living in the community:

- Eleven percent of elders reported experiencing at least one form of mistreatment — emotional, physical, sexual or potential neglect — in the past year.

- Financial exploitation by a family member in the past year was reported by 5.2 percent of elders.

- Past-year prevalence was 5.1 percent for emotional mistreatment, 1.6 percent for physical mistreatment, 0.6 percent for sexual mistreatment and 5.1 percent for potential neglect. Risk factors for elder mistreatment include:

- Low household income
- Unemployment or retirement
- Poor health
- Experiencing a prior traumatic event
- Low levels of reported social support

The Extent of Elder Abuse in Residential Care Facilities

Reports of Abuse in Assisted Living Facilities

In an NIJ-funded study of reports of abuse in assisted living facilities, verbal and psychological abuse were the most common forms of abuse reported by direct care workers. Overall, resident abuse by staff was relatively uncommon, but the study's findings indicate that there is room for improvement, especially for verbal and psychological abuse.

Findings:

- *Prevalence rates.* Researchers calculated one-year prevalence rates for resident abuse indicators. The highest rates were for items in the verbal (e.g., humiliating remarks, 203 per 1,000 residents) and psychological abuse (e.g., critical remarks, 163 per 1,000) categories. Generally, physical abuse, material exploitation and medication abuse items were less common. Sexual abuse items were the least common.

- *Factors associated with abuse.* Some facility- and individual-level factors associated with abuse were low staffing levels, residents with dementia or physical limitations, and having an administrator with a shorter tenure and lower education level.

Resident-to-Resident Abuse in Nursing Homes

Researchers and caregivers are increasingly recognizing resident-to-resident elder mistreatment as a source of abuse in residential care facilities. In an NIJ-funded study, researchers found that staff reported higher rates of resident-on-resident abuse than was documented in reports and charts.

The study sought to:

- Enhance institutional recognition of resident-to-resident abuse.

- Identify the most accurate method of reporting and detecting resident-to-resident mistreatment.

- Develop institutional guidelines for reporting resident-to-resident mistreatment in residential facilities.

Findings:

- *Prevalence.* The average number of incidents reported across the nursing homes ranged from 0 to 4.3, depending on the reporting mechanism — the direct service staff reported 4.3 incidents, but no incidents were documented in accident/incident reports.

- *Reporting accuracy.* The direct service staff were the most accurate mechanism for reporting or detecting resident-to-resident elder mistreatment. The residents themselves were the second most accurate mechanism. The facilities' accident/incident reports provided the smallest number of resident-to-resident mistreatment incidents.

  Environmental factors. Environmental factors (i.e., loud noise or congestion in public spaces due to equipment, such as walkers) may contribute to resident-on-resident mistreatment.

Recommendations

Researchers concluded that the discrepancy between staff-reported rates of resident-to-resident mistreatment and rates recorded in reports and charts illustrated the need for better documentation practices. To improve reporting, documentation and management, the researchers suggest institutional support in the form of staff training and institutional guidelines setting out standard practices for how to address resident-to-resident mistreatment.

Chapter 21

Abuse in the Lesbian, Gay, Bisexual, and Transgender (LGBT) Community

Chapter Contents

Section 21.1

Domestic Violence and LGBT Relationships

Text in this section is excerpted from "NISVS: An Overview of
2010 Findings on Victimization by Sexual Orientation," Centers for
Disease Control and Prevention (CDC), June 2013.

NISVS: An Overview of 2010 Findings on Victimization by Sexual Orientation

Little is known about the national prevalence of intimate partner
violence (IPV), sexual violence (SV), and stalking among lesbian, gay,
and bisexual women and men in the United States. The Centers for
Disease Control and Prevention's (CDC) National Intimate Partner
and Sexual Violence Survey (NISVS): 2010 Findings on Victimization
by Sexual Orientation is the first of its kind to present comparisons of
victimization by sexual orientation for women and men.

Key Findings on Victimization by Sexual Orientation

The Sexual Orientation Report indicates that individuals who
self-identify as lesbian, gay, and bisexual have an equal or higher
prevalence of experiencing IPV, SV, and stalking as compared to
self-identified heterosexuals. Bisexual women are disproportionally
impacted. They experienced a significantly higher lifetime prevalence
of rape, physical violence, and/or stalking by an intimate partner, and
rape and SV (other than rape) by any perpetrator, when compared to
both lesbian and heterosexual women.

*Sexual minority respondents reported levels of intimate partner
violence at rates equal to or higher than those of heterosexuals.*

- Forty-four percent of lesbian women, 61% of bisexual women,
  and 35% of heterosexual women experienced rape, physical violence, and/or stalking by an intimate partner in their
  lifetime.

- Twenty-six percent of gay men, 37% of bisexual men, and
  29% of heterosexual men experienced rape, physical violence,

and/or stalking by an intimate partner at some point in their lifetime.

• Approximately 1 in 5 bisexual women (22%) and nearly 1 in 10 heterosexual women (9%) have been raped by an intimate partner in their lifetime.

Rates of some form of sexual violence were higher among lesbian women, gay men, and bisexual women and men compared to heterosexual women and men.

• Approximately 1 in 8 lesbian women (13%), nearly half of bisexual women (46%), and 1 in 6 heterosexual women (17%) have been raped in their lifetime. This translates to an estimated 214,000 lesbian women, 1.5 million bisexual women, and 19 million heterosexual women.

• Four in 10 gay men (40%), nearly half of bisexual men (47%), and 1 in 5 heterosexual men (21%) have experienced SV other than rape in their lifetime. This translates into nearly 1.1 million gay men, 903,000 bisexual men, and 21.6 million heterosexual men.

Table 21.1. Lifetime prevalence of rape, physical violence, and/or stalking by an intimate partner

Women		Men	
Lesbian	44%	Gay	26%
Bisexual	61%	Bisexual	37%
Heterosexual	35%	Heterosexual	29%

Among rape victims, bisexual women experienced rape earlier in life compared to heterosexual women.

• Of those women who have been raped, almost half of bisexual women (48%) and more than a quarter of heterosexual women (28%) experienced their first completed rape between the ages of 11 and 17 years.

The rate of stalking among bisexual women is more than double the rate among heterosexual women.

• One in 3 bisexual women (37%) and 1 in 6 heterosexual women (16%) have experienced stalking victimization at some point during their lifetime in which they felt very fearful or believed that they or someone close to them would be harmed or killed. *This translates into 1.2 million bisexual women and 16.8 million heterosexual women.*

A higher percentage of bisexual women reported being concerned for their safety or injured as a result of IPV than lesbian or hetero sexual women.

- Approximately one-fifth of self-identified lesbian and heterosexual women (20% and 22%, respectively) and one-half of bisexual women (48%) reported they were concerned for their safety and/or reported at least one post-traumatic stress disorder symptom (20%, 46%, and 22%, respectively).

- Nearly 1 in 3 bisexual women (37%) and 1 in 7 heterosexual women (16%) were injured as a result of rape, physical violence, and/or stalking by an intimate partner.

Opportunities for Prevention and Action

The promotion of respectful, non violent relationships is key to preventing violence. Findings from the Sexual Orientation Report highlight the need for broad-based prevention efforts as well as services and support systems that address the specific needs of lesbian, gay, and bisexual women and men. It is important for all sectors of society, including individuals, families, and communities, to work together to end IPV, SV, and stalking. Opportunities for prevention and intervention include:

- Implementing prevention approaches that promote acceptance and recognition of healthy, respectful relationships regardless of sexual orientation.

- Including lesbian, gay, and bisexual persons in national, state, and local violence research.

- Referring victims and survivors to culturally appropriate accessible services.

Section 21.2

Bullying and LGBT Youth

Text in this section is excerpted from "You Can Stop the
Bullying of LGBT Youth," U.S. Department of Human and
Health Services (HHS), May 16, 2013.

You Can Stop the Bullying of LGBT Youth

Imagine walking down your high school hallway, knowing that
every person you passed by was judging you, marking you as someone
who does not belong. Imagine that you spent each day living for the
moment when you could go far away from everyone who mocked you,
bullied you, or treated you differently, simply because of your sexual
orientation, or perceived sexual orientation. This is the life for thousands of youth who struggle to maintain a mentally and physically
healthy life in the face of bullying and adversity while struggling with
their self-identity.

A 2011 study by the Gay, Lesbian & Straight Education Network
of 8,584 students (ages 13 to 20) found that:

- 81.9 percent of Lesbian, Gay, Bisexual and Transgender (LGBT)
  students reported being verbally harassed

- 38.3 percent reported being physically harassed

- 55.2 percent reported electronic harassment/ cyberbullying

- 18.3 percent reported being physically assaulted at school in the
  past year because of their sexual orientation

These numbers are hard to ignore. No one should feel unsafe,
unwelcome, and endure harassment and assault anywhere, especially
in a school environment. This same study found increased absenteeism, lowered educational aspirations and academic achievements,
and poorer psychological well-being in LGBT youth as a result of the
bullying they faced.

The Administration for Children and Families (ACF), in a Report
to Congress on the Runaway and Homeless Youth Programs in Fiscal
Years 2010 and 2011, cited studies that suggest 20 to 40 percent of

homeless youth identify as lesbian, gay, bisexual, transgender, or questioning. The same report stated that about one quarter of all homeless youth have run away from homes where they faced abuse and neglect. Though ACF's Family and Youth Services Bureau (FYSB) can help these homeless youth through many initiatives and centers, no child should have to face a lifetime of familial and social instability because of their sexual orientation.

Parents, schools, and communities can play an important role in creating environments where all youth can feel physically and emotionally safe. The White House and the Department of Health and Human Services have re-launched a website, StopBullying.gov. The website shows the types of bullying faced by all youth. It offers recommendations for building a safe environment for youth, whether they are heterosexual or LGBT. Included are the following:

- Build strong connections and keep the lines of communication open. Some LGBT youth often feel rejected. It is important for them to know that their families, friends, schools, and communities support them.

- Establish a safe environment at school. Schools can send a message that no one should be treated differently because they are, or are perceived to be, LGBT. Add Sexual orientation and gender identity protection to school policies.

- Create gay-straight alliances (GSAs). GSAs help create safer schools. Schools must allow these groups if they have other "non-curricular" clubs or groups.

- Protect privacy. Be careful not to disclose or discuss LGBT issues with parents or anyone else.

- We all have a responsibility to support all our youth. Department of Human and Health Services (HHS) strongly urges you to make sure you do your part to create a safe supportive environment for LGBT youth in your home, your schools, and in your community.

Section 21.3

Mistreatment of LGBT Elders

Text in this section is excerpted from "Mistreatment of
Lesbian, Gay, Bisexual, and Transgender (LGBT) Elders,"
Administration of Aging (AOA), March 2013.

Population Estimates of LGBT Elders

It has been estimated that **9 million Americans identify as
lesbian, gay, bisexual, or transgender (LGBT)**. It has also been
approximated that **1.5 million adults, aged 65 or older, are LGB**
(no transgender estimate provided).It should be noted, however, that
estimates of the LGBT population may vary depending upon measurement methods and consideration of those who may not self-identify as
LGBT due to societal stigma.

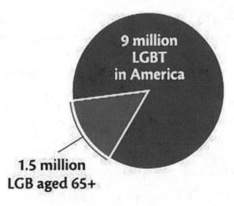

Figure 21.1. *Estimates of LGBT Elders*

LGBT Elders Face Multiple Challenges

LGBT elders face the typical challenges of aging, including the
possibility of elder abuse or domestic violence, in combination with the
**threat of discrimination and abuse due to their sexual orienta-
tion or gender identity**. In a 2006 study by Metlife Mature Market

283

Figure 21.2. *Estimates of LGBT Baby Boomers*

Institute, 27% of LGBT Baby Boomers reported that they had great concern about discrimination as they age.

Research Findings on Occurrence of Abuse

Unfortunately, prevalence and incidence studies regarding the abuse and neglect of LGBT elders are sorely lacking. Available data and information relating to the occurrence of abuse includes:

- In a survey of 416 LGB elders, aged 60 or older, **65% of respondents reported experiencing victimization due to sexual orientation** (e.g., verbal abuse, threat of violence, physical assault, sexual assault, threat of orientation disclosure, discrimination) and **29% had been physically attacked**. Men were physically attacked nearly three times more often. Those who had been physically attacked reported poorer current mental health. Many in the study were still closeted from others. Serious family or personal problems can result from disclosure of an older adult's LGB identity.

- Caregivers may not be accepting of LGBT elders. In a survey of 3,500 LGBT elders, 55 and older, **8.3% of the elders reported being abused or neglected by a caretaker because of homophobia** and **8.9% experienced blackmail or financial exploitation.**

- **Prejudice and hostility encountered by LGBT elder persons in institutional care facilities create difficult environments.** Staff may deny an LGBT elder's visitors,

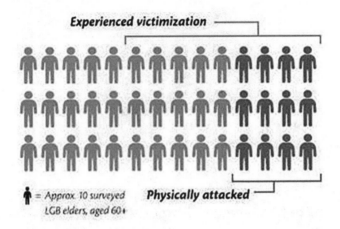

Figure 21.3. *Estimates of Abused LGBT Elders*

refuse to allow same-sex couples to share rooms, refuse to place a transgender elder in a ward that matches their gender identity, or keep partners from participation in medical decision making.

- Transphobia, or social prejudice against transgendered persons, may be more intense than that of homophobia with a **very high rate of violent victimization.**

- Cross study investigation reveals that transgender people, in general, are at high risk of abuse and violence. Initial data reported by MAP state that an average of **42% of transgender people have experienced some form of physical violence or abuse**. Further, an average **80% of transgender people have experienced verbal abuse or harassment** Therefore, it is a reasonable assumption that transgender elders may have experienced some form of abuse.

- Many transgender older adults have experienced mistreatment in long term care facilities. Examples include physical abuse, denial of personal care services, psychological abuse, being involuntarily "outed," and being prevented from dressing according to their gender identity. Others are refused admission into long-term care facilities. **The fear of discrimination and its reality result in underutilization of services.**

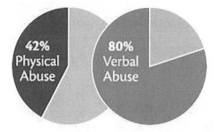

Figure 21.4. *Abuse Experienced by Transgender People*

Types of Discrimination Experienced by LGBT Elders

- Denial of visitors
- Refusal to allow same-sex couples to share rooms
- Refusal to place a transgender elder in a ward that matches their gender identity
- Keeping partners from participation in medical decision making

---

Types of Mistreatment Experienced by Transgender Elders

- Physical abuse
- Denial of personal care services
- Psychological abuse
- Being involuntarily "outed"
- Being prevented from dressing
- according to their gender identity
- Refused admission

Research Findings on Isolation as a Risk Factor

A focus group reported that the most pressing health and human service need for LGBT elders' is **dealing with social isolation**. Isolation is a risk factor for elder abuse. LGBT elders are more likely to age alone than heterosexuals.

Many LGBT older adults are at high risk for elder abuse, neglect, and various forms of exploitation because of **living in isolation and fear of the discrimination** they could encounter in mainstream aging settings.

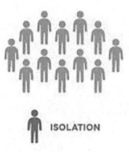

Figure 21.5. *Estimate of Isolated LDBT Elders*

Research Findings on Issues Affecting Help Seeking

- In growing up in a homophobic or transphobic environment, some LGBT elders may **go to extraordinary measures to hide their sexual orientation**. There may be such significant stigma for these elders that they will not label themselves. This may affect an abuse victims willingness to seek help, out of fear of needing to "out" themselves to authorities and face possible hostility. This may also affect their desire to enlist home care services out of fear of abuse.

- LGB adults from older generations lived under **severe stigmatization of their identities**. Many victims of attacks due to sexual orientation do not tell others of the attacks, out of fear that their sexual orientation will be disclosed or that authorities will act with hostility or indifference.

- Victimization because of sexual orientation can lead to **internalized homophobia manifested as guilt or shame**. Victims may come to believe that they are not worthy people and deserve loneliness, poor living conditions, and ill health. They may not want to seek or accept help and are at risk of self-neglect.

- For a victim of abuse in a same-sex relationship, it may be difficult to seek help because of the **personal, familial, and societal risks in coming out as gay or lesbian** and as a victim of domestic violence.

- Abusers may use victim fear of homophobia or **threaten to "out" their victims** to others as tools of control.

- **Legal discrimination** may discourage elder LGBT abuse victims from leaving abusive relationships because they may have no or limited legal rights to assets shared with the partner.

Tips for Working with LGBT Elders

- Be aware of the lack of legal protections for LGBT elders and the potential impact. For example, an elder gay man with limited income has no legal right in many states to a portion of his abusive partner's income.

- It is imperative that all who interface with the LGBT elder use the name and pronoun (e.g., he, she) used by the elder, regardless of legal identification or genitalia.

- Connect and build rapport with the LGBT elder by asking about their career/profession, friends, and personal effects.

- Listen especially carefully to the LGBT elder's input and desires.

- Be aware that not all couple relationships are heterosexual. Use the same terminology used by the elder (e.g., partner, roommate, friend) when referring to the other member of the couple. Ask the elder if the partner/roommate/friend can be counted on to provide care or financial assistance to them. Keep in mind that a large age gap between partners in a gay couple doesn't necessarily imply an exploitative relationship.

- Be prepared to be able to connect the elder to community resources for LGBT elders should they so desire (e.g., if they want to talk about being gay, lesbian, or transgendered).

- Lesbian and gay elders may have close networks of friends that may serve as a protective factor.

Gay men and lesbians tend to place high value on self-sufficiency and so may be hesitant to accept help in old age.

Section 21.4

Legal Rights for LGBT Victims of Domestic Violence

"Legal Rights for LGBT Victims of Domestic Violence,"
© 2016 Omnigraphics, Inc.
Reviewed January 2016.

Domestic violence affects all sorts of intimate relationships, including those of lesbian, gay, bisexual, and transgender (LGBT) people. In fact, research has shown that the prevalence of domestic violence among same-sex couples is between 15 and 50 percent, which is the same rate found among heterosexual couples. Yet people in same-sex relationships face a number of social and legal barriers that may limit their ability to protect themselves from domestic abuse.

One such barrier is common misconception that abuse is unlikely to occur between same-sex partners because there tends to be less disparity in their physical size and strength—or if it does occur, then it is "mutual battering." Compounding the problem, many LGBT people are reluctant to identify themselves as victims of domestic violence because they worry about encountering homophobia and discrimination. Some LGBT people believe that reporting domestic violence to law enforcement or utilizing support services could lead to involuntary outing of their sexual orientation or gender identity to family members or employers.

Civil Protection Orders

LGBT people may also find it more difficult to obtain legal protection against domestic abuse. One of the main legal tools used by survivors of domestic violence is the civil protection order (CPO). A CPO is an order issued by a family court that is intended to prevent domestic violence. Typically, the court orders the abuser to stop threatening or hurting the victim. In addition, it may order the abuser to stay away from the victim and other members of the household or family for up to five years.

Obtaining a CPO offers many benefits to survivors of domestic violence. It informs the abuser that domestic violence is a crime, and warns that any further incidents can result in arrest. It also establishes rules that the abuser must follow while the CPO is in effect, such as vacating the family home or paying child support. Finally, a CPO can stop the cycle of violence and ensure the victim's safety while they seek support and make plans for the future.

The process of obtaining a CPO generally involves two different legal hearings before a judge or magistrate. Experts recommend that people seeking a CPO hire an attorney to represent them in these proceedings. In the first one, called the *ex parte* hearing, the judge gathers information about the domestic violence complaint and decides whether the CPO request meets the requirements of state law. If so, the judge issues an *ex parte* CPO and schedules a full hearing within a week to ten days. In the full hearing, the judge hears testimony from the victim, the accused abuser, and witnesses for both sides. If a final CPO is issued, the court clerk provides certified copies to both parties, and it remains in force until the date indicated on these documents.

Same-Sex Domestic Abuse and CPOs

CPOs are important tools that empower domestic violence victims without requiring them to file criminal charges. Although it seems fair that this form of protection should be available to all citizens, in reality it can be much more difficult for LGBT people to obtain a CPO. State laws concerning CPOs vary widely in the types of relationships that qualify for protection. Some states specify that people can only seek CPOs if they are related to the abuser by blood or marriage, if they have lived with the abuser, or if they have a child together. Some states permit people who were involved in dating relationships or who shared financial and family responsibilities with the abuser to file for a CPO. But some of this statutory language excludes LGBT people.

Only one state, Hawaii, specifically makes CPOs available to "current or former same-sex partners." Most other state laws use gender-neutral language that makes the protection of LGBT domestic violence survivors subject to interpretation by the courts. A few state laws only allow people to apply for CPOs if the domestic violence occurred in a relationship with someone of the opposite sex. These laws are changing, however, with Montana dropping the opposite-sex requirement in 2013. It remains unclear how the 2015 U.S. Supreme Court ruling that legalized same-sex marriage throughout the United States will impact the legal protections granted to LGBT domestic violence victims.

References

1. "Civil Protection Order." Someplace Safe, 2012.

2. Kansler, Zach. "Same Sex Domestic Abuse and Orders of Protection." *Albany Government Law Review,* February 6, 2011.

3. "Know Your Rights: LGBT Domestic Violence Survivors." Legal Momentum, 2001.

Chapter 22

Workplace Violence

Chapter Contents

Section 22.1

What Is Workplace Violence?

Text in this section is excerpted from "Addressing Workplace
Violence," U.S. Department of Commerce (DOC), May 2014.

Introduction

Workplace violence (WPV) is a concern for agencies and employees in both the private and public sectors. WPV poses a threat to the
safety of the employees and the public and affects productivity. While
no organization is immune to WPV, it is the goal of the Department of
Commerce (Department) to reduce the impact of such occurrences on
the employees, contractors, and the public. The purpose of this policy
is to provide guidelines on recognizing and responding promptly and
effectively to potential and/or actual incidents of WPV.

Policy

It is the policy of the Department to promote and provide a safe
work environment. In furtherance of this policy, the Department, with
and through its employees, is committed to maintaining a workplace
free of violence, threats of violence, harassment, intimidation, and
other kinds of disruptive behavior.

All reports of workplace violence are taken seriously and dealt with
appropriately. Individuals who engage in workplace violence or other
disruptive behavior may be removed from the premises and may be
subject to disciplinary action (up to and including removal), criminal
penalties, or both.

Each bureau must develop and implement procedures for handling
WPV consistent with this policy.

Definitions

Workplace: Any location, either permanent or temporary, where an
employee performs work related duty. This includes, but is not limited
to, the buildings and surrounding perimeters, including parking lots,
field locations, alternate work locations, and travel to alternate work
locations while on work-related travel.

Workplace Violence: Any act of violent behavior, threats of physical violence, harassment, intimidation, bullying, verbal, or non-verbal threat, or other threatening, disruptive behavior that occurs at the workplace.

Identifying Potentially Violent Situations

It is extremely important to recognize behaviors that can lead to potentially violent situations. Indicators of potentially violent behavior may include:

- Direct or veiled threats to cause harm to self or others
- Intimidating, harassing, bullying, or other inappropriately aggressive behavior toward others
- Numerous conflicts with others; conflicts that escalate unreasonably given the circumstances
- Bringing a weapon to the workplace
- Statements showing affinity with incidents of workplace violence, statements indicating approval of the use of violence to resolve problems, or statements indicating affinity with perpetrators of workplace violence
- Statements indicating contemplating suicide, violence, or other disruptive acts in the workplace
- Habitual alcohol use/abuse or use/abuse of illegal drugs
- Extreme changes in mood or behavior

Response to Potential and/or Actual Violent Situations

Any individual who is concerned for their safety or the safety of others due to a potential or actual violent situation should contact the Department security office at their workplace, Federal Protective Service, or local police immediately.

After an individual has contacted their building security or local police department, or if they are concerned for their immediate safety o:r the safety of others, any individual who is victimized or a witness to threatening and/or intimidating behavior is strongly encouraged to report it immediately to his or her supervisor or other management official. Once reported, the supervisor or management official must then report it to the appropriate authorities identified by each bureau.

Section 22.2

Workplace Violence – The Role of the Employee

Text in this section is excerpted from "Addressing Workplace Violence," U.S. Department of Commerce (DOC), May 2014.

Department employees, managers, and supervisors are responsible for creating and maintaining a safe work environment.

Employees

Each employee is accountable for his/her own behavior and is expected to interact in a responsible manner with fellow employees, supervisors, and others.

While employees are not expected to be skilled at identifying potentially dangerous persons, employees are expected to exercise good judgment and inform their supervisor or other management official if someone exhibits behavior such as:

- Bringing a weapon into the workplace
- Displaying extreme resentment, hostility, or anger
- Making threatening remarks
- Exhibiting violent behavior
- Suicidal behavior/threats

Employees are responsible for supporting the Department policy and adhering to the procedures as defined by their bureau regarding workplace violence, threats, and emergencies. Employees are encouraged to report any known threats, physical or verbal, and/or disruptive behavior to supervisors or managers (if one's supervisor is the source of the threat, then the employee should report to a different supervisor or manager). Employees are encouraged not to confront individuals who are perceived as a threat.

Managers and Supervisors

Each manager and supervisor is accountable for his/her own behavior and is expected to interact in a responsible and

professional manner with fellow supervisors, employees, and others.

Managers and supervisors are responsible for enforcing this policy, which includes taking administrative and/or disciplinary action, as appropriate. Managers and supervisors will discuss the situation with the appropriate servicing human resources office (SHRO) and the Office of the General Counsel (OGC) prior to taking any action. Referral of employees affected by such behavior to appropriate counseling services through the Employee Assistance Program (EAP) may be included in any initial actions. Managers and supervisors should:

- Inform employees of, and enforce, the Department's workplace violence policy and appropriate bureau procedures.

- Ensure that employees adhere to specific procedures as prescribed by their bureau for dealing with workplace threats and emergencies.

- Make sure that employees with special needs are aware of emergency evacuation procedures and have assistance (as necessary) in emergency evacuation situations.

- Respond to potential threats and escalation in accordance with bureau procedures, and when appropriate, resources from law enforcement (Federal, State, and local), medical services, the Office of Security (OSY), human resources staff, and the EAP.

- Take all threats seriously.

- Report incidents to appropriate officials immediately.

- Provide assistance and guidance to employees when working with victims.

- Encourage the use of EAP.

Servicing Human Resources Offices (SHROs)

SHROs are responsible for providing advisory services and assistance to managers and supervisors. The SHROs will:

- In conjunction with OGC, provide supervisory training that includes setting clear standards of conduct and performance, address employee problems promptly and at the lowest possible level, and use the probationary period, performance counseling, discipline, alternative dispute resolution, and other management tools conscientiously.

297

- Supply technical expertise and consultation to help managers and supervisors determine if administrative and/or disciplinary action is necessary or appropriate in specific situations and assure that disciplinary action is proposed and administered in a fair and progressive manner. In consultation with OGC, advise managers and supervisors how to identify problem areas, and develop action plans to resolve problems in the early stages and at the lowest possible level.

- Determine whether sufficient evidence exists to justify taking administrative action, and, in consultation with OGC, make recommendations on appropriate discipline, once the investigation of any misconduct is complete.

- Ensure prompt coordination with the appropriate servicing security office of any administrative action deemed a concern for workplace violence (termination, suspension, or other significant adverse action).

- Convene a management group, when appropriate, to respond to potential or actual incidents of violence, including after-action review. Members should consist of SHRO, OSY, EAP, and OGC.

- Check employee references.

Employee Assistance Program (EAP) Counselors

The EAP offices are an important resource in addressing workplace violence situations and can assist managers and supervisors in strategizing and planning an effective response to violent or potentially violent incidents. Counselors bring a wealth of information and experience to situations that require expertise in dealing with many of the problems that employees, managers, and supervisors bring into their job environments from home, the workplace, and life. By intervening early in a conflict between two or more people, it may be possible to resolve problems at an early stage and at the lowest possible level.

EAP services may differ somewhat from bureau to bureau and location to location intheir structure and scope of services. Confidentiality is an important aspect and it is common practice for EAP counselors to inform clients (in writing) about the limits of confidentiality on their first visit. While employees, managers, and supervisors are afforded considerable privacy under laws, policies, and the professional ethics of EAP professionals, the EAP staff is required to take appropriate action if information about a client is received that indicates a threat to themselves or other persons. This may include the release of information without the client's consent.

Some services that EAP may provide, depending on the scope of services under contract:

- Short-term counseling and referral services at no cost

- Assistance with the prevention of workplace violence, through:

  - information dissemination;

  - early involvement in organizational change;

  - training employees, managers, and supervisors in dealing with angry co-workers and stakeholders, conflict resolution, communication skills, and training on workplace violence prevention;

  - training employees, managers, and supervisors to deal with problems as soon as they arise;

  - organizational recovery after a violent incident;

  - consulting with incident response teams upon request when a potential for violence exists or an actual incident is reported; and

  - participation in critical incident stress debriefing teams in the event of a violent situation.

Labor Organizations (Unions)

The exclusive representatives of Department bargaining unit employees have a fundamental interest in supporting the Department's policy on workplace violence. Consistent with local collective bargaining agreements and past practices, the exclusive representatives can support the Department's workplace violence policy by:

- Working to help develop the Department's efforts to prevent workplace violence;

- Reporting security issues and/or potential threats; and

- Participating with management in the development of violence prevention policies.

Section 22.3

Warning Signs of Potential Workplace Violence

Text in this section is excerpted from "A Guide for Responding to Violence or Threats in the USGS," U.S. Geological Survey (USGS), April 28, 2014.

No one can always predict when a human being will become violent. There is no absolute specific profile of a potentially dangerous individual; however, indicators of increased risk of violent behavior are available. Some of these indicators may include, but are not limited to:

- Direct or veiled threats of harm;

- Intimidating, belligerent, harassing, bullying, or other inappropriate and aggressive behavior;

- Numerous conflicts with supervisors and other employees;

- Bringing a weapon to the workplace, brandishing a weapon in the workplace, making inappropriate references to guns, or a fascination with weapons;

- Statements showing a fascination with incidents of workplace violence, statements indicating approval of the use of violence to resolve a problem, or statements indicating identification with perpetrators of workplace violence;

- Statements indicating desperation (over family, financial or other personal problems) to the point of committing suicide;

- Drug/alcohol abuse; and

- Extreme changes in behavior.

Each of these behaviors indicates the potential for escalation of violent behavior. None should be ignored. By identifying the problem and dealing with it appropriately, we may be able to prevent violence from happening. Employees who recognize these behaviors in themselves are encouraged to seek assistance from the Employee Assistance Program or their family physician. Any employees who notice the above indicators in coworkers should notify their supervisors. Supervisors who have seen the above indicators in an employee, or have received a report from one employee regarding another, should immediately contact their servicing Human Resources Office for advice and assistance in determining the appropriate course of action.

Section 22.4

Dos and Don'ts for Dealing with Potentially Violent Individuals

Text in this section is excerpted from "Workplace and Domestic Violence Prevention and Response Handbook," U.S. Department of Housing and Urban Development (HUD), June 2015.

Dos

- Do project calmness. Move and speak slowly, quietly, and confidently.
- Do listen attentively and encourage the person to talk.
- Do let the speaker know that you are interested in what he/she is saying.
- Do maintain a relaxed yet attentive posture.
- Do acknowledge the person's feelings and indicate that you can see he/she is upset.
- Do ask for small, specific favors such as asking the person to move to a quieter area.
- Do establish ground rules. State the consequences of violent or threatening behavior.
- Do employ delaying tactics that give the person time to calm down. For example, offer a glass of water.
- Do be reassuring and point out choices.

- Do help the person break down big problems into smaller, more manageable problems.

- Do accept criticism. When a complaint might be true, use statements such as, "You're probably right" or "It was my fault." If the criticism seems unwarranted, ask clarifying questions.

- Do arrange yourself so that your exit is not blocked.

- Do make sure there are three to six feet between you and the other person.

Don'ts

- Don't make sudden movements that may seem threatening.

- Don't speak rapidly, raise your volume, or use an accusatory tone.

- Don't reject all demands.

- Don't make physical contact, jab your finger at the other person, or use long periods of eye contact.

- Don't pose in challenging stances: directly opposite someone, hands on hips or with arms crossed.

- Don't challenge, threaten, or dare the individual. Never belittle the other person.

- Don't criticize or act impatient.

- Don't attempt to bargain with a threatening individual.

- Don't try to make the situation seem less serious than it is.

- Don't make false statements or promises you cannot keep.

- Don't try to impart a lot of technical or complicated information when emotions are high.

- Don't take sides or agree with distortions.

- Don't invade the individual's personal space.

Chapter 23

Abuse within the Military

Chapter Contents

Section 23.1

Prevalence of Domestic Violence among Veterans and Active Duty Servicemembers

Text in this section is excerpted from "Intimate Partner
Violence: Prevalence Among U.S. Military Veterans and Active
Duty Servicemembers and a Review of Intervention Approaches,"
Military OneSource, August 2013.

Researchers identified 13 studies that assessed IPV prevalence among U.S. active duty populations. Of these, 10 assessed perpetration outcomes and 10 assessed victimization outcomes. The most common metric of IPV across studies was prior exposure to physical violence in last year; thus, the researchers used this outcome to summarize prevalence estimates.

The researchers were able to pool six studies of IPV perpetration in the last year. Pooled estimates yielded a weighted estimated mean prevalence rate of 22 percent (95% confidence interval [CI], 17% to 27%) with significant heterogeneity ($I^2 > 90\%$). Influence analysis yielded a range of 18 percent to 23 percent for IPV perpetration among active duty servicemembers.

The researchers identified four studies that assessed victimization by physical IPV among active duty servicemembers and that met criteria for a meta-analysis. The 12-month weighted estimated mean prevalence rate of physical IPV victimization of active duty servicemembers yielded a point estimate of 30 percent (95% CI, 17% to 43%) significant heterogeneity ($I^2 > 90\%$). Influence analysis yielded a range of 25 percent to 33 percent of exposure to IPV victimization of active duty servicemembers.

The researchers conducted subgroup analyses by (1) era of cohort recruitment (pre-2001 versus post-2001), (2) IPV severity, and (3) gender to probe for group differences. All analyses showed group differences, but each pooled subgroup estimate also had high heterogeneity. Variability in prevalence is likely due to a combination of factors, including the small number of pooled studies.

IPV Among Veterans

The researchers identified 12 studies that assessed IPV prevalence among Veterans. In total, five studies assessed perpetration and eight studies assessed victimization. Populations and outcomes were too heterogeneous to meta-analyze across the perpetration studies. Samples comprised specialized populations (e.g., Veterans seeking relationship help, newly returning OEF/OIF Veterans referred to behavioral health) with a high mental health burden, or were gender-specific samples. Moreover, IPV perpetration was defined inconsistently across studies, ranging from physical abuse as measured on the CTS to any form of domestic abuse. Thus, the prevalence of IPV perpetration within the last year ranged considerably (15% to 60%) across these five studies.

Of the eight victimization studies, two reported on sexual violence only and none provided estimates for male Veterans. The most common estimate of exposure to IPV was lifetime abuse; thus, the researchers used lifetime estimates as the main outcome to syntheses theses data. Four of the eight studies were amenable to meta-analysis. The pooled lifetime weighted estimated mean prevalence rate of physical IPV victimization among women Veterans yielded a point estimate of 35 percent (95% CI, 25% to 47%). Influence analysis yielded a range of 30 percent to 41 percent victimization of women Veterans. The overall prevalence estimate had high heterogeneity, but limited data precluded moderation analysis to query for subgroup differences. Two studies reported on also reported on the on the prevalence of IPV victimization in the last year among women Veterans. Prevalence estimates in these two studies ranged from 7 percent to 12 percent.

Screening for IPV Victimization

Screening women can accurately identify those who have been exposed to IPV, can increase disclosure of IPV victimization, and incurs few adverse effects. Specific results, however, vary by screening tool, populations, and setting. Repeated screenings during pregnancy increase identification of IPV victimization. Screening interventions that included institutional support, ongoing training, and immediate access to referral services significantly increase rates of IPV screening, disclosure, and identification compared with screening interventions using a less comprehensive approach. In an emergency room environment, computerized IPV screening had high feasibility and acceptability. Screening interventions may decrease recurrence of IPV and physical and mental harms associated with IPV, but the evidence is limited. Overall based on multiple studies, there is high strength of evidence that IPV screening can detect women exposed to IPV. There is insufficient to low strength of evidence that IPV screening alone influences all other outcomes (i.e., rates of IPV, IPV-related physical or mental harms, referrals and treatment for IPV, mortality).

Behavioral Interventions

The researchers identified three SRs evaluated behavioral interventions. Two of these synthesized the evidence on behavioral interventions among women exposed to IPV, and one focused on male perpetrators of IPV. The SR that focused on perpetration synthesized the evidence on CBT for men who abuse their female partners. Compared with nonintervention controls, CBT for men who physically abuse their female partners reduced rates of IPV but did not demonstrate a statistically significant improvement across four RCTs (RR 0.86; 95% CI, 0.54 to 1.38). Overall, the evidence around interventions focusing on reducing and treating perpetration is limited; the strength of evidence is low due to imprecise estimates (wide confidence internals) and inconsistent results across the four included studies.

Of the two SRs that focused on women victims of IPV, one focused on pregnant women and identified four studies, and the other SR identified six RCTs, three of which were conducted in pregnant or postpartum women. Some studies were included in both SRs, thus there were only five unique studies among pregnant or postpartum women across the two SRs. The behavioral interventions tested in these studies were heterogonous and included home visitation, nurse management, unspecified counseling interventions plus resource card, or mentor support. Among pregnant and postpartum women, behavioral interventions that include counseling reduced IPV and improved birth outcomes. However, strength of evidence was graded as insufficient. Across these SRs, there were few studies identified, and the types of behavioral interventions were quite different from each other, which hampered drawing conclusions across this category of interventions.

Advocacy Interventions

The researchers identified one SR that assessed 10 advocacy intervention studies. Again, intervention approaches were heterogeneous and included education and support to enhance provision of legal, housing, and financial advice; promote access and use of community shelters, emergency housing, and psychological interventions; and provide safety planning. Intensive advocacy interventions (>12 hours in duration) for women recruited in domestic violence shelters reduced physical abuse 12 to 24 months postintervention (odds ratio 0.43; 95% CI, 0.43 to 0.83) but not in the year immediately following intervention. Brief interventions (<12 hours) increased the use of safety behaviors. No significant effects were found for mental harm (e.g., PTSD, depression) or use of IPV-related services. There is low strength of evidence that intensive advocacy interventions reduced IPV; results were consistent, but confidence internals were wide.

Clinical and Policy Implications

Compared with population-based studies conducted in samples not selected for active duty or Veteran status, the researchers report higher rates of 12-month IPV perpetration and victimization among active duty women servicemembers; considerably higher 12-month IPV victimization rates for active duty men; and comparable rates of both 12-month IPV perpetration among active duty men and lifetime IPV victimization among Veteran women. The researchers also found that the 12-month victimization estimate is higher among active duty men than active duty women—a pattern that has also been observed in civilian studies. Some differences between civilian and active duty or Veteran populations can be attributed to dissimilar distribution of population characteristics between the two groups (e.g., age distribution, greater proportion of African Americans and Hispanics among active duty and Veteran populations). However, factors unique to military life such as military deployments that result in family separation and reintegration issues and combat-related health issues (e.g., PTSD, head injuries) likely contribute to relationship stress and IPV among active duty servicemembers, Veterans, and their intimate partners.

Evidence from the researchers synthesis of SRs assessing IPV interventions demonstrates that standardized IPV screening interventions in a health care setting increases identification of IPV victimization. Moreover, Nelson et al. found minimal adverse effects and low levels of harm related to IPV screening for women receiving health care services. Coupled with the prevalence of IPV the researchers report here, these findings support the need to consider adopting standardized IPV screening for use in the VA. However, the researchers review also highlights the need to take a comprehensive approach to implementing such screening programs in the VA.

The researchers meta-synthesis finds that multicomponent screening interventions that include institutional support, use effective screening protocols, thorough initial and ongoing training of providers, and immediate access to referral services increase provider use of screening, patient disclosure, and, ultimately, identification of IPV. This finding suggests that establishing a screening program without building provider self-efficacy to screen and establishing sufficient support for referral and treatment mechanism will undermine the effectiveness of IPV screening programs. The researchers synthesis of the SR literature found some evidence to support behavioral counseling and advocacy interventions for women who screen positive for IPV; however, the evidence was often inconsistent—likely due to the wide variability in strategy, content, and intensity.

While primary care physicians and mental health clinicians may be ideally positioned to implement screening, successful IPV screening programs must also consider educating and enlisting the services of the entire health care team, including other providers, nurses, and social workers, to create a seamless system from screening to timely referral to appropriate services. The development of resource toolkits for clinicians that include (1) appropriate community or Veteran resources, (2) information on local and state laws regarding IPV, and (3) availability of counseling, legal, and advocacy referrals could help overcome some of the provider and institutional barriers to providing IPV screening throughout the VA healthcare system. Due to the sensitive nature of IPV screening, cultural sensitivity and confidentiality concerns would also need to be considered in the development of any IPV screening program.

The Institute of Medicine recommends that women be screened about current and past violence and abuse in a culturally sensitive and supportive manner, and assuring patient confidentiality and safety is paramount. Another consideration when planning an IPV screening program is how often to make assessments. Most screening tools were designed to detect IPV in the previous year. Thus, an annual interval may be optimal. Any screening program will need to consider the optimal use of provider and staff resources in addition to the benefit from screening for IPV victimization obtained from repeated followup screenings.

While the evidence the researchers report here on effectiveness of screening for IPV was conducted among female populations, the researchers also report considerable rates of IPV victimization among male populations. The U.S. armed services and the Veteran healthcare system currently remain largely male in population despite the growing number of female servicemembers and Veterans. The Veterans Health

Administration (VHA) provides medical and mental health care for an estimated 8.6 million Veterans each year, and only an estimated 6 percent to 8 percent of the Veterans cared for are women. Indeed, the researchers data suggest that the overall rates of IPV victimization among male active duty servicemembers are at least equal to if not higher than rates of overall IPV victimization among female active duty servicemembers. However, women are more likely to be injured or murdered as a result of IPV. This fact raises the question of whether IPV screening programs in the VA should be extended to men as well. In constructing a comprehensive national program to address IPV, consideration should be given to the prevalence of IPV victimization and perpetration, the effectiveness of interventions to decrease exposure to IPV and decrease the associated mental and physical harms, the potential benefits and harms of screening, and if universal or women-only screening should be adopted. Currently, a number of organizations recommend some form of screening to detect IPV victimization. The researchers results broadly support these recommendations; however, the researchers review highlights the need for developing an a priori detailed plan of action for treatment and followup of positive IPV screening results.

The researchers used a recommended framework to identify gaps in evidence and classify why these gaps exist (Table 23.1.). This approach considers PICOTS (population, intervention, comparator, outcomes, timing, and setting) to identify gaps and classifies them as due to (1) insufficient or imprecise information, (2) biased information, (3) inconsistency or unknown consistency, and (4) not the right information. VA and other healthcare systems should consider their clinical and policy

Table 23.1. Evidence gaps and future research

Evidence Gap	Reason	Type of Studies to Consider
Limited to no evidence for these populations and behaviors: • Male Veteran IPV perpetration • Male Veteran IPV victimization • Female Veteran IPV victimization in last year • Nationally representative samples of Veterans for both perpetration and victimization	Insufficient information	High-quality cross-sectional studies in broad populations

Table 23.1. Continued

Evidence Gap	Reason	Type of Studies to Consider
Studies that address primary prevention of IPV	Insufficient information	RCTs Observational comparative effectiveness studies
Effectiveness of screening techniques to identify males with exposure to IPV victimization	Insufficient information	Studies of diagnostic accuracy RCTs Observational comparative effectiveness studies
Effectiveness of screening techniques to identify perpetrators of current or past IPV	Insufficient information	Studies of diagnostic accuracy RCTs
Studies on interventions to reduce IPV in screen-detected populations	Insufficient information	RCTs Observational comparative effectiveness studies

needs when deciding whether to invest in research to address gaps in evidence. Specific research questions can be evaluated quantitatively, using value-of-information analysis, which uses Bayesian methods to estimate the potential benefits of gathering further information through research.

Section 23.2

The Family Advocacy Program

Text in this section is excerpted from "The Family Advocacy Program," Military OneSource, November 16, 2012.

Whether or not you've experienced domestic abuse personally, you probably know that it can have devastating consequences. Victims carry the emotional scars of abuse long after they're out of harm's way. And abusers, if not stopped, can escalate the violence until they and their victims lose everything—family, career, self-respect, and even their freedom.

The Department of Defense (DoD) is committed to addressing and ending domestic abuse. The Family Advocacy Program (FAP) works to prevent abuse by offering programs to put a stop to domestic abuse before it starts. When abuse does occur, the FAP works to ensure the safety of victims and helps military families overcome the effects of violence and change destructive behavior patterns. FAP staff members are trained to respond to incidents of abuse and neglect, support victims, and offer prevention and treatment. The following information will give you a better understanding of the FAP and how it supports families and the military mission.

The DoD is specific about what it considers domestic abuse and child abuse, and under what circumstances FAP will get involved. It defines domestic abuse as violence or a pattern of behavior resulting in emotional or psychological abuse, economic control, or interference with personal liberty directed toward a current or former spouse, a person with whom the abuser has a child, or a current or former intimate partner with whom the abuser shares or has shared a common domicile. Child abuse and neglect are defined as injury, maltreatment, or neglect to a child that harms or threatens the child's welfare. The FAP will get involved when one of the parties is a military member or, in some cases, a DoD civilian serving at an overseas installation.

For the FAP to be involved in reports of child abuse, alleged victims must be under age eighteen or incapable of self-support due to physical or mental incapacity, and in the legal care of a service member or military family member. The FAP will also intervene when a dependent military child is alleged to be the victim of abuse and neglect while in the care of a DoD-sanctioned family child care provider or installation facility such as a Child Development Center, school, or youth program.

Prevention Programs

The FAP works to prevent domestic abuse and child abuse and neglect by providing education and awareness programs for all members of the military community:

- **Classes, workshops, and seminars**. Couples communication, anger management, stress management, effective parenting, and conflict resolution are just a few of the educational programs available to help military families learn how to build positive relationships. The FAP also provides educational programs to leadership and to service members during unit training.

- **New Parent Support Program (NPSP).** Active duty service members and spouses who have or are expecting a baby may participate in the NPSP. The program offers home visitation, parenting education, and other services to help young families provide a safe and nurturing environment for their children.

- **Counseling.** Sometimes counseling is the best way for individuals and couples to understand and change attitudes, impulses, and patterns of interacting that contribute to hurtful and potentially violent behavior. One-on-one support helps parents develop positive parenting techniques, manage anger, and learn communication skills.

- **Public awareness campaigns.** The FAP works to help communities learn to recognize domestic and child abuse, where and how to report it, and how victims can get help.

When an allegation of abuse or neglect is reported, FAP professionals meet individually with suspected victims, offenders, and other family members to gather information about the allegation and the family's history. This information, along with other evidence, is used to develop recommendations for follow-up action. An important part of the program is collaboration among FAP staff, military units, law enforcement, medical and legal personnel, Family Support Centers, chaplains, and civilian agencies. This coordinated community effort is essential to prevent and respond to abusive behavior in military families.

Because abuse can take many forms and varies considerably in degree of severity, the FAP relies on a multi-disciplinary committee to evaluate reported cases and a clinical case review team to recommend a program of treatment for victims and abusers. Members of the multi-disciplinary team represent different fields, including law enforcement, health care, social services, counseling, legal services, and civilian child protective services. When allegations of abuse involve a service member, a representative from his or her command is invited to participate in the multi-disciplinary team review. When treatment is recommended for the service member, it becomes the responsibility of the command to enforce compliance with the treatment plan. Cases that meet criteria for abuse are reviewed on a regular schedule until requirements of the program of treatment have been met and victims are deemed safe from further abuse.

Victim Advocates

The FAP takes action to protect victims from further abuse and help them heal. Victim advocates support victims by providing the following services:

- **Confidentiality with a restrictive reporting option**. To encourage early identification of domestic abuse and help victims get the care they need while they decide what to do next, the military offers a restrictive reporting option for reporting abuse. With this option, victims can get assistance from an FAP victim advocate and receive medical care without it automatically resulting in an abuse investigation or notification to the service member's command. Because victim safety is a priority, victims at imminent risk of serious harm or cases involving child abuse are not eligible for restricted reporting.

- **Help finding shelter and other support**. A victim advocate may help the victim locate shelter or other safe place to stay, find legal services, refer the victim to counseling, help find child care, or help the victim find services in the local civilian community.

- **Help getting a Military Protective Order (MPO).** An MPO is issued by a military commander and may order the service member to surrender his or her weapons custody card or stay away from the family home. Commanders can tailor their orders to meet the specific needs of the victim. It is important to remember that neither a restraining order nor an MPO will prevent the abuser from returning home or entering the victim's workplace, but it does make it illegal for him or her to do so.

- **Counseling services.** Clinical counselors offer counseling services and, if appropriate, can help the victim find counseling, whether through a Military OneSource counselor or a civilian counselor in the local community.

- **Intervention with civilian agencies on behalf of victims.** Such agencies may include civilian courts, schools, and social services agencies.

- **Help preparing a safety plan.** Abuse victims need to know in advance what to do before, during, and after a domestic abuse crisis. Safety plans cover things like where to go for shelter, how to find financial and emotional support, a contingency plan for child care, and what to have ready to take with you if you have to leave home.

If you're not yet prepared to talk to someone, you can still develop a safety plan. Safety planning information is available on several Web sites, including the National Coalition Against Domestic Violence and the National Domestic Violence Hotline.

The FAP also offers abusers opportunities for rehabilitation. FAP treatment helps abusers recognize and stop their destructive behavior and begin to develop healthy family relationships.

How Involvement with the FAP May Affect a Military Career

The DoD and military Services take the position that family-member abuse will not be tolerated. In addition to the pain it causes the family, it also diminishes military performance, impacts readiness and is contrary to military values. But abuse reported to the FAP will not automatically ruin a service member's career. The first priority for the FAP and commands is to make sure victims are safe and protected from further abuse. The chain of command typically supports service members who stop abusive behavior, follow treatment recommendations, and work to achieve more positive family relationships.

With FAP intervention and treatment, many service members gain new insights into their professional and personal lives and are able to make the changes necessary for successful military service. Of course, the more extreme the violence, the more likely it is that an offender's military career will be affected. And failing to stop abusive behavior, refusing to comply with treatment plans, or causing serious injury to a family member may result in administrative discharge or court martial.

Section 23.3

Military Sexual Trauma and Harassment

Text in this section is excerpted from "Military Sexual Trauma," U.S. Department of Veterans Affairs (VA), September 2, 2015.

What Is Military Sexual Trauma (MST)?

Military sexual trauma, or MST, is the term used by the Department of Veterans Affairs (VA) to refer to experiences of sexual assault or repeated, threatening sexual harassment that a Veteran experienced during his or her military service.

The definition used by the VA comes from Federal law (Title 38 U.S. Code 1720D) and is "psychological trauma, which in the judgment of a VA mental health professional, resulted from a physical assault of a sexual nature, battery of a sexual nature, or sexual harassment which occurred while the Veteran was serving on active duty, active duty for training, or inactive duty training."

Sexual harassment is further defined as "repeated, unsolicited verbal or physical contact of a sexual nature which is threatening in character."

More concretely, MST includes any sexual activity where a Servicemember is involved against his or her will—he or she may have been pressured into sexual activities (for example, with threats of negative consequences for refusing to be sexually cooperative or with implied better treatment in exchange for sex), may have been unable to consent to sexual activities (for example, when intoxicated), or may have been physically forced into sexual activities. Other experiences that fall into the category of MST include:

- Unwanted sexual touching or grabbing

- Threatening, offensive remarks about a person's body or sexual activities

- Threatening and unwelcome sexual advances

The identity or characteristics of the perpetrator, whether the Servicemember was on or off duty at the time, and whether he or she was on or off base at the time do not matter. If these experiences occurred while an individual was on active duty or active duty for training, they are considered by VA to be MST.

How Common Is MST?

VA's national screening program, in which every Veteran seen for health care is asked whether he or she experienced MST, provides data on how common MST is among Veterans seen in VA. National data from this program reveal that about 1 in 4 women and 1 in 100 men respond "yes," that they experienced MST, when screened by their VA provider. Although rates of MST are higher among women, because there are many more men than women in the military, there are actually significant numbers of women and men seen in VA who have experienced MST.

It is important to keep in mind that these data speak only to the rate of MST among Veterans who have chosen to seek VA health care; they cannot be used to make an estimate of the actual rates of sexual assault and harassment experiences among all individuals serving in the U.S. Military. Also, although Veterans who respond "yes" when screened are asked if they are interested in learning about MST-related services available, not every Veteran who responds "yes" necessarily needs or is interested in treatment. MST is an experience, not a diagnosis, and Veterans' current treatment needs will vary.

How Can MST Affect Veterans?

MST is an experience, not a diagnosis or a mental health condition, and as with other forms of trauma, there are a variety of reactions that Veterans can have in response to MST. The type, severity, and duration of a Veteran's difficulties will all vary based on factors like:

- Whether he/she has a prior history of trauma

- The types of responses from others he/she received at the time of the MST

- Whether the MST happened once or was repeated over time

Although trauma can be a life-changing event, people are often remarkably resilient after experiencing trauma. Many individuals recover without professional help; others may generally function well in their life, but continue to experience some level of difficulties or have strong reactions in certain situations. For some Veterans, the experience of MST may continue to affect their mental and physical health in significant ways, even many years later.

Although trauma can be a life-changing event, people are often remarkably resilient after experiencing trauma. Many individual recover without professional help; others may function in general, but continue to experience some level of difficulties or have strong reactions in certain situations. For some Veterans, experiences of MST may continue to affect their mental and physical health in significant ways, even many years later.

Some of the experiences both female and male survivors of MST may have include:

- **Strong emotions:** feeling depressed; having intense, sudden emotional responses to things; feeling angry or irritable all the time

- **Feelings of numbness:** feeling emotionally "flat"; difficulty experiencing emotions like love or happiness

- **Trouble sleeping:** trouble falling or staying asleep; disturbing nightmares

- **Difficulties with attention, concentration, and memory:** trouble staying focused; frequently finding their mind wandering; having a hard time remembering things

- **Problems with alcohol or other drugs:** drinking to excess or using drugs daily; getting intoxicated or "high" to cope with memories or emotional reactions; drinking to fall asleep

- **Difficulty with things that remind them of their experiences of sexual trauma:** feeling on edge or "jumpy" all the time; difficulty feeling safe; going out of their way to avoid reminders of their experiences

- **Difficulties with relationships:** feeling isolated or disconnected from others; abusive relationships; trouble with employers or authority figures; difficulty trusting others

- **Physical health problems:** sexual difficulties; chronic pain; weight or eating problems; gastrointestinal problems

Although posttraumatic stress disorder (PTSD) is commonly associated with MST, it is not the only diagnosis that can result from MST. For example, VA medical record data indicate that in addition to PTSD, the diagnoses most frequently associated with MST among users of VA health care are depression and other mood disorders, and substance use disorders.

Fortunately, people can recover from experiences of trauma, and VA has effective services to help Veterans do this.

How Has VA Responded to the Problem of MST?

VA is strongly committed to ensuring that Veterans have access to the help they need in order to recover from MST.

- Every VA health care facility has a designated MST Coordinator who serves as a contact person for MST-related issues. This person can help Veterans find and access VA services and programs. He or she may also be aware of state and federal benefits and community resources that may be helpful.

- Recognizing that many survivors of sexual trauma do not disclose their experiences unless asked directly, VA health care

317

providers ask every Veteran whether he or she experienced MST. This is an important way of making sure Veterans know about the services available to them.

- All treatment for physical and mental health conditions related to experiences of MST is provided free of charge.

- To receive free treatment for mental and physical health conditions related to MST, Veterans do not need to be service connected (or have a VA disability rating). Veterans may be able to receive this benefit even if they are not eligible for other VA care. Veterans do not need to have reported the incident(s) when they happened or have other documentation that they occurred.

- MST-related services are available at every VA medical center and every facility has providers knowledgeable about treatment for the aftereffects of MST. MST-related counseling is also available through community-based Vet Centers. Services are designated to meet Veterans where they are at in their recovery, whether that is focusing on strategies for coping with challenging emotions and memories or, for Veterans who are ready, actually talking about their MST experiences in depth.

- Nationwide, there are programs that offer specialized sexual trauma treatment in residential or inpatient settings. These are programs for Veterans who need more intense treatment and support.

- To accommodate Veterans who do not feel comfortable in mixed-gender treatment settings, some facilities have separate programs for men and women. All residential and inpatient MST programs have separate sleeping areas for men and women.

In addition to its treatment programming, VA also provides training to staff on issues related to MST, including a mandatory training on MST for all mental health and primary care providers. VA also engages in a range of outreach activities to Veterans and conducts monitoring of MST-related screening and treatment, in order to ensure that adequate services are available.

Section 23.4

Military Protective Order

Text in this section is excerpted from "Subpart C—Offense
Reporting," U.S. Government Publishing
Office (GPO), December 1, 2015.

What Is Military Protective Order?

(a) A DD Form 2873, Military Protective Order (MPO) is a written
lawful order issued by a commander that orders a Soldier to avoid contact with those persons identified in the order. MPOs may be used to
facilitate a "cooling-off" period following domestic violence and sexual
assault incidents, to include incidents involving children. The commander should provide a written copy of the order within 24 hours of
its issuance to the person with whom the member is ordered not to
have contact and to the installation LE activity.

(b) Initial notification. In the event a MPO is issued against a Soldier and any individual involved in the order does not reside on a
Army installation at any time during the duration of the MPO, the
installation PMO/DES will notify the appropriate civilian authorities
(local magistrate courts, family courts, and local police) of:

1. The issuance of the protective order

2. The individuals involved in the order

3. Any change made in a protective order

4. The termination of the protective order

(c) A Civilian Protective Order (CPO) is an order issued by a judge,
magistrate or other authorized civilian official, ordering an individual
to avoid contact with his or her spouse or children. Pursuant to the
Armed Forces Domestic Security Act, 10 U.S.C. 1561a, a CPO has
the same force and effect on a military installation as such order has
within the jurisdiction of the court that issued the order.

Chapter 24

Abuse within Immigrant Communities

Chapter Contents

Section 24.1

Violence against Immigrant and Refugee Women

Text in this section is excerpted from "Violence against
Immigrant and Refugee Women," Office on Women's
Health (OWH), September 4, 2015.

No one deserves to be hit or mistreated. You can get help, even if
you do not have legal papers giving you permission to be in the United
States. Keep reading to learn more about getting help.

An immigrant or refugee woman may face many of the same challenges as any other abused woman. In addition, she may face some
unique challenges, such as being:

- Made to "lose face" in her community

- Taught by her culture that family duty comes first

- Accused of leaving or failing her culture and background

- Lied to about her partner's ability to have her deported and keep
  their children

- Told that in the United States the law says she must have sex
  with her partner

- Told that her abuser is allowed to hit her or use other forms of
  physical punishment

Although immigrant and refugee women may face such challenges,
they also often have strong family ties and other sources of support.
If you think you are being abused, reach out to someone who cares
about you.

Remember, violence is against the law. If your partner abuses you,
the police can make an arrest and help you leave safely. If you have
been abused, the police usually will not report you to immigration
authorities. If the police officers do not speak your language, find someone other than your abuser to translate for you.

Leaving Your Partner

If you decide to leave an abusive partner, go to a safe place such as the home of a trusted friend or relative or a local domestic violence shelter. Try to choose a place where your partner will not be able to find you. Keep in mind that shelters will help you no matter what your immigration status.

If you are leaving someone who is an immigrant, it can be helpful to have important information, so try to copy down the number on his resident card or naturalization papers. Learn more about how to get ready if you may need to leave. Take your children with you when you leave.

Court Order of Protection (Restraining Order)

If you are being abused, you can get a court order of protection to protect yourself and your children. **You don't have to be a U.S. citizen or legal resident to get a court order of protection.**

A court order of protection can:

- Order the abuser not to have any contact with you and your children

- Order the abuser to move out of your home and give you use of the car

- Order the abuser to give you money for you and your children or to continue your insurance coverage

You can get an application for a court order of protection at courthouses, women's shelters, lawyers' offices, and some police stations.

You do not need a lawyer to get a protection order. Still, you may want to get help from a lawyer if you are not legal or if you do not understand your rights. Often, a local domestic violence agency can help you find a lawyer. Some lawyers will help you at no charge.

If an order is issued and the abuser does anything that the order forbids, call the police right away. The police can arrest the abuser for not following the order.

Protecting your children

Your partner may threaten to take your children if you leave him. Here are some ways you can work to protect your children:

- **Apply for a court order of protection that says your partner has to stay away from you and your children.**

323

- **Apply for a custody order that says your children have to live with you.** You can also ask for the order to say that your partner is not allowed to take your children out of the U.S.

- **If you have a court order of protection or custody order, give a copy to your children's school.** Ask the school not to release the children to the abuser.

- **Try to prevent your abuser from leaving the country with your child using a U.S. passport.** Usually, if your child is under 16, your partner cannot get a U.S. passport for your child without your permission. Also, the U.S. Department of State has an alert program that may let you object to a passport being given to children up to the age of 18. Learn more about this passport alert program.

- **Try to prevent your child from leaving the United States using a passport from another country.** Your child may have citizenship from another country (either instead of U.S. citizenship or in addition to it). If so, contact that country's embassy in the U.S., and ask that your child not be given a passport. Include a copy of a custody order or a court order that prevents your child from leaving the country. This may help convince the embassy to grant your request.

- **Keep important items handy.** Make sure you have recent pictures of your children and their passports and birth certificates. The police can help you better if you have these items.

- **Compile contact information.** Make a list of your partner's family and friends, including their addresses and phone numbers. This can help if your partner takes your children.

You may be able to get child support from your partner. A lawyer can help you with this. Ask your local domestic violence shelter for help finding a lawyer.

Deportation Concerns

If you are a U.S. citizen **or** a legal resident **or** have a valid visa, you cannot be deported **unless** you used fake documents to enter the country, broke the rules of your visa, or committed certain crimes.

If you are undocumented (don't have legal papers to be in the U.S.) or are not sure about your immigration status, you should talk to an immigration lawyer. Your local domestic violence shelter can help you find an immigration lawyer. There are lawyers who will help you at no charge.

If you report domestic violence to the police, they usually will not report you to immigration authorities. Still, you should carry the name of an immigration lawyer in case you need it.

Becoming Legal

You should talk to an immigration lawyer before taking steps to become legal. Your local domestic violence shelter can help you find a lawyer. Some lawyers will help you at no charge if you don't have much money. Remember that your lawyer will not tell anyone what you say without your permission.

If you are married to a U.S. citizen or a lawful permanent resident, usually your spouse has to apply for legal permanent residency for you. But in cases of domestic abuse you can apply for residency for you and your children by yourself, and your partner doesn't have to know. This is called **self-petitioning**, and there are specific rules about who can apply for residency this way.

If you are already in deportation hearings and are a victim of domestic abuse, you may be able to have your deportation cancelled and become a permanent resident. This is called a **cancellation of removal** and also has specific rules about who can apply for it.

Talk to an immigration lawyer to find out more about these and other options. Also keep in mind that you should not say you are a U.S. citizen if you are not. You also should not use false papers to work in the United States.

Section 24.2

Basic Information about Residency Laws for Victims of Domestic Violence

Text in this section is excerpted from" Victims of Criminal Activity:
U Nonimmigrant Status," U.S. Citizenship and Immigration
Services (USCIS), November 12, 2015; and text from "Questions
and Answers: Battered Spouses, Children and Parents Under
the Violence Against Women Act (VAWA)," U.S. Citizenship and
Immigration Services (USCIS), July 15, 2015.

Victims of Criminal Activity: U Nonimmigrant Status

Background

The U nonimmigrant status (U visa) is set aside for victims of
certain crimes who have suffered mental or physical abuse and are
helpful to law enforcement or government officials in the investigation
or prosecution of criminal activity. Congress created the U nonimmigrant visa with the passage of the Victims of Trafficking and Violence
Protection Act (including the Battered Immigrant Women's Protection
Act) in October 2000. The legislation was intended to strengthen the
ability of law enforcement agencies to investigate and prosecute cases
of domestic violence, sexual assault, trafficking of aliens and other
crimes, while also protecting victims of crimes who have suffered substantial mental or physical abuse due to the crime and are willing to
help law enforcement authorities in the investigation or prosecution
of the criminal activity. The legislation also helps law enforcement
agencies to better serve victims of crimes.

U Nonimmigrant Eligibility

You may be eligible for a nonimmigrant visa if:

- You are the victim of qualifying criminal activity.

- You have suffered substantial physical or mental abuse as a
  result of having been a victim of criminal activity.

Table 24.1. Qualifying Criminal Activities

• Abduction	• Hostage	• Sexual Assault
• Abusive Sexual Contact	• Incest	• Sexual Exploitation
• Blackmail	• Involuntary Servitude	• Slave Trade
• Domestic Violence	• Kidnapping	• Stalking
• Extortion	• Manslaughter	• Torture
• False Imprisonment	• Murder	• Trafficking
• Female Genital Mutilation	• Obstruction of Justice	• Witness Tampering
• Felonious Assault	• Peonage	• Unlawful Criminal Restraint
• Fraud in Foreign Labor Contracting	• Perjury	• Other Related Crimes*†
	• Prostitution	*Includes any similar activity where the elements of the crime are substantially similar.
	• Rape	†Also includes attempt, conspiracy, or solicitation to commit any of the above and other related crimes.

- You have information about the criminal activity. If you are under the age of 16 or unable to provide information due to a disability, a parent, guardian, or next friend may possess the information about the crime on your behalf (see glossary for definition of 'next friend').

- You were helpful, are helpful, or are likely to be helpful to law enforcement in the investigation or prosecution of the crime. If you are under the age of 16 or unable to provide information due to a disability, a parent, guardian, or next friend may assist law enforcement on your behalf.

- The crime occurred in the United States or violated U.S. laws.

- You are admissible to the United States. If you are not admissible, you may apply for a waiver on a Form I-192, Application for Advance Permission to Enter as a Nonimmigrant.

Applying for U Nonimmigrant Status (U Visa)

To apply (petition) for a U nonimmigrant status, submit:

- Form I-918, Petition for U Nonimmigrant Status

- Form I-918, Supplement B, U Nonimmigrant Status Certification. The Form I-918, Supplement B, must be signed by and authorized official of the certifying law enforcement agency and the official must confirm that you were helpful, and currently being helpful, or will likely be helpful in the investigation or prosecution of the case.

- If any inadmissibility issues are present, you must file a Form I-192, Application for Advance Permission to Enter as Nonimmigrant, to request a waiver of the inadmissibility;

- A personal statement describing the criminal activity of which you were a victim; and

- Evidence to establish each eligibility requirement—visit the Forms section, specifically the Humanitarian Benefits Based Forms.

You may also apply (petition) for U nonimmigrant status if you are outside the United States. To do this, you must:

- File all the necessary forms for U nonimmigrant status with the Vermont Service Center.

- Follow all instructions that are sent from the Vermont Service Center, which will include having your fingerprints taken at the nearest U.S. Embassy or Consulate.

- If your petition is approved, you must consular process to enter the United States, which will include an interview with a consular officer at the nearest U.S. Embassy or Consulate.

- Information about your nearest U.S. Embassy or Consulate can be found at www.usembassy.gov.

Table 24.2. Qualifying Family Members

If you, the principal, are...	Then...
Under 21 years of age	You may petition on behalf of your spouse, children, parents and unmarried siblings under age 18
21 years of age or older	You may petition on behalf of your spouse and children.

To petition for a qualified family member, you must file a Form I-918, Supplement A, Petition for Qualifying Family Member of U-1 Recipient, at the same time as your application or at a later time.

Fees to File U Nonimmigrant Status Applications U Visa Extensions

- All U nonimmigrant status applications (petitions) and other forms related to the U petition are filed with the USCIS Vermont Service Center.

- All U nonimmigrant status applications (petitions) are free. You may request a fee waiver for any other form that is necessary for your U nonimmigrant status application (petition) by filing a Form I-912, Request for Fee Waiver, or by including your own written request for a fee waiver with your application or petition.

U Visa Extensions

When U nonimmigrant status is granted, it is valid for four years. However, extensions are available in certain, limited circumstances if the extension is:

- Needed based on a request from law enforcement,

- Needed based on exceptional circumstances,

- Needed due to delays in consular processing or

- Automatically extended upon the filing and pendency of an application for adjustment (application for a Green Card).

U Visa Cap

- The limit on the number of U visas that may be granted to principal petitioners each year is 10,000. However, there is no cap for family members deriving status from the principal applicant, such as spouses, children, or other eligible family members.

- If the cap is reached before all U nonimmigrant petitions have been adjudicated, USCIS will create a waiting list for any eligible principal or derivative petitioners that are awaiting a final decision and a U visa. Petitioners placed on the waiting list will be granted deferred action or parole and are eligible to apply for work authorization while waiting for additional U visas to become available.

- Once additional visas become available, those petitioners on the waiting list will receive their visa in the order in which their petition was received. Petitioners on the waiting list do not have to take any additional steps to request the U visa. USCIS will notify the petitioner of the approval and the accompanying U visa.

Applying for a Green Card

You may be eligible to apply for a Green Card (adjustment of status/permanent residence) if you meet certain requirements, including:

- You have been physically present in the United States for a continuous period of at least three years while in U nonimmigrant status, and

- You have not unreasonably refused to provide assistance to law enforcement since you received your U visa.

- To apply for permanent residence (a Green Card) for yourself or a qualifying family member, visit our Green Card for a U Nonimmigrant page.

- PLEASE NOTE: Any qualifying family member who does not have a derivative U visa when the principal U nonimmigrant receives a Green Card is no longer eligible for a derivative U visa, but may still be eligible to apply for lawful permanent residence.

- For information on extending your principal U visa to ensure your family member remains eligible for a U visa, please visit the T and U visa extension memorandum.

Family Members Deriving Status

If the family member deriving status based on your status has met the eligibility requirements for a Green Card, they may apply for lawful permanent residence by filing their own Form I-485, Application to Register Permanent Residence or Adjust Status, and following the instructions on the Form I-485, Supplement E.

Even if your family members never had U nonimmigrant status or a U visa, they may still be eligible for a Green Card.

- First, you must file a Form I-929, Petition for Qualifying Family Member of U-1 Nonimmigrant, for each eligible family member.

- You may file the Form I-929 at the same time or after you file your Form I-485.

If the Form I-929 for your family member(s) is approved:

- Family members in the United States may file the Form I-485 to apply for a Green Card.

- Family members outside the United States must first visit a U.S. embassy or consulate to obtain their immigrant visa. Information for the local U.S. embassy or consulate and the procedures for obtaining a visa to enter the United States may be found at www.usembassy.gov.

The Form I-929 is the form that is used to establish whether your family member is eligible to apply for a Green Card based on your U visa based lawful permanent resident status. This does not mean that your family member will receive a Green Card. Even if the Form I-929 is approved, your family member is not automatically eligible for work authorization. They are eligible to work once they have received their Green Card.

Fees to File Form I-929

- All Form I-929 applications are sent to the USCIS Vermont Service Center.

- There is a filing fee for the Form I-929. If you are unable to pay the fee, you may request a fee waiver by also filing a Form I-912, or by submitting a separate written request for a fee waiver.

Questions and Answers: Battered Spouses, Children and Parents Under the Violence Against Women Act (VAWA)

What if my Form I-360, petition for amerasian, widow(er), or special immigrant, is denied?

If your petition is denied the denial letter will tell you how to file an appeal. You may file a Notice of Appeal along with the required fee at the Vermont Service Center within 33 days of receiving the denial. Once the fee is collected and the form is processed at the service center, the appeal will be referred to the Administrative Appeals Office in Washington, D.C.

Can a man file a petition for himself under the Violence Against Women Act?

Yes, VAWA applies equally to victims of either sex.

Do I have to remain married to my abusive spouse until my Form I-360 is approved?

Effective October 28, 2000, you may file a Form I-360 if you are still married to your abusive spouse or, in certain circumstances, if you are not still married to your abusive spouse. If you are not still married to your abusive spouse when you file Form I-360, you must meet one of the following exceptions:

- You believed you were legally married to your abusive spouse but the marriage is not legitimate solely because of the bigamy of your abusive spouse.

- Your abusive spouse died within 2 years of filing the petition.

- Your abusive spouse lost or renounce his citizenship or lawful resident status due to an incident of domestic violence

- Your marriage to your abusive spouse was terminated within the 2 years prior to filing of the petition, and there is a connection between the termination of the marriage and the battery or extreme cruelty.

The actual grounds for the termination of the marriage do not need to explicitly cite battery or extreme cruelty. After your petition has been filed, legal termination of the marriage will not usually affect the status of your petition. Unfortunately, current USCIS regulations do not reflect these statutory changes and still state that you must be married at the time of filing. USCIS is obligated to follow the statute, and you are no longer required to be married to your abusive spouse at the time of filing. You may wish to seek advice from an immigration attorney or legal advocate regarding this provision.

Can a divorced spouse seek relief by filing a Form I-360?

Yes. Effective October 28, 2000, you may file a Form I-360 if the marriage was terminated within 2 years prior to the date of filing, if you can demonstrate a connection between the termination of the marriage and the battery or extreme cruelty. A battered spouse who cannot demonstrate such a connection may be eligible for battered spouse cancellation of removal. To qualify for battered spouse cancellation of removal, you must meet the other requirements that would be necessary for approval of a self-petition. In addition, you must have been physically present in the United States for 3 years immediately preceding the filing of the application for cancellation of removal, and you must demonstrate that your removal from the United States would result in extreme hardship to you or your child.

Your Form I-360 will be denied if you re-marry prior to the approval of the Form I-360. Remarriage after the Form I-360 has been approved will not affect the validity of the petition.

What if my abusive U.S. citizen or permanent resident spouse or parent (or U.S. citizen son or daughter) filed a form I-130, petition for alien relative, on my behalf, which is still pending or was withdrawn?

If you are the beneficiary of a Form I-130 filed by the abusive spouse, parent or child, you will be able to transfer the priority date of the Form I-130 to the Form I-360. This is extremely important for you if since it may result in an earlier priority date and a shorter waiting time for getting a green card.

Can anyone else assist me?

If you need additional advice, you may contact the USCIS field office nearest your home for a list of community-based, non-profit organizations that may be able to assist you in applying for an immigration benefit. Please see the "Find a USCIS Office" page for more information on contacting USCIS offices. In addition, see the "finding legal advice" link to the right for information on free or low cost legal advice.

You should also know that help is available to you through the National Domestic Violence Hotline at 1-800-799-7233 or 1-800-787-3224 [TDD]. The hotline has information about shelters, mental health care, legal advice and other types of assistance, including information about self-petitioning for immigration status.

Chapter 25

Human Trafficking

Chapter Contents

Section 25.1

What Is Human Trafficking?

Text in this section is excerpted from "What Is Human Trafficking?"
U.S. Department of Homeland Security (DHS), September 14, 2015.

Human trafficking is a modern-day form of slavery involving the illegal trade of people for exploitation or commercial gain. Every year, millions of men, women, and children are trafficked in countries around the world, including the United States. It is estimated that human trafficking generates many billions of dollars of profit per year, second only to drug trafficking as the most profitable form of transnational crime.

Human trafficking is a hidden crime as victims rarely come forward to seek help because of language barriers, fear of the traffickers, and/or fear of law enforcement.

Traffickers use force, fraud, or coercion to lure their victims and force them into labor or commercial sexual exploitation. They look for people who are susceptible for a variety of reasons, including psychological or emotional vulnerability, economic hardship, lack of a social safety net, natural disasters, or political instability. The trauma caused by the traffickers can be so great that many may not identify themselves as victims or ask for help, even in highly public settings.

Many myths and misconceptions exist. Recognizing key indicators of human trafficking is the first step in identifying victims and can help save a life. Not all indicators listed are present in every human trafficking situation, and the presence or absence of any of the indicators is not necessarily proof of human trafficking.

The safety of the public as well as the victim is paramount. **Do not attempt to confront a suspected trafficker directly or alert a victim to any suspicions.** It is up to law enforcement to investigate suspected cases of human trafficking.

Section 25.2

Child Welfare and Human Trafficking

Text in this section is excerpted from "Child Welfare and Human Trafficking," Child Welfare Information Gateway, July 2015.

The growing awareness of human trafficking in the United States and abroad requires government and human services agencies to rethink old policies and develop new ones for identifying and serving victims.

Child welfare agencies are on the front lines of these changes: Children and youth involved with the child welfare system due to abuse or neglect and then placed in foster care or group homes—as well as youth who are involved with the justice system, are homeless, or have run away—are all at high risk of being trafficked. Often, the lack of stability in their living situation, physical distance from friends and family, and emotional vulnerability put them at risk for traffickers who are actively seeking children and teens to exploit.

This issue brief provides a broad overview of the crossover between the child welfare field and the work currently being done to prevent and respond to human trafficking of children and youth in the United States.

There is a particular focus on sex trafficking of children and youth, because that trafficking type is more likely to affect the child welfare population. This issue brief provides basic background information, including highlights of federal legislation, and then discusses the needs of victims and the ways that child welfare agencies can address the problem of the trafficking of children.

Definitions of Trafficking

Both U.S. citizens and foreign national children and youth can be victims of sex and/or labor trafficking within the United States.

Sex trafficking

According to the Victims of Trafficking and Violence Protection Act of 2000, all children under the age of 18 who are induced to engage in commercial sex are victims of sex trafficking (U.S. Department of State, 2000).

Children cannot consent to trafficking, so there is no need to demonstrate "force, fraud, or coercion" as is necessary for labor trafficking. However, there are some inconsistencies between the Federal definition and common practices in the States. Many States still prosecute minors for prostitution, despite State laws and the contradiction of charging children with an act for which they are too young to consent, rather than approaching them as victims of sex trafficking (Broughton, 2012).

In addition, working definitions of sex trafficking may differ for child welfare and law enforcement professionals. Many States have also established their own definitions of commercial sexual exploitation and sexually exploited children. These definitions impact how these children are treated (as victims or as delinquents), the involvement of child welfare, and their eligibility for services. Examples of commercial sex trafficking that may involve minors include prostitution, pornography, and sex tourism.

Labor trafficking

The definition of labor trafficking does not distinguish between children and adults. The use of "force, fraud, or coercion for the purpose of subjection to involuntary servitude, peonage, debt bondage, or slavery" has to be present for children to be defined as victims of labor trafficking (U.S. Department of State, 2000).

Examples of labor trafficking include agricultural or domestic service workers who are underpaid or not paid at all, physically abusive traveling sales crews that force children to sell legal items (e.g., magazines) or illegal items (e.g., drugs) or to beg, and workers in restaurants and hair and nail salons who are abused, confined, and/or not paid.

Numbers of Children and Youth Who Are Trafficked

There are a number of sources that estimate trafficking statistics, but none provides a complete picture:

- In 2014, the National Human Trafficking Resource Center (NHTRC), operated by the Polaris Project, was contacted 24,062 times by persons of all ages seeking help or reporting possible instances of trafficking, and 5,042 incidents of potential trafficking were reported. Of these, 3,598 were instances of sex trafficking, 818 were instances of labor trafficking, and the remainder were either combinations of sex and labor trafficking or unspecified (NHTRC, 2015).

- The National Center for Missing and Exploited Children (NCMEC) estimated that one in six endangered runaways were likely sex trafficking victims in 2014. This is an increase from one in seven endangered runaways in 2013 (NCMEC, 2014).

- A 2011 bulletin from the Federal Bureau of Investigation (FBI) cites an earlier estimate (Estes & Weiner, 2001) that 293,000 youth are at risk for being trafficked in North America because they live on the streets or in particularly vulnerable situations (WalkerRodriguez & Hill).

While the true prevalence of sex and labor trafficking is unknown, most service providers believe that these statistics are underestimated. Challenges in identifying victims, collecting and cross-referencing data, and deciding on common definitions contribute to a lack of accurate statistics. In addition, many youth do not see themselves as victims or they may be reluctant to admit to victimization due to fears of deportation, jail, and sometimes deadly retribution from traffickers. The trauma caused by trafficking and the overall drive for survival also serve as strong deterrents to self-identification as a trafficking victim.

Section 25.3

Sex Trafficking

Text in this section is excerpted from "Fact Sheet:
Sex Trafficking," U.S. Department of Health and Human
Services (HHS), December 31, 2015.

Sex trafficking is a modern-day form of slavery in which a commercial sex act is induced by force, fraud, or coercion, or in which the person induced to perform such an act is under the age of 18 years. Enactment of the Trafficking Victims Protection Act of 2000 (TVPA) made sex trafficking a serious violation of Federal law. As defined by the TVPA, the term "commercial sex act" means any sex act on account of which anything of value is given to or received by any person.

The TVPA recognizes that traffickers use psychological and well as physical coercion and bondage, and it defines coercion to include:

- threats of serious harm to or physical restraint against any person;

- any scheme, plan, or pattern intended to cause a person to believe that failure to perform an act would result in serious harm to or physical restraint against any person; or

- the abuse or threatened abuse of the legal process.

Victims of Sex Trafficking and What They Face

Victims of sex trafficking can be women or men, girls or boys, but the majority are women and girls. There are a number of common patterns for luring victims into situations of sex trafficking, including:

- A promise of a good job in another country

- A false marriage proposal turned into a bondage situation

- Being sold into the sex trade by parents, husbands, or boyfriends

- Being kidnapped by traffickers

Sex traffickers frequently subject their victims to debt-bondage, an illegal practice in which the traffickers tell their victims that they owe money (often relating to the victims' living expenses and transport into the country) and that they must pledge their personal services to repay the debt.

Sex traffickers use a variety of methods to "condition" their victims including starvation, confinement, beatings, physical abuse, rape, gang rape, threats of violence to the victims and the victims' families, forced drug use and the threat of shaming their victims by revealing their activities to their family and their families' friends.

Victims face numerous health risks. Physical risks include drug and alcohol addiction; physical injuries (broken bones, concussions, burns, vaginal/anal tearings); traumatic brain injury (TBI) resulting in memory loss, dizziness, headaches, numbness; sexually transmitted diseases (e.g., HIV/AIDS, gonorrhea, syphilis, UTIs, pubic lice); sterility, miscarriages, menstrual problems; other diseases (e.g., TB, hepatitis, malaria, pneumonia); and forced or coerced abortions.

Psychological harms include mind/body separation/disassociated ego states, shame, grief, fear, distrust, hatred of men, self-hatred, suicide, and suicidal thoughts. Victims are at risk for Posttraumatic Stress Disorder (PTSD) – acute anxiety, depression, insomnia, physical hyper-alertness, self-loathing that is long-lasting and resistant to change (complex-PTSD). Victims may also suffer from traumatic bonding – a form of coercive control in which the perpetrator instills in the victim fear as well as gratitude for being allowed to live.

Types of Sex Trafficking

Victims of trafficking are forced into various forms of commercial sexual exploitation including prostitution, pornography, stripping, live-sex shows, mail-order brides, military prostitution and sex tourism.

Victims trafficked into prostitution and pornography are usually involved in the most exploitive forms of commercial sex operations. Sex trafficking operations can be found in highly-visible venues such as street prostitution, as well as more underground systems such as closed-brothels that operate out of residential homes. Sex trafficking also takes place in a variety of public and private locations such as massage parlors, spas, strip clubs and other fronts for prostitution. Victims may start off dancing or stripping in clubs and then be coerced into situations of prostitution and pornography.

Assistance for Victims of Sex Trafficking

When victims of trafficking are identified, the U.S. government can help them adjust their immigration status, and obtain support and assistance in rebuilding their lives in the United States through various programs. By certifying victims of trafficking, the U.S. Department of Health and Human Services (HHS) enables trafficking victims who are non-U.S. citizens to receive Federally funded benefits and services to the same extent as a refugee. Victims of trafficking who are U.S. citizens do not need to be certified to receive benefits. As U.S. citizens, they may already be eligible for many benefits.

Through HHS, victims can access benefits and services including food, health care and employment assistance. Certified victims of trafficking can obtain access to services that provide English language instruction and skills training for job placement. Since many victims are reluctant to come forward for fear of being deported, one of HHS' most important roles is to connect victims with non-profit organizations prepared to assist them and address their specific needs. These organizations can provide counseling, case management and benefit coordination.

If you think you have come in contact with a victim of human trafficking, call the National Human Trafficking Resource Center at 1.888.373.7888. This hotline will help you determine if you have encountered victims of human trafficking, will identify local resources available in your community to help victims, and will help you coordinate with local social service organizations to help protect and serve victims so they can begin the process of restoring their lives.

Section 25.4

Labor Trafficking

Text in this section is excerpted from "Fact Sheet: Labor Trafficking," U.S. Department of Health and Human Services (HHS), December 31, 2015.

The Trafficking Victims Protection Act of 2000 (TVPA) defines labor trafficking as: "The recruitment, harboring, transportation, provision, or obtaining of a person for labor or services, through the use of force, fraud or coercion for the purpose of subjection to involuntary servitude, peonage, debt bondage or slavery." The TVPA also recognizes sex trafficking, which is discussed in a separate fact sheet. A modern-day form of slavery, labor trafficking is a fundamental violation of human rights.

Forms of Labor Trafficking

There are several forms of exploitative practices linked to labor trafficking, including bonded labor, forced labor and child labor.

Bonded Labor

Bonded labor, or debt bondage, is probably the least known form of labor trafficking today, and yet it is the most widely used method of enslaving people. Victims become bonded laborers when their labor is demanded as a means of repayment for a loan or service in which its terms and conditions have not been defined or in which the value of the victims' services as reasonably assessed is not applied toward the liquidation of the debt. The value of their work is greater than the original sum of money "borrowed."

Forced Labor

Forced labor is a situation in which victims are forced to work against their own will, under the threat of violence or some other form of punishment, their freedom is restricted and a degree of ownership is exerted. Forms of forced labor can include domestic servitude; agricultural labor; sweatshop factory labor; janitorial, food service and other service industry labor; and begging.

Child Labor

Child labor is a form of work that is likely to be hazardous to the health and/or physical, mental, spiritual, moral or social development of children and can interfere with their education. The International Labor Organization estimates worldwide that there are 246 million exploited children aged between 5 and 17 involved in debt bondage, forced recruitment for armed conflict, prostitution, pornography, the illegal drug trade, the illegal arms trade and other illicit activities around the world.

Identifying Victims of Labor Trafficking

Victims of labor trafficking are not a homogenous group of people. Victims are young children, teenagers, men and women. Some of them enter the country legally on worker visas for domestic, "entertainment," computer and agricultural work, while others enter illegally. Some work in legal occupations such as domestic, factory or construction work, while others toil in illegal industries such as the drug and arms trade or panhandling. Although there is no single way to identify victims of labor trafficking, some common patterns include:

- Victims are often kept isolated to prevent them from getting help. Their activities are restricted and are typically watched, escorted or guarded by associates of traffickers. Traffickers may "coach" them to answer questions with a cover story about being a student or tourist.

- Victims may be blackmailed by traffickers using the victims' status as an undocumented alien or their participation in an "illegal" industry. By threatening to report them to law enforcement or immigration officials, traffickers keep victims compliant.

- People who are trafficked often come from unstable and economically devastated places as traffickers frequently identify vulnerable populations characterized by oppression, high rates of illiteracy, little social mobility and few economic opportunities.

- Women and children are overwhelmingly trafficked in labor arenas because of their relative lack of power, social marginalization, and their overall status as compared to men.

Health Impacts of Labor Trafficking

In addition to the human rights abuses that define their involuntary servitude, victims of labor trafficking suffer from a variety of physical and mental health problems:

- Various methods of forced labor expose victims of labor trafficking to physical abuse such as scars, headaches, hearing loss, cardiovascular/respiratory problems, and limb amputation. Victims of labor trafficking may also develop chronic back, visual and respiratory problems from working in agriculture, construction or manufacturing under dangerous conditions.

- The psychological effects of torture are helplessness, shame and humiliation, shock, denial and disbelief, disorientation and confusion, and anxiety disorders including posttraumatic stress disorder (PTSD), phobias, panic attacks, and depression.

- Many victims also develop Traumatic Bonding or "Stockholm Syndrome," which is characterized by cognitive distortions where reciprocal positive feelings develop between captors and their hostages. This bond is a type of human survival instinct and helps the victim cope with the captivity.

- Child victims of labor trafficking are often malnourished to the extent that they may never reach their full height, they may have poorly formed or rotting teeth, and later they may experience reproductive problems.

Assistance for Victims of Labor Trafficking

When victims of trafficking are identified, the U.S. government can help them stabilize their immigration status, and obtain support and assistance in rebuilding their lives in the United States through various programs. By certifying victims of trafficking, the U.S. Department of Health and Human Services (HHS) enables trafficking victims who are non-U.S. citizens to receive federally funded benefits and services to the same extent as a refugee. Victims of trafficking who are U.S. citizens do not need to be certified to receive benefits. As U.S. citizens, they may already be eligible for many benefits.

As a result of the certification or eligibility letters issued by HHS, victims can access benefits and services including food, health care and employment assistance. Certified victims of trafficking can obtain access to services that provide English language instruction and skills training for job placement. Since many victims are reluctant to come forward for fear of being deported, one of HHS' most important roles is to connect victims with non-profit organizations prepared to assist them and address their specific needs. These organizations can provide counseling, case management and benefit coordination.

If you think you have come in contact with a victim of human trafficking, call the National Human Trafficking Resource Center at 1-888-373-7888. This hotline will help you determine if you have encountered victims of human trafficking, will identify local resources available in your community to help victims, and will help you coordinate with local social service organizations to help protect and serve victims so they can begin the process of restoring their lives.

Section 25.5

Victim Assistance

Text in this section is excerpted from "Fact Sheet: Victim Assistance," Office of Refugee Resettlement, August 7, 2012.

Under the Trafficking Victims Protection Act of 2000 (TVPA), the U.S. Department of Health and Human Services (HHS) is the sole Federal agency authorized to certify foreign adult victims of human trafficking so that they are eligible for federal and State benefits and services to the same extent as refugees admitted to the United States. Similarly, it is the sole Federal agency authorized to determine the eligibility of foreign minor victims of trafficking for the benefits and services available to refugees. Certification and Eligibility Letters are issued by the HHS Office of Refugee Resettlement (ORR).

U.S. citizen and Lawful Permanent Resident (LPR) victims do not need to be certified or receive a letter of eligibility to be eligible for similar benefits and services.

The Certification for Adult Victims of Trafficking and Child Victims of Human Trafficking fact sheets provide more information about HHS/ORR certification and eligibility determinations.

ORR also provides funding for services to foreign victims of trafficking and potential victims in the United States. The ORR National Human Trafficking Victim Assistance Program funds comprehensive case management to foreign victims of trafficking and potential victims in the United States seeking HHS/ORR certification through a network of sub-awardees in locations throughout the country.

Benefits and Services Available to Victims of Human Trafficking

Certified and eligible victims of human trafficking can receive benefits and services necessary for their safety, protection, and basic well-being. These include:

- Housing assistance
- Food assistance
- Income assistance
- Employment assistance
- English language training
- Health care
- Mental health services
- Foster care

Temporary Immigration Status and Relief

The TVPA created the T visa, a nonimmigrant status that allows a foreign victim of human trafficking to remain in the United States for up to four years. The law also allows certain members of a T visa holder's family to apply for derivative T visa status.

There are several benefits to a T visa, including the following:

- Employment authorization (EAD);
- Possibility of adjusting status to Lawful Permanent Resident; and

- Ability of certain family members to obtain nonimmigrant status as T visa derivatives.

Eligible family members of trafficking victims who have received T nonimmigrant status can apply for a special T visa for derivatives. These family members include the spouse, child, parent, or an unmarried minor sibling of a victim of trafficking victim who is under 21 years of age, or the spouse or child of a victim of trafficking who is 21 years of age or older. Like certified trafficking victims, T visa derivatives are eligible for Federal and State benefits and services to the same extent as refugees. Also, derivatives can apply for EADs.

Continued Presence (CP) is a one-year form of immigration relief that Federal law enforcement officials request on behalf of a victim of a severe form of trafficking who is also a potential witness. Continued Presence allows the victim to remain in the United States during the course of an investigation or prosecution as well as obtain an Employment Authorization Document (EAD). Both CP and T nonimmigrant status are granted by the U.S. Department of Homeland Security.

The following are some of the specific benefit programs for which trafficking victims with a Certification or Eligibility Letter can apply.

- **Temporary Assistance for Needy Families (TANF)** – A federally subsidized, State-run cash-benefit and work-opportunities program for needy families with children when the parents or other caretaker relatives are unable to provide for the family's basic needs, and for pregnant women.

- **Supplemental Security Income (SSI)** – A monthly benefit for persons who are blind or disabled, or are at least 65 years old and have limited income and resources.

- **Refugee Cash Assistance (RCA)** – HHS/ORR program available to victims who are ineligible for TANF and SSI. RCA benefits are available for up to eight months from the date of ORR certification. RCA recipients must register for employment services and participate in employability service programs unless specifically exempted by State criteria. Minors who cannot comply with the employability service requirements cannot receive RCA.

- **Supplemental Nutrition Assistance Program (SNAP), formerly Food Stamps** – Federal benefits to buy food that is provided to low-income individuals and families through an electronic card that is used like an ATM card at participating grocery stores.

- **Women, Infants and Children (WIC)** – Provides supplemental food packages for nutritionally at-risk, low-income pregnant, breastfeeding, and postpartum women; infants; and children up to five years of age.

- **Medicaid** – The federally subsidized State-run program that provides health coverage for low-income pregnant women, children, parents, adults, and those with disabilities who may have no insurance or inadequate medical insurance.

- **Children's Health Insurance Program (CHIP)** – The public health insurance program for low-income, uninsured children 18 years of age or younger who do not qualify for Medicaid.

- **Refugee Medical Assistance (RMA)** – HHS/ORR program available to victims who are ineligible for Medicaid or CHIP. RMA benefits are available for up to eight months from the date of ORR certification, or the date of eligibility if the victim is a minor.

- **Medical Screening** – Conducted by State or local health departments or their proxies for the diagnosis, treatment and prevention of communicable diseases and other conditions of public health importance. This usually includes screening for tuberculosis (TB), parasites, and hepatitis B, as well as school vaccinations.

- **One-Stop Career Center System** – Department of Labor (DOL)-funded nationwide network of employment centers that provide information and assistance for people who are looking for jobs, or who need education and training to get a job. Services include training referrals, career counseling, job listings, and other employment services.

- **Job Corps** – DOL-funded centers to help eligible youth aged 16-24 achieve employment, earn a high school diploma or GED and/ or learn a vocational trade.

- **Matching Grant** – HHS/ORR self-sufficiency program administered by private agencies as an alternative to public assistance and designed to enable clients to become self-sufficient within four to six months from the date of certification or eligibility. Provides case management; cash assistance and housing, when needed; and employment services. Clients must complete enrollment in Matching Grant within 31 days of the date of certification or eligibility.

- **Housing** – Eligibility for affordable rental housing for low-income families, the elderly, and persons with disabilities, and Housing Choice Vouchers issued by low-income housing agencies to very low-income individuals and families so that they can lease privately owned rental housing.

- **Unaccompanied Refugee Minors (URM) Program** – Provides specialized, culturally appropriate foster care or other licensed care settings according to children's individual needs. Provides family reunification assistance when appropriate.

Part Four

Preventing and Intervening in Domestic Violence

Chapter 26

Healthy Relationships Are Key to Preventing Domestic Violence

Chapter Contents

Section 26.1

What Should I Look For in a Boy- or Girlfriend?

Text in this section is excerpted from "Dating," Office on Women's Health (OWH), September 22, 2009. Reviewed January 2016.

Dating

Dating relationships can be a fun and exciting part of your life. They can also be confusing, especially if dating is new to you. Once you know that the person that you like also likes you, you may not know what to do next. You can start by learning about what makes a dating relationship healthy and safe.

When Do Teens Start Dating?

There is no best age for teens to start dating. Every person will be ready for a dating relationship at a different time. Different families may have their own rules about dating, too. When you decide to start a dating relationship, it should be because you care about someone and not because other people are dating. A dating relationship is a special chance to get to know someone, and it should happen only when you are really ready and your parents/guardians are okay with it.

What Is a Healthy Dating Relationship?

Healthy dating relationships should start with the same things that healthy friendships start with: good communication, honesty, and respect. Dating relationships are a little different because they may include physical ways of showing you care, like hugging, kissing, or holding hands. You may find yourself wanting to spend all of your time with your crush, but it is important to spend some time apart, too. This will let you have a healthy relationship with your crush and with your friends and family at the same time.

Why Should I Date Someone Close to My Age?

It may not seem like a big deal to date someone more than 2 years older than you, but it can be. It's possible that someone older than you might want a more physical relationship than you do.

What If I Feel Pressure to Do Something I Do Not Want to Do?

Respecting your right to say no means that your date will stop if you say "no."

You should NEVER feel pressured to do something that you don't want to do. Your crush should always respect your right to say no to anything that doesn't feel right. Talk to your crush ahead of time about what you will and will not do.

Tips for Having Healthy and Safe Relationships

- Get to know a person by talking on the phone or at school before you go out for the first time.

- Go out with a group of friends to a public place the first few times you go out.

- Plan fun activities like going to the movies or the mall, on a picnic or for a walk.

- Tell the other person what you feel okay doing. Also, tell the person what time your parents/guardians want you to be home.

- Tell at least one friend and your parents/guardians who you are going out with and where you are going. Also tell them how to reach you.

Communication, trust, and respect are key to healthy relationships. Healthy relationships make you feel good about who YOU are and SAFE with the other person. Feel good about yourself and get to know what makes you happy. The more you love yourself, the easier it will be to find healthy relationships.

Section 26.2

Building Healthy Relationships

Text in this section is excerpted from "Healthy Relationships,"
Office on Women's Health (OWH), September 22, 2009.
Reviewed January 2016; and text from "Opportunities for
Healthy Relationships for Teens," Centers for Disease Control
and Prevention (CDC), July 22, 2015.

What Makes a Relationship Healthy?

Healthy relationships are fun and make you feel good about yourself. You can have a healthy relationship with anyone in your life—family, friends, and the people you date. Relationships take time and care to make them healthy. The relationships you have as a teen are a special part of your life and will teach you good lessons about who you are.

Communication and Sharing

The most important part of any healthy relationship is communication. Communication means that you are able to share things about yourself and your feelings. It also means that you listen to what the other person shares. This can happen by talking, emailing, writing, texting, or even using body language. When you are talking to someone, look him or her in the eye to show you are listening.

When you have healthy communication, everyone feels calm. You can share your feelings with the other person. You know that he or she will be there to listen, support you, and keep personal things that you share private. The other person will feel safe with you, too. In healthy relationships, people do not tell lies.

Respect and Trust

Fights can still happen in healthy relationships. In healthy relationships, though, people stay calm and talk about how they feel. Talking calmly helps you see the real reason you are not getting along. This makes it easier to figure out how to fix the problem. In healthy relationships, working through problems often makes the relationship stronger. People feel good about one another when they work through tough times rather than give up too easily.

Self-Esteem

Feeling good about yourself—having good self-esteem—and knowing that you deserve a healthy relationship is also very important.

Negotiation and Compromise

In a healthy relationship, negotiation and compromise are always present. **Negotiation** means talking until you agree with each other. **Compromise** means each person gives up a little bit of what they want until both persons can agree. For example, say Jane wants to go to a movie, but Kara already saw the movie Jane wants to see. Jane and Kara can negotiate and compromise until they find something they both want to do. This way, it's a 'win-win' situation and everyone is happy.

There may be some issues which are **non-negotiable** within your family. **Non-negotiable** means they are rules that will not change. These rules are likely in place to keep you safe. (Some of these items may be no underage drinking or no missing curfew, for example.)

Be Assertive, Not Aggressive

Don't be afraid to ask for what you want, but remember to respect your partner. Being assertive means asking for what you want clearly and respectfully, without threats, intimidation, or physical force. Assertive communication means respecting the rights of others, as well as your own rights.

How Do I Know That I Have a Healthy Relationship with Someone?

- You feel good about yourself when you are with that person.
- You think that both people work hard to treat the other person well.
- You feel safe around the other person.
- You like being with the other person.
- You feel that you can trust him or her with your secrets.

Opportunities for Healthy Relationships for Teens

Table 26.1. Opportunities for Healthy Relationships for Teens

Relationship Type	Defining the Relationship	Potential Benefit(s)	Opportunities for Observation/ Interaction
Peers	These individuals are better known as friends	Learning to make and keep friendships also builds skills needed for healthy dating relationships. A strong network of healthy friendships is linked to lower rates of dating violence.	In hallways, at lunch, and other times teens are together, you can see how they interact with each other and encourage positive social skills and behaviors.
Parents	For many teens, this is the first example of an intimate relationship they observe.	If they have conversations with a teen around how to build healthy, respectful relationships and model those behaviors, this connection can impact how a teen communicates and deals with conflict/ stress in a dating relationship.	Learning about a student's home life and family bonds can give you valuable insight. Coordination between school and home is also linked to better school performance
Educators	These individuals help teens learn how to navigate the world beyond their home and family in school and other learning environments.	Students engaged at school tend to have more positive outcomes later in life.	Besides the classroom, other learning environments where these individuals can be observed include sites where teens participate in extracurricular activities and/or school-sponsored programs. This may be your chance to see what successfully engages a teen and what does not.

Table 26.1. Continued

Relationship Type	Defining the Relationship	Potential Benefit(s)	Opportunities for Observation/ Interaction
Dating Partners	Adolescents may spend a great deal of time thinking about these relationships, even if they don't have one. Teens will have the least experience with this relationship type.	This relationship type can be another source of support for a teen, if it is healthy.	Teens don't always have private spaces to be alone with other teens. Unfortunately, this may mean more private behavior happening in public. You may be in a position to guide healthier behavior.
Other Trusted Adults	These individuals are mentors and family friends who may not have an official role in the lives of teens, but they have taken the time to show interest and build trust.	When problems arise with parents, friends, or dating partners, having someone who is not as closely involved can be helpful. The outsider status of these individuals can make it easier for teens to share concerns and accept advice.	If you know a teen is struggling but you are not close to the teen, you may want to look for these connections in their neighborhoods or communities.

Section 26.3

Tips for Being a Nurturing Parent

Text in this section is excerpted from "Family Checkup: Positive
Parenting Prevents Drug Abuse," National Institute on Drug
Abuse (NIDA), National Institutes of Health (NIH), August 2015.

Communication

Are You Able to Communicate Calmly and Clearly with Your Teenager regarding Relationship Problems, Such as Jealousy or Need for Attention?

Good communication between parents and children is the foundation of strong family relationships. Developing good communication skills helps parents catch problems early, support positive behavior, and stay aware of what is happening in their children's lives.

Relationship Problems and Clear Communication

- Negative example: Mom gets defensive
- Positive example: Mom is understanding

Before you begin:

- Be sure it's a good time to talk and you can focus one hundred percent on communicating with your child.
- Have a plan.
- Gather your thoughts before you approach your child.
- Be calm and patient.
- Limit distractions.

Key Communication Skills Include:

Questioning

The kind of information you receive depends a lot on how you ask the question.

- **Show interest/concern.** Don't blame/accuse. For example, instead of, "How do you get yourself into these situations?" say, "That sounds like a difficult situation. Were you confused?"

- **Encourage problem-solving/thinking.** For example: Instead of, "What did you think was going to happen when you don't think?" say, "So, what do you think would have been a better way to handle that?"

Listening and Observing

- Youth feel more comfortable bringing issues and situations to their parents when they know they will be listened to and not be accused.

Extra Tips

- Be present and tuned in.

- Show understanding.

- Listen with respect.

- Be interested.

- Avoid negative emotions.

- Give encouragement.

Reducing Emotions

Sometimes, talking with children brings up strong feelings that interfere with clear thinking. Following the CALM steps can help a parent keep the conversation moving in the right direction:

- **C**ontrol your thoughts and your actions.

- **A**ssess and decide if you are too upset to continue.

- **L**eave the situation if you are feeling too angry or upset.

- **M**ake a plan to deal with the situation within 24 hours.

Practice Skill

When listening to your child, remember:

- Show understanding.

- Repeat back or summarize what your child said.

- Practice patience.

- Emphasize positive behaviors and choices.

Encouragement

Do You Encourage Positive Behavior Habits in Your Teenager on a Daily Basis?

Encouragement is key to building confidence and a strong sense of self. Consistent encouragement helps youth feel good about themselves and gives them confidence to: try new activities, develop new friendships, explore their creativity, and tackle difficult tasks. It also helps parents promote cooperation and reduce conflict.

Underachievement in School and Daily Encouragement

- Negative example: Dad reacts to failure
- Positive example: Dad builds on success

Encouragement promotes a strong sense of self because it sends three main messages to your child:

1. You can do it!

Youth believe they can do things if parents:

- help them break a problem down into smaller parts
- remind them of their strengths and past successes
- encourage them by sharing how they have dealt with challenges

Examples of Encouraging Words

- "I know that wasn't easy."
- "You did such an awesome job."
- "Keep on trying."
- "You are very good at that."
- "You are learning a lot."
- "I like the way you did that."
- "I can tell you've been practicing."
- "It's great to see you working so hard."
- "I'm so proud of you."

2. You have good ideas!

Youth believe they have good ideas if parents:

- ask them to share their opinions and feelings
- listen to what they have to say
- ask them for input concerning family plans and events
- ask them for ideas to solve family problems

3. You are important!

Youth know they are important if parents:

- remember what they have told them
- make time for them each day
- attend school functions and extracurricular activities
- let them know that they are thinking about them when they can't be with them
- display things they have made and recognitions they receive from school or the community

Practices That Are Discouraging

- Being sarcastic or negative about a child's ability to be successful
- Comparing a child to brothers and sisters
- Taking over when a child's progress is slow
- Reminding a child of past failures

When Giving Praise for Cooperation:

- Make it simple: "Thank you."
- Do it right away.
- Be specific about what you like.
- Never miss an opportunity to encourage behavior or acts you would like to see repeated.

When Reviewing Behavior Change Plans:

- Check each step of the plan.

- Praise positive behaviors.

- Give incentives immediately.

- Remember to review the plan with your child every day.

Negotiation

Are You Able to Negotiate Emotional Conflicts with Your Teenager and Work toward a Solution?

Negotiating solutions offers parents a way to work together to solve problems; make changes; promote and improve cooperation; and teach youth how to focus on solutions rather than problems, think through possible outcomes of behavior, and develop communication skills.

Destructive Behavior and Negotiation

- Negative example: Dad gets angry

- Positive example: Dad stays calm

Set Up for Success

When. Select an unemotional or regularly scheduled time (not in the middle of a problem).

Where. Choose a neutral place with few distractions.

How:

- Choose problems that are small and specific.

- State the problem neutrally.

- Recognize the other person's positive behavior.

- Accept part of the responsibility for the problem.

- Restate what you hear, show understanding, and stop if you get too upset.

The Steps to Problem-Solving

Brainstorm—Open Your Mind to All Ideas

- Try to come up with three ideas each.

- Any idea is good—even ones that seem silly.

- Take turns coming up with ideas.

Problem-Solving Traps

- Don't try to solve hot issues.
- Don't blame the other person or put the other person down.
- Don't defend yourself—try to let it go.
- Don't make assumptions about another person's intentions.
- Don't bring up the past—avoid using words such as "always" and "never."
- Don't lecture—a simple statement will get your point across better.

Evaluate Your List of Ideas. Go through and list the pluses and minuses of each idea.

Choose a Solution:

- Combine ideas if needed.
- All of you should agree on the chosen solution.

Practice Skills

Follow Up

- Check in with each other after you have tried your solution a couple of times to see how it is working.
- If it isn't working, go back to your list of ideas.
- If necessary, start over with some more brainstorming.

When Making Neutral Problem Statements:

- Be brief.
- Be specific.
- Use a neutral tone of voice.
- Lead with something positive.

Negotiating Steps:

- Make neutral problem statements.
- Generate possible solutions.

- Evaluate solutions.

- Choose a solution.

- Follow up to see if it is working.

Setting Limits

Are You Able to Calmly Set Limits When Your Teenager Is Defiant or Disrespectful? Are You Able to Set Limits on More Serious Problem Behavior Such as Drug Use, If or When It Occurs?

Setting limits helps parents teach self-control and responsibility, show caring, and provide safe boundaries. It also provides youth with guidelines and teaches them that following rules is important for their success in life.

Defiance/Disrespect and Setting Limits

- Negative example: Mom argues

- Positive example: Mom stays in control

Teenage Drug Use and Setting Limits

- Negative example: Mom overreacts

- Positive example: Mom stays reasonable

A Two-Step Process

Step 1: Setting Rules

- Make clear, simple, and specific rules.

- Make sure your child understands your rules.

- Have a list of consequences.

- Be ready to follow through.

Step 2: Following Up

- Research shows that parents are most effective in setting limits when they follow up right away, giving consequences when rules are broken and offering encouragement when rules are followed. Youth are more likely to follow rules if they know parents are checking up on them and will enforce the consequences consistently.

Testing Limits

Testing limits is a natural part of growing up, but it presents a special challenge for parents. Often our first reactions may come from fear for our child's safety, or anger at being disobeyed. The **SANE** guidelines can help parents establish appropriate consequences when youth break rules.

- **S**mall consequences are better
- **A**void consequences that punish you
- **N**on-abusive responses
- **E**ffective consequences (are under your control and non-rewarding to your child)

Youth may get angry, act out, or become isolated when parents enforce consequences. Your child is testing you and your limits. Don't react. Be consistent with your rules.

Extra Tips

- State the limit and the consequence clearly.
- Catch the problem early.
- Avoid arguments and threats.
- Remember to use a firm and calm tone of voice.
- Follow through each time a limit is stretched or a rule is broken.
- Offer encouragement each time a rule is followed.

Practice Skills

When Stating Rules:

- Be calm.
- Be specific.
- State only one rule at a time.
- Remember to stay involved and notice when your child follows the rule.

When giving consequences, remember:

- Label the problem behavior in terms of your rule.

- State the consequence clearly.

- Avoid arguing.

- Ignore trivia.

- Remember it is normal for kids and teens to react negatively when they receive a consequence.

To make effective requests:

- Be specific.

- Make only one request at a time.

- Focus on what you want, not what you don't.

- Remember to make sure your child does what is asked and give praise when he or she does.

Supervision

Do You Monitor Your Teenager to Assure That He or She Does Not Spend Too Much Unsupervised Time with Peers?

Childhood is a period of major growth and change. Youth tend to be uncertain about themselves and how they "fit in," and at times they can feel overwhelmed by a need to please and impress their friends. These feelings can leave children open to peer pressure. Knowing your child's friends and peers helps parents improve communication, reduce conflict, and teach responsibility.

Unsupervised Time with Peers and Monitoring

- Negative example: Dad doesn't pay attention

- Positive example: Dad follows up

You Can Help Your Child and Increase Your Influence By:

- knowing your child's friends in the neighborhood and at school

- staying involved in your child's activities

- talking to your child when a concern comes up

Peer Influence

Youth do not always make wise choices in picking friends. Help them see what qualities they should value in friends—such as honesty, school involvement, and respect.

Supervision

When youth begin to spend more and more time away from home, monitoring their behavior and whereabouts is challenging. Supervision helps parents recognize developing problems, promote safety, and stay involved.

The 4 Cs of Supervision Can Help You with This Difficult Task:

- **Clear Rules**—Have a few non-negotiable rules about your child's behavior and state them clearly!

- **Communication**—Regular communication with other parents and teachers keeps you involved in your child's activities, creates resources to deal with problems by building a strong safety network for your child, and informs you of dangerous places or people.

- **Checking Up**—This lets your child know that you care about his or her safety and that your rules are important. This is hard for some of us because we want to trust our children and they may resist our efforts.

- **Consistency**—Supervision is most effective when parents set clear limits and follow through with consequences for misbehavior. Also, be consistent with giving praise and incentives when a rule is followed.

How Do You Supervise When You Are Not at Home?

- Know your child's schedule.

- Call your child at varying times.

- Have your child check in with you or other caregivers when he or she reaches home.

- Have your child check in when he or she reaches his or her destination.

- Surprise your child with a random visit or call.
- Remain in communication with adults who interact with your child.

Extra Tips

- Keep lines of communication open.
- Be patient and observe; don't react—it may pass.
- Stay involved.
- Spend time listening to your child.
- Know who your child's friends are and watch your child interact with them and others.
- Talk to the parent(s) of your child's friends.

Practice Skills

When Asking Your Child Questions:

- Choose a good time.
- Use a neutral or positive tone.
- Show interest and understanding.
- Paraphrase what your child says.

Chapter 27

Men's Role in Domestic Violence Prevention

It is now widely accepted that strategies to end violence against women and girls (VAWG) must include work with men and boys. Much of the evidence relating to such strategies comes from the health sector. Ending VAWG, however, requires coordinated work across many sectors. The need for a multisectoral response to the challenge of ending VAWG has focused attention on the opportunities for and challenges of male engagement strategies outside of the health sector. This report reviews documentation of work, outside the health sector, with men and boys on VAWG to identify promising approaches to, and emerging lessons from, these efforts.

Such approaches are grounded in an understanding of the links between social constructions of masculinity and men's use of violence. Social constructions of gender almost always confer a higher social value on men than women, and privilege the masculine over the feminine. Male violence against women and girls is born of this privilege. The term "positive masculinities," which is used in this report, has emerged in recent years as a way to characterize the values, norms, and practices that gender-based work with men and boys seeks to promote in order to end VAWG.

Text in this chapter is excerpted from "Working with Men and Boys to End Violence Against Women and Girls: Approaches, Challenges, and Lessons," United States Agency for International Development (USAID), February 2015.

This chapter reviews the published and grey literature on male engagement strategies for ending VAWG in five sectors from across the Global South. Sectors reviewed include economic growth, trade and agriculture; education; governance, law enforcement and justice systems; conflict, post conflict and humanitarian assistance; and social development. A broad definition of such violence was used. Violence against men and boys, much of which could be considered gender based, was not considered as part of this review in accordance with stipulated terms of reference. Programs were included in this review on the basis of evaluated impact, lessons learned documentation, and/or innovative program design. Findings from the review are summarized below in relation to the five sectors considered.

Ending Violence against Women and Girls Requires Work with Men and Boys

It is now widely accepted that strategies to end violence against women and girls must include work with men and boys. In recent years, the proliferation of interventions involving men and boys has been motivated by a desire to address men's role in violence perpetration and recognition that patriarchal norms of masculinity are implicated in violence. In its 2008 report to the United States Congress on Response and Policy Issues with respect to international Violence Against Women, the Congressional Research Service identified "The Role of Men and Boys" as the first of its current and emerging areas in violence against women research, prevention, and treatment, observing that:

Research on VAW has evolved to include not only treatment and prevalence but also root causes. As a result, many experts and policymakers have increasingly focused on the role of men and boys in preventing violence against women.

This recognition of the importance of male engagement strategies to end VAWG is part of a broader acknowledgement of the roles that men and boys can and must play in work to establish and maintain gender equality. Such roles have gained significant attention from the international community over the past decade, including the 1995 Beijing Platform for Action, the 2000 review of the Programme of Action of the World Summit on Social Development and the 48th Session of the United Nations Commission on the Status of Women in 2004.

Not only has the importance of work with men and boys for ending VAWG been established, there is a growing body of evidence from male engagement interventions about the best ways to work with men and boys on changing gender inequitable attitudes, practices, norms and policies. Much of this evidence comes from the health sector, as it is within the fields of sexual and reproductive health (SRH) and HIV and AIDS that much of the early work with men on gender equality was established and where it has been best documented.

Ending VAWG, however, requires coordinated work across many sectors, as recent analyses of gender based violence prevention have emphasized. The need for a multi-sectoral response to the challenge of ending VAWG has focused attention on the opportunities for and challenges of male engagement strategies outside of the health sector. This review has been commissioned by the United States Agency for International Development (USAID) to investigate the available documentation of work with men and boys on VAWG outside the health sector and to identify promising approaches to, and emerging lessons from, this work that can guide future funding priorities and program development.

Men, Masculinities, and Violence against Women and Girls

Violence against women and girls is the most widespread form of abuse worldwide, affecting one third of all women in their lifetime. Such violence takes many forms (physical, sexual, emotional and economic) and is rooted in women's political, economic, and social subordination. Rape and intimate partner violence (IPV) are found in all societies, with varying prevalence, and culturally specific forms of VAWG may be locally common, such as honor killings or female genital mutilation. However, women's experience of such violence is far from uniform as it is shaped not only by patriarchal norms and institutions, but also by other forms of inequality and discrimination linked to factors such as class, ethnicity, age, sexuality, and disability. Women's and girls' exposure to different forms of violence, their experience of that violence, and their access to justice, health services and social support in response to that violence are all affected by these multiple and linked forms of inequality that they face. The frequency and severity of VAWG may also increase during periods of conflict and humanitarian emergencies, as well as in the aftermath of such crises.

While it is true that not all men are violent and that some men have been active for many years in working to end VAWG and to promote gender equality, it remains the case that the vast majority of violence experienced by women and girls is perpetrated by men and boys, whether as individuals or as part of male-dominated institutions. Research also suggests that men's use of violence against girls and women is closely related to their use of violence against other men. Studies indicate that men who have themselves experienced violence are more likely to perpetrate intimate partner violence or rape, although the majority of male survivors of violence do not subsequently go on to perpetrate violence.

The biology of the Y chromosome is not an adequate explanation for male violence against women and girls, for there are great global differences in prevalence and patterns, and individual differences between men in any one setting. But a growing body of empirical research and program expertise has developed in recent years addressing the connections between social constructions of masculinity and men's use of violence. Although differing in degree across different societies, social constructions of gender almost always confer a higher social value on men than women and privilege the masculine over the feminine.

Male violence against women and girls is born of this privilege, whether because men feel entitled to use violence against those who are 'less' than them, or because they fear the loss of such privilege or feel unable to live up to the expectations associated with being the dominant gender. In many societies, boys are raised to be men learning that violence is a way to demonstrate their masculinity and prove themselves to be "real men," often at great cost not only to the women and girls in their lives but also to themselves.

These links between social constructions of masculinity and male violence have been starkly illustrated by several large-scale research projects. Over 10,000 men participated in a recent United Nations (UN) study in Asia and the Pacific, providing valuable insights into factors associated with men's perpetration of VAWG, and complementing research conducted through the International Men and Gender Equality Survey (IMAGES).

Key factors strongly associated with perpetration of IPV and non-partner rape included controlling behaviors towards women and inequitable gender attitudes, behaviors that emphasized (hetero)sexual prowess (transactional sex and having multiple sexual partners), and involvement in violence with other men. Men struggling to live up to the ideals of manhood because of social exclusion and poverty, and men who had been traumatized through harsh childhoods and violence in adulthood, were also at increased risk of perpetration.

The concept of "hegemonic masculinity," originally developed by Australian sociologist Raewyn Connell, is now widely used to characterize those ideas about and expressions of masculinity associated with male domination and male violence against women and girls. In this sense, the practices and norms of hegemonic masculinity help to keep patriarchy in place. This phenomenon has been emphasized with reference to the male behaviors associated with IPV and non-partner rape identified by the research findings above:

Many of these behaviors are rooted in expected practices or entitlements that flow from hegemonic ideals of men who are strong, tough, in control over women and their bodies, heterosexual and sexually dominant.

The concept of hegemonic masculinity has proved particularly useful in work with men on ending VAWG, both because it emphasizes that men's gender identities and practices are learned and thus can be changed, and because there are other masculinities available to men (i.e., other ways of being a man) that do not conform to these hegemonic ideals but instead focus on more equitable, respectful and harmonious gender relations. This emphasis on masculinities as both multiple and changeable has been used in working with men to critically reflect on their socialization, power, privilege, and the costs to themselves as well as to women and girls of conforming to the norms of hegemonic masculinity.

It suggests that there are alternative, more 'positive' ways of being a man that do not involve VAWG that can be linked to culturally significant values of trust, respect, and equality that exist in a given community. Importantly, it also highlights the gravity of working with women, as women often take for granted men's power over them. As a result, there is a need to empower women not just economically but socially and individually and to raise their consciousness, so that women understand their role in male gender socialization and demand more equitable relationships.

The term "positive masculinities," which is used in this report, has emerged in recent years as a way to characterize the values, norms and practices that gender-based work with men and boys seeks to promote in order to end VAWG. Often this is taken to refer simply to more equitable, non-violent relations between men and women. However, as the widespread violence against lesbian, gay, bisexual, transgender, and intersex (LGBTI) people—whether perpetrated by individuals or institutions—makes clear, hegemonic masculinity is not simply about men's domination of women, but also the subordination of those whose gender identities and sexual orientations do not conform to the heterosexual hegemonic ideal.

The emphasis on different, non-violent ways of being a man that is central to work on "positive masculinities" must also seek to support the diversity and multiplicity of gender identities and sexual orientations, in culturally meaningful ways, in order to foster societies where any violence rooted in hegemonic norms of gender and sexuality is no longer tolerated.

375

Recommendations

There is now widespread agreement among practitioners, policy advocates, and researchers that action to prevent and respond to violence against women and girls must work across the 'social ecology' of individual, community, institutional, and societal levels to effect change. Thus, the following synthesis of a set of recommendations across the different sectors included in this wide-ranging review uses a modified social ecological framework to discuss key findings from this review at each of the following four levels of change:

- Individual level attitudes and behaviors

- Community level norms and practices

- Institutional level policies and cultures

- Societal level laws and government policy

Presenting the recommendations in this way is also intended to highlight the importance of linking work across different sectors in order to effect change at these different levels of the social ecology.

Working with Men and Boys for Change at the Individual Level

Start Young. The male engagement interventions reviewed here make clear the value of working with younger adolescents, at a time when both their gender identities and their attitudes towards and skills in gender relations are being formed. This is clearly an important emphasis of male engagement programming on violence within the Education sector, but it also suggests a need to extend male engagement programming in other sectors to younger men and boys were possible.

Adapt Effective Group-work Methodologies. Well-tested, evidence-based group-work methodologies focused on positive masculinities have been successfully adapted for use in many different sectoral contexts. Successful adaptation relies on adequate investments in situational assessments and engaging the participation of targeted communities and stakeholders in the adaptation process. Skilled facilitation is crucial to the effectiveness of such group-work, emphasizing the need for investments in capacity building and mentoring for facilitators. Although most of the male-targeted group-work reviewed here was led by male facilitators, there are indications that mixed-gender facilitation teams can prove beneficial in helping to model more equitable gender relations.

Highlight Men's Roles in Care Work. Focusing work with men on the roles they can play as caregivers within their own families and in the broader community as a whole is a promising practice for promoting more positive, nonviolent masculinities. Not only is this approach validated by research on the associations between men's care giving involvement and more gender equitable attitudes, but focusing on men's involvement with their families has been found to be an important component of supporting their social reintegration in post-conflict situations.

Address Men's Multiple Interests in Change. Much of the work with men and boys on VAWG focuses on their gender interests in change with respect to the benefits of more positive masculinities for both themselves and women and girls. Yet, much of this work is targeted at poor and socially marginalized communities, within which many women and men share similar interests (based on class and/or ethnicity and/or other aspects of social marginalization) in struggling for a better life for themselves and their families. Addressing GBV as that which fractures families and communities and jeopardizes their shared struggle for a better life and more social justice is one way to engage women and men in working together to end such violence. Furthermore, while this review has focused specifically on efforts to prevent and respond to VAWG, many different programs found that work with men and boys on such violence is more effective when it acknowledges and addresses men's and boys' own experiences with male violence.

Working with Men and Boys for Change at the Community Level

Nurture Supportive Male Peer Groups. Fostering alternative male peer groups are an important way to sustain men's adoption of more equitable masculinities, by creating networks of both support and accountability for men to help them in dealing with peer pressures to conform to dominant and harmful norms of masculinity.

Engage Men In Collective Action. Organizing men to undertake action for change at the community level is a way to both sustain and broaden the impact of a program. While much of the positive masculinities work discussed in this review focuses exclusively on changing men's own attitudes and individual behaviors, there are indications that this individual level change can be better sustained when men are organized to take specific actions to change aspects of community life that increase women's and girls' vulnerability to violence or inhibit them from accessing needed services.

Increase the Focus on Men's Roles in Responding to VAW. The overall sense from the programs reviewed for this report is that much of the male engagement work concerned with VAWG has focused on prevention, and given less attention to men's multiple roles in improving the support given to women and girl survivors. Whether this is as active bystanders intervening to address situations of vulnerability or as referral agents to available health, legal, and social welfare services, male engagement programming can better equip men to play an active role in response. As a recent report has emphasized:

Experience in the field shows that violence prevention cannot be undertaken successfully without provision of services for survivors and showing that social institutions care about violence against women and girls, it requires empowerment of women both as individuals, within relationships and across society, and transforming masculinities must be framed as a complement to these.

Address Broader Social Influences Shaping Norms of Masculinity. The evidence suggests that male engagement programming on ending VAWG is more effective when it combines strategies focusing on individual level change and nurturing alternative peer groups, with strategies that target broader social influences promoting harmful norms of masculinity. Building the capacity of programs to design and implement strategies using social marketing, media advocacy, and cultural work is an important priority for this work.

Work 'With The Grain' of Male Community Leadership but Stay Connected to Goals for Women's Empowerment. As work with male community and religious leaders to address harmful traditional practices or reform aspects of alternative justice mechanisms indicates, it is both necessary and possible to engage male leaders in changing aspects of community life without challenging the patriarchal basis of their authority. In seeking to change a practice that is based on inequitable gender norms, and in using but not seeking to change the patriarchal power that men in positions of community leadership have to make this change, this work is both gender transformative and gender aware. Nevertheless, in order to contribute to the broader gender transformative goals of women's empowerment work, it is important that this male engagement work with male leaders is connected to ongoing efforts to strengthen women's leadership and power within such communities.

Working with Men and Boys for Change at the Institutional Level

Strengthen Program Capacity to Work for Institutional Level Change. A common finding across the different sectors reviewed for this report is that individual and community level strategies for change must be complemented by initiatives directed at reforming the institutions that shape people's lives and affect women's and girls' vulnerability to violence and their ability to access needed services. From workplaces to schools to law enforcement and justice systems, these institutions not only tend to be led by men but are often infused with the very patriarchal norms and 'cultures' that underpin VAWG. Reforming the policies and 'cultures' of male-dominated institutions is an important priority for male engagement programming to end VAWG.

Use Institutional Hierarchies to Facilitate Institutional Reform. Institutional reform requires internal champions. Male engagement programming must identify and nurture internal male champions who can provide the necessary leadership to initiate and sustain institutional reform. The need to move beyond externally led pilot initiatives and mainstream gender training as part of institutional reform processes is also widely recognized. Programs reviewed for this report undertook different strategies to accomplish this mainstreaming. Yet there was a common concern that mainstreaming risked dilution of training impact, especially when the training was focused on more participatory and experiential methodologies. This suggests a need to invest sufficient time and resources to train and then mentor the internal training capacity that is required to fully mainstream such gender training.

Work with the 'Whole' Person and Not Only Their Professional Responsibility. Workshops on women's rights, gender equality, and institutional responsibilities with respect to VAW are one of the most common approaches to institutional reform. A common finding across several such initiatives is that such training is more effective when it focuses not only on the professional responsibilities of men within a given institution, but also on men's own experiences with gender socialization, harmful norms of masculinity, and their own experiences of male violence (in terms of the women and girls in their lives). Working with the 'whole' person is important in motivating and sustaining men's commitment to changing institutional culture and practice concerning VAWG.

Strengthen Oversight and Accountability Mechanisms. While much of the emphasis in reform processes to improve institutional responses to VAW focused on training, a consistent finding reported from differing sectoral contexts was that such training would have limited impact unless it was complemented by oversight and account-ability mechanisms. It is clear that more work is needed to develop such mechanisms. Linked to the above, men's organizations have a role to play in keeping up the pressure to hold institutions account-able to their reform agenda. Fortunately, there are promising exam-ples of organizations that work with men on gender equality taking action collaboratively with women's rights organizations to ensure such accountability (e.g., demanding women's access to justice from law enforcement and justice systems). Supporting men's organizations to collaborate with women's rights organizations in this way is an important priority.

Working with Men and Boys for Change at the Societal Level

Use a Masculinities 'Lens' for Policy Advocacy on VAWG. The promising results of Men Engage Africa's policy audits and associated advocacy efforts highlights the value of focusing a mas-culinities 'lens' at the policy level as a contribution to the ongoing advocacy of women's rights groups to improve policy and its imple-mentation on GBV and women's empowerment more broadly. While much of the investment in capacity building for male engagement work has focused on skills needed for individual and community level work, this suggests a need also to build the advocacy and campaigning skills of organizations working with men on gender equality.

Hold Male Authority Figures Accountable for Their Public Discourse. Another promising and relatively neglected area of work with men on ending VAW is to address the role that men, and the organizations that support men in working for gender equality, can play to create a more conducive public environment for efforts to end VAW. The principle of men holding other men accountable for their patriarchal behavior should be extended to holding male authority figures accountable for their public discourse.

Link Male Engagement Programming with Broader Movements for Gender Equality and Social Justice: Sustained action to challenge inequitable norms and practices of masculinity requires a movement-building perspective to designing and developing interventions. The challenge of sustaining impact was identified by many of the programs reviewed for this report.

One response has been to look at how male engagement programming can contribute to a broader and ongoing movement for change in a given community or society. This requires attention to fostering links between organizations and investing in movement-building opportunities, not least in terms of building closer relationships between initiatives focused exclusively on working with men on positive masculinities and those working on women's empowerment.

The challenge of ending VAWG is the challenge of changing unequal relations of political, economic, and social power. Supporting the efforts of social movements, which are campaigning for gender justice as part of their social justice work, and targeting male engagement work at men within such social movements to enlist their support as allies in this work, is an important direction for male engagement programming to take.

Chapter 28

Preventing Dating Violence

Chapter Contents

Section 28.1

Parents' Role in Preventing Dating Violence: Talking to Your Teen about Dating Violence

Text in this section is excerpted from "Talk with Your
Teen about Healthy Relationships," U.S. Department of
Health and Human Services (HHS), July 15, 2015.

The Basics

You can help your teen build strong, respectful relationships. Start
by teaching your son or daughter about healthy relationships.

Unfortunately, many teens have relationships that are unhealthy.
More than 1 in 10 teens who have been on a date have also been:

- Physically abused (hit, pushed, or slapped) by someone they've
  gone out with

- Sexually abused (kissed, touched, or forced to have sex without
  wanting to) by someone they've dated

- You can help your kids:

- Develop skills for healthy and safe relationships

- Set expectations for how they want to be treated

- Recognize when a relationship is unhealthy

Talking about healthy relationships is a great way to show that you
are available to listen and answer questions—so make sure to check
in often with your teen. Together, you can agree on clear rules about
dating to help keep your teen safe.

When Should I Start Talking with My Child about Relationships?

It's never too early to teach your child about healthy relationships.
You've probably been doing it all along. When you taught your child to
say "please" and "thank you" as a toddler, you were teaching respect
and kindness.

Your own relationships also teach your kids how to treat others. When you treat your kids, partner, and friends in healthy, supportive ways, your kids learn from your choices.

Kids learn from unhealthy experiences, too. When kids experience violence at home or in the community, they are more likely to be in unhealthy relationships later on.

When Should I Start Talking about Dating?

It's best to start talking about healthy dating relationships before your child starts dating. Start conversations about what to look for in a romantic partner. For example, you could ask your child:

- How do you want to be treated?

- How do you want to feel about yourself when you are with that person?

What Makes a Relationship Healthy?

In a healthy relationship:

- Both people feel respected, supported, and valued
- Both partners make decisions together
- Both people have friends and interests outside of the relationship
- The couple settles disagreements with open and honest communication
- There are more good times than bad

What Makes a Relationship Unhealthy?

In an unhealthy relationship:

- One person tries to change the other
- One person makes most or all of the decisions
- One or both people drop friends and interests outside of the relationship
- One or both people yell, threaten, hit, or throw things during arguments
- One person makes fun of the other's opinions or interests

- One person keeps track of the other all the time by calling, texting, or checking in with friends

- There are more bad times than good

People in unhealthy relationships may make many excuses to try to explain away the hurtful parts of the relationship. If you see any of these signs, talk to your teen.

What Is Dating Violence?

Dating violence is when one person in a romantic relationship is abusive to the other person. This includes:

- Stalking

- Emotional, physical, and sexual abuse

Abuse can happen in person, online, or with cell phones. And it can happen in any relationship, whether it's an opposite-sex (straight) or same-sex relationship.

Both boys and girls can be unhealthy or unsafe in a relationship. Sometimes, both partners act in unhealthy or unsafe ways. It's important to talk to all kids about how to have respectful, healthy relationships.

Who Is at Risk for Dating Violence?

Dating violence can happen to anyone. Teens may be more at risk of being in unhealthy relationships if they:

- Use alcohol or drugs

- Are depressed

- Hang out with friends who are violent

- Have trouble controlling their anger

- Struggle with learning in school

- Have sex with more than one person

- Have experienced violence at home or in the community

What Are the Warning Signs of Dating Violence?

It's common for teens to have mood swings or try out different behaviors. But sudden changes in your teen's attitude or behavior could mean that something more serious is going on. If you are worried, talk to your teen to find out more.

Watch for Signs That Your Teen's Partner May Be Violent.

If your teen is in a relationship with someone who uses violence, your teen may:

- Avoid friends, family, and school activities
- Make excuses for a partner's behavior
- Look uncomfortable or fearful around a partner
- Lose interest in favorite activities
- Get lower grades in school
- Have unexplained injuries, like bruises or scratches

Watch for Signs That Your Teen May Be Violent.

Teens who use physical, emotional, or sexual violence to control their partners need help to stop. Start a conversation if your teen:

- Is jealous and possessive
- Blames other people for anything that goes wrong
- Damages or ruins a partner's things
- Wants to control someone else's decisions
- Constantly texts or calls a partner
- Posts embarrassing information about a partner on websites like Facebook (including sexual information or pictures)

Help Your Teen Stay Healthy.

Dating violence can have long-term effects for both partners – even after the relationship ends. By helping your teen develop the skills for healthy relationships, you can help prevent these long-term effects of dating violence.

Someone who has experienced dating violence may struggle with:

- Depression
- Low self-confidence
- Eating disorders

- Drug or alcohol abuse

- Other violent relationships

A partner who has been violent may experience:

- Loss of respect from others

- Suspension or expulsion from school

- Loneliness

- Trouble with the law

Watch for signs of dating violence and help your teen stay healthy now and in the future.

Take Action!

Talk with your kids to help them develop realistic and healthy expectations for relationships.

Help Your Teen Develop Problem-Solving Skills.

Help your teen think about healthy relationships by asking how he'd handle different situations. You might ask, "What would you do if:

- you think your friend's partner isn't treating him right?"

- your partner calls you to come over whenever you try to hang out with your friends?"

- your friend yells at his girlfriend in front of everyone at a party?"

It may help to use examples from TV shows, movies, or songs on the radio to start the conversation.

Be sure to listen respectfully to your teen's answer, even if you don't agree. Then you can offer your opinion and explore other options together.

Set Rules for Dating.

As kids get older, they gain more independence and freedom. But teens still need parents to set boundaries and expectations for behavior. Here are some things to talk about with your teen:

- Are friends allowed to come over when you aren't home?

- Can your son go on a date with someone you haven't met?

- How can your daughter reach you if she needs a ride home?

Be a Role Model.

You can teach your kids a lot by treating them and others with respect. As you talk with your teen about healthy relationships, think about your own behavior. Does it match the values you are talking about?

Treating your kids with respect also helps you build stronger relationships with them. This can make it easier to communicate with your teen about important issues like staying safe.

Talk to Your Kids about Sex.

Teens who have sex with more than one person are at higher risk of being in an unhealthy relationship. Talk with your teen about your values and expectations.

Talk to Your Kids about Preventing STDs.

About half of all STD cases in the United States happen in young people ages 15 to 24.

Talk with Your Kids about Alcohol and Other Drugs.

Alcohol and drugs don't cause violence or unhealthy relationships – but they can make it harder to make smart choices. Talk to your kids about the dangers of alcohol and drugs.

If You Are Worried, Talk to Your Teen.

If you think your teen's relationship might be violent, you can:

- Write down the reasons you are worried.

- Tell your teen why you are concerned. Point out specific things that don't seem right to you.

- Listen to your teen calmly, and thank her or him for opening up.

Section 28.2

Prevention and Intervention of Teen Dating Violence

Text in this section is excerpted from "Prevention and Intervention of Teen Dating Violence," National Institute of Justice (NIJ), February 13, 2014.

Overview

The ultimate goal of prevention and intervention is to stop dating violence before it begins. During the preteen and teen years, young people are learning the skills they need to form positive, healthy relationships with others. This is an ideal time to promote healthy relationships and prevent patterns of relationship violence that can last into adulthood.

Studies investigating the effectiveness of programs to prevent dating violence are beginning to show positive results. Most programs focus on changing knowledge, attitudes and behaviors linked with dating violence while focusing on the skills needed to build healthy relationships.

Effective School Level Interventions

In one rigorous NIJ-funded study, school-level interventions in 30 New York City public middle schools reduced dating violence by up to 50 percent.

Researchers evaluated dating violence and sexual harassment interventions by randomly assigning classes to receive:

- Classroom-level interventions

- School-level interventions

- A combination of classroom- and school-level interventions

- No intervention (i.e., the control group)

Youth exposed to domestic violence are at greater risk for being both a victim and the perpetrator of dating violence. Classroom-level interventions were delivered in six sessions, using a curriculum emphasizing the consequences for perpetrators, state laws and penalties, the construction of gender roles, and healthy relationships.

School-level interventions included the use of temporary school-based restraining orders, higher levels of faculty and security presence in "hot spots," and raising awareness schoolwide.

Researchers found that, compared with the control group who received no intervention, students who received the school-level intervention or both the school- and classroom-level interventions experienced reduced levels of dating violence and sexual harassment. The researchers noted that the classroom-level intervention alone was not effective in improving these outcomes. In addition, students in the school-level intervention were more likely to intend to intervene as bystanders if they witnessed abusive behavior between their peers.

These findings are important in several ways:

- This is one of the first studies to document the effectiveness of such prevention programs among middle school students.

- Given the large size of the study (with more than 2,500 students) and the ethnic diversity of these students, the program may be applicable to a broad range of populations.

The success of the school-level intervention is particularly important because it can be implemented with very few extra costs to schools.

Family-Based Interventions for High-Risk Youth

Youth exposed to domestic violence are at increased risk to be both a victim and perpetrator of dating violence.

Yet we currently have no violence intervention protocols for this vulnerable group. To help fill the gap, NIJ funded an effort to adapt the successes of an existing evidence-based program, Families for Safe Dates, so it would be applicable to teens who are exposed to domestic violence.

To adapt Families for Safe Dates for teens exposed to domestic violence, the researcher recruited 28 women (and 35 of their 12- to 15-year-old children) from four counties, either when the women were in court filing a domestic violence protection order or when the women were seeking services through public or community-based programs. To be eligible, women had to have been victims of domestic violence but no longer living with their partners and to have a child 12 to 15 years old.

The researchers adjusted the protocol recruitment strategies, data collection procedures, measures, and program administration, and

391

eliminated the follow-up calls from the health educator. They also determined that the intervention was reaching the high-risk group: teens who had been exposed to an average of seven years of domestic violence and had high rates of dating violence compared with national averages. These teens also had high rates of exposure to bullying, sexual harassment and peer aggression, as both victims and perpetrators.

Overall, the mothers and youth reported that they enjoyed the booklets and found them helpful and informative. Given low rates of booklet completion and follow-up, however, the researchers could not decisively determine what effects the booklet had.

The pilot study was instrumental in guiding the development, refinement and implementation of a larger, ongoing efficacy trial of the intervention that is being funded by the Centers for Disease Control and Prevention (CDC).

Group-Based Interventions for High-Risk Youth

Adolescents who are maltreated and become involved in the child welfare system are at risk for being re-victimized by romantic partners. To better understand how to prevent re-victimization among this high-risk group, NIJ funded a study to evaluate the effectiveness of two prevention curriculums. The study focused on girls because they sometimes face more serious consequences of dating violence (e.g., injuries, pregnancy) than boys do.

Participants included 176 adolescent girls involved in child welfare services. The girls were assigned randomly to receive one of two curriculums:

- A group of 67 girls received a social learning/feminist curriculum designed to help girls develop healthy relational skills, understand power dynamics and understand societal pressures that can lead to violence.

- A group of 67 girls participated in a risk detection/executive functioning curriculum designed to improve their ability to recognize and maintain attention to environmental danger cues, recognize different emotions and know how to respond in risky relational situations.

A third group of 42 girls were enrolled in the study but did not participate in a curriculum intervention.

Overall, the girls reported positive experiences about participating in a curriculum. The study found no significant differences in re-victimization rates for girls who completed the social learning/feminist curriculum compared with those who completed the risk detection/executive functioning curriculum. In addition, compared with girls who did not participate in a curriculum, the odds of not being re-victimized (sexually or physically) were two to five times greater for girls who received the risk detection/executive functioning or social learning curriculum.

The study suggests that high-risk girls can successfully participate in and benefit from relational programming.

Chapter 29

Preventing and Intervening in Child Abuse

Chapter Contents

Section 29.1

When You Suspect Child Abuse or Neglect

Text in this section is excerpted from "When You
Suspect Child Abuse or Neglect," Federal Bureau of
Investigation (FBI), February 23, 2015.

If You Have Reason to Believe That a Child Is Being, or Has Been, Abused

DO NOT confront the abuser. **DO** report your reasonable suspicions. However, if you are witnessing a child being abused, do what you can to safely stop the abuse (e.g., call 911) and safeguard the child until authorities arrive.

Even if your report does not bring decisive action, it may help establish a pattern that will eventually be enough to help the child.

The signs of abuse described below do not by themselves necessarily indicate abuse. You might talk to the child a little to see if there is a simple or innocent explanation for what you have observed but do not overwhelm the child with questions. It is not up to you to determine whether your suspicions are true or not. A trained investigator will evaluate the child's situation.

You Should Suspect Physical Abuse

When you see . . .

- Frequent injuries such as bruises, cuts, black eyes or burns, especially when the child cannot adequately explain their causes

- Burns or bruises in an unusual pattern that may indicate the use of an instrument or a human bite; ligature marks on the wrists/ankles or gag marks on the side of the mouth

- Cigarette burns on any part of a child's body; unusual patterns of scalding (glove or sock patterns on hands or feet)

- Injuries that are unusual for the child's age (fractures in a child under age 4)

- Defensive injuries on backs of arms and hands

- Frequent complaints of pain without obvious injury, which may indicate internal injuries or injuries covered by clothing
- Aggressive, disruptive, and destructive behavior
- Lack of reaction to pain
- Passive, withdrawn, emotionless behavior
- Fear of going home or seeing parents, family members or others who know the child
- Injuries that appear after the child has not been seen for several days
- Unseasonable clothes hiding injuries to arms or legs

Physical discipline, such as spanking or paddling, is not considered abuse as long as it is reasonable and does not cause harm or injury and does not expose the child to substantial harm or injury. Punching, beating, kicking, biting, shaking, throwing, stabbing, choking, hitting, and burning are considered to be abuse, not reasonable discipline.

You Should Suspect Neglect

When you see. . .

- Obvious malnourishment
- A child who is consistently dirty or has torn and/or dirty clothes and has severe body odor
- Obvious fatigue and listlessness
- A child unattended for long periods of time
- Need for glasses, dental care or other medical attention
- Stealing or begging for food
- Frequent absence or tardiness from school
- Lack of sufficient clothing for the weather

You Should Suspect Sexual Abuse

When you see. . .

- Difficulty in sitting or walking
- Sudden changes in behavior or school performance

- Sudden change in appetite

- Refusal to change for gym or to participate in physical activities

- Extreme fear of being alone with adults, especially if of a particular gender

- Sexually suggestive, age inappropriate or promiscuous behavior

- Sudden reporting of nightmares or bed-wetting

- Knowledge about sexual relations beyond what is appropriate for the child's age

- Sexual victimization of other children

- Complaints of painful urination

- Pregnancy or venereal disease, particularly if under age 14

Sexual abuse may involve fondling, lewd and lascivious behavior, intercourse, sodomy, oral copulation, penetration of a genital or anal opening, child pornography, child prostitution, or any other sexual conduct that is harmful to a child's mental, emotional, and physical welfare. These acts may be forced upon the child, or the child may be coaxed, seduced, and persuaded to cooperate. A child, however, cannot legally consent to such acts. The absence of force or other discernable coercion does not diminish the abusive nature of the conduct, but it may cause the child to feel responsible for what occurred.

When a Child Discloses

If you are the first person the child tells about sexual abuse, your testimony as an "outcry witness" may be especially important in future legal proceedings. What you say the child told you is not considered hearsay evidence in most states but is admissible evidence in a trial involving a sexual offense against a child. This exception generally applies only to the first person the child approaches.

Emotional Injury

The law recognizes both physical and emotional injury. An angry parent who physically assaults their child is likely to assault them verbally, too. Emotional injury is a common result of all types of abuse and neglect. Emotional injury can be subtle and harder to prove, yet it can be just as devastating and lead to some of the costliest and long term effects on children: substance abuse, crime, suicide, and perpetuation of violence within families. Emotional abuse can involve constant blaming, berating, and belittling of a child, extremely unpredictable responses and unreasonable demands, and emotional deprivation when a parent withholds or withdraws affection, attention, and approval. Emotionally injured children may withdraw and become depressed or apathetic, attempt suicide, become overly compliant and fearful about not exactly following instructions, or act out in negative ways to get attention. A child's behavior problems may be a fulfillment of the negative labels ("worthless" or "no good") the abuser has applied to the child.

You Are Legally Responsible for the Safety of Your Own Child

Sometimes abusers are close relatives, but the fact that the abuser is a parent or other family member does not remove your obligation to protect the child. If you permit your child to be in a situation where you knew, or should have known, he or she would be willfully, recklessly or negligently injured, you may be prosecuted for child abuse or neglect.

If you are frightened for your own safety or that of your child, call 911, the local child abuse hotline, or a domestic violence hotline.

You are legally responsible for the care of your child. You must either provide your child with safe and adequate food, clothing, shelter, protection, medical care and supervision or arrange for someone else to provide these basic necessities. Failure to do so may be considered neglect.

If you are uneasy about your own behavior toward your child, you can contact the Employee Assistance Unit. Parents Anonymous is a non-profit organization that provides support and training on parenting and coping with stress, and can be contacted through their toll-free hotline at: 800-554-2323.

Section 29.2

Talking to Your Child about Sexual Abuse

Text in this section is excerpted from "Information for
Parents and Guardians of Children: Talking to Your Child,"
U.S. Department of Justice (DOJ), March 29, 2015.

When you empower your children to say "no" to unwanted touch and teach them that they can come to you with questions and concerns, you take critical steps to preventing child sexual abuse.

- Talk to your children about sexuality and sexual abuse in age-appropriate terms. Talking openly and directly about sexuality teaches children that it is okay to talk to you when they have questions.

- Teach children the names of their body parts so that they have the language to ask questions and express concerns about those body parts.

- Teach children that some parts of their bodies are private.

  - Let children know that other people should not be touching or looking at their private parts unless they need to touch them to provide care. If someone does need to touch them in those private areas, a parent or trusted caregiver should be there when it happens.

  - Tell children that if someone tries to touch those private areas or wants to look at them OR if someone tries to show them his or her own private parts, they should tell a trusted adult as soon as possible.

- Teach your child boundaries and that it's okay to say "no" to touches that make him or her uncomfortable or scared.

  - Teach your child how to say "no" when he or she is uncomfortable or scared and that he or she should tell a trusted adult as soon as possible.

  - Respect a child's boundaries in play, teasing, and affection.

- Assure your child that it is okay to get help, even if someone he or she cares about might be upset or embarrassed.

- Know that telling a trusted adult can lead to a slightly embarrassing situation for you, your child, and those involved.

- A child who then says he or she does not want to give a relative a hug or kiss can create tension. Do not force the child to give the relative a hug or a kiss, because it is sending the wrong message to the child and teaches the child to ignore his or her confusing or uncomfortable feelings to the point where he or she does it anyway. Work with your child to find ways to greet people that do not involve uncomfortable kinds of touch.

- Talk openly about sexuality and sexual abuse to teach your child that these topics do not need to be "secret." Abusers will sometimes tell a child that the abuse should be kept a secret. Let your child know that if someone is touching him or her or talking to him or her in ways that make him or her uncomfortable or scared, that it should not stay a secret.

  - Abusers rely on the child's likelihood of not telling an adult.

  - Assure your child that he or she will not get into trouble if he or she tells you this kind of secret.

- Do not try to put all this information into one big "talk" about sex.

  - Talking about sexuality and sexual abuse should be routine conversations.

  - Use everyday issues to begin conversations to help avoid a big "talk" about sex.

Be Involved in Your Child's Life.

- Be engaged in your child's activities.

  - Ask your child about the people he or she goes to school with or plays with.

  - If your child is involved in sports, go to games and practices. Get to know the other parents and coaches.

- If your child is involved in after-school activities or day care, ask him or her what he or she did during the day.
- Know the other adults that your child might talk to.
  - Children sometimes feel that they cannot talk to their parents.
  - Identify and tell your child who the other trusted adults are in his or her life.
- Talk about the media and technology.
  - If your child watches a lot of television or plays video games, watch or play with him or her.
  - Ask him or her questions about technology you do not understand.
  - Many TV shows show sexual violence of different kinds.
  - Some video games allow the user to engage in sexual violence.
  - Discuss the Internet, the child's surfing habits, and online safety tips.
  - Use examples from TV or games that you have watched or played together to start up conversations about sexuality and sexual abuse.

Be Available.

- Make time to spend with your child.
- Let your child know that he or she can come to you if he or she has questions or if someone is talking to him or her in a way that makes him or her feel uncomfortable or scared.
  - Make time to talk to your child when he or she comes to you with concerns or questions.

Discussing Sexual Abuse with Teens

The discussion about sexuality and sexual abuse should start way before a child begins puberty. The following tips are provided with the understanding that preventative discussions have occurred with your child years earlier. If you have not discussed sexual abuse with your child, start today.

When it comes to sexual abuse, protecting teens is complicated. Teenagers seek relationships outside the family for friendship, security, and even advice. In addition, they may be confused or embarrassed about their own developing sexuality, which makes communication difficult and protecting them nearly impossible.

Be Realistic and Educate Yourself.

- Know that most abusers are known by the victim.
- Realize teens are learning about sex. Often their sources may not be the best places to get the facts on sex. Sources include their friends, pornography, or firsthand experiences.
- Learn more so you can help and inform your child.
  - If your teen comes to you with a question and you respond by giving him or her a pamphlet of information, he or she may think you are not open to further conversation.
  - Educational pamphlets can be helpful, many times for you as a parent. Creating open communication is a better way for teens to learn about sexuality and sexual abuse.

Do Not Put Off Discussions.

- Before communication lines shut down or something happens, talk to your child.
- Open the lines of communication and talk to your child about his or her personal rights and personal boundaries in an age-appropriate manner.

Help Teens Define Their Personal Rights.

- Believe it or not, many teens who get caught up in an inappropriate relationship with an adult (or even someone their own age who is an abuser) blame themselves. They do not know what their personal rights are or what kind of behavior to expect from adults. Teach your children that it is okay to say no and that they do not have to do anything they do not want to do. Often, kids think they are supposed to respect their elders and be nice, so they go along with things that make them uncomfortable because they feel obligated.

- Teens should understand that:
  - Their bodies are theirs.
  - Past permission does not obligate them to future activity.
  - They do not have to do anything they do not want to do.
  - They should trust their instincts.
  - It is not okay for them to engage in sexual behavior with adults.
  - It is not okay for adults to take pictures or videos of them in sexual positions or unclothed.
  - Regardless of how they dress or talk, it does not constitute permission.
  - Pornography is not an accurate depiction of real life.
  - They deserve to be spoken to with respect and never feel coerced.
  - Alcohol and drugs may make it hard for them to maintain their boundaries and can cloud their judgment.
  - Touching someone sexually while they are drunk is abuse.
  - Adults should not discuss their sexual fantasies or share pornography with minors.
  - No one has the right to touch them without their permission.
- If they are in a relationship, they should also understand that:
  - Both parties respect each other's personal rights and boundaries in a healthy relationship.
  - They should decline sexual relations with anyone who refuses to use proper protection.
  - Not everyone is having sex. Many teens wait and that is perfectly okay.

Help Them Build Up Their Self-Esteem.

Often, low self-esteem is a pivotal factor in risky teen behavior. Teens who do not feel good about themselves or who are at odds with their family may turn to other adults for support. This type of behavior is extremely dangerous; this is exactly what abusers are looking for. They approach teens and take advantage of their low self-esteem, give gifts like liquor or drugs, further isolate them from the family, and attempt to become their "friend." In addition, teens that do not have money are also often a target and may be bribed with gifts or money.

- Encourage your teen to get involved in a hobby, sport, work, or art.

- Teach your teen how to earn money legitimately without having to give up his or her pride or self-worth.

- Teach your teen how to take care of himself or herself.

- Empower your teen to be in control of his or her own life rather than feeling like a victim.

- Give your teen responsibility.

- Communicate how much you value his or her independence, accomplishments, and ability to be responsible, while letting him or her know you are supportive and available.

Need Help? Get Help.

- Know that it is never too late to seek help.

- Talk to school administrators, counselors, teachers, and community outreach program representatives for assistance.

- Affirm to yourself that abuse is something that needs to be stopped, not ignored.

- Report abuse as soon as possible. Silence protects the abuser and shows the child that abuse is acceptable and may convey that it is his or her fault.

- Do not blame the child for the abuse.

- Seek counseling for abused children to help alleviate confusion, anger, and possible self-esteem issues.

- Seek counseling for you to learn how to get through the hurt and anger, and find ways to help your child and family connections heal.

Talking to Your Child If You Suspect That He or She Is Being Sexually Abused

Parents are surrounded by messages about child sexual abuse. Talk shows and TV news warn parents about dangers on the Internet, at school, and at home. However, parents do not get much advice on how to talk to their children if they are concerned that sexual abuse is occurring.

Talk to Your Child Directly.

- Pick your time and place carefully!

  - Have this conversation somewhere that your child feels comfortable.

  - DO NOT ask your child about child abuse in front of the person you think may be abusing the child!

Ask If Anyone Has Been Touching Your Child in Ways That Do Not Feel Okay or That Make Him or Her Feel Uncomfortable.

- Know that sexual abuse can feel good to the victim, so asking your child if someone is hurting him or her may not get the information that you are looking for.

- Follow up on whatever made you concerned. If there was something your child said or did that made you concerned, ask about that.

- Ask in a nonjudgmental way, and take care to avoid shaming your child as you ask questions.

  - "I" questions can be very helpful. Rather than beginning your conversation by saying, "You (the child) did something/ said something that made me worry...," consider starting your inquiry with the word "I." For example: "I am concerned because I heard you say that you are not allowed to close the bathroom door."

  - Make sure that your child knows that he or she is not in trouble, and that you are simply trying to gather more information.

- Talk with your child about secrets.

  - Sometimes abusers will tell children that sexual abuse is a secret just between them. They may ask the child to promise to keep it secret.

  - When you talk to your child, talk about times that it is okay not to keep a secret, even if he or she made a promise.

Build a Trusting Relationship with Your Child.

- Let your child know that it is okay to come to you if someone is making him or her uncomfortable.

  - Be sure to follow up on any promises you make—if you tell your child that he or she can talk to you, be sure to make time for him or her when he or she does come to you!

- All children should know that it's okay to say "no" to touches that make them uncomfortable or if someone is touching them in ways that make them uncomfortable and that they should tell a trusted adult as soon as possible.

  - Let your child know that you will not get angry at him or her if he or she tells someone "no." Children are often afraid that they will get into trouble if they tell someone not to touch them.

Teach Your Child That Some Parts of His or Her Body Are Private.

- Tell your child that if someone tries to touch those private areas or wants to look at them OR if someone tries to show the child his or her own private parts, your child should tell a trusted adult as soon as possible.

- Let your child know that he or she will not be in trouble if he or she tells you about inappropriate touching.

- Make sure to follow through on this if your child does tell you about inappropriate touching! Try not to react with anger towards the child.

If you have reason to be concerned about sexual abuse, there may be other signs of sexual abuse as well. This Website provides a list of warning sign for parents. Additionally, RAINN's Web site provides a comprehensive list of signs that indicate child sexual abuse. As you talk to your child about sexual abuse, remember to focus on creating a safe place for your child. Even if he or she does not tell you about sexual abuse at the time of the conversation, you are laying a foundation for future conversations.

Section 29.3

Parenting a Child Who Has Experienced Abuse or Neglect

Text in this section is excerpted from "Parenting a
Child Who Has Experienced Abuse or Neglect,"
Child Welfare Information Gateway, December 2013.

Introduction

Children who have been abused or neglected need safe and nurturing relationships that address the effects of child maltreatment. If you are parenting a child who has been abused or neglected, you might have questions about your child's experiences and the effects of those experiences. This factsheet is intended to help parents (birth, foster, and adoptive) and other caregivers better understand the challenges of caring for a child who has experienced maltreatment and learn about the resources available for support. (In some cases, the term "birth" parent is used to distinguish parents with children involved with child welfare from kin or foster or adoptive parents.)

What Should I Know about My Child?

Learning about your child's unique history is an important first step for all parents and caregivers in providing a healing environment for children who have experienced abuse or neglect. Try to consider the child's background and history from the child's point of view. What has happened in the child's life—both good and bad—and how might this impact the child's behavior and family adjustment? This history is one of many variables that will affect how you can help your child heal and thrive. For instance, your history with the child and other factors specific to the maltreatment (e.g., type of abuse or neglect), specific to the child (e.g., age, resilience), and specific to you (e.g., parenting experience) all come into play.

Parents who reunite with a child who was in out-of-home care, relatives that provide care for the child of a family member, and foster and adoptive parents may confront different challenges when raising a child who has experienced maltreatment. The amount and types of information you are able to obtain about your child's history may also depend on the type of parent-child relationship.

For birth parents. Many children whose parents are reported for child maltreatment are not removed from their homes; instead, the family receives in-home services. For children who do enter foster care, the primary goal is usually family reunification, and the majority of children who enter foster care due to child abuse or neglect eventually return home. In both cases, the goal is to reconnect and build strong parent-child relationships in a safe home environment that promotes child and family well-being. While birth parents may know just about all there is to know about their child's background, they may need to learn more about any foster care or kinship care experiences that their child has had, and they may need to learn more about the possible impact of abuse or neglect on their child. You may wish to talk with your social worker about your child's history, and sharing your concerns will help your social worker help you and your family, including help seeking professional mental health services.

For kinship caregivers. Some children who have been abused or neglected enter formal or informal kinship care with a grandparent, aunt, or other relative. Kinship caregivers may become responsible for a child unexpectedly or may confront issues that didn't exist when they raised their own children. Kinship caregivers may or may not have a good history of their child's background and any maltreatment experiences. They may not have received training in providing out-of-home care and may need to be brought up to date on what has happened to the child, as well as any possible impact of abuse or neglect.

For foster and adoptive parents. Foster and adoptive parents may not be aware of their child's past traumas or the extent of the abuse or neglect. Although they have received training to prepare them to care for the child, they may not be completely ready for the unique situation of a particular child. While child welfare agencies are required to provide all available information about a child, some information may not be obtainable, and some children may not feel comfortable disclosing past abuse or neglect.

Educating yourself about your child's history and about child abuse and neglect and the services available for help will better prepare you and your family to face the challenges ahead and continue down the road toward healing.

What Are the Effects of Child Abuse and Neglect?

Research shows that abuse and neglect can affect a child's ability to learn, form relationships, and problem solve, and children who have experienced maltreatment are at risk for many illnesses and poor health later in life. Knowing how maltreatment may have affected your child may help you recognize the effects of abuse or neglect and seek the appropriate assessments and help.

Effects on Child Development

A great deal of research in recent years has examined child and adolescent brain development. We now know that the way the brain develops can change when a child has experienced stress from severe or ongoing abuse or neglect. Maltreatment can delay or affect the ways a child is able to control his or her emotions, see right from wrong, identify consequences of actions, and learn from mistakes.

Most children experience developmental milestones along the same general timelines. Typically, children from birth to 5 acquire the ability to soothe themselves when they are stressed; children ages 6–7 have more control over their emotions and behaviors; and adolescents ages 11–14 might have frequent mood swings, but they learn to accept disappointments and overcome failures. Abuse or neglect can impair this healthy development. Some causes for concern about developmental delays include:

- A child ages birth–5 who exhibits an inability to relax or manage stress

- A child ages 6–7 who is frequently sad, worried, afraid, or withdrawn

- A child ages 11–14 who has strong negative thoughts about him or herself, or has an extreme need for approval and social support

It's important to remember that although crucial brain development occurs during the first 3 years of life, our brains continue to develop into adulthood. The brain development that takes place at age 2 is quite different from the development that happens at age 14. In fact, the brain experiences a growth spurt right before puberty that affects a preteen's ability to plan, reason, and control impulses and emotions.

It is normal for teenagers to act impulsively and take risks, because the part of their brain that regulates impulse control—the frontal lobe—is not fully matured. Adolescents who have experienced abuse, neglect, or other trauma, however, may be more impulsive. Teens who have been maltreated may:

- Struggle academically and socially

- Have difficulty with tasks requiring a higher level of thinking

- Experiment with drugs or criminal activity

A caring adult who provides healthy guidance to youth can offer the opportunity for them to model appropriate behaviors and develop the skills necessary for healthy adult relationships.

Effects on Health

While child abuse and neglect can leave physical scars, there also can be a number of underlying, less visible effects. Several studies have demonstrated a link between negative experiences during childhood and poor adult health outcomes that can lead to early death, including:

- Heart, lung, and liver diseases

- High blood pressure, diabetes, asthma, and obesity

- Alcohol and other drug abuse

- Sexually transmitted diseases

Social, Psychological, and Behavioral Effects

Children and youth who have experienced abuse or neglect may also experience one or more of the following psychological and behavioral effects:

- Borderline personality disorder, depression, and/or anxiety

- Attachment issues or affectionate behaviors with unknown/little-known people

- Inappropriate modeling of adult behavior, aggression, and other antisocial traits

- Juvenile delinquency or adult criminality

- Future abusive behavior such as interpersonal violence or domestic abuse

How Can I Help My Child Heal?

Knowing the possible effects of child abuse and neglect is a first step. This section explores some strategies for helping your child or youth overcome these traumas, including some techniques for discipline that can help prevent future abuse or retraumatization.

Building Resilience and Promoting Protective Factors

Resilience is a child or youth's ability to cope, and even thrive, following a negative experience. This is not an inherent trait but something that has to be developed and nurtured.

Some of the ways you can help your child build resilience include:

- **Build strong connections** with friends and family that can support children during challenges and teach them to think about and consider other people's feelings.

- **Allow children to feel their feelings.** Teach them how to describe those feelings, and commend them for expressing feelings of hurt or sadness without acting out.

- **Be consistent.** If you say you'll be there, be there. If you say you'll listen to concerns, listen. This will help to teach your child that people can be trusted.

- **Be patient.** Children's reactions to trauma vary as widely as the types of trauma one can experience. There isn't a one-size-fits-all solution.

- **Express your support.** Express love and support for your child verbally and physically. Express your love through words, notes, and hugs.

- **Teach your child the importance of healthy behaviors.** Have open and honest talks about the dangers of drugs and alcohol, smoking, and sexual promiscuity. Teach your child the importance of eating properly and exercising.

Experiencing abuse or neglect doesn't mean your child *will* develop poor health or negative well-being outcomes. When caregivers and parents foster protective factors—circumstances in families and communities that increase the health and well-being of children and families—it may lessen the negative effects of maltreatment. A strong and secure emotional bond between children and their caregivers is critical for children's physical, social, and emotional development, including their ability to form trusting relationships, exhibit positive behaviors, and heal from past traumas.

The healing process is not always a clear, straight path, and it takes time. Some things you can do to help your child heal include:

- Address the child's physical safety first by letting him or her know that no one will physically lash out. This will help the child create feelings of trust and open up to psychological and emotional healing.

- Address the past as the past. Help the child identify elements of his or her current life that are different from the past. Use this as an opportunity to discuss new boundaries and expectations to encourage feelings of belonging and.

Building a Strong Relationship with Your Child

A child's earliest relationships are some of the most important. Attachment is the sense of security and safety a child feels with caregivers and is important for your child's physical, emotional, mental, and psychological development. It is formed through consistent, positive affection and emotional interactions. The issues and challenges most caregivers face with children who have experienced maltreatment is the result of a break in attachment during the first 3 years of life.

To foster a secure relationship with a child:

- **Be available.** Provide consistent support to build feelings of trust and safety.

- **Offer comfort.** Support the child when he or she is upset, modeling appropriate displays of affection and building the child's self-esteem.

- **Be respectful.** Let your child know that you will keep him or her safe.

What Is the Difference between Child Abuse and Child Discipline?

It is normal for children to act out and challenge a parent or caregiver's authority. Toddlers throw tantrums. Teenagers argue. The ways in which parents guide a child and discipline poor behavior is critical to shaping more positive behavior. Children learn control and self-discipline from their caregivers, and discipline should never be harmful to a child. In fact, severe punishment won't accomplish your goals and can do more harm than good. For children who have experienced abuse or neglect, aggressive punishment could elicit memories of past trauma or cause retraumatization.

Discipline and punishment, while often used interchangeably, are actually quite different.

- **Discipline** is the act of *teaching* children the difference between acceptable and unacceptable behavior. This can be accomplished by talking to children about misbehavior and requiring children to take responsibility for its consequences, like being responsible for cleaning up a mess or apologizing for hurting someone's feelings. You also can guide your child by positively reinforcing and encouraging their good behaviors and not just correcting their poor behaviors.

- **Punishment** is an approach to discipline that can be physical—a slap on the hand—or psychological—the loss of TV time, or other freedoms.

A misbehaving child can be frustrating, but using physical force to teach a lesson or relieve aggravation is always wrong. Factors like sleep and diet can cause tensions to rise. If your child is acting out and you feel overwhelmed, consider whether he or she is hungry, tired, or expressing a reaction to an underlying issue like fear or anxiety.

Practical Discipline Tips or Techniques

The following tips may help you safely discipline your child:

- **Role modeling:** Children learn more about behavior by watching adults than in any other way. Be a positive example for expressing emotions and dealing with frustration. Stay calm instead of yelling.

- **Encouragement:** Let children know what they are doing right as well as pointing out the mistakes they make.

- **Rules:** Set routines for bedtimes, meals, and chores. Knowing what will happen next can be very important to a child whose life once felt chaotic.

- **Set limits:** Be very clear about your limits.

- **Attention-ignore:** Ignoring behavior is simply pretending that the behavior is not occurring. The parent does not look at, talk to, or respond to the child until the inappropriate behavior ends. When a child breaks a rule, stay calm and do what is fair. Sometimes, your child can help you decide what is fair to do when a rule is broken.

- **Never hit or shake a child:** Hitting is not a useful discipline tool for your children. Besides the potential physical abuse and injury, hitting and other physical punishments are not effective ways to discipline. They teach children that it is acceptable to hurt people, and they make children much too angry to be sorry for what they've done.

- **Gear the discipline to the child's developmental stage:** Don't expect a child of any age to perform something he or she is not ready for. Allow your child to learn at his or her own pace. Break tasks down into small, manageable steps, so that he or she feels a sense of success and accomplishment.

Where Can I Find Support?

Recovering from child maltreatment is a journey that affects the entire family, and parents and caregivers need support, too. Learning as much as you can about child maltreatment and bolstering your parenting skills can go a long way in promoting your child's well-being and building a healthy family.

Parent Education and Training

Parent education programs are geared toward reinforcing your parenting skills and teaching you new strategies. They foster parent leadership and empower you to shape your family and advocate for their needs.

These support programs and training programs not only offer you strategies for tackling difficult situations and enhancing your problem-solving skills, they may also help reduce children's misbehaviors. Parent education programs can be online, in-person, involve one-to-one instruction, or take place in a group setting. Whether you prefer a course with direct instruction, videos, or in another format, successful programs will:

- Promote positive family interaction

- Involve fathers

- Use interactive training techniques

- Offer opportunities to practice new skills

- Teach emotional communication skills

- Encourage peer support

Therapy or Support Groups

Dealing with the effects of maltreatment can be challenging, and you and your family may wish to seek professional help. Therapy, counseling, and support groups can provide children and caregivers with the skills necessary to build healthy relationships, overcome past trauma, and prevent reoccurring or future trauma.

Take your time when searching for a mental health professional to ensure you find the right fit. If you and your family are receiving child welfare services, your agency or caseworker may provide you with a referral to a therapist. If you are selecting a therapist on your own, you can call prospective therapists or schedule an initial interview to gather basic information. Some therapists will even offer an initial brief consultation that is free of charge. It's important that the professionals you choose to work with are specifically trained to effectively address the unique needs of your family—as mentioned earlier, the issues that affect parents differ from those affecting kinship caregivers, which differ still from issues faced by adoptive or foster families. Some things to keep in mind include:

- Your therapists should be knowledgeable about the impact of trauma on children and families.

- Your therapists should allow and encourage your participation in treatment.

- You should be wary of therapies that restrain a child or intrude on his or her physical space, as children who have been maltreated need to develop clear boundaries to feel safe and prevent retraumatization.

Just like there are different types of parent education programs, there are different approaches to therapy. From group or family therapy to individual psychotherapy or cognitive therapy, it's important that the type of treatment you seek fits the needs of your family. One type of therapy proven effective for abused children between the ages of 2 and 8 is parent-child interaction therapy. In this approach, therapists coach parents while they interact with their children, teaching parents strategies for promoting positive behaviors.

Child Welfare Services

The child welfare system offers support to prevent child abuse or neglect and provides services to families that need help protecting and caring for their children. Agencies will arrange for children to live

416

with kin or with foster families when they are not safe at home. When formal assessment is not warranted, families often can benefit from services to prevent future reports of abuse or neglect.

Sometimes, a family might benefit from respite services, counseling, or other help for which a child welfare agency might provide a referral.

- **Prevention services**, like parent education programs, are those that aim to reduce the risk of child abuse and neglect or the reoccurrence of maltreatment.

- **Family preservation services** are short-term services for families in crisis that are intended to keep families safely together in their own home.

- **Postadoption services** can help children and families dealing with a range of issues after an adoption is finalized, such as loss or grief, birth family connections, adjusting to family dynamics, and more.

Sometimes, parents and caregivers just need a break. Respite care is just one of the family support services that can provide relief and support to families in crisis. There is a variety of respite services, and finding one that fits your family's needs is key. The ARCH National Respite Network and Resource Center offers a national respite locator to help you find services in your State: http://archrespite.org/respitelocator

Making Your Community Safer

Helping children and families heal from maltreatment, or prevent abuse from happening in the first place, is not the sole responsibility of parents and caregivers. Just like children and youth need permanent connections to help them thrive, families need strong communities. There are things you can do to help make your neighborhoods safe—not just for your family, but for the benefit of all the children in your community.

Parent and community cafés are a helpful tool for bolstering community support. Cafés can include parents, neighbors, school professionals, church members, and other adults in your community who are concerned with the health and well-being of children. These gatherings should be intimate and designed to ignite conversation among participants about the presence of—or lack of—protective factors in their own lives. Communities with committed parents who have taken on a leadership role have improved their neighborhoods and improved child safety. Programs like Circle of Parents® can help strengthen communities. Other things you can do to engage your community in preventing child abuse and neglect include:

- **Building partnerships** to enhance support for parents and caregivers

- **Educating community members** about the stages of child development

- **Promoting a community responsibility** for the health and wellbeing of children

- **Developing a consistent language** within your community about protective factors and the signs of abuse and neglect

- **Building awareness** about the available services and supports for families and children

Conclusion

If you are the parent or caregiver of a child who has experienced maltreatment, helping him or her through that pain can be daunting, yet there are resources available to help. It's important to remember that many children who have been abused or neglected do not grow up to abuse others and can live happy and healthy lives. You and your family will play an important role in your child's healing, and the more knowledge you acquire about maltreatment and the services available for support, the better prepared you will be to help your child through this difficult time.

Chapter 30

How the Legal System Can Help

Chapter Contents

Section 30.1

Common Legal Intervention Strategies and Their Effectiveness

Text in this section is excerpted from "Practical Implications of
Current Intimate Partner Violence Research for Victim Advocates
and Service Providers," National Criminal Justice Reference
Service (NCJRS), December 2013.

Is Arrest an Effective Criminal Justice Response to Reported IPV?

An analysis of arrest studies in five urban jurisdictions found that
arrest deters repeat reabuse. In none of the sites was arrest associated
with increased reabuse against intimate partners. Approximately 50
percent of the abusers did not commit further IPV during the follow-up
period. A major study, based on 2,564 partner assaults reported in the
NCVS (1992-2002), found that whether police arrested the suspect or
not, their involvement had a strong deterrent effect.

The positive effects of police involvement and arrest did not
depend on whether the victim or a third party reported the incident
to law enforcement. Neither did they depend on the seriousness of
the incident assault, whether a misdemeanor or a felony. A Berkeley
arrest study found similarly that all actions taken by responding
officers, including arrest, providing victims with information pamphlets, taking down witness statements, and helping victims secure
protective orders, were associated with reduced reabuse. By contrast,
the highest reabuse rates were found where the responding officers
left it to the victim to make a "citizen arrest," swearing out a complaint herself.

Research has shown that police response also significantly increases
the likelihood that victims will secure protective orders.

Research also reveals that, by and large, the vast majority of victims
report satisfaction with the arrest of their abuser when interviewed
after the fact. In Massachusetts, 82 percent of victims were either very
or somewhat satisfied with police arrest response, and 85.4 percent
said they would call police again for a similar incident.

A study of courts in California, Oregon, Nebraska and Washington found that 76 percent of the victims said they wanted their abusers arrested. Also, important to note is that police arrests in spite of victims' objections do not reduce the likelihood of victims reporting new abuse to police.

Victims may want police to arrest their violent partners, not necessarily for the purpose of prosecution or incarceration, but rather to remove abusers from the home temporarily or permanently.

What Should Law Enforcement's Response Be If the Suspect Is Gone When Officers Arrive?

A large percentage of alleged abusers leave the crime scene before law enforcement arrives. Where noted, absence rates range from 42 to 66 percent. Pursuing alleged abusers, including the issuance of warrants, is associated with reduced re-victimization. Pursuing absent suspects may be of particular utility because limited research finds that suspects who flee the scene before police arrive are significantly more likely to have prior criminal histories and to reabuse than those arrested at the scene. Similarly, another study finds higher reabuse **if the victim is gone** when officers arrive.

According to a national survey, 68 percent of police departments have specific policies that cover procedures for responding law enforcement officers if the alleged perpetrator is gone when they arrive.

In a study of the south shore communities of Massachusetts, researchers documented that police arrested 100 percent of abusers present at the scene and arrested or issued warrants for a majority (54 percent) who left the scene, for a total arrest or warrant rate of about 75 percent. Similarly, a statewide New York study found that half of the domestic violence suspects fled the scene, but local police ultimately arrested 60 percent of those who fled.

State laws vary, with some limiting police arrest powers for misdemeanor IPV after passage of time.

Does IPV Prosecution Increase Victim Safety?

The research on the effectiveness of prosecution of domestic violence has found mixed results in terms of stopping abusers from reabusing their victims. Regardless of the victim's wishes to proceed with prosecution or not, research has found that contact with the prosecutor may be protective against future IPV-related police calls or emergency room use.

A large, longitudinal, mixed-methods study examining to what extent female IPV victim participation in prosecution is associated with their future safety, found that victim communication with a prosecutor appears to be protective against future IPV.

This finding holds across both the pre- and post-disposition periods. Specifically, researchers found that direct victim contact with the prosecutor's office (in person or by phone) was associated with a victim being 37 percent less likely to have a subsequent police-reported IPV incident, without any increase in the risk of emergency room visits for IPV or injury. If prosecutors dropped cases against victim wishes, those victims were twice as likely as those who had their case prosecuted to return to the prosecutor's office for a subsequent event. Victims were also more likely to apply for a protective order in the civil court system for a future IPV event. Victims who wanted to drop the case—and the case was dropped—were more likely to go to the emergency room for a subsequent IPV event compared to women who wanted and secured prosecution of their cases.

Other researchers suggest that direct contact or communication with the prosecutor's office may provide victims a type of legal leverage necessary to "rebalance" power in relationships. "Actual prosecution of the criminal act is probably less important to (some) victims than the power they gain (in the relationship with the batterer) through bargaining with significant threats of prosecution and punishment."

A 2008 re-examination of a large Ohio prosecution data set found the prosecution of domestic violence arrestees was associated with less repeat offending, as was conviction and sentencing to probation. However, sentencing to a treatment program or sentencing to jail was not. In fact, the researchers found that among convicted offenders, being sentenced to jail was associated with **more** repeat offending. The same researchers recently completed a review of 31 prosecution studies and found **no** consistent evidence that prosecution had a deterrent effect over arrest without prosecution; prosecution without conviction, or conviction regardless of sentence severity.

The Indianapolis experiment assessing the efficacy of prosecution of IPV perpetrators found that in victim-initiated complaints of IPV where suspects were subsequently arrested on warrants were least likely to suffer future abuse. One researcher suggests that "coercive (prosecution) policies may be less effective (against recidivism) than efforts to empower a victim by informing and supporting her choices with respect to prosecution and her need for safety."

Victim participation in prosecution does not appear to lead to retaliatory violence.

More recent research has re-examined IPV prosecutions in the broader context of how abusers' non-IPV cases are prosecuted compared to their IPV cases. As most repeat abusers also commit many non-IPV crimes, the researchers wanted to see if differential prosecution and sentencing severity between IPV and non-IPV cases impacted on likelihood of repeat IPV arrests.

The researchers found that if the IPV cases during the first several years of an abuser's criminal career were prosecuted and sentenced more severely than non-IPV cases, the abusers were significantly less likely to continue to commit new IPV cases (or committed fewer IPV cases) over the rest of their criminal careers than if their IPV cases were prosecuted less severely than the non-IPV cases. On the other hand, if the IPV cases were prosecuted less severely than the non-IPV cases, reabuse rates were unaffected.

Section 30.2

Laws on Violence against Women

Text in this section is excerpted from "Laws on Violence against Women," Office on Women's Health (OWH), September 30, 2015.

The U.S. Congress has passed two main laws related to violence against women, the Violence Against Women Act and the Family Violence Prevention and Services Act.

1. The Violence Against Women Act (VAWA)

The Violence Against Women Act (VAWA) was the first major law to help government agencies and victim advocates work together to fight domestic violence, sexual assault, and other types of violence against women. It created new punishments for certain crimes and started programs to prevent violence and help victims. Over the years, the law has been expanded to provide more programs and services. Currently, some included items are:

- Violence prevention programs in communities

- Protections for victims who are evicted from their homes because of events related to domestic violence or stalking

- Funding for victim assistance services like rape crisis centers and hotlines

- Programs to meet the needs of immigrant women and women of different races or ethnicities

- Programs and services for victims with disabilities

- Legal aid for survivors of violence

- Services for children and teens

The National Advisory Committee on Violence against Women works to help promote the goals and vision of VAWA. The committee is a joint effort between the U.S. Department of Justice and the U.S. Department of Health and Human Services. Examples of the committee's efforts include the Community Checklist initiative to make sure each community has domestic violence programs and the Toolkit to End Violence against Women, which has chapters for specific audiences.

2. The Family Violence Prevention and Services Act (FVPSA)

The Family Violence Prevention and Services Act (FVPSA) provides the main federal funding to help victims of domestic violence and their dependents (such as children). Programs funded through FVPSA provide shelter and related help. They also offer violence prevention activities and try to improve how service agencies work together in communities. FVPSA works through a few main ways:

- **Formula Grants.** This money helps states, territories, and tribes create and support programs that work to help victims and prevent family violence. The amount of money is determined by a formula based partly on population. The states, territories, and tribes distribute the money to thousands of domestic violence shelters and programs.

- **The National Domestic Violence Hotline.** This is a 24-hour, confidential, toll-free hotline. Hotline staff connect the caller to a local service provider. Trained advocates provide support, information, referrals, safety planning, and crisis intervention in more than 170 languages to hundreds of thousands of domestic violence victims each year.

- **The Domestic Violence Prevention Enhancements and Leadership Through Alliances (DELTA) Program.** Like many public health problems, intimate partner violence is not simply an individual problem—it is a community problem. DELTA supports local programs that teach people ways to prevent violence.

Section 30.3

Mandatory Reporters of Child Abuse and Neglect

Text in this section is excerpted from "Mandatory Reporters of Child Abuse and Neglect," U.S. Department of Health and Human Services (HHS), November 2013.

All States, the District of Columbia, American Samoa, Guam, the Northern Mariana Islands, Puerto Rico, and the U.S. Virgin Islands have statutes identifying persons who are required to report suspected child maltreatment to an appropriate agency, such as child protective services, a law enforcement agency, or a State's toll-free child abuse reporting hotline.

Professionals Required to Report

Approximately 48 States, the District of Columbia, American Samoa, Guam, the Northern Mariana Islands, Puerto Rico, and the Virgin Islands designate professions whose members are mandated by law to report child maltreatment. Individuals designated as mandatory reporters typically have frequent contact with children. Such individuals may include:

- Social workers

- Teachers, principals, and other school personnel

- Physicians, nurses, and other health-care workers

- Counselors, therapists, and other mental health professionals

- Child care providers
- Medical examiners or coroners
- Law enforcement officers

Some other professions frequently mandated across the States include commercial film or photograph processors (in 12 States, Guam, and Puerto Rico) and computer technicians (in six States). Substance abuse counselors are required to report in 14 States, and probation or parole officers are mandatory reporters in 17 States. Directors, employees, and volunteers at entities that provide organized activities for children, such as camps, day camps, youth centers, and recreation centers, are required to report in 12 States. Seven States and the District of Columbia include domestic violence workers on the list of mandated reporters, while seven States and the District of Columbia include animal control or humane officers. Court-appointed special advocates are mandatory reporters in 10 States. Members of the clergy now are required to report in 27 States and Guam.

Ten States now have designated as mandatory reporters faculty, administrators, athletics staff, and other employees and volunteers at institutions of higher learning, including public and private colleges and universities and vocational and technical schools.

Reporting by Other Persons

In approximately 18 States and Puerto Rico, any person who suspects child abuse or neglect is required to report. Of these 18 States, 16 States and Puerto Rico specify certain professionals who must report but also require all persons to report suspected abuse or neglect, regardless of profession. New Jersey and Wyoming require all persons to report without specifying any professions. In all other States, territories, and the District of Columbia, any person is permitted to report. These voluntary reporters of abuse are often referred to as "permissive reporters."

Institutional Responsibility to Report

The term "institutional reporting" refers to those situations in which the mandated reporter is working (or volunteering) as a staff member of an institution, such as a school or hospital, at the time he or she gains the knowledge that leads him or her to suspect that abuse or neglect has occurred. Many institutions have internal policies and procedures for handling reports of abuse, and these usually require the person who suspects abuse to notify the head of the institution that abuse has been discovered or is suspected and needs to be reported to child protective services or other appropriate authorities.

Statutes in 32 States, the District of Columbia, and the Virgin Islands provide procedures that must be followed in those cases. In 18 States, the District of Columbia, and the Virgin Islands, any staff member who suspects abuse must notify the head of the institution when the staff member feels that abuse or possible abuse should be reported to an appropriate authority. In 10 States, the District of Columbia, and the Virgin Islands, the staff member who suspects abuse notifies the head of the institution first, and then the head or his or her designee is required to make the report. In eight States, the individual reporter must make the report to the appropriate authority first and then notify the institution that a report has been made.

Laws in 14 States make clear that, regardless of any policies within the organization, the mandatory reporter is not relieved of his or her responsibility to report. In 15 States, an employer is expressly prohibited from taking any action to prevent or discourage an employee from making a report.

Standards for Making a Report

The circumstances under which a mandatory reporter must make a report vary from State to State. Typically, a report must be made when the reporter, in his or her official capacity, suspects or has reason to believe that a child has been abused or neglected. Another standard frequently used is in situations in which the reporter has knowledge of, or observes a child being subjected to, conditions that would reasonably result in harm to the child. Permissive reporters follow the same standards when electing to make a report.

Privileged Communications

Mandatory reporting statutes also may specify when a communication is privileged. "Privileged communications" is the statutory recognition of the right to maintain confidential communications between professionals and their clients, patients, or congregants. To enable States to provide protection to maltreated children, the reporting laws in most States and territories restrict this privilege for mandated reporters. All but three States and Puerto Rico currently address the issue of privileged communications within their reporting laws, either affirming the privilege or denying it (i.e., not allowing privilege to be grounds for failing to report). For instance:

- The physician-patient and husband-wife privileges are the most common to be denied by States.

- The attorney-client privilege is most commonly affirmed.

- The clergy-penitent privilege is also widely affirmed, although that privilege usually is limited to confessional communications and, in some States, denied altogether.

Inclusion of the Reporter's Name in the Report

Most States maintain toll-free telephone numbers for receiving reports of abuse or neglect. Reports may be made anonymously to most of these reporting numbers, but States find it helpful to their investigations to know the identity of reporters. Approximately 18 States, the District of Columbia, American Samoa, Guam, and the Virgin Islands currently require mandatory reporters to provide their names and contact information, either at the time of the initial oral report or as part of a written report. The laws in Connecticut, Delaware, and Washington allow child protection workers to request the name of the reporter. In Wyoming, the reporter does not have to provide his or her identity as part of the written report, but if the person takes and submits photographs or X-rays of the child, his or her name must be provided.

Disclosure of the Reporter's Identity

All jurisdictions have provisions in statute to maintain the confidentiality of abuse and neglect records. The identity of the reporter is specifically protected from disclosure to the alleged perpetrator in 39 States, the District of Columbia, Puerto Rico, American Samoa, Guam, and the Northern Mariana Islands. This protection is maintained even when other information from the report may be disclosed.

Release of the reporter's identity is allowed in some jurisdictions under specific circumstances or to specific departments or officials, for example, when information is needed for conducting an investigation or family assessment or upon a finding that the reporter knowingly made a false report (in Alabama, Arkansas, Connecticut, Kentucky, Louisiana, Minnesota, Nevada, South Dakota, Vermont, and Virginia). In some jurisdictions (California, Florida, Minnesota, Tennessee, Texas,

Vermont, the District of Columbia, and Guam), the reporter can waive confidentiality and give consent to the release of his or her name.

Section 30.4

Clergy as Mandatory Reporters of Child Abuse and Neglect

Text in this section is excerpted from "Clergy as Mandatory Reporters of Child Abuse and Neglect," U.S. Department of Health and Human Services (HHS), November 2013.

Every State, the District of Columbia, American Samoa, Guam, the Northern Mariana Islands, Puerto Rico, and the U.S. Virgin Islands have statutes that identify persons who are required to report child maltreatment under specific circumstances. Approximately 27 States and Guam currently include members of the clergy among those professionals specifically mandated by law to report known or suspected instances of child abuse or neglect. In approximately 18 States and Puerto Rico, any person who suspects child abuse or neglect is required to report it. This inclusive language appears to include clergy but may be interpreted otherwise.

Privileged Communications

As a doctrine of some faiths, clergy must maintain the confidentiality of pastoral communications. This is sometimes referred to as "clergy-penitent privilege," where "penitent" refers to the person consulting the clergy. Mandatory reporting statutes in some States specify the circumstances under which a communication is "privileged" or allowed to remain confidential. Privileged communications may be exempt from the requirement to report suspected abuse or neglect. The privilege of maintaining this confidentiality under State law must be provided by statute. Most States do provide the privilege, typically in rules of evidence or civil procedure. If the issue of privilege is not addressed in the reporting laws, it does not mean that privilege is not granted; it may be granted in other parts of State statutes.

This privilege, however, is not absolute. While clergy penitent privilege is frequently recognized within the reporting laws, it is typically interpreted narrowly in the context of child abuse or neglect. The circumstances under which it is allowed vary from State to State, and in some States it is denied altogether. For example, among the States that list clergy as mandated reporters, Guam, New Hampshire, and West Virginia deny the clergy-penitent privilege in cases of child abuse or neglect. Four of the States that enumerate "any person" as a mandated reporter (North Carolina, Oklahoma, Rhode Island, and Texas) also deny clergy-penitent privilege in child abuse cases.

In States where neither clergy members nor "any person" are enumerated as mandated reporters, it is less clear whether clergy are included as mandated reporters within other broad categories of professionals who work with children. For example, in Virginia and Washington, clergy are not enumerated as mandated reporters, but the clergy-penitent privilege is affirmed within the reporting laws.

Many States and territories include Christian Science practitioners or religious healers among professionals who are mandated to report suspected child maltreatment. In most instances, they appear to be regarded as a type of health-care provider. Only nine States (Arizona, Arkansas, Louisiana, Massachusetts, Missouri, Montana, Nevada, South Carolina, and Vermont) explicitly include Christian Science practitioners among classes of clergy required to report. In those States, the clergy-penitent privilege is also extended to those practitioners by statute.

The following table summarizes how States have or have not addressed the issue of clergy as mandated reporters (either specifically or as part of a broad category) and/or clergy-penitent privilege (either limiting or denying the privilege) within their reporting laws.

Table 30.1

	Privilege granted but limited to pastoral communications	Privilege denied in cases of suspected child abuse or neglect	Privilege not addressed in the reporting laws
Clergy enumerated as mandated reporters	Alabama, Arizona, Arkansas, California, Colorado, Georgia, Illinois, Louisiana, Maine, Massachusetts, Michigan, Minnesota, Missouri, Montana, Nevada, New Mexico, North Dakota, Ohio, Oregon, Pennsylvania, South Carolina, Vermont, Wisconsin	Guam, New Hampshire, West Virginia	Connecticut, Mississippi
Clergy not enumerated as mandated reporters but may be included with "any person" designation	Delaware, Florida, Idaho, Kentucky, Maryland, Utah, Wyoming	North Carolina, Oklahoma, Rhode Island, Texas	Indiana, Nebraska, New Jersey, Tennessee, Puerto Rico
Neither clergy nor "any person" enumerated as mandated reporters	Virginia, Washington	Not applicable	Alaska, American Samoa, District of Columbia, Hawaii, Iowa, Kansas, New York, Northern Mariana Islands, South Dakota, Virgin Islands

Chapter 31

How You Can Help Someone Who Is in an Abusive Situation

Chapter Contents

Section 31.1

How to Help a Friend Who Is Being Abused?

This section includes excerpts from "How to Help a Friend Who Is Being Abused?" Office on Women's Health (OWH), September 4, 2015; and text from "Help Someone in an Unhealthy Relationship: Quick Tips," U.S. Department of Health and Human Services (HHS), May 28, 2015.

Here are some ways to help a friend who is being abused:

- **Set up a time to talk.** Try to make sure you have privacy and won't be distracted or interrupted

- **Let your friend know you're concerned about her safety.** Be honest. Tell her about times when you were worried about her. Help her see that what she's going through is not right. Let her know you want to help.

- **Be supportive.** Listen to your friend. Keep in mind that it may be very hard for her to talk about the abuse. Tell her that she is not alone, and that people want to help.

- **Offer specific help.** You might say you are willing to just listen, to help her with childcare, or to provide transportation, for example.

- **Don't place shame, blame, or guilt on your friend.** Don't say, "You just need to leave." Instead, say something like, "I get scared thinking about what might happen to you." Tell her you understand that her situation is very difficult.

- **Help her make a safety plan.** Safety planning includes picking a place to go and packing important items.

- **Encourage your friend to talk to someone who can help.** Offer to help her find a local domestic violence agency. Offer to go with her to the agency, the police, or court.

- **If your friend decides to stay, continue to be supportive.** Your friend may decide to stay in the relationship, or she may leave and then go back many times. It may be hard for you to understand, but people stay in abusive relationships for many reasons. Be supportive, no matter what your friend decides to do.

- **Encourage your friend to do things outside of the relationship.** It's important for her to see friends and family.

- **If your friend decides to leave, continue to offer support.** Even though the relationship was abusive, she may feel sad and lonely once it is over. She also may need help getting services from agencies or community groups.

- **Keep in mind that you can't "rescue" your friend.** She has to be the one to decide it's time to get help. Support her no matter what her decision.

- **Let your friend know that you will always be there no matter what.**

Help Someone in an Unhealthy Relationship: Quick Tips

It can be hard to know what to do when someone you care about is in a controlling or violent relationship. These tips can help.

Watch for signs of abuse.

Make a list of anything you see that doesn't seem right. For example, watch for signs of:

- Controlling behavior, like demanding all of your loved one's time

- Physical abuse, like bruises or cuts

- Emotional abuse, like put-downs or name-calling

Find out about local resources.

Before you talk with your friend or family member, call 1-800-799-SAFE FREE (1-800-799-7233 FREE) to get the address and phone number of the nearest domestic violence agency. This way, you'll be able to share the information if the person is ready for it.

You can offer to help your friend or family member call the agency. You can also suggest visiting the domestic violence agency, talking to the police, or going to the doctor together.

Set up a time to talk.

Make sure you can have your conversation in a safe, private place.

Be specific about why you are worried.

Does your friend or loved one:

- Spend less time with friends or doing things he used to enjoy?
- Make excuses for his partner's behavior?
- Have unexplained cuts or bruises?

Does your friend or loved one's partner:

- Yell at or make fun of her?
- Try to control her by making all of the decisions?
- Check up on her when she's at work or school?
- Force her to do sexual things she doesn't want to do?
- Threaten to hurt himself if she ever breaks up with him?

Try to help your loved one understand that being treated this way isn't right. The more specific you can be, the better.

Plan for safety

People whose partners are controlling or violent may be in danger when they leave the relationship.

If your friend or loved one is ready to leave an abusive partner, help him make a plan for getting out of the relationship as safely as possible. A domestic violence counselor can help with making a safety plan.

If someone is in immediate danger, don't wait—call 911.

Be patient

Do your best to share your concerns with your friend or loved one – but understand that she will decide what's right for her, even if it doesn't make sense to you.

It can take time for someone to be ready to talk. Let her know that you are available to talk again whenever she is ready.

Section 31.2

How the Child Welfare System Works

Text in this section is excerpted from "How the Child Welfare
System Works," U.S. Department of Health and
Human Services (HHS), February 2013.

Introduction

The child welfare system is a group of services designed to promote
the well-being of children by ensuring safety, achieving permanency, and
strengthening families to care for their children successfully. While the
primary responsibility for child welfare services rests with the States, the
Federal Government plays a major role in supporting States in the delivery of services through funding of programs and legislative initiatives.

The primary responsibility for implementing Federal child and
family legislation rests with the Children's Bureau, within the Administration on Children, Youth and Families, Administration for Children and Families, U.S. Department of Health and Human Services
(HHS). The Children's Bureau works with State and local agencies to
develop programs that focus on preventing child abuse and neglect by
strengthening families, protecting children from further maltreatment,
reuniting children safely with their families, or finding permanent
families for children who cannot safely return home.

Most families first become involved with their local child welfare
system because of a report of suspected child abuse or neglect (sometimes called "child maltreatment"). Child maltreatment is defined by
CAPTA as serious harm (neglect, physical abuse, sexual abuse, and
emotional abuse or neglect) caused to children by parents or primary
caregivers, such as extended family members or babysitters. Child
maltreatment also can include harm that a caregiver allows to happen or does not prevent from happening to a child. In general, child
welfare agencies do not intervene in cases of harm to children caused
by acquaintances or strangers. These cases are the responsibility of
law enforcement.

The child welfare system is not a single entity. Many organizations in each community work together to strengthen families and

437

keep children safe. Public agencies, such as departments of social services or child and family services, often contract and collaborate with private child welfare agencies and community-based organizations to provide services to families, such as in-home family preservation services, foster care, residential treatment, mental health care, substance abuse treatment, parenting skills classes, domestic violence services, employment assistance, and financial or housing assistance.

The Child Abuse Prevention and Treatment Act

The Child Abuse Prevention and Treatment Act (CAPTA), originally passed in 1974, brought national attention to the need to protect vulnerable children in the United States. CAPTA provides Federal funding to States in support of prevention, assessment, investigation, prosecution, and treatment activities as well as grants to public agencies and nonprofit organizations for demonstration programs and projects. Additionally, CAPTA identifies the Federal role in supporting research, evaluation, technical assistance, and data collection activities. CAPTA also sets forth a minimum definition of child abuse and neglect. Since it was signed into law, CAPTA has been amended several times. It was most recently amended and reauthorized on December 20, 2010, by the CAPTA Reauthorization Act of 2010.

Child welfare systems are complex, and their specific procedures vary widely by State. The purpose of this factsheet is to give a brief overview of the purposes and functions of child welfare from a national perspective.

Child welfare systems typically:

- Receive and investigate reports of possible child abuse and neglect

- Provide services to families that need assistance in the protection and care of their children

- Arrange for children to live with kin or with foster families when they are not safe at home

- Arrange for reunification, adoption, or other permanent family connections for children leaving foster care

What Happens When Possible Abuse or Neglect Is Reported?

Any concerned person can report suspicions of child abuse or neglect. Most reports are made by "mandatory reporters"—people who are required by State law to report suspicions of child abuse and neglect. As of August 2012, statutes in approximately 18 States and Puerto Rico require any person who suspects child abuse or neglect to report it. These reports are generally received by child protective services (CPS) workers and are either "screened in" or "screened out." A report is screened in when there is sufficient information to suggest an investigation is warranted. A report may be screened out if there is not enough information on which to follow up or if the situation reported does not meet the State's legal definition of abuse or neglect. In these instances, the worker may refer the person reporting the incident to other community services or law enforcement for additional help.

What Happens after a Report Is "Screened In"?

CPS caseworkers, often called investigators or assessment workers, respond within a particular time period, which may be anywhere from a few hours to a few days, depending on the type of maltreatment alleged, the potential severity of the situation, and requirements under State law. They may speak with the parents and other people in contact with the child, such as doctors, teachers, or child care providers. They also may speak with the child, alone or in the presence of caregivers, depending on the child's age and level of risk.

Children who are believed to be in immediate danger may be moved to a shelter, a foster home, or a relative's home during the investigation and while court proceedings are pending. An investigator also engages the family, assessing strengths and needs and initiating connections to community resources and services.

Some jurisdictions now employ an alternative, or differential, response system. In these jurisdictions, when the risk to the children involved is considered low, the CPS caseworker focuses on assessing family strengths, resources, and difficulties and on identifying supports and services needed, rather than on gathering evidence to confirm the occurrence of abuse or neglect.

At the end of an investigation, CPS caseworkers typically make one of two findings—unsubstantiated (unfounded) or substantiated (founded). These terms vary from State to State. Typically, a finding of unsubstantiated means there is insufficient evidence for the worker to conclude that a child was abused or neglected, or what happened

439

does not meet the legal definition of child abuse or neglect. A finding of substantiated typically means that an incident of child abuse or neglect, as defined by State law, is believed to have occurred.

Some States have additional categories, such as "unable to determine," that suggest there was not enough evidence to either confirm or refute that abuse or neglect occurred.

The agency will initiate a court action if it determines that the authority of the juvenile court (through a child protection or dependency proceeding) is necessary to keep the child safe. To protect the child, the court can issue temporary orders placing the child in shelter care during the investigation, ordering services, or ordering certain individuals to have no contact with the child.

At an adjudicatory hearing, the court hears evidence and decides whether maltreatment occurred and whether the child should be under the continuing jurisdiction of the court. The court then enters a disposition, either at that hearing or at a separate hearing, which may result in the court ordering a parent to comply with services necessary to alleviate the abuse or neglect. Orders can also contain provisions regarding visitation between the parent and the child, agency obligations to provide the parent with services, and services needed by the child.

What Happens in Substantiated (Founded) Cases?

If a child has been abused or neglected, the course of action depends on State policy, the severity of the maltreatment, an assessment of the child's immediate safety, the risk of continued or future maltreatment, the services available to address the family's needs, and whether the child was removed from the home and a court action to protect the child was initiated. The following general options are available:

- **No or low risk**—The family's case may be closed with no services if the maltreatment was a one-time incident, the child is considered to be safe, there is no or low risk of future incidents, and any services the family needs will not be provided through the child welfare agency but through other community based resources and service systems.

- **Low to moderate risk**—Referrals may be made to community-based or voluntary in-home child welfare services if the CPS worker believes the family would benefit from these services and the child's present and future safety would be enhanced. This may happen even when no abuse or neglect is found, if the family needs and is willing to participate in services.

- **Moderate to high risk**—The family may again be offered voluntary in-home services to address safety concerns and help reduce the risks. If these are refused, the agency may seek intervention by the juvenile dependency court. Once there is a judicial determination that abuse or neglect occurred, juvenile dependency court may require the family to cooperate with in-home services if it is believed that the child can remain safely at home while the family addresses the issues contributing to the risk of future maltreatment. If the child has been seriously harmed, is considered to be at high risk of serious harm, or the child's safety is threatened, the court may order the child's removal from the home or affirm the agency's prior removal of the child. The child may be placed with a relative or in foster care.

What Happens to Parents?

Caregivers who are found to have abused or neglected a child are generally offered support and treatment services or are required by a juvenile dependency court to participate in services that will help keep their children safe. In cases of low risk, in-home services and supports may be provided, including parent education, child care, counseling, safety planning, and more.

In more severe cases or fatalities, police are called on to investigate and may file charges in criminal court against the perpetrators of child maltreatment. In many States, certain types of abuse, such as sexual abuse and serious physical abuse, are routinely referred to law enforcement.

Whether or not criminal charges are filed, the name of the person committing the abuse or neglect may be placed on a State child maltreatment registry if abuse or neglect is confirmed. A registry is a central database that collects information about maltreated children and individuals who are found to have abused or neglected those children. These registries are usually confidential and used for internal child protective purposes only. However, they may be used in background checks for certain professions that involve working with children to protect children from contact with individuals who may mistreat them.

What Happens to Children?

Depending on the severity of the case, children may remain at home or be removed into foster care.

In-Home

In low-risk cases, children may remain in their own homes with their families, and the families may receive in-home services and supports. These may include parent education, safety planning, counseling, and more. Families may also be connected with community services that provide concrete help (e.g., housing, food) as well as services such as therapy, parent training, and support groups.

Out-of-Home

Most children in foster care are placed with relatives or foster families, but some may be placed in a group or residential setting. While a child is in foster care, he or she attends school and should receive medical care and other services as needed. The child's family also receives services to support their efforts to reduce the risk of future maltreatment and to help them, in most cases, be reunited with their child. Visits between parents and their children and between siblings are encouraged and supported, following a set plan.

Every child in foster care should have a permanency plan. Families typically participate in developing a permanency plan for the child and a service plan for the family, and these plans guide the agency's work. Family reunification, except in unusual and extreme circumstances, is the permanency plan for most children. In some cases, when prospects for reunification appear less likely, a concurrent permanency plan is developed. If the efforts toward reunification are not successful, the plan may be changed to another permanent arrangement, such as adoption or transfer of custody to a relative.

Federal law requires the court to hold a permanency hearing, which determines the permanent plan for the child, within 12 months after the child enters foster care and every 12 months thereafter. Many courts review each case more frequently to ensure that the agency is actively pursuing permanency for the child.

Whether or not they are adopted, older youth in foster care should receive support in developing some form of permanent family connection, in addition to transitional or Independent Living services, to assist them in being self-sufficient when they leave foster care between the ages of 18 and 21.

Summary

The goal of child welfare is to promote the well-being, permanency, and safety of children and families by helping families care for their children successfully or, when that is not possible, helping children find permanency with kin or adoptive families. Among children who enter foster care, most will return safely to the care of their own families or go to live with relatives or an adoptive family.

Chapter 32

The Role of the Office on Women's Health (OWH) in Helping Prevent Violence against Women

Violence against Women

Government in action on violence against women

About OWH's programs

The Office on Women's Health (OWH) of the U.S. Department of Health and Human Services (HHS) works to stop violence against women and girls. The OWH do this through model programs, policy work, and communications.

Through leadership of the HHS Steering Committee on Violence Against Women, OWH coordinates partnerships within HHS and with other federal, state, and local agencies.

The OWH also serve as the point of contact for HHS on violence against women issues. In that role they direct citizens, colleagues, and

---

The text in this chapter is excerpted from "Violence against Women," Office of Women's Health (OWH), January 27, 2015.

organizations to the appropriate office or agency to respond to inquiries and provide resources.

Through the work of the OWH Regional Women's Health Offices, they have had an impact on domestic violence, sexual assault, and violence against women and girls throughout the country. The Regional Women's Health Coordinators have done groundbreaking work on the issues faced by women in prison, tribal women, and women in the U.S. territories.

Some of the coordinator's work focuses on examining how violence affects women with disabilities, engaging men as partners in prevention of violence, and enhancing college and university curricula to include domestic violence and sexual assault issues.

"It's On Us" sexual assault prevention campaign

The HHS Office on Women's Health has partnered with the White House Council on Women and Girls and the Center for American Progress to launch the It's On Us campaign. The campaign will fundamentally shift the way we think about sexual assault. Sexual assault is not only a crime, but a societal problem in which all of us have a role to play. Stopping sexual assault is the responsibility of all of us.

Project Connect: A coordinated public health initiative to prevent violence against women

Project Connect is a national initiative to change how adolescent health, reproductive health, and Native health services respond to sexual and domestic violence. Research demonstrates that programs like Project Connect can help improve maternal and adolescent health and decrease the risks for unplanned pregnancy, poor pregnancy outcomes, and further abuse.

OWH and Futures Without Violence provide technical assistance and monitor the grantees selected for Project Connect. Project Connect grantees are committed to providing innovative, effective, and culturally relevant services to traditionally underserved communities, including African-American women, Native women, Latinas, LGBTQ youth, and rural women living in poverty. The University of Pittsburgh School of Medicine is implementing an evaluation plan to measure the effectiveness of both the clinical intervention and policy change efforts.

Over the past five years, Project Connect has trained nearly 11,000 health care providers in specific interventions to assess for and respond to domestic and sexual violence in their clinical settings. The initiative has helped establish partnerships between public health programs and domestic and sexual violence advocates to effectively identify and refer victims of abuse. Project Connect teams have also had a significant impact on state-level policies, including instituting assessment of domestic and sexual violence into statewide protocols, improving data collection by adding new questions about domestic violence to statewide surveillance systems, increasing funding statewide for clinics that address violence, and requiring annual training on violence in key state programs.

Chapter 33

Interventions and Help for Abusers

Chapter Contents

Section 33.1

Batterer Interventions

"Batterer Interventions," © 2016 Omnigraphics, Inc.
Reviewed January 2016.

Batterer Interventions: What Are They?

Whether or not a person who behaves abusively toward an intimate partner can change is a question that has long interested researchers— as well as couples and families. Some studies have suggested that most perpetrators of verbal, emotional, physical, or sexual abuse cannot effectively change the deep-seated feelings, attitudes, and behaviors that contribute to domestic violence. Other studies have indicated that meaningful change is possible for some abusers, but that achieving healthy relationships is a long and difficult process. One type of program that is intended to stop domestic abuse and rehabilitate abusers is known as a batterer intervention program (BIP). As is the case with other efforts to reform domestic violence offenders, the results of BIP have been mixed.

Identifying Abusers

The first step toward ending domestic abuse is recognizing that certain types or patterns of behavior are abusive. Both perpetrators and victims of domestic violence need to be aware of the common traits of domestic abusers, including:

- extreme jealousy, possessiveness, or controlling behavior

- demanding commitment very quickly

- isolating victims from family and friends, limiting their social interaction, and insisting that the intimate relationship should fulfill all of their needs

- being easily insulted or overly sensitive to criticism

- harboring unrealistic expectations of perfection in relationships

- believing in rigid, stereotypical gender roles or holding negative attitudes toward the opposite sex

- making cruel, hurtful, degrading remarks to partners or belittling their accomplishments

- shifting blame and refusing to take responsibility for problems

- threatening violence, breaking objects, or using force of any kind during an argument

- having a past history of violence in relationships

- being cruel or neglectful toward animals or children

- abusing alcohol or drugs

- showing extreme, Jekyll-and-Hyde shifts in personality or behavior.

People who are wondering whether their behavior constitutes abuse should consider whether they treat others—such as friends, neighbors, or co-workers—in the same way they treat their intimate partners. They should also try to view their behavior from the perspective of someone outside of the relationship, and consider how they would feel if they saw another person treating a loved one in that manner. Finally, if an intimate partner has ever described certain behaviors as abusive or threatened to leave the relationship, then it seems likely that some interactions may have crossed the line into domestic abuse.

Changing Abusive Behavior

In order to end abusive behavior, the abuser must have a deep desire to change as well as a full commitment to what can be a long and challenging process. Abusive behavior is often rooted in attitudes and feelings that originated in childhood and developed over the course of many years. As a result, it can be extremely difficult to dislodge these longstanding issues and affect true change.

The first step for abusers is admitting that their behavior is wrong and harmful. Abusers often deflect blame onto others, so taking direct personal responsibility for their actions is a vital part of the change process. Some tips for people who are committed to ending abusive behavior include:

- View violence as a choice. Remember that there is no excuse for abuse. Admit the abuse, take full responsibility for it, and avoid blaming others.

- Realize that physical violence is not the only form of domestic abuse. Verbal and emotional abuse also have no place in a healthy, respectful relationship.

- Recognize that abusive behavior hurts others. Respect an intimate partner's right to a safe and healthy relationship.

- Accept the consequences of abusive actions, including legal consequences.

- Work to identify underlying attitudes and patterns of behavior involved in abuse.

- Develop new methods of dealing with conflicts and responding to an intimate partner's grievances, criticisms, and anger.

- Make amends for past abuse and develop kind, supportive, respectful, and loving behaviors.

- Avoid seeking recognition or credit for any improvements in behavior.

- Seek help and support from friends, family members, and intervention programs.

- Recognize that achieving change is very difficult, and overcoming abusiveness is a long-term process. Do not expect immediate results and do not give up trying to change.

Batterer Intervention Programs

Professional help is essential in learning to avoid abusive behaviors and treat intimate partners with respect. Batterer Intervention Programs (BIP) are tools that were developed to aid in this process. BIP originated in the 1980s, when increased enforcement of domestic violence laws led to rising numbers of accused batterers in the criminal justice system. The courts discovered that some victims of domestic violence did not want their abusive partners put in jail. Instead, they only wanted the abuse to stop. BIP were developed to meet the demand for programs to help abusers reform and potentially return to their families. Many courts began requiring offenders to attend BIP as a condition of probation.

There are several types of BIP based on different theoretical approaches to domestic violence. The most common type of BIP is the Duluth model, a psychoeducational program based on the idea that domestic violence stems from patriarchal ideas that equate masculinity with strength, power, and dominance. This theory claims that cultural norms of masculinity encourage men to exert control over their intimate partners, which sometimes results in abuse. The Duluth model helps abusers confront such attitudes and develop new, more respectful methods of relating to their partners.

Individual and group psychotherapy are also used to treat domestic abusers. These approaches explain domestic violence as stemming from an underlying emotional problem or traumatic childhood experience. They focus on helping abusers uncover the unconscious sources of their behavior and resolve them consciously in order to stop battering. Cognitive-behavioral intervention is another type of BIP. It focuses on training abusers in anger management and other skills to help them change their ways of thinking about relationships and dealing with problems. Other types of BIP tailor their approaches to specific attributes or typologies of batterers, such as ethnicity or socioeconomic group.

Couples or family therapy is also employed in BIP. This approach treats domestic violence as part of a larger pattern of relationship dysfunction and involves all parties in the effort to end the abuse. It has aroused controversy because it appears to assign a share of the blame to victims of abuse. Although some studies have found that BIP can be effective in helping end abusive behavior, other studies have suggested that a very low percentage of abusers succeed in making permanent changes.

References

1. "Can I Stop Being Abusive?" Love Is Respect, 2013.

2. "I Think I'm Abusive." Hidden Hurt, 2015.

3. Jackson, Shelly. "Batterer Intervention Programs." U.S. Department of Justice, June 2003.

4. Robinson, Kathryn. "Is Change Possible in an Abuser?" National Domestic Violence Hotline, September 5, 2013.

Section 33.2

Effectiveness of Batterer Intervention Programs

Text in this section is excerpted from "Practical Implications of Current Intimate Partner Violence Research for Victim Advocates and Service Providers," National Criminal Justice Reference Service (NCJRS), December 2013.

Do Batterer Intervention Programs Prevent Reabuse?

Commonly, whether diverted, placed on probation or jailed, many domestic violence offenders are required to attend batterer intervention programs. These programs have increased dramatically over the past several decades. There have been more than 35 evaluations of batterer intervention programs, but they have yielded inconsistent results.

The largest multistate study of four batterer programs concluded that approximately a quarter of batterers appeared unresponsive and resistant to batterer intervention regardless of batterer treatment programs. In this long-term study, based on victim and/or abuser interviews and/or police arrests, approximately half of the batterers reassaulted their initial or new partners sometime during the study's 30-month follow-up. Most of the reassaults occurred within the first six months of program intake.

Nearly a quarter of the batterers repeatedly assaulted their partners during the follow-up, and these offenders accounted for nearly all of the severe assaults and injuries. The leading researcher suggests that "the system matters." BIPs that incorporate enhanced "support and notification to partners, program orientation sessions, open-ended enrollments, curricula that are designed for open-ended enrollments, 'voluntary' post-program sessions, and on-going risk management that identifies and responds to problematic cases and dropout" may achieve better outcomes.

Several meta-analyses of the more rigorous batterer program studies find the programs have, at best, a "modest" treatment effect, producing a minimal reduction in re-arrests for domestic violence. In one of the meta-analyses, the treatment effect translated to a five percent improvement rate in cessation of reassaults due to the treatment. In the other, it ranged from none to 0.26, roughly representing a reduction in recidivism from 13 to 20 percent.

A randomized, experimental evaluation of an "early intervention" BIP with male IPV suspects who had minimal DV criminal history and were detained in a county jail pending trial found that a one week intervention appeared to reduce controlling behavior and alcohol and drug use in the 6 months after the program. However, the BIP did not have an effect on physical, sexual, and psychological abuse, threats and the injuries inflicted on victims. Victim partners reported that the intervention did not create problems for them. Participant and victim follow-up data were collected 6 months after the BIP, and police reports were tracked from 6−12 months thereafter. The "system" in which the BIP program was delivered included a daily, 3 hour, Duluth Model-based educational workshop for 5 days, mandatory detention in a special DV jail unit, supervision by correction officers who had specialized DV training, daily Twelve-Step Drug/Alcohol addiction support groups, and strict regulations on TV watching (special non-violent education programs were the only available programs).

The rate of recidivism 8 years following the last class of the DAIP Men's program attended by 353 men in Duluth revealed that men enrolling in the DAIP Men's program recidivate at a rate of 28%, with non-completers reoffending at 31% and completers at 25%. There is a significant difference in the number of re-offenses; non-completers commit 63% more re-offenses than men who complete the program. Recidivism was measured by arrests, citations for DV, and protection orders issued against program participants by intimate partners or former partners. The DAIP is embedded in the Duluth CCR such that the deterrence must be viewed as a result of the entire criminal justice process rather than just of the DAIP Men's program.

On the other hand, a few studies have found that batterer intervention programs are associated with higher rates of reabuse or have found no reduction in abuse at all. A meta-analysis of four randomized trials involving more than 2,300 batterers comparing those who received Cognitive Behavioral Therapy (CBT) and those who had no intervention found the positive difference obtained by the CBT participants in terms of reabuse to be so slight that researchers could not conclude there was any clear evidence for an effect. Another single study compared CBT with process psychodynamic group treatment and found equivocal differences, although the process-psychodynamic treatment proved marginally better.

Does the Type or Length of Batterer Intervention Programs Make a Difference?

Several studies have found that the type of batterer intervention program, whether feminist, psycho-educational, or cognitive-behavioral, does not affect reabuse. One study also found that a "culturally focused" program specifically designed for black male abusers did no better than the program offered to all abusers. In fact, those assigned to a conventional, racially mixed group were half as likely to be arrested for reassaults compared to those assigned to a black culturally focused counseling group or a conventional group of all blacks.

As to duration of the BIP program, in the 4 state, multisite study, similar reassault rates were found for the participants in the shorter BIP (13 sessions over 3 months) as for those in longer ones (9 month), except that the reported reassaults were less severe in the 9 month program that included some alcohol treatments. The shorter BIP outcomes appeared to be related to the swift and certain actions of the court (judicial reviews) and the higher completion rates.

However, a rigorous study based in New York City found the length of the program (26 weeks compared to 8 weeks) may make a difference, with the longer program proving more effective at deterring reabuse. The researchers suggest that the longer program's increased effectiveness was due to its longer "suppression effect" while abusers were mandated to attend, whether or not they actually attended. In other words, whether or not they actually attended the program, while they were under court supervision they were more likely to be on their best behavior.

Are Court-Referred Batterers Likely to Complete Batterer Programs?

Multiple studies of disparate programs around the country have found high non-completion rates ranging from 25 percent to 89 percent, with most at around 50 percent. Rates vary because different programs have different standards for monitoring attendance as well as different policies regarding re-enrollment, missed meetings, and so on. A study in California found that, of 10 counties examined, only one maintained a database to track offender participation in the mandated batterer intervention program; it reported that 89 percent did not complete the program. Not surprisingly, requiring additional treatment programs increases non-completion. For example, although 42 percent of the referred batterers in the Bronx court study failed to complete the batterer intervention program, that number increased to 67 percent for those also required to complete drug treatment. For those required to complete drug treatment alone, the non-completion rate was lower at 60 percent.

High rates of technical violations are common for probationers sentenced for IPV, including violations of no-contact orders, drug abstinence, and failure to attend batterer intervention programs. Various probation studies have found technical violation (noncrime) rates ranging from 34 percent of those sentenced in the Brooklyn felony domestic violence court, 41 percent in Colorado, to 61 percent in Champaign County, Ill. Rates of technical violations may vary based on the practices of the probation officers or others charged with monitoring the probationers. For example, technical violations were found to be 25% in Rhode Island for those abusers supervised in regular mixed caseloads, but 44% in specialized IPV only caseloads.

Do Those Who Complete Batterer Programs Do Better than Those Who Fail?

Abusers who complete batterer programs are less likely to reabuse than those who fail to attend, are noncompliant, or drop out. The differences have been found to be significant.

A Chicago study of more than 500 court-referred batterers referred to 30 different programs found that recidivism after an average of 2.4 years was 14.3 percent for those who completed the program, whereas recidivism for those who did not complete the programs was more than twice that (34.6 percent). Those who did not complete their program mandate in the Bronx court study were four times more likely to recidivate than those who completed their program.

A multistate study of four programs found that abusers who completed the programs reduced their risk of reassault in a range of 46 to 66 percent. A Florida study found that the odds that abusers who completed the program would be rearrested were half those of a control group not assigned to the program, whereas the odds of rearrest for those who failed to attend were two and one-half times higher than the control group.

A Massachusetts study found that, over a six-year period, those who completed a certified batterer intervention program were significantly less likely to be rearraigned for any type of offense, a violent offense, or a protection order violation. The rate differences for these offenses, between those who completed a program and those who did not, was as follows: 47.7 vs. 83.6 percent for any crime, 33.7 vs. 64.2 percent for a violent crime, and 17.4 vs. 41.8 percent for violation of a protective order. A Dallas study found that twice as many program dropouts as program completers were rearrested within 13 months: 39.7 vs. 17.9 percent for any charge, and 8.1 vs. 2.8 percent for assault arrests. An

Alexandria, Va., study of almost 2,000 domestic violence defendants found that noncompliance with court-ordered treatment was associated significantly with being a repeat offender.

A few studies have found less dramatic reductions, for example, in Broward County, the difference was only four percent vs. five percent, and in Brooklyn, it was 16 percent vs. 26 percent for completers compared to non-completers.

Which Batterers Are Likely to Fail to Attend Mandated Batterer Intervention Treatment?

Researchers generally agree that there are a number of variables associated with failure to complete programs. They include being younger, having less education, having greater criminal histories and violence in their family of origin, being less often employed and less motivated to change, having substance abuse problems, having children, and lacking court sanctions for noncompliance.

A number of studies emphasize the positive correlation between program completion and "stakes in conformity," including the variables of age (being older), marital status (being married) and employment (being employed).

Studies also find that many of the same variables that predict non-completion also predict reabuse or general recidivism. In the Florida probation study, an examination of court referred batterers found that the same characteristics that predicted rearrest (including prior criminal history and stakes in conformity) also predicted missing at least one court mandated program session. Other studies, including a study of two Brooklyn batterer intervention programs, also found that employment correlated both positively with completion and negatively with rearrest.

However, prior criminal history remains the strongest and most consistent predictor of both non-completion and new arrests. In the Brooklyn study, defendants with a prior arrest history were found to be four times more likely to fail to complete programs than defendants without prior arrests. The Bronx court study similarly found that prior arrests as well as a history of drug abuse predicted both non-completion and recidivism and found background demographics to be less important.

When Are Noncompliant Abusers Likely to Drop out of Batterer Programs?

Several studies have found that batterers who do not complete batterer intervention programs are likely to be noncompliant from the start. Furthermore, these studies found that noncompliance at the first court monitoring predicted both program failure and recidivism. In the Brooklyn study, the strongest predictor of program failure was early noncompliance. Defendants who had not enrolled in a program by the time of their first compliance hearing were significantly less likely to complete the program than those enrolled by the first hearing. These findings are similar to those found in the Bronx study.

Defendants who were not in compliance at their first monitoring appearance were six times more likely to fail to complete the program than those in compliance at that time. Attrition may even occur before enrollment in BIPS. In a study of the use of polygraphs in BIP programs, researchers reported that 46 percent of the "high-risk" abusers did not report to probation or enroll in the BIP.

These findings are consistent with extensive research indicating that the largest proportion of court-identified abusers who reabuse are likely to reabuse sooner rather than later.

What Should the Court's Response Be If Court-Referred Abusers Are Noncompliant with Programs?

The Rhode Island probation study that compared probationers in specialized probation supervision caseloads with those in less stringent general caseloads found that the former committed significantly less reabuse over one year. The difference, however, applied only to what researchers called "lower risk" probationers, those without prior arrest histories. Although there were several differences in how the two caseloads were supervised, enforcement of batterer intervention program attendance was one of the major differences. The specialized group's program was more rigidly enforced, as measured by significantly more probation sanctions for nonattendance. As a result of the court violation hearings, most of the noncompliant probationers were required to attend weekly compliance court sessions until they completed the program.

An evaluation of two OVW demonstration domestic violence courts found that abusers who participated in the specialized DV court with considerably more probation revocations for noncompliance (12 percent vs. only 1 percent in the other court) were significantly less likely to reabuse than those in the comparison court. In the court with more revocations, victims reported a lower frequency of physical assaults for up to 11 months after the study incident. The offenders in the court with the higher revocation rates had a significantly higher number of prior arrests than the defendants in the comparison court (8.3 vs.

3.7 percent). Researchers posited that lower rates of recidivism were obtained primarily through early detection and incarceration of probationers who either continued to reabuse or failed to comply with conditions.

Broward County probation study researchers concluded that if abusers are not afraid of violating their court orders, they are also not afraid of the consequences of committing new offenses.

Are Victims Satisfied with Batterer Intervention Program Referrals?

Studies find that most victims are satisfied with their abuser's referral to a batterer intervention program. In the Bronx study, 77 percent of victims were satisfied with the sentence imposed by the court if the abuser was ordered to attend a BIP, compared to only 55 percent of victims who were satisfied when the abuser was not required to attend a program. A survey of victims of men attending batterer intervention programs throughout Rhode Island found most female victims enthusiastic about the batterer programs. Some victims were enthusiastic and felt that the program improved their situation even though they were reassaulted.

Victims may be more likely to remain with their abusers if their abusers are in treatment programs and are hopeful that the abusers will "get better." For some victims, the failure of abusers to attend and complete mandated BIPs is a key component in their decisions to terminate relationships with violent partners.

Many IPV victims want help for their intimate partners. Victims consider BIP participation by abusers an important opportunity to learn and to choose to stop abuse. Listening sessions with African American and Latina women revealed that participants strongly support programming that will assist their abusive partners in stopping IPV. Participants added that services should be offered in community settings apart from traditional DV services and that community engagement should address the economic fragility of the environments in which they live to build safeguards against IPV.

Chapter 34

Workplace Violence: Prevention and Intervention

Chapter Contents

Section 34.1

Deterring Workplace Violence

Text in this section is excerpted from "Addressing Workplace
Violence," U.S. Department of Commerce (DOC), May 2014.

A successful effort to deter workplace violence consists of management and employees using a number of resources. These include:

Pre-Employment Screening

Management and supervisors, with the assistance of its Servicing
Human Resources Offices's (SHRO), and Office of Security (OSY), will
determine any pre-employment screening techniques that may be utilized,
such as background and reference checks, provided those techniques are
non-discriminatory, job-related, and consistent with business necessity,
and drug testing, if the position is a testing designated position.

Security

Managers and supervisors will comply with existing OSY Manual
of Security Policies and Procedures to ensure that appropriate security measures are in place. Access control systems, wearing of issued
badges, effective guard service, and liaison with law enforcement are
deterrents to workplace violence. OSY will also provide guidance in the
development of Occupant Emergency and Lockdown plans for owned
and leased Department facilities.

Alternative Dispute Resolution (ADR)

ADR may be effective in resolving disputes when a conflict has
been identified before potential workplace violence erupts by using
one of these techniques: facilitation, mediation, interest based problem
solving, or peer review.

Incident Management

SHROs will, when appropriate, convene a management group
to discuss the potential for workplace violence incidents. Issues of

concern such as planned personnel actions, for example, RIF, furlough, adverse action, termination, and EAP-required disclosures should be discussed. Members should consist of SHRO, OSY, EAP, and OGC. The management group should also meet after a workplace violence incident for after-action review.

Section 34.2

Prevention Strategies

This section includes excerpts from "The Phenomena of Workplace Violence," Federal Bureau of Investigation (FBI), August 6, 2013; and text from "Violence in the Workplace," The National Institute for Occupational Safety and Health (NIOSH), Centers for Disease Control and Prevention (CDC), June 6, 2014.

Preventing Incidents

Crisis consultants have improved radically in handling two aspects of workplace violence. The first involves assessing the likelihood that a person who makes a threat will act on it. The second area is in the response—more specifically, responding in ways that both defuse the threat and protect those most vulnerable.

Several best practices can help prevent violence in the workplace. These include setting additional security in place; notifying law enforcement; seeking a temporary restraining order (TRO) against the person who poses the threat; and, if the person is an employee, referring the individual to an employee assistance program (EAP). However, these actions are not foolproof. For example, with regard to added security, authorities must consider the length of time the security will remain in place, the rationale behind eventually discontinuing its use, and the measures established to prevent the person who made the threat from reappearing once the security no longer is present.

Law enforcement agencies are limited to a certain degree until the threatening person actually commits a crime. Police officers cannot arrest someone for what that person may do in the future. A TRO is only effective if the restrained person honors it. If individuals decide to act irrespective of a court order, the piece of paper will not stop them. Also, EAPs provide only limited information to an organization regarding one of its employees. Additionally, EAP professionals frequently lack necessary expertise in handling workplace violence.

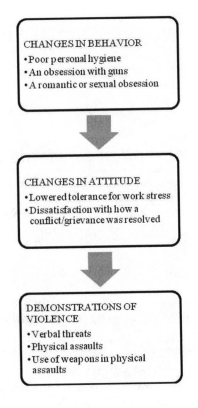

CHANGES IN BEHAVIOR
- Poor personal hygiene
- An obsession with guns
- A romantic or sexual obsession

CHANGES IN ATTITUDE
- Lowered tolerance for work stress
- Dissatisfaction with how a conflict/grievance was resolved

DEMONSTRATIONS OF VIOLENCE
- Verbal threats
- Physical assaults
- Use of weapons in physical assaults

Figure 34.1. Structural Flow of Behaviour and Attitude Changes

Warning Signs

Managers can help prevent workplace violence by identifying the warning signs that an employee may become violent. As shown in Figure 34.1, three apparent indicators are changes in behavior, shifts in attitude, and demonstrations of violence. Other signs may include few friends and little social support, unexplained absences, lack of adequate housing or health care, addictions, and depression. Managers recognizing these warning signs can work with the angry employee through a 12-step process, shown in Figure 34.2. In addition to being aware of warning signs, it is important to be conscious of triggering events that may lead to acts of violence.

- Submission of a grievance that was ignored
- Termination of employment (fired or laid off), passed over for promotion, or suspended
- A personal crisis, such as a failed romance
- Escalation of domestic problems
- Disciplinary action, a poor performance review, or criticism from a boss or coworker
- Bank or court action, such as a foreclosure, restraining order, or custody hearing
- Benchmark date, such as an anniversary, birthday, or date of a high-profile bombing

Creating a safer physical environment also is an ideal way to enhance workplace violence prevention. This may involve restricting areas accessible to the public; modifying the landscape by increasing visibility around buildings and improving lighting; limiting the amount of cash kept on hand; and installing a security system. More so, training employees in interpersonal communications so they can deal effectively with disgruntled peers also is helpful. A progressive system of discipline for personnel can be established to this end. For instance, in step one, a warning may be issued when an angry outburst occurs; step two may involve asking the person to leave the premises; step three may call for the intervention of security personnel or the police.

Hiring Right

Workplace violence prevention starts with hiring. The process begins with requiring potential employees to thoroughly answer the questions on their job applications. The wording of the application should warn that giving false or misleading information will result in either rejection of the application or termination of employment. An applicant background check also should be conducted, focusing on any criminal history, verification of past employment, and confirmation of the person's social security number and driver's license. The investigative and screening efforts made on behalf of the potential employee should be documented, even if all the information received is favorable.

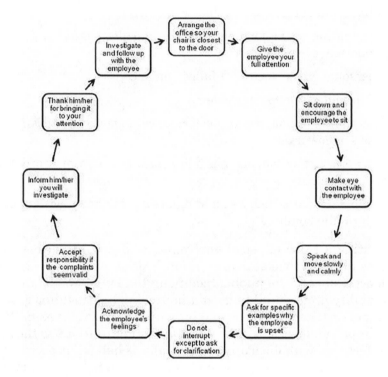

Figure 34.2. *Administration in office*

Employers can be held responsible for the harm their employees cause. Several legal theories may be used to try to impose liability on the employer for the intentional and negligent violent acts of employees, citing negligence in hiring and negligent retention. While a thorough analysis of the liability an employer may face is outside the scope of this article, reference to a few basic steps that can be taken to help minimize the risk of liability, as well as harm to others, should be noted.

In addition to screening out unsuitable applicants with the background check process, employers should focus on adopting effective workplace policies and practices to address unacceptable behavior. One example is a zero-tolerance policy towards violence in the workplace. Such a policy should include a preassigned contact person in the event an employee becomes aware of a potentially threatening situation or individual, a nonretaliation statement, and guidelines for managers when they become aware of a policy violation.

Prevention Strategies

Environmental Designs

Commonly implemented cash-handling policies in retail settings include procedures such as using locked drop safes, carrying small amounts of cash, and posting signs and printing notices that limited cash is available. It may also be useful to explore the feasibility of cashless transactions in taxicabs and retail settings through the use of machines that accommodate automatic teller account cards or debit cards. These approaches could be used in any setting where cash is currently exchanged between workers and customers.

Physical separation of workers from customers, clients, and the general public through the use of bullet-resistant barriers or enclosures has been proposed for retail settings such as gas stations and convenience stores, hospital emergency departments, and social service agency claims areas. The height and depth of counters (with or without bullet-resistant barriers) are also important considerations in protecting workers, since they introduce physical distance between workers and potential attackers. Consideration must nonetheless be given to the continued ease of conducting business; a safety device that increases frustration for workers or for customers, clients, or patients may be self-defeating.

Visibility and lighting are also important environmental design considerations. Making high-risk areas visible to more people and installing good external lighting should decrease the risk of workplace assaults.

Access to and egress from the workplace are also important areas to assess. The number of entrances and exits, the ease with which non-employees can gain access to work areas because doors are unlocked, and the number of areas where potential attackers can hide are issues that should be addressed. This issue has implications for the design of buildings and parking areas, landscaping, and the placement of garbage areas, outdoor refrigeration areas, and other storage facilities that workers must use during a work shift.

Numerous security devices may reduce the risk for assaults against workers and facilitate the identification and apprehension of perpetrators. These include closed-circuit cameras, alarms, two-way mirrors, card-key access systems, panic-bar doors locked from the outside only, and trouble lights or geographic locating devices in taxicabs and other mobile workplaces.

Personal protective equipment such as body armor has been used effectively by public safety personnel to mitigate the effects of workplace violence. For example, the lives of more than 1,800 police officers have been saved by Kevlar® vests.

Administrative Controls

Staffing plans and work practices (such as escorting patients and prohibiting unsupervised movement within and between clinic areas) are included in the California Occupational Safety and Health Administration Guidelines for the Security and Safety of Health Care and Community Service Workers [State of California 1993]. Increasing the number of staff on duty may also be appropriate in any number of service and retail settings. The use of security guards or receptionists to screen persons entering the workplace and controlling access to actual work areas has also been suggested by security experts.

Work practices and staffing patterns during the opening and closing of establishments and during money drops and pickups should be carefully reviewed for the increased risk of assault they pose to workers. These practices include having workers take out garbage, dispose of grease, store food or other items in external storage areas, and transport or store money.

Policies and procedures for assessing and reporting threats allow employers to track and assess threats and violent incidents in the workplace. Such policies clearly indicate a zero tolerance of workplace violence and provide mechanisms by which incidents can be reported and handled. In addition, such information allows employers to assess whether prevention strategies are appropriate and effective.

These policies should also include guidance on recognizing the potential for violence, methods for defusing or de-escalating potentially violent situations, and instruction about the use of security devices and protective equipment. Procedures for obtaining medical care and psychological support following violent incidents should also be addressed. Training and education efforts are clearly needed to accompany such policies.

Behavioral Strategies

Training employees in nonviolent response and conflict resolution has been suggested to reduce the risk that volatile situations will escalate to physical violence. Also critical is training that addresses hazards associated with specific tasks or worksites and relevant prevention strategies. Training should not be regarded as the sole prevention strategy but as a component in a comprehensive approach to reducing workplace violence.

To increase vigilance and compliance with stated violence prevention policies, training should emphasize the appropriate use and maintenance of protective equipment, adherence to administrative controls, and increased knowledge and awareness of the risk of workplace violence.

Section 34.3

What to Do When a Colleague Discloses Abuse?

Sometimes people who are experiencing domestic abuse need to tell an outsider about their situation. If they do not trust family members or friends to listen in an unbiased, nonjudgmental way, they may instead choose to confide in someone at work. Likewise, co-workers who see each other every day may be among the first to notice signs of domestic abuse, such as unexplained injuries, repeated absences, sudden declines in productivity, or unusual anxiety or isolation. Either way, a co-worker may be the first to learn that a fellow employee is experiencing domestic violence.

If a colleague is being abused, they may not have told anyone about it before. They may have conflicting emotions about their abusive partner that they are struggling to understand. Although the situation may be affecting their work performance, they may not feel comfortable discussing their home life with supervisors or human resources representatives. Finding the courage to confide in a co-worker is a big step, and how the co-worker reacts can have a major impact on their ability to trust others and seek additional support. Thus, it is important to know how to respond in a sensitive manner if a colleague shows signs of domestic violence or discloses abuse.

Supportive Responses

If you suspect that a co-worker may be experiencing domestic violence, it is better to express concern rather than make accusations. Gently mention specific things you may have noticed. If the person denies that there is a problem or offers a different explanation for their injuries, do not push for a confession. Instead, make it clear that no one deserves to be hurt, and offer to listen or provide the phone number of a confidential domestic violence hotline if they ever want to talk about it.

If a colleague discloses abuse, one of the best ways to help is by listening. Although you may be tempted to ask questions and offer advice, you should not push them to take action or try to fix the problem for them. Instead, experts suggest providing a supportive, sympathetic ear and offering to help them find resources or access support services when they feel ready.

As you talk your co-worker, it is important to remember that people become trapped in abusive relationships by their partners' use of violence and coercion. The victim of abuse is in no way responsible for what is happening to them. Experts suggest responding in a nonjudgmental way, reassuring your colleague that it is not their fault and that you are there to support them. Some possible things to say include:

- I know it was difficult to tell me, but I'm glad you did.

- I believe you.

- I care about your health and safety.

- I'm sorry you are in this situation.

- No one has the right to hurt you.

- It's not your fault.

- No one deserves to be treated this way.

- What's happening to you is against the law.

- I understand that it may take some time to figure out what to do.

- There are people who can help you.

- I will keep this information confidential.

- I will support you no matter what you decide to do.

If your colleague is having problems at work due to ongoing abuse—such as absenteeism or a loss of productivity—they may need reassurance about their job security. They may also need to take some time off from work for doctor appointments, legal consultations, or counseling sessions. Confiding in a supportive colleague at work can help give them the time and resources they need to get out of an abusive situation.

References

1. "Domestic Abuse: How to Respond." Stanford Medicine, 2016.

2. "An Employee/Co-Worker Has Just Disclosed They Experienced Historic Abuse, What Should I Do?" Live Fear Free, n.d.

3. "If You Suspect Abuse." University of Michigan, 2009.

Section 34.4

Preventing Workplace Violence for Healthcare and Social Service Workers

Text in this section is excerpted from "Guidelines for Preventing Workplace Violence for Healthcare and Social Service Workers," Occupational Health and Safety Administration (OSHA), 2014.

Healthcare and social service workers face a significant risk of job-related violence. The National Institute for Occupational Safety and Health (NIOSH) defines workplace violence as "violent acts (including physical assaults and threats of assaults) directed toward persons at work or on duty."

According to the Bureau of Labor Statistics (BLS), 27 out of the 100 fatalities in healthcare and social service settings that occurred in 2013 were due to assaults and violent acts.

While media attention tends to focus on reports of workplace homicides, the vast majority of workplace violence incidents result in non-fatal, yet serious injuries. Statistics based on the Bureau of Labor

Statistics (BLS) and National Crime Victimization Survey (NCVS) data both reveal that workplace violence is a threat to those in the healthcare and social service settings. BLS data show that the majority of injuries from assaults at work that required days away from work occurred in the healthcare and social services settings. Between 2011 and 2013, workplace assaults ranged from 23,540 and 25,630 annually, with 70 to 74% occurring in healthcare and social service settings. For healthcare workers, assaults comprise 10-11% of workplace injuries involving days away from work, as compared to 3% of injuries of all private sector employees.

The workplace violence rates highlighted in BLS data are corroborated by the NCVS, which estimates that between 1993 and 2009 healthcare workers had a 20% (6.5 per 1,000) overall higher rate of workplace violence than all other workers (5.1 per 1,000).3 In addition, workplace violence in the medical occupations represented 10.2% of all workplace violence incidents. It should also be noted that research has found that workplace violence is underreported—suggesting that the actual rates may be much higher.

Risk Factors: Identifying and Assessing

Workplace Violence Hazards Healthcare and social service workers face an increased risk of work-related assaults resulting primarily from violent behavior of their patients, clients and/or residents. While no specific diagnosis or type of patient predicts future violence, epidemiological studies consistently demonstrate that inpatient and acute psychiatric services, geriatric long term care settings, high volume urban emergency departments and residential and day social services present the highest risks. Pain, devastating prognoses, unfamiliar surroundings, mind and mood altering medications and drugs, and disease progression can also cause agitation and violent behaviors.

While the individual risk factors will vary, depending on the type and location of a healthcare or social service setting, as well as the type of organization, some of the risk factors include:

Patient, Client and Setting-Related Risk Factors

- Working directly with people who have a history of violence, abuse drugs or alcohol, gang members, and relatives of patients or clients;

- Transporting patients and clients;

- Working alone in a facility or in patients' homes;
- Poor environmental design of the workplace that may block employees' vision or interfere with their escape from a violent incident;
- Poorly lit corridors, rooms, parking lots and other areas;
- Lack of means of emergency communication;
- Prevalence of firearms, knives and other weapons among patients and their families and friends; and
- Working in neighborhoods with high crime rates.

Organizational Risk Factors

- Lack of facility policies and staff training for recognizing and managing escalating hostile and assaultive behaviors from patients, clients, visitors, or staff;
- Working when understaffed—especially during mealtimes and visiting hours;
- High worker turnover;
- Inadequate security and mental health personnel on site;
- Long waits for patients or clients and overcrowded, uncomfortable waiting rooms;
- Unrestricted movement of the public in clinics and hospitals; and
- Perception that violence is tolerated and victims will not be able to report the incident to police and/or press charges.

Violence Prevention Programs

A written program for workplace violence prevention, incorporated into an organization's overall safety and health program, offers an effective approach to reduce or eliminate the risk of violence in the workplace. The building blocks for developing an effective workplace violence prevention program include:

1. Management commitment and employee participation,
2. Worksite analysis,
3. Hazard prevention and control,

4.   Safety and health training, and

5.   Recordkeeping and program evaluation.

A violence prevention program focuses on developing processes and procedures appropriate for the workplace in question.

Specifically, a workplace's violence prevention program should have clear goals and objectives for preventing workplace violence, be suitable for the size and complexity of operations and be adaptable to specific situations and specific facilities or units. The components are interdependent and require regular reassessment and adjustment to respond to changes occurring within an organization, such as expanding a facility or changes in managers, clients, or procedures. And, as with any occupational safety and health program, it should be evaluated and reassessed on a regular basis. Those developing a workplace violence prevention program should also check for applicable state requirements. Several states have passed legislation and developed requirements that address workplace violence.

1. Management Commitment and Worker Participation

Management commitment and worker participation are essential elements of an effective violence prevention program. The leadership of management in providing full support for the development of the workplace's program, combined with worker involvement is critical for the success of the program. Developing procedures to ensure that management and employees are involved in the creation and operation of a workplace violence prevention program can be achieved through regular meetings— possibly as a team or committee.

Effective management leadership begins by recognizing that workplace violence is a safety and health hazard.

Management commitment, including the endorsement and visible involvement of top management, provides the motivation and resources for workers and employers to deal effectively with workplace violence.

2. Worksite Analysis and Hazard Identification

A worksite analysis involves a mutual step-by-step assessment of the workplace to find existing or potential hazards that may lead to incidents of workplace violence. Cooperation between workers and employers in identifying and assessing hazards is the foundation of a successful violence prevention program. The assessment should be made by a team that includes senior management, supervisors and workers. Although management is responsible for controlling hazards, workers have a critical role to play in helping to identify and assess workplace hazards, because of their knowledge and familiarity with facility operations, process activities and potential threats.

Depending on the size and structure of the organization, the team may also include representatives from operations; employee assistance; security; occupational safety and health; legal; and human resources staff. The assessment should include a records review, a review of the procedures and operations for different jobs, employee surveys and workplace security analysis.

Once the worksite analysis is complete, it should be used to identify the types of hazard prevention and control measures needed to reduce or eliminate the possibility of a workplace violence incident occurring. In addition, it should assist in the identification or development of appropriate training. The assessment team should also determine how often and under what circumstances worksite analyses should be conducted. For example, the team may determine that a comprehensive annual worksite analysis should be conducted, but require that an investigative analysis occur after every incident or near miss.

Additionally, those conducting the worksite analysis should periodically inspect the workplace and evaluate worker tasks in order to identify hazards, conditions, operations and situations that could lead to potential violence. The advice of independent reviewers, such as safety and health professionals, law enforcement or security specialists, and insurance safety auditors may be solicited to strengthen programs. These experts often provide a different perspective that serves to improve a program.

Information is generally collected through: (1) records analysis; (2) job hazard analysis; (3) employee surveys; and (4) patient/ client surveys.

3. Hazard Prevention and Control

After the systematic worksite analysis is complete, the employer should take the appropriate steps to prevent or control the hazards that were identified. To do this, the employer should:

- Identify and evaluate control options for workplace hazards;

- Select effective and feasible controls to eliminate or reduce hazards;

- Implement these controls in the workplace;

- Follow up to confirm that these controls are being used and maintained properly; and

- Evaluate the effectiveness of controls and improve, expand, or update them as needed.

In the field of industrial hygiene, these steps are generally categorized, in order of effectiveness, as

- Substitution;

- Engineering controls; and

- Administrative and work practice controls.

These principles, which are described in more detail below, can also be applied to the field of workplace violence. In addition, employers should ensure that, if an incident of workplace violence occurs, post-incident procedures and services are in place and/or immediately made available.

Substitution

The best way to eliminate a hazard is to eliminate it or substitute a safer work practice. While these substitutions may be difficult in the therapeutic healthcare environment, an example may be transferring a client or patient to a more appropriate facility if the client has a history of violent behavior that may not be appropriate in a less secure therapeutic environment.

Engineering controls and workplace adaptations to minimize risk

Engineering controls are physical changes that either remove the hazard from the workplace or create a barrier between the worker and the hazard. In facilities where it is appropriate, there are several engineering control measures that can effectively prevent or control workplace hazards. Engineering control strategies include:

1. using physical barriers (such as enclosures or guards) or door locks to reduce employee exposure to the hazard;

2. metal detectors;

3. panic buttons,

4. better or additional lighting; and

5. more accessible exits (where appropriate).

Administrative and work practice controls

Administrative and work practice controls are appropriate when engineering controls are not feasible or not completely protective.

These controls affect the way staff perform jobs or tasks. Changes in work practices and administrative procedures can help prevent violent incidents. As with engineering controls, the practices chosen to abate workplace violence should be appropriate to the type of site and in response to hazards identified.

Post-incident procedures and services

Post-incident response and evaluation are important components to an effective violence prevention program. Investigating incidents of workplace violence thoroughly will provide a roadmap to avoiding fatalities and injuries associated with future incidents. The purpose of the investigation should be to identify the "root cause" of the incident. Root causes, if not corrected, will inevitably recreate the conditions for another incident to occur.

When an incident occurs, the immediate first steps are to provide first aid and emergency care for the injured worker(s) and to take any measures necessary to prevent others from being injured. All workplace violence programs should provide comprehensive treatment for workers who are victimized personally or may be traumatized by witnessing a workplace violence incident. Injured staff should receive prompt treatment and psychological evaluation whenever an assault takes place, regardless of its severity—free of charge. Also, injured workers should be provided transportation to medical care if not available on site.

Investigation of incidents

Once these immediate needs are taken care of, the investigation should begin promptly. The basic steps in conducting incident investigations are:

- Report as required. Determine who needs to be notified, both within the organization and outside (e.g., authorities), when there is an incident. Understand what types of incidents must be reported, and what information needs to be included. If the incident involves hazardous materials additional reporting requirements may apply.

  - Involve workers in the incident investigation. The employees who work most closely in the area where the event occurred may have special insight into the causes and solutions.

  - Identify Root Causes: Identify the root causes of the incident. Don't stop an investigation at "worker error" or "unpredictable event." Ask "why" the patient or client acted, "why" the worker responded in a certain way, etc.

- Collect and review other information.

- Depending on the nature of the incident, records related to training, maintenance, inspections, audits, and past incident reports may be relevant to review.

- Investigate Near Misses. In addition to investigating all incidents resulting in a fatality, injury or illness, any near miss (a situation that could potentially have resulted in death, injury, or illness) should be promptly investigated as well. Near misses are caused by the same conditions that produce more serious outcomes, and signal that some hazards are not being adequately controlled, or that previously unidentified hazards exist.

4. Safety and Health Training

Education and training are key elements of a workplace violence protection program, and help ensure that all staff members are aware of potential hazards and how to protect themselves and their coworkers through established policies and procedures. Such training can be part of a broader type of instruction that includes protecting patients and clients (such as training on de-escalation techniques). However, employers should ensure that worker safety is a separate component that is thoroughly addressed. Training for all workers

Training can: (1) help raise the overall safety and health knowledge across the workforce, (2) provide employees with the tools needed to identify workplace safety and security hazards, and (3) address potential problems before they arise and ultimately reduce the likelihood of workers being assaulted.

The training program should involve all workers, including contract workers, supervisors, and managers. Workers who may face safety and security hazards should receive formal instruction on any specific or potential hazards associated with the unit or job and the facility. Such training may include information on the types of injuries or problems identified in the facility and the methods to control the specific hazards. It may also include instructions to limit physical interventions in workplace altercations whenever possible.

Every worker should understand the concept of "universal precautions for violence"— that is, that violence should be expected but can be avoided or mitigated through preparation. In addition, workers should understand the importance of a culture of respect, dignity, and active mutual engagement in preventing workplace violence.

New and reassigned workers should receive an initial orientation before being assigned their job duties. All workers should receive required training annually. In high-risk settings and institutions, refresher training may be needed more frequently, perhaps monthly or quarterly, to effectively reach and inform all workers. Visiting staff, such as physicians, should receive the same training as permanent staff and contract workers. Qualified trainers should instruct at the comprehension level appropriate for the staff. Effective training programs should involve role-playing, simulations and drills.

Training topics

Training topics may include management of assaultive behavior, professional/police assault-response training, or personal safety training on how to prevent and avoid assaults. A combination of training programs may be used, depending on the severity of the risk. In general, training should cover the policies and procedures for a facility as well as de-escalation and self-defense techniques. Both de-escalation and self-defense training should include a hands-on component. The following provides a list of possible topics:

- The workplace violence prevention policy;

- Risk factors that cause or contribute to assaults;

- Policies and procedures for documenting patients' or clients' change in behavior;

- The location, operation, and coverage of safety devices such as alarm systems, along with the required maintenance schedules and procedures;

- Early recognition of escalating behavior or recognition of warning signs or situations that may lead to assaults;

- Ways to recognize, prevent or diffuse volatile situations or aggressive behavior, manage anger and appropriately use medications;

- Ways to deal with hostile people other than patients and clients, such as relatives and visitors;

- Proper use of safe rooms—areas where staff can find shelter from a violent incident;

- A standard response action plan for violent situations, including the availability of assistance, response to alarm systems and communication procedures;

- Self-defense procedures where appropriate;

- Progressive behavior control methods and when and how to apply restraints properly and safety when necessary;

- Ways to protect oneself and coworkers, including use of the "buddy system";

- Policies and procedures for reporting and recordkeeping;

- Policies and procedures for obtaining medical care, trauma-informed care, counseling, workers' compensation or legal assistance after a violent episode or injury.

Guidelines for Preventing Workplace Violence for Healthcare and Social Service Workers

Training for supervisors and managers

Supervisors and managers must be trained to recognize high-risk situations, so they can ensure that workers are not placed in assignments that compromise their safety. Such training should include encouraging workers to report incidents and to seek the appropriate care after experiencing a violent incident.

Supervisors and managers should learn how to reduce safety hazards and ensure that workers receive appropriate training. Following training, supervisors and managers should be able to recognize a potentially hazardous situation and make any necessary changes in the physical plant, patient care treatment program and staffing policy, and procedures to reduce or eliminate the hazards.

Training for security personnel

Security personnel need specific training from the hospital or clinic, including the psychological components of handling aggressive and abusive clients, and ways to handle aggression and defuse hostile situations.

Evaluation of training

The training program should also include an evaluation. At least annually, the team or coordinator responsible for the program should review its content, methods and the frequency of training. Program evaluation may involve supervisor and employee interviews, testing, observing and reviewing reports of behavior of individuals in threatening situations.

5. Recordkeeping and Program Evaluation

Recordkeeping and evaluation of the violence prevention program are necessary to determine its overall effectiveness and identify any deficiencies or changes that should be made. Accurate records of injuries, illnesses, incidents, assaults, hazards, corrective actions, patient histories and training can help employers determine the severity of the problem; identify any developing trends or patterns in particular locations, jobs or departments; evaluate methods of hazard control; identify training needs and develop solutions for an effective program. Records can be especially useful to large organizations and for members of a trade association that "pool" data. Key records include:

- OSHA Log of Work-Related Injuries and Illnesses (OSHA Form 300). Covered employers are required to prepare and maintain records of serious occupational injuries and illnesses, using the OSHA 300 Log. As of January 2015, all employers must report: (1) all work-related fatalities within 8 hours and (2) all work-related inpatient hospitalizations, all amputations and all losses of an eye within 24 hours. Injuries caused by assaults must be entered on the log if they meet the recording criteria.

- Medical reports of work injury, workers' compensation reports and supervisors' reports for each recorded assault. These records should describe the type of assault, such as an unprovoked sudden attack or patient-to-patient altercation, who was assaulted, and all other circumstances of the incident. The records should include a description of the environment or location, lost work time that resulted and the nature of injuries sustained. These medical records are confidential documents and should be kept in a locked location under the direct responsibility of a healthcare professional.

- Records of incidents of abuse, reports conducted by security personnel, verbal attacks or aggressive behavior that may be threatening, such as pushing or shouting and acts of aggression toward other clients. This may be kept as part of an assaultive incident report. Ensure that the affected department evaluates these records routinely.

- Information on patients with a history of past violence, drug abuse or criminal activity recorded on the patient's chart. Anyone who cares for a potentially aggressive, abusive or violent client should be aware of the person's background and history, including triggers and de-escalation responses. Log the admission of violent patients to help determine potential risks. Log violent events on patients' charts and flagged charts.

- Documentation of minutes of safety meetings, records of hazard analyses and corrective actions recommended and taken.

- Records of all training programs, attendees, and qualifications of trainers.

Section 34.5

Manager's Guide for Workplace Sexual Harassment Prevention

Text in this section is excerpted from "Manager Workplace Sexual Harassment Prevention Toolkit (Your Guide to Preventing and Addressing Sexual Harassment in the Workplace)," Office of Equity, Diversity, and Inclusion, National Institutes of Health (NIH), May 2014.

What Course of Action Should a Manager Take If a Sexual Harassment Claim Is Brought to Him or Her?

As a manager you must initiate an immediate administrative inquiry process by contacting your employee relations specialist who will assist you in conducting an investigation intended to gather information to determine what action, if legal or criminal prosecution.

What Course of Action Should a Manager Take If a Sexual Harassment Claim Is against Him or Her?

If a sexual harassment claim has been brought against you, your behavior will be under increased scrutiny. To avoid exacerbating the situation you should not engage in the behavior cited in the complaint. The National Institutes of Health (NIH) is committed to promoting and maintaining a work environment free from discrimination and retaliation. Reprisal for participation in the EEO process is prohibited. Therefore, any retaliation against the complainant is barred.

It is strongly advised that any behavior that could be perceived as retaliatory be strictly avoided. It is imperative that you be supportive and cooperative of the resolution process and maintain a record of relevant communications and events.

What Course of Action Should a Manager Take If the Victim Elects to Not Pursue the Complaint?

The National Institutes of Health (NIH) is legally obligated to investigate any potential allegations of sexual harassment once it is notified of its existence. Once management is made aware of potentially unlawful behavior it is duty bound to investigate regardless of the victim's wishes.

Suppose the Employee Wants to Talk about the Sexual Harassment but Does Not Want the Manager to Do Anything about It?

Once a manager is on notice that there is workplace sexual harassment you are obligated to act. A manager's knowledge of the situation puts the agency on official notice that illegal discrimination is occurring. The manager should tell the employee that now that they know what is going on that they have an obligation to conduct an administrative inquiry into the matter and to take action if inappropriate behavior is found.

What Course of Action Should a Manager Take If He or She Witnesses Sexual Harassment?

Any manager who witnesses an act of potential sexual harassment is required to initiate an immediate administrative inquiry process.

What Course of Action Should a Manager Take If He or She Learned of the Sexual Harassment via Informal Channels Such as Gossip or Rumors?

To prevent sexual harassment in the workplace management must take a proactive, not reactive, stance to sexual harassment. Being proactive means adopting the NIH's zero tolerance harassment policy.

Managers should investigate all allegations of sexual harassment regardless of how he or she was made aware of the allegations.

What You Should Know, but Probably Don't

- The National Institutes of Health (NIH) is automatically liable for sexual harassment that results in a significant change in an individual's employment status (hiring, firing, promotions, demotions, undesirable reassignment) regardless of upper management's level of knowledge.
- A victim's submission to sexual activity is not a defense to avoid liability.
- Sexual harassment is an abuse of power it is not an expression of sexual attraction.

How to Prevent Workplace Harassment

- Post the NIH's EEO policy in a highly visible physical or electronic location.

- Disseminate the NIH's EEO policy to everyone and often.

- Firmly and consistently enforce the NIH's EEO policy.

- Monitor behavior. Acquire a sense of what is normal and abnormal workplace behavior for your employees.

- Respond to all allegations immediately.

- Once a manager is put on notice that an employee or applicant finds a behavior objectionable the manager should promptly put an end to the behavior.

- Treat all complaints seriously, consistently, and confidentially

- Be sensitive but neutral.

- Follow up with both the harasser(s) and the victim.

- Document your actions.

- Avoid even the appearance of retaliation. For example if an employee must be removed from the workplace do not remove the alleged victim.

Chapter 35

Intervention by Faith Communities

The Religious Imperative to End Violence against Women

Religious principles of the world's major faiths affirm the position of religion as a force for good and human dignity. Universal religious principles can be used in services or events with religious communities in order to show that violence against women is of particular concern for the community because it goes against the beliefs of faith. These examples can help to enforce the positive potential of religion to promote peace for every human being. Religious leaders can search through their own sacred texts and teachings as well to find examples that show the need to respect and value women, which can help in the effort to eliminate violence against women.

Religious communities have a unique responsibility to preserve the dignity of women and girls, many who have been traumatized by violence. The first section has outlined the devastating forms of violence against women and how they are linked with other urgent global problems. The second section takes that impulse to act and offers tools, resources and suggestions for how people of faith can

Text in this section is excerpted from "Restoring Dignity: A Toolkit for Religious Communities to End Violence against Women," U.S. Agency for International Development, October 24, 2011. Reviewed January 2016.

work together to eliminate violence against women in pursuit of a brighter tomorrow. This chapter includes resources that can be utilized to help educate and raise awareness, prevent violence against women, organize advocacy initiatives, and support and care for survivors. Faith Communities and religious leaders can use these tools and develop new ones to effect change as they unite across faith lines and around the globe to defend and restore the inviolable rights and dignity of women and girls.

> Religious principles express an inspiring message of non-violence in the hope of a more equal and peaceful world. They demonstrate a strong ethical position on the dignity of women and mandate that women be valued in society. Faith communities are the right people to address violence against women, a tremendous crisis that threatens the preservation of all these principles.

Education and Awareness

Religious leaders and communities are well positioned to educate themselves and others on how to overcome the devastating incidence of violence against women. Education and awareness can help shape shared values on the dignity of the human person that mandates respect for women. It is a powerful tool to critically analyze the root causes of violence and break down ignorance and prejudice—both dangerous preconditions for violence against women.

- **Facilitate education for healing and leadership- building:** This may include conducting trauma healing, empowerment and socio-economic skills-building workshops for survivors of violence to become community leaders. Sharing real-life people's experiences of violence against women in a safe and confidential manner is also an effective tool in this pursuit.

- **Support religious and inter-religious educational programs for people of faith:** Train religious teachers and clergy on violence against women and the empowerment of women and girls. Organize facilitated interactive dialogues aimed at increasing public knowledge, influencing attitudes and opinions on non-violence as well as promoting a code for living with respect for women and girls.

- **Conduct religious and spiritual educational events:**
  Organize educational prayer or worship services and ensure
  that prayers, songs, meditations, messages or religious rituals
  support education on eradicating violence against women and
  supporting survivors. Speak out through educational talks or
  sermons that raise awareness, influence public opinion, shape
  social values and reject the misuses of religion for violence.

- **Develop and disseminate relevant educational and awareness materials:** These tools should mobilize religious assets
  and resources to end violence against women. Such educational
  resources can include fact-sheets, educational quilts, posters,
  informational brochures, or a collage of educational photographs.

> By helping to mobilize religious and spiritual resources and
> motivations for peaceful co-existence, multi-religious education
> can promote dialogue and action from the grassroots to the
> global level to end violence against women. One example of a
> way to start the dialogue is by having an inter-religious educa-
> tion and awareness week radio program.

Prevention

Religious leaders have tremendous moral and spiritual influence
and thus have a unique and unparalleled potential to not only react
to violence against women but to change people's thinking and actions
before they act. Taking a strong stance can prevent someone from
committing an act of violence against women or sway others to join in
eliminating this terrible crime.

- **Encourage involvement of both men and women:** While
  the perpetrators of violence against women are usually men,
  their involvement is key to prevent future violence. One way
  to involve men more is to make them the focus of sensitization
  efforts and awareness campaigns or to solicit influential male
  partners, including clergy, in these prevention efforts.

- **Collaborate with other religious leaders and communities:** Multi-faith cooperation is particularly powerful because it
  shows solidarity and strength and allows diverse communities
  to pool resources and talents for a common goal. Multi-faith

cooperation also demonstrates that while different faiths have many diverse traditions, all faiths value that sanctity and dignity of every human life. Multi-faith activities can be organized through local Inter-religious Councils or with leaders of other local places of worship. Consider holding special multi-religious services or vigils where ending violence against women is the universal and unifying goal.

- **Incorporate violence against women into religious gatherings:** Putting violence against women on the agenda not only at community events but also within the services or spiritual meetings that happen on a regular basis sends a strong message about the role of religious communities in preventing violence against women.

- **Focus on talking to youth:** Some young people today might become perpetrators of violence against women but they also could become the positive leaders of tomorrow. As figures of great influence, religious leaders can target youth and tap into their potential to pick up the work of ending violence against women wherever it's left off. The next generation is a crucial factor in building a new culture of cooperation and respect for all.

Prevention of violence against women and girls is a serious commitment to change the reality we live in and improve the lives of women and girls who are suffering around the world. Sharing a statement of religious commitment to ending violence against women during a sermon or event can have a tremendous impact on enlisting more people to work to prevent violence before it starts.

Advocacy

Advocacy is working actively to influence certain outcomes such as changing public policy and public opinion. Religious leaders, as highly respected figures in their communities, are uniquely equipped to lead activism that will address violence against women. Right now religious leaders can and must act out against interpretations and practices that threaten the well- being of any woman or girl; advocacy is a perfect way to do that.

- **Act to recover religion as a force for peace:** Act to recover religion as a force for peace: Promote policies, religious texts and doctrines that respect the dignity of all persons and defend the sanctity of life. Condemn all practices—traditional and otherwise—that endanger the physical, emotional, mental and/ or spiritual wellbeing of women and girls. Speak out against anyone that tries to manipulate or use religion as an excuse for violence or ill- treatment of women.

- **Hold a community meeting:** Religious leaders, women's organizations, youth organizations, schools and other faith- based groups can take an active role in breaking the silence together. Call a communal meeting to mobilize all the resources and assets of these different groups; this can increase the effectiveness of a united effort to change the status quo.

- **Speak with community and governmental leaders:** Find out from these representatives what is most needed in the community and what can be done as a religious leader to eliminate violence against women. This can help to make religious leaders more visible in the community, and it holds the government accountable for their own involvement and promises to eradicate violence against women as well.

- **Schedule lobbying days:** Religious leaders and their communities can use these days to approach decision makers and talk about what is needed on the ground in their communities—services, laws, policies, implementation of existing policies etc.

> Advocacy is a highly effective means to merge the assets of the religious community with other organizations and leaders so that real changes can be made collectively that will help end violence against women. An inter-religious campaign is a great way to broadcast a message of hope and action that will bring all these communities together in pursuit of a common goal to end violence against women.

Support and Care

One of the most powerful ways that religious leaders can respond to violence against women is by supporting and caring for survivors, working with perpetrators and comforting those in fear of violence. All too often people live with their emotions bottled up inside and after such a traumatic experience it is crucial that survivors have strong leaders and communities to support them and hear their voices.

- **Listen to survivors' stories:** Providing a safe and confidential space is essential, as survivors may feel voiceless or fearful that speaking about their experiences will lead to further violence and social stigma. Allow survivors to talk freely about their rage, fears, assumptions, and experiences related to violence against women; in many contexts, religious leaders serve as one of the only safe listeners for survivors, and their voices must be heard to get the appropriate support.

- **Form support groups:** Facilitating group reflections about violence against women can help survivors feel less isolated and powerless. A sense of solidarity may empower survivors to recognize that they in no way deserve to be abused, and that they have a sacred right to live healthy and dignified lives.

- **Link to health care agencies or organizations:** Guiding survivors towards quality health care providers in the community is a critical way to address the physical and psychological effects of violence against women. All too often inadequate health care aggravates issues related to violence against women and securing survivors with a good provider can help in recovery and preventing further violence and complications.

- **Provide guidance and support to individuals living in fear of aggression:** Counseling men and women who are experiencing relationship problems can help address conflicts before they become violent. Listen to people and let them freely share their emotions. It will give them a necessary outlet to share their feelings; having that outlet may make the difference between a healthy relationship and an abusive one.

> Grounded in the spiritual and moral richness of their own faith traditions, religious leaders can help transform cultures of violence into cultures of healing and reconciliation, one person at a time. Tips for listening and talking to violence against women survivors can be a tool to help in facilitating that process of healing.

Tips for Listening and Talking to Violence against Women Survivors

- **Confidentiality and Disclosure:** A survivor must be completely clear that it's her choice what she wants to share, knowing that the information will remain completely confidential. Disclosing is a very difficult step to take and power shifts when information is shared. The listener should remind the survivor of both risks and benefits of sharing when she is deciding how much to disclose and to whom.

- **Concerns:** Consider some of the major concerns survivors may have when disclosing information and acknowledge them in the conversation. These concerns include, but are certainly not restricted to, fear of shame and social stigma, concern about safety, damage to one's identity in recognizing what happened to them and loss of control from sharing their story.

- **Support:** A survivor may be feeling a range of complicated and intense emotions, such as fear, anger, anxiety, guilt, shame, vulnerability, denial, depression, powerlessness or guilt. It is useful to identify these feelings and also to try to help counteract them. Tell her that she has been through an extremely upsetting and frightening experience, and assure her that she is not to blame for what happened and that she is in a safe place now.

- **Non-Judgmental Listening:** The listener may have his or her own thoughts about what has happened to the survivor, what they have done in response, etc. but it is crucial to reserve that judgment. Listening is a very meaningful act and for a survivor to just be heard without someone giving their opinion is hugely beneficial for them. Put the power in their hands as much as possible and be there for them as a support.

- **Do:** Believe the survivor's story, assure the survivor of divine love and presence, respect the survivor's choices, help the survivor with any religious concerns, pray with the survivor if she wants and give the survivor referral information so she knows what further services are available to her.

- **Don't:** Don't tell the survivor what to do, don't blame the survivor for the violence, don't encourage the survivor to forgive her abuser, don't allow the survivor to become too dependent on the listener and don't do nothing—religious leaders have tremendous potential to be a positive force in her recovery.

Addressing Justice: Ending Impunity

What Can Religious Leaders Do about Perpetrators of Violence against Women?

Religions recognize human rights of every individual with a nucleus to values, duties and responsibilities. These include the need to promote justice and provide redress so that individuals can be protected and perpetrators of violence can be held accountable and sanctioned. Religious institutions have sometimes limited the scope for achieving justice when nobody is called to account for the suffering of women and girls who experience violence.

- **Take a strong stance:** Faith leaders know not to condone any act of violence against women but rather to take necessary steps to lead perpetrators on a path toward rehabilitation.

- **Preserve religion as a source for good:** Make clear that violence against women is never tolerated by any sacred text or faith tradition and be part of the transformation of perpetrators of these crimes into agents for social good.

- **Connect with rehabilitation agencies or organizations:** Perpetrators may require professional assistance beyond what religious leaders are trained to provide. Referring individuals to effective rehabilitation centers is important so that perpetrators of violence against women do not become repeat offenders.

- **Call the government to take action:** Build alliances with other organizations and even other faith communities and then encourage the government to take action regarding perpetrators and provide serious rehabilitation to prevent future cases.

Actions to ensure punitive consequences of violators enhance security not only for individuals, but for the entire community, because it proves that victims will be protected and perpetrators of violence against women will be caught, tried and punished. Quotes from different faiths condemning the violation of women's rights may be used to demonstrate the multi-faith commitment to upholding women's rights and the need to punish perpetrators. The following quotes from faith leaders can help break the silence and stigma surrounding violence against women.

Chapter 36

Intervention by Healthcare Providers

What Role Do Health Care Providers Play in Responding to Intimate Partner Violence (IPV)?

Many victims regularly come into contact with medical and health care providers although the providers may not identify their patients as victims of IPV. In fact, early help-seeking by battered women is often with health care providers. Health care providers are in the position to assess victim health needs (related to abuser violence and victim isolation, depression or suicidality), to assist in safety planning, to provide preventive health care, follow-up consultations, and information-sharing about legal options and supportive community resources.

Research suggests, however, that women victims of IPV may not seek health care when they encounter providers who appear "uninterested, uncaring, or uncomfortable" about domestic violence. In addition, screening and risk assessment by health care providers makes little sense if they have no idea what to do once IPV is assessed.

Text in this section is excerpted from "Practical Implications of Current Intimate Partner Violence Research for Victim Advocates and Service Providers," National Criminal Justice Reference Service (NCJRS), December 2013; and text from "Documenting Domestic Violence: How Health Care Providers Can Help Victims," U.S. Department of Justice (DOJ), September 2001. Reviewed January 2016.

Recognizing the importance of effective screening, risk assessment, continuing health care and informed referrals to community agencies, researchers undertook a quasi-experimental study of emergency departments, primary care facilities, and pediatric clinics in a Midwest, university city to determine if explicit changes in health care practice (ire., screening; improvements in confidential care; internal advocacy by nursing staff; enhanced capacity of doctors and nurses to discuss sensitive and complex issues related to violence against women; upgraded referral practice; and routine communication with victim service staff) would improve health care delivery to battered women. The study anticipated improved health and safety outcomes for those domestic violence (DV) patients in the "intervention" group rather than those in the "as usual" group.

The design of the study—"Health care Can Change From Within" (HCCW)—was change generated within the health sector. It was posited that institutionalizing a change model within the health care system could better produce change that would be effective, sustained and modified through on-going evaluation. The model created an internal network of professionals within each participating health sector who would advocate for essential reforms. The methods of change employed were: saturated training of all staff, adoption of parallel policies and procedures, development of relationships with community victim services personnel, continuous evaluation of changes, and primary prevention.

Researchers reported that prior efforts at significant change of the health care system had generally been initiated by victim advocates and services providers. As a result, adoption of methods of change was uneven. Outcomes for providers and victims were unsatisfactory. Attrition was high. The health of victims appeared compromised over the lifespan, even after the abuse terminated, due to the lack of continuing access to health care, among other factors.

As to benefits for victims in the "intervention" as contrasted with the "as usual" group, the results were not as strong as expected. However, the "intervention" and the "as usual" battered women experienced significantly lower rates of violence during the study. The two groups engaged in similar, but modest, increased rates of help-seeking, safety-planning, cultivation of relationships and connections within the community, improvement of health, or satisfaction with health care services.

The researchers suggest that participation in research interviews may have created an unintentional positive intervention related to help-seeking and community connection for the "as usual" group.

How Health Care Providers Can Help Victims

Physicians and other health care providers know that often the first thing victims of domestic violence need is medical attention. They also know they may have a legal obligation to inform the police when they suspect the patient they are treating has been abused. What they may not know is that they can help the patient win her case in court against the abuser by carefully documenting her injuries.

In the past decade, a great deal has been done to improve the way the health care community responds to domestic violence. One way that effort has paid off is in medical documentation of abuse. Many health care protocols and training programs now note the importance of such documentation. But only if medical documentation is accurate and comprehensive can it serve as objective, third party evidence useful in legal proceedings.

For a number of reasons, documentation is not as strong as it could be in providing evidence, so medical records are not used in legal proceedings to the extent they could be. In addition to being difficult to obtain, the records are often incomplete or inaccurate and the handwriting may be illegible. These flaws can make medical records more harmful than helpful.

Health care providers have received little information about how medical records can help domestic violence victims take legal action against their abusers. They often are not aware that admissibility is affected by subtle differences in the way they record the injuries. By making some fairly simple changes in documentation, physicians and other health care professionals can dramatically increase the usefulness of the information they record and thereby help their patients obtain the legal remedies they seek.

What Health Care Providers Can Do

Medical records could be much more useful to domestic violence victims in legal proceedings if some minor changes were made in documentation.

Clinicians can do the following:

- Take photographs of injuries known or suspected to have resulted from domestic violence.

- Write legibly. Computers can also help overcome the common problem of illegible handwriting.

- Set off the patient's own words in quotation marks or use such phrases as "patient states" or "patient reports" to indicate that the information recorded reflects the patient's words. To write "patient was kicked in abdomen" obscures the identity of the speaker.

- Avoid such phrases as "patient claims" or "patient alleges," which imply doubt about the patient's reliability. If the clinician's observations conflict with the patient's statements, the clinician should record the reason for the difference.

- Use medical terms and avoid legal terms such as "alleged perpetrator," "assailant," and "assault."

- Describe the person who hurt the patient by using quotation marks to set off the statement. The clinician would write, for example: The patient stated, "My boyfriend kicked and punched me."

- Avoid summarizing a patient's report of abuse in conclusive terms. If such language as "patient is a battered woman," "assault and battery," or "rape" lacks sufficient accompanying factual information, it is inadmissible.

- Do not place the term "domestic violence" or abbreviations such as "DV" in the diagnosis section of the medical record. Such terms do not convey factual information and are not medical terminology. Whether domestic violence has occurred is determined by the court.

- Describe the patient's demeanor, indicating, for example, whether she is crying or shaking or seems angry, agitated, upset, calm, or happy. Even if the patient's demeanor belies the evidence of abuse, the clinician's observations of that demeanor should be recorded.

- Record the time of day the patient is examined and, if possible, indicate how much time has elapsed since the abuse occurred. For example, the clinician might write, Patient states that early this morning his boyfriend hit him.

Chapter 37

The Affordable Care Act and Domestic Violence

How the Affordable Care Act Benefits Domestic Violence Survivors the Affordable Care Act Benefits Domestic Violence Survivors

By making insurance affordable and easier to obtain, the Affordable Care Act allows survivors of domestic violence access to services to treat chronic health conditions often associated with abuse, and referrals to resources to prevent further violence. Additionally, it helps women who feel trapped in abusive relationships due to economic dependency, which can include health insurance through their partner, to leave that partner and seek safety. Here are some key changes to health coverage that will benefit domestic violence survivors

Prohibits Pre-Existing Condition Exclusion Based on Domestic Violence History

- Beginning on January 1, 2014, the Affordable Care Act will prohibit insurance companies, health care providers, and health programs that receive federal financial assistance from denying

Text in this section is excerpted from "The Affordable Care Act and Maternity Care," U.S. Department of Health and Human Services (HHS), May 13, 2015; and text from "The Affordable Care Act & Women's Health," U.S. Department of Health and Human Services (HHS), December 2013.

coverage to women based on many factors, including being a survivor of domestic or sexual violence.

- Before this protection, seven states allowed insurers to deny health coverage to domestic violence survivors, and only 22 states had enacted adequate domestic violence insurance discrimination protections.

Exempts Survivors of Domestic Violence from Penalty Fee for Not Having Insurance

- Starting in 2014, most people must have health coverage or pay a fee known as the "individual shared responsibility payment." If you can afford health insurance but choose not to buy it, you must pay this fee.

- Survivors of domestic violence who have recently experienced abuse are not required to pay the fee; they qualify for a hardship exemption.

Requires Coverage of Mental Health and Substance Abuse Disorder Treatment

- The Affordable Care Act will require most health insurance plans on the Health Insurance Marketplace to cover mental health and substance use disorder services. Under the Affordable Care Act, non-grandfathered health plans must cover preventive services like depression screening for adults and behavioral assessments for children at no cost. Starting in 2014, most plans will not be able to deny patients coverage or charge more due to pre-existing health conditions, including mental illnesses.

- Mental health coverage will significantly benefit survivors. According to the CDC, 63% of female victims of intimate partner violence experienced at least one symptom of Post-Traumatic-Stress-Disorder (PTSD), and research shows that intimate partner violence is a major risk factor for depression, deliberate self-harm, and suicide.

Increases Support for Native Survivors

- The Affordable Care Act established a new program for behavioral health in the Indian Health Service (IHS) that addresses violence and abuse, expanding treatment and prevention for Native survivors, their children and partners.

Part Five

Emergency Management, Moving Out, and Moving On

Chapter 38

Why Do Victims Stay with Their Abusers?

Why some women don't leave?

People who have never been in an abusive relationship may wonder, "Why doesn't she just leave?" There are many reasons why a woman may stay in an abusive relationship. She may have little or no money and worry about supporting herself and her children. It may be hard for her to contact friends and family who could help her. Or she may feel too frightened, confused, or embarrassed to leave.

If you are in an abusive relationship and are not sure if you are ready to leave, keep in mind that:

- Abuse often gets worse. It may be possible for a partner to change, but it takes work and time. If your partner is blaming you or other factors for his or her behavior, your partner probably is not ready to change.

- You deserve to be safe and happy.

- Even if you are not ready to leave, you can still contact a domestic violence hotline or a local shelter for support, safety planning, and services.

This chapter includes excerpts from "Domestic and Intimate Partner Violence," Office on Women's Health (OWH), September 30, 2015; and text from "Intimate Partner Violence in Rural America," Health Resources and Services Administration (HRSA), March 2015.

- People want to help. Many services are available at no cost, including childcare, temporary housing, job training, and legal aid.

- You need support. Reach out to people you trust.

If a friend or loved one is not leaving an abusive relationship, you may feel frustrated at times. Remember that your friend needs your support.

Challenges Facing Older Women

Older women who are abused often face the same challenges as younger women, but they face additional ones, too. These may include:

- Having grown up and married during a time when domestic abuse was tolerated or ignored

- Having lived with abuse for many years, which can lead to problems like poor self-esteem

- Feeling a duty to take care of an aging partner

- Not knowing a lot about risks of sexually transmitted infections, how to use a condom, or how to negotiate with a partner to use a condom

- Feeling afraid to live alone after being with someone for many years

- Having less of a support network, such as when friends retire and move away

Rural Poverty and IPV

Women who are affected by IPV in rural areas may have a more difficult time becoming economically independent than those in urban areas. Rural America on the whole has higher rates of poverty than other geographies. There may be fewer economic opportunities in some rural areas for women seeking to be independent from a partner. For those who can find jobs, rural women are disadvantaged by both an urban-rural wage gap and a male-female wage gap. A brief from the nonprofit Wider Opportunities for Women notes that rural women earn on average 25 percent less than their rural male counterparts and 16 percent less than their metropolitan female counterparts. In addition, rural residents are more likely to have fewer liquid assets—50 percent of rural residents are asset poor compared to approximately 30 percent of urban residents. Rural Americans are also less likely to have employer-based benefits such as paid sick days, health insurance and unemployment insurance, and they on average face higher health insurance costs. All of these factors can make it difficult for a woman to initially leave a violent partner and also make it difficult for her to become economically secure once she has left.

Rural IPV service providers may have trouble accessing sources of private-sector funding to support their services. The Committee heard from executive directors at the stakeholder meeting about their concern that many rural NGOs in South Dakota cannot meet the State's matching requirement due to the fact that they have limited donors (e.g., corporations and businesses) to request unrestricted funding and limited staff to complete the paperwork for each prorate requirement.

Rural Human Services Infrastructure and IPV

Women who have experienced IPV face the same challenges in accessing human services in rural America as the rest of the rural population. Long travel times, a lack of providers, and a lack of access to certain amenities, such as transportation and telecommunications, can prevent rural women from seeking human services. A study conducted in Illinois on service use by rural and urban women who have experienced IPV indicates that rural survivors are more likely to need a range of social services, including education, transportation, and housing services than their urban counterparts.

Rural women experiencing IPV may face the additional barrier of their abuser controlling the family's transportation and communication channels, preventing them from leaving the relationship or seeking help. One study stated that "(o)ver 25 percent of women in small rural and isolated areas lived more than 40 miles from the closest [IPV] program, compared with less than 1 percent of women living in urban areas." Without a vehicle, women may have trouble accessing health and human services providers as well as securing employment.

In one qualitative study, a woman recounted having a spouse who disabled the car by removing the keys or the spark plugs to prevent her from leaving. Transportation challenges affect advocates too; advocates present at the community stakeholder meeting in Sioux Falls mentioned that oftentimes they are not reimbursed for fuel needed to travel many miles for their work. Additionally, limited access to telecommunications in many rural areas may create barriers to service. Qualitative studies suggest that some abusers may control phone use. Without cell phone service or an Internet connection, isolated rural women experiencing IPV may have trouble seeking help and applying for employment even after they have left violent partners.

Chapter 39

Staying Safe with an Abuser

In an ideal world, anyone who experienced domestic violence would be able to get out of harm's way by leaving the abusive relationship. In reality, however, some people must remain in abusive relationships—whether due to fear for their safety, manipulation or coercion by their abusive partners, or concerns about housing, finances, or child custody. Until they are able to get out of the violent situation, victims of domestic abuse may benefit from the following strategies designed to help them and their children stay safe.

Safety at Home

- Watch for patterns of abuse in order to recognize signs that your partner may become violent. If the situation appears dangerous, try to leave before any violence occurs.

- Know where any weapons are kept. If possible, lock them away, hide them, or make them difficult to access. In addition to guns and knives, potential weapons may include other heavy or sharp objects, such as a hammer, baseball bat, or ice pick.

- Avoid wearing necklaces or scarves that could be used to choke you.

- Figure out the safest places in the home. Avoid the kitchen and garage, which are likely to contain objects that can be used as weapons, as well as rooms with hardwood or tile floors. Try to get to a room with a lock on the door or a window to escape from, and stay out of small, enclosed spaces where you can be cornered.

- Keep a phone somewhere that you can reach it quickly. Memorize the numbers for police emergency response (911), the National Domestic Violence Hotline (1-800-799-SAFE), and the nearest battered women's shelter.

- If physical violence is imminent, make yourself as small as possible and protect vital areas. Go into a corner, curl up in a ball, and lock your fingers behind your head.

- Tell a trusted friend or neighbor about the abuse. Arrange a signal so they will know when you need help. Make a plan so they will understand what to do in these situations.

- Make copies of important documents—such as birth certificates, passports, bank statements, and medical records—that you would need if you had to leave home in an emergency. Put them in a bag along with money and spare car keys. Keep the bag in a safe place or give it to a friend or neighbor to hold for you.

Keeping Children Safe

- When physical abuse occurs, try to stay away from the part of the house where the children are. Tell them not to get involved or try to help you, as their efforts may result in them getting hurt as well.

- Designate a safe place in the house for the children to go during a violent incident.

- Practice various methods of getting out of the house safely. Create a code word to let the children know that they should leave the house and get help. Teach them to call 911 and give your address to emergency responders.

- Let the children know that violence is always wrong, even when it is done by someone they love, and that it is never their fault.

Leaving an abusive relationship or getting a civil protection order does not guarantee that survivors of domestic violence will remain safe. It is important to take the following precautions to limit the abusive partner's access to you at home, at work, and during court appearances.

Safety at Home and School

- Get an unlisted telephone number. Do not answer the phone unless you recognize the caller; otherwise, let it go to voicemail.
- Change the locks on all doors, put bars on windows, and install a home-security system and motion-sensor outdoor lighting.
- Never open the door to someone you do not know.
- Ask your neighbors to call the police if they see the abuser in the neighbourhood or at your home.
- Ask the school or daycare provider not to release the children to anyone without checking with you first. Provide them with copies of restraining orders or custody papers, as well as a photograph of the abusive partner.

Safety in the Workplace

- Vary your routines. Avoid leaving for work or doing your grocery shopping at the same time every day.
- Carpool to work with a colleague or have a friend accompany you to the bus stop.
- Give a photograph of your abusive partner to the receptionist or security personnel at work, and ask them to notify you or call the police if they see that person.
- Save any emails or voicemails if the abuser tries to contact you at work.
- When leaving work, have someone walk you to your car. Be wary in the parking lot, and check inside, around, and under the car for danger.
- If your abusive partner follows your car, drive to a police or fire station and honk the horn. Keep a sign in the car that says "CALL POLICE."

Safety in Court

- Ask a friend or relative to accompany you to any court hearings.
- Inquire whether the court has a private waiting area or a separate entrance for victims of domestic violence.

- Sit as far away from your abusive partner as possible and avoid interaction.

- If you fear for your safety in a public place, studies show that yelling "Fire!" is the most effective way to get a quick response.

References

1. "Staying Safe with an Abuser." WomensLaw.org, 2008.

2. "Keeping Safe in Abusive Relationships or While Trying to Leave." Hidden Hurt, 2015.

Chapter 40

Managing a Domestic Violence Emergency

Chapter Contents

Section 40.1

Calling the Police

Text in this section is excerpted from "Reporting Abuse,"
Administration on Aging (AOA), February 28, 2013.

Reporting Abuse

Each one of us has a responsibility to keep vulnerable elders safe
from harm. The laws in most states require helping professions in the
front lines—such as doctors and home health providers—to report
suspected abuse or neglect. These professionals are called mandated
reporters. Under the laws of eight states, "any person" is required to
report a suspicion of mistreatment.

*Call the police or 9-1-1 immediately if someone you know is in
immediate, life-threatening danger.*

If you have been the victim of abuse, exploitation, or neglect, you
are not alone. Many people care and can help. Please tell your doctor,
a friend, or a family member you trust, or call the Adult Protective
Services program in your area. Relay your concerns to the local Adult
Protective Services, Long-term Care Ombudsman, or police. If the
danger is not immediate, but you suspect that abuse has occurred or
is occurring, please tell someone.

**You do not need to prove that abuse is occurring; it is up to
the professionals to investigate the suspicions.**

When making the call, be ready to give the name, address, and
contact information of the person you suspect is abused or neglected,
and details about why you are concerned.

You may be asked a series of questions to gain more insight into
the nature of the situation.

- Are there any known medical problems (including confusion or
  memory loss)?

- What kinds of family or social supports are there?

- Have you seen or heard incidents of yelling, hitting, or other
  abusive behavior?

You will be asked for your name, address, telephone number, etc., but most states will take the report even if you do not identify yourself.

The professionals receiving your report are prohibited from releasing your information as reporter. They may not disclose your identity to the alleged abuser or victim.

Section 40.2

Preserving and Collecting Forensic Evidence after a Sexual Assault

This section includes excerpts from "Violence against Women," Office on Women's Health (OWH), September 30, 2015; text from "A Guide for Victim Service Providers," National Criminal Justice Reference Service (NCJRS), 2015; and text from "Sexual Assault Kits," National Institute of Justice (NIJ), September 10, 2015.

Preserving and Collecting Forensic Evidence after a Sexual Assault

If you have been assaulted, get away from the attacker and find a safe place as fast as you can. Call 911. Call someone you trust or a hotline, such as the National Sexual Assault Hotline at 800-656-HOPE (4673). Protect any evidence.

The Value of DNA Evidence

DNA is a powerful investigative tool because, with the exception of identical twins, no two people have the same DNA. Therefore, DNA evidence collected from a crime scene can be linked to a suspect or can eliminate a suspect from suspicion. During a sexual assault, for example, biological evidence such as hair, skin cells, semen, or blood can be left on the victim's body or other parts of the crime scene. Properly collected DNA can be compared with known samples to place a suspect at the scene of the crime. In addition, if no suspect exists, a DNA profile from crime scene evidence can be entered into the FBI's Combined DNA Index System (CODIS) to identify a suspect anywhere in the United States or to link serial crimes to each other.

The effective use of DNA as evidence may also require the collection and analysis of elimination samples to determine the exact source of the DNA. Elimination samples may be taken from anyone who had lawful access to the crime scene and may have left biological material. When investigating a rape case, for example, it may be necessary to obtain an elimination sample from everyone who had consensual intercourse with the victim within 72 hours of the alleged assault to account for all of the DNA found on the victim or at the crime scene. Comparing DNA profiles from the evidence with elimination samples may help clarify the results.

Evidence Collection

If DNA evidence is not initially identified at the crime scene or on the victim, it may not be collected, or it may become contaminated or degraded.

To assist in collection, victims of sexual assault should not

- change clothes,

- shower, or

- wash any part of their body after the assault.

Such evidence as semen, saliva, and skin cells may be found on clothing or bedding, under fingernails, or in the vaginal, anal, or mouth region.

Evidence on or inside a victim's body should be collected by a physician or sexual assault nurse examiner. A medical examination should be conducted immediately after the assault to treat any injuries, test for sexually transmitted diseases, and collect forensic evidence, such as fingernail scrapings and hair. Typically, the vaginal cavity, mouth, anus, or other parts of the body that may have come into contact with the assailant are examined.

The examiner should also take a reference sample of blood or saliva from the victim to serve as a control standard. Reference samples of the victim's head and pubic hair may also be collected if hair analysis is required. A control standard is used to compare known DNA from the victim with that of other DNA evidence found at the crime scene to determine possible suspect(s).

Given the sensitive nature of DNA evidence, victim service providers should always contact crime laboratory personnel or evidence technicians when procedural collection questions arise.

Possible Location of DNA Evidence

- Bite mark or area licked

- Fingernail scrapings

- Inside or outside surface of used condom

- Blankets, sheets, pillows, or other bed linens

- Clothing, including under-garments worn during and after the assault

- Hat, bandanna, or mask

- Tissue, washcloth, or similar item

- Cigarette butt; toothpick; or rim of bottle, can, or glass

- Dental floss

- Tape or ligature

What is a Safe Exam?

A sexual assault medical forensic exam (SAFE) is conducted by a specially trained Sexual Assault Nurse Examiner (SANE) or other medical professional. The exam includes gathering a complete medical history, coordinating the treatment of injuries, documenting and collecting biological and physical evidence, and referring the victim to other medical or nonmedical support.

What Is a Sexual Assault Kit and How Is It Used?

A sexual assault kit (SAK) is a collection of evidence gathered from the victim by a medical professional, often a specially trained Sexual Assault Nurse Examiner (SANE). The type of evidence collected depends on what occurred during the assault. The contents of a kit vary by jurisdiction, but generally include swabs, test tubes, microscopic slides, and evidence collection envelopes for hairs and fibers.

The sexual assault kit evidence may contribute to investigations, prosecutions and exonerations in sexual assault cases.

Testing a SAK is one part of the investigative process, but testing does not always result in a new investigative lead. For example, the suspect may already be known, or the evidence in the kit does not contain any or enough biological evidence to yield a DNA profile.

515

The medical examination is highly invasive and can last several hours. The victim is swabbed for any biological evidence that may contain the perpetrator's DNA (e.g., skin, saliva, semen). The examiner also photographs any bruising or other injuries, collects the victim's clothing, and provides the victim with medicine to prevent infection or pregnancy, if the victim chooses. Evidence collected from the victim goes into the sexual assault kit. The SAK and other crime scene evidence, such as bedding, can be tested in an effort to identify the perpetrator.

Typically, after the examination is completed, the SAK is transferred to an authorized law enforcement agency to be logged into evidence. Protocols vary among jurisdictions regarding whether and when the SAK is sent to the lab for testing. Identifying reasons why some SAKs, historically, were not submitted for testing and researching new ways to improve the processing of sexual assault kits have been goals of recent NIJ efforts, such as the action research projects with Detroit and Houston.

Chapter 41

Getting Help in the Aftermath of Abuse

Chapter Contents

Section 41.1

Sources of Help for Victims of Domestic Violence

Text in this section is excerpted from "Getting Help with
Domestic Violence," U.S. Department of Health and Human
Services (HHS), October 1, 2014.

Getting Help with Domestic Violence

More than 1 in 3 women and 1 in 4 men across the United States
have experienced violence from an intimate partner. If you or someone
you know has experienced domestic violence, you are not alone. The
Family Violence Prevention and Services Program (FVPSA), is the
primary Federal funding stream for a national network of domestic
violence shelters and programs.

Reaching out for help to stop domestic violence in your relationship,
and navigating the complex resources in your community can be difficult. It can be hard to know where to go for the help you want and it
may not be clear how these programs can support your efforts to live
a life free of violence and abuse—but you are not alone! The resources
listed below are great places to start your journey towards safety, hope
and healing. Many of these national organizations can guide you to
more in-depth and knowledgeable resources in your community and
surrounding areas.

National Hotlines

These hotlines offer support from well trained, caring advocates
24/7/365 (including holidays). Advocates help victims and survivors of
domestic violence and rape or sexual violence find support and assistance in their communities, even if you only need someone to talk to
before making that first step.

- National Domestic Violence Hotline – 1-800-799-7233 or TTY
  1-800-787-3224 – Secure online chat at http://www.thehotline.
  org/what-is-live-chat

- National Teen Dating Abuse Helpline – 1-866-331-9474 or TTY 1-866-331-8453 – Secure online chat at http://www.loveisrespect. org/get-help/contact-us/chat-with-us

- National Sexual Assault Hotline (RAINN) – 1-800-656-4673 Choose #1 to talk to a counselor – Secure online private chat at https://ohl.rainn.org/online

- Stalking Resource Center – Access online resources to learn things you can do if you or someone you know is being stalked

By calling any of the national hotlines, a trained advocate will be able to connect you to a program in your community. As you make decisions about how to get away from the abuse and ensure your own safety, developing a safety plan becomes more and more important. Caring advocates on the hotline and in your local program can help you think through how to be safe in an emergency, during a domestic violence incident, while getting help from resources in the community, and when you're with your children—this is called a "safety plan."

State Domestic Violence and Sexual Assault Coalitions

There is a state domestic violence coalition for every State and United States Territory. Each Coalition represents the domestic violence and sexual violence service providers in their state or territory; they are connected to more than 2,000 local domestic violence programs and shelters. You can find the domestic violence coalition working with programs in your state at the National Network to End Domestic Violence's website. Select your state from the list and then look for the link to their members or programs for a listing of the resources in your city or county.

Local / Community-based Domestic Violence and Sexual Assault Programs

In addition to offering safe, emergency shelter, there are many ways that local domestic violence programs and advocates can partner with you to live a life free of violence and abuse. Services may vary from place to place, but most include:

- Safety planning assistance;

- Legal assistance and referrals for obtaining protection orders (which may include evicting an abusive partner from a shared

home, obtaining emergency child custody, and many such remedies to increase your safety);

- Counseling and support groups for survivors and their children;

- Help applying for public assistance and housing subsidies;

- Transitional housing; and

- Referrals to counseling, mental health, and addiction services.

National Resource Centers and Culturally Specific Institutes

All of the service providers listed above—the hotlines, shelters,
state coalitions, and tribal programs—work together and receive training, assistance, guidance, and support from several national resource
center and culturally specific institutes. These organizations make up
the Domestic Violence Resource Network (DVRN), which is funded
by the U.S. Department of Health and Human Services to inform and
strengthen domestic violence intervention and prevention efforts at
the individual, community, and societal levels.

There are two national resource centers working collaboratively to
promote practices and strategies to improve our nation's response to
domestic violence:

1. The National Resource Center on Domestic Violence

2. The National Indigenous Women's Resource Center

   There is a national network of specialized resource centers
   that work to address domestic violence responses across these
   specific systems:

3. Criminal and Civil Justice Systems;

4. Child Protection System and Child Custody; and

5. Mental Health Systems.

There is also a network of culturally specific resource centers that
works to address the impact of domestic violence within and culturally relevant responses for the following ethnic and racially specific
communities:

- African American Communities;

- Asian and Pacific Islander Communities; and

- Hispanic and Latina Communities.

Section 41.2

The Family Violence Prevention and Services Program

This section includes excerpts from "Family Violence Prevention and Services Program," U.S. Department of Health and Human Services (HHS), August 25, 2015; and text from "America's Youngest Outcasts," Substance Abuse and Mental Health Services Administration (SAMHSA), November 2014.

Family Violence Prevention and Services Program

The **Family Violence Prevention and Services Program** administers the Family Violence Prevention and Services Act (FVPSA), the primary federal funding stream dedicated to the support of emergency shelter and related assistance for victims of domestic violence and their children.

The Family Violence Prevention and Services Program is committed to:

- **Providing shelter** and other supportive services for victims and their children

- **Coordinating statewide improvements** within local communities, social service systems, and programming regarding the prevention and intervention of domestic violence through the leadership of State Domestic Violence Coalitions and FVPSA State Administrators

- Increasing **public awareness** about the prevalence of domestic violence, dating violence and family violence

- **Supporting** local and community-based domestic violence programs with specialized **technical assistance** addressing emerging issues such as trauma-informed care; the co-occurrence of domestic violence and child maltreatment; culturally specific domestic violence services; and effective interventions for children exposed to domestic violence

To accomplish this work the FVPSA Program provides grants to states, territories, tribes, state domestic violence coalitions, and national resource centers.

Family Violence Prevention and Services Formula Grants to States and Territories

The FVPSA formula grants to states and territories fund more than 1,600 local public, private, nonprofit and faith-based organizations and programs demonstrating effectiveness in the field of domestic violence services and prevention. These domestic violence programs provide victims of domestic and dating violence and their children with:

- Shelter

- Safety planning

- Crisis counseling

- Information and referral

- Legal advocacy

- Additional support services

The Need for Services

- 40% of American Indian or Alaska Native women have experienced rape, physical violence or stalking.

- 10% of FVPSA grants are dedicated to Tribes and distributed based on population.

- Approximately 12.6 million people in the United States experienced rape, physical violence and/or stalking by a current or former spouse, boyfriend or girlfriend.

- Nearly 30% of women and 10% of men in the United States have experienced rape, physical violence, and/or stalking by an intimate partner and reported at least one impact related to experiencing these or other forms of violent behavior in the relationship (e.g., being fearful, concerned for safety, post traumatic stress disorder (PTSD) symptoms, need for health care, injury, contacting a crisis hotline, need for housing services, need for victim's advocate services, need for legal services, missed at least one day of work or school).

- Almost 10% of children witnessed family violence in the past year.

- Men exposed to physical abuse, sexual abuse, and domestic violence as children were almost four times more likely than other men to have perpetrated domestic violence as adults.

Serving Families in Crisis

FVPSA formula grants are awarded to every State and Territory and over 200 Tribes. These funds reach almost 1,600 domestic violence shelters and over 1,100 non-residential service sites, providing both a safe haven and an array of supportive services to intervene in and prevent abuse. Each year, FVPSA-funded programs served over 1.3 million victims and their children and respond to 2.7 million crisis calls. FVPSA-funded programs do not just serve victims, they reach their communities; in 2013, programs provided almost 166,000 presentations reaching 4.7 million people, of which over half were youth.

The National Domestic Violence Hotline provides a compassionate and caring response to thousands of victims and survivors of domestic violence, their families and friends and concerned others. Each month, the Hotline answers about 17,500 calls. The Hotline provides crisis intervention, counseling and safety planning and can directly connect the caller to a seamless referral system of over 4,500 community programs across the U.S., Puerto Rico, Guam and the U.S. Virgin Islands. The Hotline operates 24 hours a day, 7 days a week and is available in 170 languages. It also provides services to deaf and hard of hearing callers.

Domestic Violence Resource Network

FVPSA supports two national resource centers on domestic violence, along with special issue and culturally specific resource centers. These organizations ensure that victims of domestic violence, advocates, community-based programs, educators, legal assistance providers, justice personnel, health care providers, policy makers, and government leaders at the local, state, tribal and federal levels have access to up-to-date information on best practices, policies, research and victim resources.

Discretionary Programs

- Each year, FYSB funds a range of discretionary programs coordinated by the Family Violence Prevention and Services Program. These programs aim to:

- Improve the prevention and intervention of domestic violence, dating violence and family violence Enhance available support and resources for victims and their children

- Ensure that services are accessible

- Foster practice changes within the domestic violence field

- Support research and data collection on the incidence of domestic violence, dating violence and family violence

- Enhance public awareness of issues related to domestic violence including the life-time health impact, advocacy within culturally specific communities, and the co-occurrence of domestic violence and child maltreatment

Housing First

"Housing first" and "rapid re-housing" are designed to help homeless households access housing as quickly as possible. USICH describes housing first as "an approach that offers permanent, affordable housing as quickly as possible for individuals and families experiencing homelessness, and then provides the supportive services and connections to the community-based supports people need to keep their housing and avoid returning to homelessness" (USICH, 2014b).

- The variation in housing first and rapid re-housing approaches stem from differing interpretations of the model.

- For example, programs may construe "as quickly as possible" to mean:

  - As soon as medical or behavioral health crises are stabilized.

  - As soon as eligibility for program assistance is established.

  - As soon as viable sources of financial support for food, utilities, housing, and other essentials are in place.

  - As soon as appropriate sources of post-placement support services are identified and engaged.

  - As soon as housing leased or operated by the program becomes available.

  - As soon as the household is able to identify and lease housing they can afford, and want to live in, that meets programmatic requirements, and the owner is willing to rent to them.

Similarly, programs may interpret "supportive services and connections to the community-based supports" differently. The program may:

- Limit rental assistance to six or twelve or 24 months, or limit the time that supportive services are provided.

- Determine the scope, magnitude, and availability of supportive services, or the needs the program can address, and the types of participants it can serve. For example:

  - Scattered site programs in rural settings might provide case management by phone or electronically.

  - Meetings with case managers or program staff might be scheduled on a weekly, semi-weekly, or monthly basis, or might be arranged by request of the participant.

  - Some programs may provide a rich array of clinical and non-clinical supportive services; other programs may operate in a very constrained service environment.

  - Some programs may define "success" as reducing participants' dependence on government assistance or services; other programs may maximize client participation in public benefits and community services.

  - Some programs focus services on the adult head of household, and see the parent as the gatekeeper in identifying and addressing the needs of the children; other programs see children as full-fledged program clients.

Apart from the idea that stability occurs when a family has obtained their own housing and has access to case management, there are few set rules about what constitutes the necessary elements of housing first or rapid re-housing. However, one-size-fits-all is not a meaningful framework for responding to the wide range of needs among families experiencing homelessness. To succeed in housing, families with more extensive needs may require more assistance.

Chapter 42

Safety Planning for Victims of Domestic Violence

Chapter Contents

Section 42.1

Planning for Safety: Personal Safety and Safety of Children and Pets

"Planning for Safety: Personal Safety and Safety of Children and Pets,"
© 2016 Omnigraphics, Inc.
Reviewed January 2016.

People who experience domestic violence may be able to increase their safety through advance planning. Experts suggest creating an emergency escape plan for personal safety, along with safety plans to protect children and pets. Safety plans may include a variety of actions designed to help victims of domestic violence stay safe during a crisis, as well as preparations to help them leave an abusive situation.

Emergency Escape Plan

If you need to get away from an abuser quickly, it may be helpful to make the following preparations in advance:

- Plan and practice your escape, including what doors or windows you will use, where you will go, and how you will get there.

- Make copies of important documents, such as your birth certificate, passport, driver's license, car registration, mortgage or rental agreement, insurance policies, bank account numbers, medical records, custody agreements, restraining orders, and divorce papers. Put them in a safe place, such as a friend's house, your lawyer's office, or a safe deposit box.

- Pack an emergency suitcase with extra clothing, spare keys, money, and medications. Keep it somewhere you can get to it quickly.

- Open a savings account in your own name at a different bank than the one you usually use. Make sure statements are sent to a friend's address, your workplace, or a post office box rather than to your home.

- Keep a record of physical abuse, including dates, circumstances, witnesses, and photographs of injuries. If you get medical attention, ask the doctor or hospital to document your visit.

- Tell a trusted friend or neighbor about the abuse. Arrange a signal or code word so they will know when you need them to call the police.

- To facilitate a quick getaway, make a habit of backing the car into the driveway. Always keep the car keys handy and the gas tank full.

- Consider asking a friend or family member to accompany you when you leave, or request a police escort.

- Do not tell your partner where you are going. Clear your phone of recently dialed numbers. Have a backup plan in place in case your partner learns of your destination.

- File for a restraining order to prevent your partner from contacting you. Consult with an attorney about other legal means of protection.

Safety Plan for Children

Domestic violence can be very traumatic for children who experience or witness it in their homes. Developing a safety plan can help limit the damage to their physical and emotional health. It is important to emphasize to children that violence is always wrong, even when it is done by someone they love, and that it is never their fault. The following strategies may also help protect children from the effects of domestic violence:

- Tell them not to get involved or try to help you when physical abuse occurs, as their efforts may result in them getting hurt as well. Instead, they should leave the room and implement the safety plan.

- Identify a safe place in the home for the children to go. An ideal place would be a locked room with a telephone in it.

- Tell the children to avoid hiding in closets or other small spaces where they could become trapped, and to stay out of the kitchen, garage, and other rooms that contain objects that could be used as weapons.

- Practice various methods of getting out of the house safely. Create a code word to let the children know that they should leave the house and get help.

- Designate a safe place for the children to go in an emergency, such as the home of a friend, relative, or neighbor.

- Teach children to call 911 and give your address to emergency responders. Rehearse exactly what they should say on the phone, such as "Someone is hurting my mom."

Safety Plan for Pets

Domestic violence can also endanger pets in the household. Pets may be abused or neglected, or the abusive partner may use threats to the pets' well-being as a way to control or manipulate members of the family. Creating a safety plan for pets can help protect them from the effects of domestic violence. Some possible steps to take include:

- Know the location and phone number of the nearest twenty-four-hour veterinary clinic.

- Establish ownership of pets by putting adoption or purchase papers, licenses, and veterinary records in your name.

- Pack a bag with emergency pet supplies, such as food, medicine, toys, leash, license, and copies of ownership papers and health records. Keep it somewhere safe and accessible, such as a friend's house.

- Identify a safe emergency shelter for your pets where your abusive partner will not be able to find them.

- After you have left an abusive situation, be careful to keep pets indoors whenever possible, avoid leaving them outdoors alone, pick a safe time and place to exercise them, and switch to a new veterinarian.

References

1. "Develop a Safety Plan." Center for Relationship Abuse Awareness, 2015.

2. "Safety for My Children." The Healing Journey, 2006.

3. "Safety Planning for Pets of Domestic Violence Victims." Animal Welfare Institute, 2016.

Section 42.2

Safety Packing List

The text in this section is excerpted from "Safety Planning for Abusive Situations," Office on Women's Health (OWH), May 18, 2011. Reviewed January 2016.

If you are in an abusive relationship, it is important to create a safety plan. Domestic violence advocates and teen dating abuse advocates are people who are trained to help you create a safety plan. Advocates can:

- Figure out ways for you to leave an abuser

- Discuss how to deal with emergencies

- Suggest safe places to go, such as a shelter or the home of a friend or family member where your abuser might not look

- Help you learn about a court order of protection, which requires your abuser to stay away from you

- Suggest services and provide support

Call a help hotline to find advocates. You can call the National Domestic Violence Hotline at 800-799-SAFE (7233) or TDD 800-787-3224. You can call the National Teen Dating Abuse Helpline at 866-331-9794 or TDD 866-331-8453.

Abused women are not necessarily safe just because they leave an abuser. In fact, sometimes the danger is greatest right after leaving. Once you have a new home, learn ways to make it safer with locks and other security measures.

If you are leaving an abusive situation, take your children and, if possible, your pets. Put together the items listed below. Hide them someplace where you can get them quickly, or leave them with a friend. If you are in immediate danger, though, leave without these items.

Safety Packing List

Identification for Yourself and Your Children

- Birth certificates

- Social Security cards (or numbers written on paper if you can't find the cards)

- Driver's license

- Photo identification or passports

- Welfare benefits card

- Green card

Important papers

- Marriage certificate

- Divorce papers

- Custody orders

- Legal protection or restraining orders

- Health insurance papers and medical cards

- Medical records for all family members

- Children's school records

- Investment papers/records and account numbers

- Work permits

- Immigration papers

- Rental agreement/lease or house deed

- Car title, registration, and insurance information

- Records of police reports you have filed or other evidence of abuse

Money and other ways to get by

- Cash

- Credit cards

- ATM card

- Checkbook and bankbook (with deposit slips)
- Jewelry or small objects you can sell

Keys

- House
- Car
- Safety deposit box or Post Office box

Ways to communicate

- Phone calling card*
- Cellphone*
- Address book

Medications

- At least one month's supply for all medicines you and your children are taking
- A copy of any prescriptions

Things to help you cope

- Pictures
- Keepsakes
- Children's small toys or books

* Don't share a calling card or cellphone plan with an abuser, because they can be used to find you. And if you already have a shared card or phone plan, try not to use them after you've left.

Section 42.3

Safety Planning with Adult and Child Victims

Text in this section is excerpted from "Child Protection in Families
Experiencing Domestic Violence," U.S. Department of Health and
Human Services (HHS), 2003. Reviewed January 2016.

Safety planning is an individualized plan developed to reduce
the immediate and long-term risks faced by the victim and their
children. Ideally, safety planning should begin at assessment and
continue through case closure. The plan includes strategies that
reduce the risk of physical violence and harm by the perpetrator
and enhance the protection of the victim and the children. It also
contains strategies that address other barriers to safety such as
income, housing, health care, child care, and education.

Risk assessment and safety planning for domestic violence should
be ongoing and should occur concurrently with risk assessment and
safety planning for child maltreatment. The safety plans of victims
of domestic violence will vary depending on whether they are separated from the abuser, thinking about leaving, or returning to or
remaining in the relationship.

CPS caseworkers should involve the victim in developing safety
plans. Otherwise, it is merely one more thing being done "to" the victim and is not really a service plan. Specific safety planning activities
can include:

- Engaging the victim in a discussion about the options available
  to keep him or her and the children safe, including what has
  been tried before.

- Exploring the benefits and disadvantages of specific options, and
  creating individualized solutions for each family.

- Collecting and gathering important documents and various personal items that will be necessary for relocation of the victim
  and the children.

- Determining who to call, where to go, and what to do when a violent situation begins or is occurring.

- Developing a security plan that might involve changing or adding door and window locks, installing a security system, or having additional outside lighting.

- Informing friends, coworkers, school personnel, and neighbors of the situation and restraining orders that are in effect.

- Writing down a list of phone numbers of neighbors, friends, family, and community service providers that the victim can contact for safety, resources, and services. This requires CPS caseworkers to stay current about resources, contacts, and legal options.

Additionally, CPS caseworkers can help victims develop a safety plan with their children. This often depends on the child's age and circumstances—some children feel that developing a safety plan helps them feel safer and can provide life-saving strategies, while others need to know that their parents can protect them. CPS caseworkers also should review and practice the safety plan steps with the children.

Children's safety plans can include how to:

- Find a safe adult and ask for help whenever they experience violence. This may involve calling supportive family members, friends, or community agencies for help.

- Escape from the house if an assault is imminent or in progress. If they cannot escape, discuss where they can go to be safe in the house.

- Avoid being in the middle of the domestic violence.

- Find a place to go in an emergency and the steps to take to find safety.

- Call the police.

Safety plans are not intended to hold victims responsible for possible future abuse. Instead, these plans can help victims feel empowered and provide concrete steps to help avoid or positively respond to abusive actions. Incorporating domestic violence safety plans into service plans provides realistic and relevant actions for family members living with abuse. The safety plans of victims and children should not be shared with the perpetrator. This is especially true if the plan involves the victim leaving the abusive relationship. In fact, some victims will need to hide their safety plans to avoid potential harm by the abuser.

In some cases, safety planning can be conducted with the abuser as a way to hold him or her responsible and should include steps to take to stop the violence (e.g., honoring protection orders, leaving the house, time-outs, going to abuser intervention groups).

Chapter 43

Issues in Internet Safety

Chapter Contents

Section 43.1

Internet Safety Tips

Text in this section is excerpted from "Internet Safety," Central Intelligence Agency (CIA), June 18, 2013; and text from "Technology Tips for Domestic Violence and Stalking Victims," Federal Trade Commission (FTC), February 5, 2015.

Internet Safety Tips for Your Children

- Tell your children to never give out personal information (e.g., their name, home address, school name or telephone number) in a chat room, on online bulletin boards, or to online pen pals that you have never actually met.

- Explain to your children that the Internet provides anonymity and allows people to misrepresent themselves. Tell your children never to set up a meeting with someone without your permission.

- Encourage your children to alert you if anyone has made them feel uncomfortable or frightened in online correspondence. Discourage them from sending a personal picture to anyone without your permission.

Additional suggestions to help your children stay safe on the Internet are listed below:

- Instruct your children to create hard-to-guess passwords at least eight characters long, using both letters and numbers.

- Update anti-virus software regularly, and install firewall software or hardware, particularly for high-speed use.

- Make sure you or your children never open any attachments from senders you don't know.

- Have your children alert you when something bad happens, and also notify your Internet service provider or software vendor, if necessary.

- Surf the Internet with your children at times and talk to them about the sites they visit.

- Review the privacy policy of websites your children regularly use and discuss with them the information the sites collect about them. Remember, if a site has information about you or your children that you don't want them to have, you can ask the website to delete the information.

Technology Tips for Domestic Violence and Stalking Victims

We love technology. So it's disturbing when it's used to threaten or harass people – especially domestic violence and stalking victims.

With computers and mobile phones, abusers have more tools for stalking. They can install spyware to hack into your email, use Bluetooth or GPS to track your every move, even secretly turn on your device's camera or microphone to watch and listen to you.

Online safety is important for everyone but for domestic violence victims, these tips may be particularly useful:

- Use strong passwords and change them frequently. Make sure you have passwords on your phone, computer and all online accounts. Keep your passwords private.

- If you think someone may be monitoring you, then try to use a safer computer – one that the abuser does not have access to. It's especially important to use a safer computer if you are researching an escape plan, new jobs or a place to live.

- Change usernames and passwords of your online accounts on the safer computer. Then, don't log into those accounts on any computer that you think is monitored.

Abusers may not stop at your computer. If you're using a mobile phone, here are a few more things to consider:

- Know where your phone is at all times. Malware, spyware and tracking apps can be installed in just a few minutes.

- Check your phone's settings. Bluetooth and GPS can be used to track you. A victim advocate can help strategize a specific tech safety plan for your situation.

- If you think your phone is being monitored, get a new one. The safest thing is to get a new phone with an account that the abuser does not have access to. Remember to put a password on your new phone, then disable Bluetooth and GPS.

Section 43.2

Cyberstalking

Text in this section is excerpted from "Stalking," Office on
Women's Health (OWH), September 30, 2015.

Cyberstalking is using the Internet, email, or other electronic communications to stalk someone. Examples of cyberstalking include:

- Sending unwanted, frightening, or obscene emails, text messages, or instant messages (IMs)
- Harassing or threatening someone in a chat room
- Posting improper messages on a message board
- Tracking your computer and Internet use
- Sending electronic viruses
- Pretending to be you in a chat room

If you are cyberstalked:

- Send the person a clear, written warning not to contact you again
- If the stalking continues, get help from the police. You also can contact a domestic violence shelter and the National Center for Victims of Crime Helpline for support and suggestions.
- Print out copies of evidence such as emails. Keep a record of the stalking and any contact with police.
- Consider blocking messages from the harasser
- Change your email address
- File a complaint with the person's Internet Service Provider (ISP)
- Never post online profiles or messages with details that could be used to identify or locate you (such as age, sex, address, workplace, phone number, school, or places you hang out)

Section 43.3

Social Networking Safety

Text in this section is excerpted from "Social Network Safety: How to Protect Your Identity Online?" U.S. Army, December 15, 2014; and text from "Six Tips For Keeping Teens Safe On Social Media," U.S. General Services Administration, October 1, 2015.

Social network safety: How to protect your identity online?

Social media platforms such as Facebook, Twitter and LinkedIn are powerful tools that can help bring communities together. However, an individual's online profile can provide cyber criminals with an endless pool of personal information and potential targets to be exploited.

Social Networking Safety Tips:

Things to Know

1. The Internet does not forget. Once something is posted on a social networking website it can spread quickly, and no amount of effort can delete it. Do not post anything you would be embarrassed to see on the evening news.

2. You are not anonymous. Cyber criminals have the capability to gather and exploit both individuals and organizations if the information is out there.

3. More isn't always better. Participating in multiple social networking sites significantly increases a person's risk, and affords cyber criminal alternate avenues to strike and gather information.

How to Protect Yourself:

- Know the terms on social networking websites. Facebook, Twitter, LinkedIn and other social networking sites frequently change their privacy and user policies. Social networking sites privacy settings default to everyone. This means anyone, can view your profile, not just the people you know. Securely configuring one's account will minimize who can see your information.

- Safe social networking. Never disclose private information when using social networking websites. Be very selective who you invite or accept invitations from as criminals often use false or spoofed profiles to gain access to personal and private information, such as birthdates, marital status, and photographs. Social media posts that contain personal identifying information (PII), digital photos that contain metadata (i.e., information written into the digital photo file such as who owns it, contact information, location, and Internet search terms) can be used against you and your family.

- Click with caution. Always use caution when clicking on links in social networking posts, even from someone you know. Reports of personal social networking accounts being hacked by criminals have increased in recent years. Clicking on a link that appears to be benign in nature may in fact contain embedded malware that can compromise your device. Once compromised, any data on your device can be exploited.

- Hide your profile from search engines. This can be accomplished by going to the social networking site account settings and unchecking the "Public Search Results" box. This will remove your public preview from Google, Bing, and Yahoo search returns.

- Check-out and tag-out. Do not use check-ins or post your specific location on social media. Also, prevent people from "tagging" you in photos and videos.

- Login No No's. Do not use your social networking site to login to other sites or use the save password, remember me, and keep me logged in options from a public or shared device. Use strong, unique passwords and never use the same password for all online accounts.

- Install/Update your anti-virus/firewall software. Antivirus and firewall software is a must for anyone to safely navigate online. Always keep your security software up to date in order to provide the most complete protection from malicious programs as thousands of new viruses are detected every year. Also, ensure your antivirus software program updates automatically and scans your computer on a recurring schedule.

Six Tips For Keeping Teens Safe On Social Media

Going back to school is about more than shiny shoes and trendy notebooks. It's also about kids making new friends and adding those friends on social network sites like Facebook, Twitter and Instagram.

More than 60 percent of teens in the United States have at least one social media account, according to the American Academy of Child and Adolescent Psychiatry. And while being online is a good way to keep in touch with friends, it's important for parents to be proactive about Internet safety.

Unfortunately, there are people who can use your child's personal information to steal identities, bully them or begin an inappropriate relationship. Help protect students from online dangers by following these safety tips:

1. Keep your child's profile private so that only family and people you know see photos, important dates and other information.

2. Make sure they're not posting personal details, including phone numbers, home address, and the name of their school or Social Security number.

3. Only allow them to publish photos and videos that don't jeopardize their safety or their integrity.

4. Make sure they choose a strong password that can't be guessed, and that it gets changed every three months.

5. Never allow them to accept friend requests from people they don't know.

6. Keep an open dialogue with your children. Ask them to let you know if they've received private messages from a stranger, or from someone at school who is teasing, harassing or threatening them. Those could be signs of cyber-bullying or even a sexual predator.

Chapter 44

Navigating the Legal System

Chapter Contents

Section 44.1

Questions to Ask before You Hire an Attorney

"Questions to Ask before You Hire an Attorney,"
© 2016 Omnigraphics, Inc.
Reviewed January 2016.

In relationships affected by domestic violence, it often becomes necessary for survivors to hire an attorney to assist them with divorce, child custody, or criminal assault cases. After gathering the names of possible attorneys from personal recommendations, state bar associations, and other sources, the next step is to schedule a meeting with each candidate to learn more about their background, qualifications, skills, experience, approach, strategy, and fees. Although the process of choosing an attorney may seem overwhelming, asking detailed questions during the initial consultation can help people make an informed decision.

Some examples of good questions to ask about a family law attorney's background and experience include:

- Where did you attend law school?

- How long have you been practicing family law?

- Do you only handle divorce and family law cases?

- How many cases do you handle annually?

- Have you handled many cases similar to mine?

- How much experience do you have with courtroom litigation?

To assess whether an attorney's legal philosophy and approach to family law is a good fit with the circumstances of a specific case, some recommended questions to ask include:

- How would you describe your overall philosophy as an attorney?

- Do you offer your clients options and allow them to decide, or do you tell them what to do?

- How would you assess my case?

- What approach would you take?

- What problems might I encounter?

- Do you think my case will go to trial?

- What outcomes can I expect?

- How long do you think it will take to resolve the case?

Since family law practices can range from large firms to sole practitioners, it may also be valuable to ask questions concerning how the case will be managed, such as:

- Will you be managing my case personally, or will another attorney take primary responsibility?

- Who will handle court appearances and negotiations?

- Who else will be involved with my case, and what will their roles be?

- How often will I receive updates on the status of my case?

- How will we communicate about the case?

- How quickly can I expect responses to my questions?

Legal Fees

Hiring a family law attorney can be an expensive proposition. Before signing an agreement for representation, it is important to understand exactly what types of legal fees the attorney will charge. In general, the fees will depend on the attorney's skill and experience in handling family law or domestic violence cases, as well as the complexity of the specific case. Although it may be more expensive to hire a highly experienced attorney, the extra cost may be worthwhile if it increases the likelihood of achieving the desired outcome. In addition, a less experienced lawyer might require more billable hours to complete the necessary work.

There are many different types of legal fees that may be charged in family law cases. It is important to be aware that some attorneys charge a fee for the initial consultation, even before a potential client decides whether or not to hire them. Although some attorneys charge a flat fee for straightforward cases, such as a summary dissolution of a marriage, most charge an hourly rate for their work on a case. While a flat fee may seem attractive, it is not generally recommended for cases that are contested or may require multiple court appearances.

Before hiring an attorney, experts suggest asking for a written retainer agreement that lays out the hourly rate and any additional fees, as well as the amount of the initial deposit and the schedule for payment. Some other questions to ask an attorney about legal costs include:

- How exactly do you charge for your services?

- What other fees and expenses will I be expected to pay?

- Do you require a retainer payment?

- How often do you send out bills?

- What is your estimate of the total cost of my case?

References

1. Farzad, B. Robert. "What Are Questions to Ask a Divorce Lawyer at the Consultation and Before Hiring One?" Farzad Family Law, June 28, 2014.

2. "Questions to Ask Before Hiring Child Custody Lawyers." Attorneys.com, 2016.

3. "Watch Out for the Cost of a Domestic Violence Suit." Laws.com, 2015.

Section 44.2

Restraining Orders

"Restraining Orders," © 2016 Omnigraphics, Inc.
Reviewed January 2016.

A restraining order, also known as a civil protection order, is an order issued by a family court that is intended to protect people from domestic violence. In a typical restraining order, the court orders an abuser to stop contacting, harassing, stalking, threatening, or harming their intimate partner or other members of the family. Obtaining a restraining order offers many benefits to survivors of domestic violence. It informs the abuser that domestic violence is a crime, and it warns that any further incidents can result in arrest. In addition, a restraining order can help stop the cycle of violence and ensure the victim's safety while they seek support and make plans for the future.

Although the specific rules vary by state, restraining orders are usually available to protect applicants who are or were formerly married to, living with, or dating the person named in the order. They also usually protect applicants who have a child in common with the respondent. When dependent children are involved, the court may issue additional orders of maintenance that are intended to ensure the safety and meet the basic needs of the family. An order may specify, for instance, that the respondent must vacate the family home, make rent or mortgage payments, maintain utilities and insurance, pay child support, or provide bank statements, tax forms, or other financial documents.

Obtaining a Restraining Order

The process of obtaining a restraining order begins when victims of domestic violence apply to a judge asking for a court order directing their abusers to stay away from them. An applicant must fill out a form called an Application for Relief from Abuse, which is available at the nearest family court. In addition to the full names, addresses, and dates of birth of everyone involved in the case, the form also requires the applicant to submit an affidavit explaining why they need a restraining order. This sworn statement must provide information to support a claim of domestic abuse and convince a judge that a restraining order is necessary to protect the applicant from imminent harm.

After the application is completed, it must be filed with the clerk of the family court that is closest to where the applicant lives. There is no fee involved in filing for a restraining order. The clerk submits the form to a judge or magistrate, who holds an *ex parte* hearing to gather additional information about the domestic violence complaint and decide whether the applicant's request meets the requirements of state law. If so, the judge issues a temporary restraining order and schedules a full hearing within two weeks.

In the meantime, legal documentation of the request for a restraining order must be served to the person who is being accused of domestic violence. A marshal will serve a copy of the court papers free of charge. Applicants who feel that revealing their whereabouts to the respondent will put their safety at risk can file a request to keep their contact information private.

In the full hearing, the judge hears testimony from the victim, the accused abuser, and witnesses for both sides. The person seeking the restraining order must convince the judge that their allegations of domestic violence are true by a preponderance of the evidence. Experts recommend that people seeking a restraining order hire an attorney to represent them in these proceedings, especially if the respondent brings an attorney. If the judge decides to issue a final restraining order, the court clerk provides certified copies to both parties, and it remains in force until the date indicated on these documents.

Although some states allow judges to issue permanent restraining orders, most states set a time limit for their duration—often five years. Family courts may grant extensions, however, and restraining orders can be modified by filing a request with a judge. To extend a restraining order, applicants should file a motion with the family court clerk at least one month before the original order expires. Copies of the motion should also be sent to the respondent and their attorney. The court will then schedule a new hearing to decide whether to extend the duration of the restraining order.

References

1. Connecticut Network for Legal Aid. "Court Orders Can Protect You From Domestic Violence." CTLawHelp.org, March 2015.

2. Portman, Janet. "What Is a Restraining Order or Protection Order?" Lawyers.com, 2016.

Section 44.3

General Information for Victims and Witnesses

Text in this section is excerpted from "Understanding Your Rights and the Federal Court System," U.S. Department of Justice (DOJ), June 10, 2015.

Participants in the Criminal Justice System

- **Federal Judge:** The individual who presides over a court proceeding. Sometimes a Federal Magistrate Judge presides over the proceeding. He/she has some, but not all, of the powers of a judge.

- **The United States Attorney (U.S.A.):** The chief prosecutor for violations of federal laws of the United States. The USA is appointed by the President of the United States and confirmed by the United States Senate. The United States Attorney's offices are part of the United States Department of Justice.

- **Assistant United States Attorneys (A.U.S.A.):** Government lawyers in the United States Attorneys' offices who prosecute cases on behalf of the United States.

- **Victim-Witness Coordinator / Advocate:** The person(s) in the United States Attorneys' offices who will assist you in your journey through the criminal justice system process.

- **Witness:** A person who has information or evidence concerning a crime and provides information regarding his/her knowledge to a law enforcement agency.

- **Victim:** An individual who has suffered direct physical, emotional, or economic harm as a result of the commission of a crime.

- **Defendant:** The person accused of committing a crime.

The Victim-Witness Program

Each United States Attorney's office has a Victim-Witness program which is staffed by at least one Victim-Witness Coordinator or Victim

Advocate. The goal of the Federal Victim-Witness Program is to ensure that victims and witnesses of federal crimes are treated fairly, that their privacy is respected, and that they are treated with dignity and respect. Victim-Witness Coordinators and Victim Advocates work to make sure victims are kept informed of the status of a case and help victims find services to assist them in recovering from the crime.

Information for Witnesses

General Witness Information

If you are required to testify as a witness in a trial or other proceeding, you will receive a subpoena telling you when and where to go to court. A subpoena is a formal court order telling you to appear in court, and there are serious penalties for disobeying a subpoena. If you know in advance of anything that might keep you from attending a required court appearance, let the United States Attorney's Office know immediately so that an attempt may be made to adjust the schedule. However, scheduling is at the discretion of the court and sometimes cannot be changed.

Will this be at my expense?

- **Witnesses:** If you are a witness, you will receive a witness fee for each day that you are required to attend court in connection with the case, including time spent waiting to testify.

- **Local witnesses:** If you are a local witness, you are entitled to parking and mileage reimbursement, in addition to the witness fee for the days you are asked to be in court.

- **Out-of-town witnesses:** If you are an out-of-town witness, you may receive reimbursement for certain travel expenses, in addition to the daily witness fee. Out-of-town witnesses will be contacted by a representative from the United States Attorney's Office who will make all witness travel and lodging arrangements.

- **Witnesses who are federal government employees:** If you are a federal Government employee, the United States Attorney's Office will assist you in advising your employer that you are required to be present in court. This will enable you to receive your regular salary, notwithstanding your absence from your job. You will not collect a witness fee in addition to that salary.

How do I receive my reimbursement?

- **Witness voucher:** At the conclusion of your testimony, you will be assisted in completing a witness voucher to make a claim for your fees and expenses. Generally, a check for all fees will be mailed to you by the U.S. Marshal when the case is over.

Frequently Asked Questions

The criminal justice process can be complex and lengthy. Federal and tribal law enforcement agencies, and staff from the United States Attorney's offices will provide you with a variety of notification and assistance services to keep you informed on the status of your case.

The Victim-Witness Coordinator at the United States Attorney's Office will be your main contact throughout the prosecution phase of the case. Please contact the Coordinator if you have any questions.

Listed below are answers to some questions that are frequently asked by victims and witnesses:

What kind of support services or assistance can the Victim-Witness Coordinator offer?

1. **Referrals:** Victim-Witness Coordinators can provide victims with referrals to existing agencies for shelter, counseling, financial compensation, and other types of assistance services.

2. **Accompaniment to court:** In certain cases, the Victim-Witness Coordinator or Victim-Witness Assistant may be available to accompany you to court to provide support.

3. **Assistance with employers or creditors:** If your participation in the prosecution causes you to be absent from work, the Victim-Witness Coordinator can, at your request, contact your employer and explain your role in the case. Likewise, if the crime, or your participation in the prosecution makes you unable to pay your bills on time, the Victim-Witness Coordinator can, at your request, contact creditors for you, or assist you in doing so yourself. While creditors are not obligated to take your participation in the case into consideration, they may chose to do so, particularly if there is a possibility that you may receive restitution from the defendant.

How will I find out information about the case?

The United States Attorney's Office will provide you with information throughout the progress of the case, including notification of the filing of charges against a suspected offender or the dismissal of any or all charges; notification of a plea agreement; and notification of the date set for sentencing if the offender is found guilty, as well as the sentence imposed.

The Victim-Witness Coordinator will routinely provide information or assistance concerning transportation, parking, lodging, translators, and related services. In addition, every effort will be made to inform you about changes in the court's schedules.

If you have questions about the case in which you are involved, you are welcome to call the Victim-Witness Coordinator or the Assistant United States Attorney who is handling the case. The Assistant United States Attorney may also be contacting you for information at various stages of the proceedings.

How can I tell the court how this crime has affected me?

During a trial, it may seem as if most of the attention is paid to the defendant and not to the affects the crime has had on the victim. However, if the defendant is found guilty or pleads guilty to a crime in which you are a victim, you may have an opportunity to let the court know how the crime affected your life. A victim may submit a Victim Impact Statement, a written statement of the affects of the crime and his/her feelings about the crime, to the probation officer. This statement will be included in the pre-sentence report prepared by the probation officer for the judge prior to sentencing.

Victims may attend the sentencing hearing, and victims of violent crimes or crimes involving sexual abuse will also have the opportunity to address the court at this time. This is called victim allocution, and is discussed further in The Sentencing Hearing section. The Assistant United States Attorney or the Victim-Witness Coordinator will tell you if such an opportunity exists for you, and will talk to you about the aspects of a presentation.

How do I know when the offender in my case may be released from prison?

1. **Federal Bureau of Prisons Notification Program:** If the defendant is sentenced to a period of time in a federal prison, victims may receive notice from the Bureau of Prisons notification program. Once enrolled, you will receive information directly from the Bureau of Prisons. You will be notified of the death, escape, or furlough of the inmate, and you will be notified if the inmate is transferred to a halfway house.

Finally, you will be notified of the inmate's eventual release date. The Victim-Witness Coordinator will provide victims with the information needed to enroll in this program. Once you are enrolled in the Bureau of Prisons Notification Program, you must keep the appropriate officials notified of any address or telephone number change so that they may readily contact you with information about the defendant's status.

2.   Victim contact information is placed in the inmate's central file. This information is kept confidential, and the inmate does not have access to this information.

3.   You may call the Inmate Locator phone number at (202) 307-3126 to ascertain the federal facility where the inmate is held or log onto http://www.BOP.gov, and click on "Inmate Information" to obtain location and projected release date.

What do I do if I am being threatened by the defendant or others acting on behalf of the defendant?

If anyone threatens you at any time while you are involved with the case, or you feel that you are being harassed because of your connection to the case, you should immediately notify the federal law enforcement agency conducting the investigation or the United States Attorney's Office. These telephone numbers are listed in your telephone directory under United States Government. In emergency situations, always contact your local law enforcement (911) first.

What is a bond and what factors are considered when releasing a defendant?

There are two main factors the court considers when deciding whether or not to release a defendant pending trial: Risk of flight, and risk of danger to the community.

If the court is satisfied that the defendant will appear in court and that the defendant does not pose a threat to the community, the court may release the defendant while he or she is awaiting trial.

Sometimes the court may require the defendant, or someone acting on his/her behalf, to post cash or property which is known as a bond; or it may simply require the defendant to promise to appear. Since most federal criminal defendants are released on bond pending trial, you should not be surprised if you happen to see the defendant prior to trial.

Can I observe the trial?

- **Witnesses:** As a general rule, witnesses are not permitted to watch court proceedings. This rule helps to ensure that a witness' testimony is based solely on his or her own knowledge, and not on things he or she heard another witness testify about or on things he or she heard the judge or the lawyers say during court proceedings.

- **Victims that are testifying at the trial:** although victims have a right to attend public court proceedings, they lose this right if a judge decides that the victim's testimony would be affected by hearing other testimony at the trial.

- **Victims that are not testifying at the trial:** Not all victims are required to be witnesses at the trial. According to the Victim's Rights Clarification Act of 1997, the judge is not allowed to order a victim to be excluded from the trial simply because that victim may testify or allocute at the sentencing hearing.

Am I entitled to a witness fee for every day that I am required to appear in court in connection with the case?

Victims: Victims will only receive a witness fee for the days they testify. If they are not testifying and are there only to observe the proceeding, they will not receive a witness fee.

Witnesses: Information for Witnesses.

Can I discuss the case with others?

Defense attorneys and investigators working for defendants often contact victims and witnesses. It is not unusual or inappropriate for the defense lawyer or an investigator for the defense to contact you for an interview. While you may discuss the case with them if you wish to do so, you do not have to talk to them. The choice is entirely yours.

The Assistant United States Attorney may discuss some parts of the case with you to inform you and prepare you for testifying. However, there may be some instances when the Assistant United States Attorney may not be able to answer some of your questions because it may endanger the case or other witnesses.

After you testify in court, you are not allowed to tell other witnesses what was said during the testimony until after the case is over. Please do not ask other witnesses about their testimony, and do not volunteer information about your own testimony.

Below are some general suggestions and tips when discussing the case:

1. Know to whom you are talking when you discuss the case. The department encourage you not to discuss the case with members of the press before or during the trial as the defendant's right to a fair trial could be jeopardized by any publicity.

2. Please let the United States Attorney's Office know if you have agreed to be interviewed by the defense attorney or investigator. You may want to bring an additional person, chosen by you, to witness the interview.

3. Always tell "the truth, the whole truth, and nothing but the truth."

My property is being held as evidence. How, and when, can I get it back?

Sometimes, law enforcement officers hold property belonging to victims and witnesses as evidence for trial. If your property is being held as evidence and you would like to try to get your property back before the case is over, notify the law enforcement officer or the Assistant United States Attorney who is handling the case.

In some, but not all cases, arrangements can be made for early release of property. In any event, at the conclusion of the case, your property should be returned to you promptly. In those instances where this is not possible, the Assistant United States Attorney will explain the reasons for not returning the property.

How can I get my money back?

Many people lose money as a result of being victimized. There are two possible ways for you to recover your losses; Compensation and Restitution. There is, however, no guarantee that your losses will be recovered.

Compensation: Crime victims' compensation programs are administered by each state, territory, and the District of Columbia and provide financial assistance to victims and survivors of victims of criminal violence who are not otherwise covered by insurance. These funds are intended to cover:

- Medical expenses, including expenses for mental health counseling and care

- Loss of wages resulting from a physical injury

- Funeral expenses for a death resulting from a compensable crime

- Eyeglasses or other corrective lenses

- Dental services and devices

- Prosthetic devices

Each compensation program has its own rules regarding the types of losses for which victims may recover and the amount of money victims may recover. Also, each compensation program has its own instructions for applying for crime victims' compensation. Consult with your Victim-Witness Coordinator to determine how to apply for compensation.

Restitution: After a defendant is convicted of certain types of crimes, the judge may order the defendant to pay restitution as part of the sentence. Restitution occurs when an offender gives back the thing(s) he or she stole (or damaged) or when the offender pays the victim for his or her loss. Restitution can be either discretionary or, in some cases, the judge is required by law to award the victim restitution for the full amount of the victim's losses. Examples of these cases include child support recovery, sexual abuse, domestic violence, telemarketing fraud, sexual exploitation and other abuses of children, consumer product tampering, most violent crimes, and most crimes against property, including fraud.

Receiving restitution payments: You will normally receive your restitution payments from the Clerk of the District Court. The defendant should not make payments directly to you. The court clerk of courts maintains a record of payments and disbursements on all court-ordered restitution for accountability purposes. You may receive one large lump sum payment, but more than likely you will receive smaller payments from time to time. This will depend on the defendant's ability to repay the restitution and on the number of other victims involved.

It is your responsibility to keep the U.S. District Clerk of Court informed of your current address. If you move, you should contact the Clerk of Court immediately so that any restitution payments can be forwarded to you at your new address.

Section 44.4

How Cases Are Resolved

Text in this section is excerpted from "Understanding
Your Rights and the Federal Court System," U.S. Department
of Justice (DOJ), June 10, 2015.

Although many criminal cases go to trial, many other criminal cases
end without a trial. For example, a defendant may plead guilty to the
crime, or the Government may dismiss the case (not try the case) for
a variety of reasons. Different scenarios are discussed below:

Declination: When the United States Attorney chooses not to
prosecute a particular case, this is called declination.

An Assistant United States Attorney has the discretion to decline
to prosecute a case based on several considerations, some of which
the Assistant United States Attorney may not be able to discuss with
you. The Assistant United States Attorney is ethically bound not to
bring criminal charges unless the legally admissible evidence is likely
to be enough to obtain a conviction. However, even when the evidence
is sufficient, the Assistant United States Attorney may decide that
there is not a sufficient federal interest served by prosecuting the
particular defendant in a federal case. In many cases, the defendant
may be subject to prosecution in another state, local, or tribal court
(including a state court for the prosecution of juvenile delinquents)
and prosecution in this other forum might be more appropriate than
prosecution in federal court.

Dismissal: When the United States Attorney or the court chooses
to dismiss the case after it has been filed with the court, this is called
dismissal.

The Assistant United States Attorney may ask the court to dismiss
a case that has been filed in court. The Assistant United States Attorney may do this because the court will not allow critical evidence to be
part of the case, or because witnesses have become unavailable. There
are times when evidence that weakens the case may come to light
after the case has started. In other instances, the court may dismiss a

case over the objection of the Assistant United States Attorney if the court determines that the evidence is insufficient to find the defendant guilty.

Pre-trial Diversion: When the United States Attorney decides not to try a defendant right away, or not to bring charges immediately, a defendant may be placed in a Pre-trial Diversion Program.

Under this program, the United States and the defendant enter into a contract in which the defendant agrees to comply with certain conditions, and agrees to be supervised by the United States Probation Office for a period of time. If the defendant successfully complies with all of the conditions, no charges will be brought. However, if the defendant fails to meet a condition, charges may be filed.

The Pretrial Diversion Program is designed for those defendants who do not appear likely to engage in further criminal conduct, and who appear to be susceptible to rehabilitation. The objective of the program is to prevent future criminal activity by certain defendants who would benefit more from community supervision and services than from traditional punishment.

Plea Agreements: When the United States Attorney reaches an agreement with a defendant, a plea agreement is established. A guilty plea can take place at any time, and can even take place after trial has begun.

To the public and to many victims, plea bargaining has a negative image. In reality, it is a very good tool to resolving a case and making sure a conviction is certain. Criminal cases always involve risks and uncertainties. A jury verdict of guilty is never a sure thing. With a plea agreement, a conviction is guaranteed, and a sentence is imposed. By pleading guilty, the defendant waives his or her right to trial.

Trial: Many cases do go to trial.

Chapter 45

Identity Protection for Abuse Victims

Chapter Contents

Section 45.1

Tips for Protecting Your Identity

"Tips for Protecting Your Identity,"
© 2016 Omnigraphics, Inc.
Reviewed January 2016.

Even after leaving an abusive relationship, survivors of domestic violence may still be vulnerable to an abuser's efforts to harass or control them. An increasingly common method abusers may use to continue to exert power in the relationship is identity theft. For instance, an abuser may use a survivor's personal information—such as Social Security number, credit cards, or bank accounts—without their knowledge to incur debts, commit crimes, and ruin the survivor's credit or reputation. Abusers may also use information posted on social media sites to locate and stalk their former partners.

The following tips can help survivors of domestic violence protect their identity and maintain their safety and independence:

- Consider getting a post office box to prevent an abuser from stealing your mail and accessing your personal information. Or arrange to have paperless statements sent to you online.

- Open an account at a new bank and get a new credit card in your own name. Check bank statements and credit card bills as soon as you receive them. If bills do not arrive on time, call the company to inquire whether someone may have changed the contact information for the account. Report any unauthorized withdrawals or charges immediately.

- Shred your mail before throwing it away to prevent an abuser from gaining access to personal information by going through your garbage. Opt out of pre-approved credit card offers, which may enable an identity thief to open accounts in your name, by calling 1-888-5OPTOUT or visiting www.optoutpre-screen.com.

- Obtain a free credit report once a year by calling 1-877-322-8228 or visiting www.annualcreditreport.com. Check the reports carefully. If you suspect fraudulent activity, close the account immediately and notify the Federal Trade Commission at 1-877-ID-THEFT.

- Contact the major credit bureaus (Equifax, Experian, and TransUnion) to place a fraud alert on your credit report, which makes it more difficult for an identity thief to open new lines of credit in your name.

- Protect your personal information, especially your Social Security number. Do not provide the number to anyone who calls or emails you claiming to be a store, bank, or government agency. Most legitimate businesses will never request the information in this manner.

- Use firewall, antivirus, and spyware protection programs on your computers and smartphones and keep the programs updated. Make strong passwords using a mix of at least eight letters, numbers, and symbols, and use a different password for each account.

- Be careful about sharing personal information on social media sites, such as Facebook and Twitter. Never publish your home address, workplace address, daily schedule, current whereabouts, or vacation plans. All of this information can reveal your location to an abusive partner and enable them to stalk you.

References

1. "How to Protect Your Identity." DomesticShelters.org, July 7, 2014.

2. "Top 10 Tips for Identity Theft Protection." State of California Department of Justice, 2015.

Section 45.2

Address Confidentiality Programs

Text in this section is excerpted from "Domestic Violence Awareness
Month: Focus on Resources, Collaboration and Confidentiality," U.S.
Department of Health and Human Services (HHS), October 3, 2014.

Confidentiality

Confidentiality is a key concern for survivors of domestic violence. A
survivor must be able to flee from violence without being located. It is
vitally important that engagement with a child support program does
not inadvertently endanger a family by disclosing information. Carefully considered data sharing protocols and safeguarding are essential.

Family Violence Indicator ("FVI") policies are not a complete
approach to protecting the identity of or information about a victim of
violence nor are they a complete domestic violence policy. The FVI is
just one protection provided victims seeking child support. Under federal law, states are required to have an FVI process (Section 453(b)(2)
and 454(26) of the Social Security Act). The law prohibits the release
of specific information when evidence of domestic violence or child
abuse exists. The FVI prevents any information from being released
from the FPLS.

While states have taken great care in crafting policies and practices
for the placement and removal of an FVI, such efforts do not ensure
total confidentiality. The presence or absence of an FVI is not definitive of whether or not there is a history of domestic violence, particularly as family circumstances (and trust of the child support program)
may change over time. Additionally, policies and practices regarding
placement and removal of the FVI are only one component of a child
support program's domestic violence plan or policies. Apart from the
FVI, a comprehensive domestic violence plan should address disclosure, training, confidentiality, referrals, legal practice, and internal
procedures for responding to domestic violence.

To further assist with the safety issues raised in seeking child
support, child support programs can provide information and assist
victims through address confidentiality programs. PIQ 12-02, expressly

states that child support programs can "use FFP [Federal Financial Participation] to develop alternative address/confidentiality systems for survivors in the child support program. This may be in partnership with family violence service organizations." Additionally, many states have existing address confidentiality programs. Enhanced safeguards and attention to confidentiality are especially necessary in interstate cases and interstate communications. For example, court documents protected in one jurisdiction may be public in another system.

Apart from data sharing where there are safety concerns, child support professionals must be careful not to communicate any information about child support customers unless they are required to by law. Even when child support programs pay careful attention to the safety needs of families, there will always be risks to engaging with the child support system. Therefore, it is important not to promise total safety or confidentiality, particularly given the prevalence of information on the Internet. OCSE recommends ongoing review of existing confidentiality policies.

Section 45.3

Applying for a New Social Security Number

Text in this section is excerpted from "New Numbers for
Domestic Violence Victims," Social Security
Administration (SSA), August 2015.

New Numbers for Domestic Violence Victims

Anyone can be a victim of domestic violence. If you're a victim of family violence, harassment, abuse, or life-endangering situations, Social Security may be able to help you.

Public awareness campaigns stress how important it is for victims to develop safety plans that include gathering personal papers and choosing a safe place to go. Sometimes, the best way to evade an abuser and reduce the risk of further violence may be to relocate and establish a new identity. Following these changes, getting a new Social Security number may also be helpful.

Although Social Security doesn't routinely assign new numbers, the Social Security Administration (SSA), does so when evidence shows you are being harassed or abused, or your life is endangered.

Applying for a new number is a big decision. Your ability to interact with federal and state agencies, employers, and others may be affected; your financial, medical, employment, and other records will be under your former Social Security number and name (if you change your name). If you expect to change your name, please do so before applying for a new number.

How to apply for a new number?

You must apply in person at any Social Security office. The Social Security Administration (SSA) helps you complete a statement explaining why you need a new number and an application for a new number.

In addition, you must present:

- Evidence documenting the harassment, abuse, or life endangerment;

- Your current Social Security number;

- Evidence documents establishing your:

  - U.S. citizenship or work-authorized immigration status;

  - Age; and

  - Identity.

- Evidence of your legal name change if you've changed your name.

Also, the Social Security Administration (SSA) need to see documents showing you have custody of any children for whom you're requesting new numbers and documentation proving their U.S. citizenship, ages, and identities.

All documents must be either originals or copies certified by the issuing agency. The Social Security Administration (SSA) can't accept photocopies or notarized copies of documents. The Social Security Administration (SSA) may use one document for two purposes. For example, the Social Security Administration (SSA) may use your U.S. passport as proof of both citizenship and identity. Or, the Social Security Administration (SSA) may use your U.S. birth certificate as proof of age and citizenship. **However, you must provide at least two separate documents.**

The Social Security Administration (SSA) mail your number and card as soon as the Social Security Administration (SSA) have all of your information and have verified your documents with the issuing offices.

Citizenship or immigration status

U.S. citizen: The Social Security Administration (SSA) can accept only certain documents as proof of U.S. citizenship. These include a U.S. birth certificate or a U.S. passport. Noncitizen: To prove your U.S. Immigration status, show the Social Security Administration (SSA) your current immigration document such as your I-94, Arrival/Departure Record, showing a class of admission permitting work, or your Form I-766, Employment Authorization Document (EAD, work permit). If you're an F-1 or M-1 student, you also must show the Social Security Administration (SSA) your I-20, Certificate of Eligibility for Nonimmigrant Student Status. If you're a J-1 or J-2 exchange visitor, show the Social Security Administration (SSA) your DS-2019, Certificate of Eligibility for Exchange Visitor Status.

Age

U.S. born: You must present your birth certificate if you have one. If you don't have a birth certificate, the Social Security Administration (SSA) may be able to accept your:

- Religious record made before age 5 showing the date of birth;
- U.S. hospital record or birth; or
- U.S. passport.

Foreign born: You must present your foreign birth certificate if you have it or can get a copy within 10 business days. If you can't get it, the Social Security Administration (SSA) may be able to accept your:

- Foreign passport;
- I-551, Permanent Resident Card; or
- I-94 Arrival/Departure Record.

Identity

The Social Security Administration (SSA) can accept only certain documents as proof of identity. An acceptable document must be current (not expired) and show your name, identifying information and preferably a recent photograph.

U.S. citizen: Social Security will ask to see a U.S. driver's license, U.S. state-issued non-driver identification card, or U.S. passport as proof of identity. If you don't have the specific documents the Social Security Administration (SSA) asks for, we'll ask to see other documents, including:

- Employee identification card;

- School identification card;

- Health insurance card (not a Medicare card);

- U.S. military identification card.

Noncitizen: Social Security will ask to see your current U.S. immigration documents. Acceptable immigration documents include your:

- I-551, Permanent Resident Card;

- I-94, Arrival/Departure Record with your unexpired foreign passport; or

- I-766, Employment Authorization Card (EAD, work permit) from DHS.

Changing your name on your card

We can accept only a court-order-approved legal name change document that supports your requested name change.

Providing the evidence you need

The best evidence of abuse comes from third parties, such as police or medical personnel, and describes the nature and extent of harassment, abuse, or life endangerment. Other evidence may include court restraining orders and letters from shelters, family members, friends, counselors, or others who have knowledge of the domestic violence or abuse. We'll help you get any additional evidence needed.

Blocking access to your record

You can choose to block electronic access to your Social Security record. When you do this, no one, including you, will be able to get or change your personal information online or through the Social Security Administration's (SSA) automated telephone service. If you block access to your record, and then change your mind, you can contact Social Security and ask us to unblock it.

Chapter 46

Life after Abuse:
Looking after Yourself and
Moving On

Getting out of an abusive relationship requires a great deal of courage and resiliency. But leaving is often only the first step in what can be a long and difficult recovery process. Domestic violence harms victims emotionally and mentally as well as physically. Many survivors struggle to move on and regain their self-confidence long after their physical injuries have healed.

Struggling to Move On

In an abusive relationship, the abuser controls you through manipulation, coercion, or violence. You are forced to surrender your power and independence. Even after leaving an abusive situation, you may still feel bound to the abuser and struggle to regain control of your own life. You may find yourself on an emotional roller-coaster, as your thoughts, feelings, and emotions seem to fluctuate wildly. You may blame yourself for the abuse and second guess your decision to leave the relationship. You may wonder if you did something wrong, or if you could have tried harder. All of these feelings are normal.

"Life after Abuse: Looking after Yourself and Moving On," © 2016 Omnigraphics, Inc. Reviewed January 2016.

Many survivors of domestic violence experience feelings of loss, depression, or guilt. It is not uncommon for survivors to have symptoms of posttraumatic stress disorder, such as anxiety, insomnia, and being easily startled or frightened. They may also feel emotionally numb and have trouble reconnecting with friends and maintaining relationships. Although experiencing domestic violence can cause lasting damage, it is important to remember that anyone who manages to get out of an abusive relationship has tremendous strength. The key to healing and moving on is channeling that strength into rebuilding your self-esteem and forging a happy and healthy future.

Tips for Looking Forward

Moving forward after an abusive relationship is a gradual process. It involves accepting that you were not to blame, forgiving yourself for loving and believing in a person who hurt you, and understanding that you are a worthwhile person who deserves to feel safe and happy. Following the steps below may aid in your recovery:

- Ensure that you remain safe and beyond the abuser's control. You may need to cut off all contact with the abuser, obtain a civil protection order, change your phone number, or even move away from the area. If the abuser ever harasses, threatens, or frightens you, keep a detailed written record of each incident and contact the police if necessary.

- Deal with emotional turmoil in a healthy way. Feelings of anger, sadness, or grief are normal at the end of any relationship. Expressing those feelings in a healthy manner—such as writing poetry, painting, dancing, singing, or exercising—can increase your sense of power and control over your life.

- Start by making small choices. When the abuser was in control, you may not have been allowed to make decisions for yourself. As a result, the many choices you face every day may seem overwhelming. It may be helpful to start by making small decisions, such as what to eat for lunch or what to watch on television, to begin reestablishing control over your life. Then you can move on to bigger decisions as you grow more confident and independent.

- Acknowledge and celebrate your successes. Give yourself credit for the tremendous courage and determination it took to end an abusive relationship. Write down even minor achievements on your road to recovery. Look back on them and feel proud of how far you have come.

- Take care of your health. Eating a balanced diet, exercising daily, and getting plenty of sleep will help ensure that you have the physical and mental energy you need to rebuild your life. If you relied upon drugs or alcohol to cope with the abuse, try to cut back or quit.

- Establish a support network. Many abusers isolate their victims from family and friends in order to solidify their control. Getting back in touch with these people can provide a valuable source of support in your recovery and help you reconnect with ordinary life. It may also be helpful to talk to people who have been through similar experiences through online forums or local support groups for victims of domestic violence.

- If you have children, work to rebuild your relationship with them. Sometimes going for a walk, tossing a ball, or having a picnic in the park will reduce the pressure on children and make it easier for them to talk about their feelings and experiences.

- Help other people. Volunteering in a school, church, or community center is a great way to feel useful and valued, give back to the community, and meet new people in a casual atmosphere. Taking a class, learning a skill, or joining a team can also help rebuild self-esteem.

References

1. "Take Your Power Back: Life after Abuse." CheriSpeak, October 29, 2013.

2. "Tips for Life after Violence and Abuse." Single Parent Action Network, 2016.

3. "Why Am I Struggling to Move On after Abuse?" Love Is Respect, July 31, 2013.

Part Six

Additional Help and Information

Chapter 47

Glossary of Terms Related to Domestic Violence

There may be other definitions for these words but these are the meanings used in relation to domestic violence.

abandonment: When a parent leaves a child without adequate care, supervision, support, or parental contact for an excessive period of time.

affidavit: A written statement of facts confirmed by the oath of the party making it. Affidavits must be notarized or administered by an officer of the court with such authority.

affirmed: Judgment by appellate courts where the decree or order is declared valid and will stand as decided in the lower court.

aggravated assault: Unlawful, intentional causing of serious bodily injury with or without a deadly weapon, or unlawful, intentional attempting or threatening of serious bodily injury or death with a deadly or dangerous weapon.

batterer: An individual who uses abusive tactics over his intimate partner in order to exercise power and control over his partner. Other terms used are perpetrator and abuser.

child abuse: Maltreatment or neglect of a child, including nonaccidental physical injuries, sexual abuse/exploitation, severe or general

---

This glossary contains terms excerpted from documents produced by several sources deemed reliable.

neglect, unjustifiable mental suffering/emotional abuse, and willful cruelty or unjustifiable punishment of a child.

contract: An agreement between two or more persons that creates an obligation to do or not to do a particular thing.

cyberbullying: Hurting someone again and again using a computer, a cellphone, or another kind of electronic technology.

dating violence: Is defined as the physical, sexual, psychological, or emotional violence within a dating relationship, including stalking. It can occur in person or electronically and might occur between a current or former dating partner.

defendant: In a civil suit, the person complained against; in a criminal case, the person accused of the crime.

economic abuse: Is defined as making or attempting to make an individual financially dependent by maintaining total control over financial resources, withholding one's access to money, or forbidding one's attendance at school or employment.

elder abuse: Abuse perpetrated by a caretaker on an elderly individual who depends on others for support and assistance.

emotional abuse: Undermining an individual's sense of self-worth and/or self-esteem is abusive.

ex parte: A proceeding brought before a court by one party only, without notice to or challenge by the other side.

felony: A serious crime, usually punishable by at least one year in prison.

gang violence: Criminal acts committed by a group of three or more individuals who regularly engage in criminal activity and identify themselves with a common name or sign.

human traffic: Sex trafficking in which a commercial sex act is induced by force, fraud, or coercion, or in which the person induced to perform such act has not attained 18 years of age; or the recruitment, harboring, transportation, provision, or obtaining of a person for labor or services, through the use of force, fraud, or coercion, for the purpose of subjection to involuntary servitude, peonage, debt bondage, or slavery.

litigation: A case, controversy, or lawsuit. Participants (plaintiffs and defendants) in lawsuits are called litigants.

misdemeanor: An offense punishable by one year of imprisonment or less.

perpetrator: A perpetrator is an individual who commits or threatens to commit an act of domestic violence, sexual assault, and/or stalking.

petitioner: A person who presents a petition to the court; a person who files legal forms to start a court case.

physical abuse: Hitting, slapping, shoving, grabbing, pinching, biting, hair pulling, etc. are types of physical abuse.

probation: A sentencing alternative to imprisonment in which the court releases convicted defendants under supervision as long as certain conditions are observed.

prosecute: To charge someone with a crime. A prosecutor tries a criminal case on behalf of the government.

psychological abuse: Elements of psychological abuse include—but are not limited to—causing fear by intimidation; threatening physical harm to self, partner, children, or partner's family or friends; destruction of pets and property; and forcing isolation from family, friends, or school and/or work.

remand: When an appellate court sends a case back to a lower court for further proceedings.

respondent: If you are the person that answers the original petition, you are the respondent. Even if you later file an action of your own in that case, you are still the respondent for as long as the case is open.

restitution: Giving something back to its owner. Or, giving the owner something with the same value, like paying to fix his or her property.

restraining order: A court order that tells a person to stop doing something for a certain amount of time, usually until a court hearing is held.

safety plan: Guidelines for stalking victims that, if implemented, may reduce the odds of physical or emotional harm from a stalker.

sentence: The punishment ordered by a court for a defendant convicted of a crime.

settlement: Parties to a lawsuit resolve their dispute without having a trial. Settlements often involve the payment of compensation by one party in at least partial satisfaction of the other party's claims, but usually do not include the admission of fault.

sexual abuse: Coercing or attempting to coerce any sexual contact or behavior without consent.

sexual assault: Means a Rape, Aggravated Sexual Assault, or Sexual Assault as defined in the *Peace Corps Consolidated Incident Reporting Guide.*

stalking: Any unwanted contact between two people that directly or indirectly communicates a threat or places the victim in fear.

status quo: A child's usual place of residence, current schedule and daily routine for at least the last three months.

subpoena: A command to a witness to appear and give testimony.

temporary restraining order: Akin to a preliminary injunction, it is a judge's short-term order forbidding certain actions until a full hearing can be conducted. Often referred to as a TRO.

threat: Any oral, written expression, or gesture that could be interpreted by a reasonable person as conveying intent to cause physical harm to persons or property.

verdict: The decision of a trial jury or a judge that determines the guilt or innocence of a criminal defendant, or that determines the final outcome of a civil case.

victim safety: Means a plan developed by Designated Staff and a Volunteer to address the immediate and ongoing personal safety and emotional needs of the Volunteer following a Sexual Assault, including, when necessary, housing changes.

visitation: The time that third parties, often grandparents or step-parents, will spend with children. When the time with children is for parents, it is called parenting time.

warrant: Court authorization, most often for law enforcement officers, to conduct a search or make an arrest.

witness: A person who has information or evidence concerning a crime and provides information regarding his/her knowledge to a law enforcement agency.

workplace violence: Any act of violent behavior, threats of physical violence, harassment, intimidation, bullying, verbal, or non-verbal threat, or other threatening, disruptive behavior that occurs at the workplace.

youth violence: Youth violence is a serious problem that can have lasting harmful effects on victims and their family, friends, and communities.

Chapter 48

Directory of Domestic Violence Resources

AbuseofPower.info
Website: www.abuseofpower.info

Abused Deaf Women's Advocacy Services
8623 Roosevelt Way N.E.
Seattle, WA 98115
Phone: 206-922-7088
Phone: 206-518-9361
(Hotline—Videophone)
Fax: 206-726-0017
TTY: 206-726-0093
Website: www.adwas.org
E-mail: adwas@adwas.org

Alabama Coalition Against Domestic Violence
Phone: 334-832-4842
Toll-Free: 800-650-6522
Website: www.acadv.org
E-mail: info@acadv.org

Asian & Pacific Islander Institute on Domestic Violence
450 Sutter St., Ste. 600
San Francisco, CA 94108
Phone: 415-568-3315
Fax: 415-954-9999
Website: www.api-gbv.org
E-mail: info@apiidv.org

Aurora Center for Advocacy and Education
University of Minnesota
407 Boynton Health Services
410 Church St.
Minneapolis, MN 55455
Phone: 612-626-2929
Phone: 612-626-9111 (Help Line)
Fax: 612-626-9933
Website: www1.umn.edu/aurora
E-mail: aurora@umn.edu

Information in this chapter was compiled from sources deemed accurate. All contact information was verified and updated in January 2016.

579

Break the Cycle
5777 W. Century Blvd.
Ste. 1150
Los Angeles, CA 90045
Phone: 310-286-3383
Fax: 310-286-3386
Website: www.breakthecycle.org
E-mail: info@breakthecycle.org

Centers for Disease Control and Prevention (CDC) National Center for Injury Prevention and Control (NCIPC)
4770 Buford Hwy N.E.
MS F-63
Atlanta, GA 30341-3717
Toll-Free: 800-CDC-INFO
(800-232-4636)
Toll-Free TTY: 888-232-6348
Website: www.cdc.gov
E-mail: cdcinfo@cdc.gov

Centre for Research and Education on Violence Against Women and Children
1137 Western Rd.
Rm. 1118
London, Ontario N6G 1G7
Canada
Phone: 519-661-4040
Fax: 519-850-2464
Website: www.
learningtoendabuse.ca

Child Witness to Violence Project
Website: www.
childwitnesstoviolence.org

Corporate Alliance to End Partner Violence
2416 E. Washington St.
Ste. E
Bloomington, IL 61704
Phone: 309-664-0667
Fax: 309-664-0747
Website: www.caepv.org
E-mail: caepv@caepv.org

FaithTrust Institute
2900 Eastlake Ave. E.
Ste. 200
Seattle, WA 98102
Phone: 206-634-1903
Fax: 206-634-0115
Website: www.
faithtrustinstitute.org

Florida Council Against Sexual Violence
1820 E. Park Ave.
Ste. 100
Tallahassee, FL 32301
Phone: 850-297-2000
Fax: 850-297-2002
Toll-Free: 888-956-7273
Website: www.fcasv.org
E-mail: information@fcasv.org

Futures Without Violence
100 Montgomery St.
San Francisco, CA 94129
Phone: 415-678-5500
Fax: 415-529-2930
Toll-Free TTY: 800-595-4889
Website: www.
futureswithoutviolence.org

Gay Men's Domestic Violence Project
955 Massachusetts Ave.
PMB 131
Cambridge, MA 02139
Phone: 617-354-6056
Fax: 617-354-6072
Toll-Free: 800-832-1901 (Hotline)
Website: www.glbtqdvp.org
E-mail: support@gmdvp.org

Houston Area Women's Center
1010 Waugh Dr.
Houston, TX 77019
Phone: 713-528-2121 (Domestic Violence Hotline)
Phone: 713-528-7273 (Sexual Assault Hotline)
Toll-Free: 800-256-0551 (Domestic Violence Hotline)
Toll-Free: 800-256-0661 (Sexual Assault Hotline)
TDD: 713-528-3625 (Domestic Violence Hotline)
TDD: 713-528-3691 (Sexual Assault Hotline)
Website: www.hawc.org

Institute on Domestic Violence in the African American Community University of Minnesota School of Social Work
290 Peters Hall
1404 Gortner Ave.
St. Paul, MN 55108-6142
Phone: 612-624-5357
Fax: 612-624-9201
Toll-Free: 877-643-8222
Website: www.idvaac.org
E-mail: info@idvaac.org

Loveisrespect.org
Toll-Free: 866-331-9474
Toll-Free TTY: 866-331-8453
Website: www.loveisrespect.org

Minnesota Coalition for Battered Women
60 E. Plato Blvd.
Ste. 130
St. Paul, MN 55107
Phone: 651-646-6177
Fax: 651-646-1527
Toll-Free: 800-289-6177
Website: www.mcbw.org

Muslim Advocacy Network Against Domestic Violence (MANADV)
Peaceful Families Project
P.O. Box 771
Great Falls, VA 22066
Phone: 703-474-6870
Website: www.api-gbv.org/organizing/manadv.php
E-mail: info@manadv.org or info@peacefulfamilies.org

National Center for Victims of Crime
2000 M St.
N.W. Ste. 480
Washington, DC 20036
Phone: 202-467-8700
Fax: 202-467-8701
Website: www.victimsofcrime.org

National Center on Domestic and Sexual Violence
4612 Shoal Creek Blvd.
Austin, TX 78756
Phone/Fax: 512-407-9020
Phone: 206-787-3224 (Video Phone Hotline)
Toll-Free: 800-799-SAFE
(800-799-7233)
Toll-Free TTY: 800-787-3224
Website: www.ncdsv.org

National Coalition Against Domestic Violence
One Broadway
Ste. B210
Denver, CO 80203
Phone: 303-839-1852
Fax: 303-831-9251
TTY: 303-839-8459
Website: www.ncadv.org
E-mail: mainoffice@ncadv.org

National Council on Child Abuse & Family Violence
1025 Connecticut Ave. N.W.
Ste. 1000
Washington, DC 20036
Phone: 202-429-6695
Fax: 202-521-3479
Website: www.nccafv.org
E-mail: info@nccafv.org

National Crime Prevention Council
2001 Jefferson Davis Hwy
Ste. 901
Arlington, VA 22202
Phone: 202-466-6272
Fax: 202-296-1356
Website: www.ncpc.org

National Latino Alliance for the Elimination of Domestic Violence (Alianza)
Phone: 505-753-3334
Fax: 505-753-3347
Website: www.dvalianza.org
E-mail: info@dvalianza.org

National Network to End Domestic Violence
2001 S. St.
N.W. Ste. 400
Washington, DC 20009
Phone: 202-543-5566
Fax: 202-543-5626
Website: nnedv.org

National Resource Center on Domestic Violence
Website: www.nrcdv.org

New York City Alliance Against Sexual Assault
32 Broadway
Ste. 1101
New York, NY 10004
Phone: 212-229-0345
Fax: 212-229-0676 fax
Website: www.svfreenyc.org
E-mail: contact-us@svfreenyc.org

New York State Coalition Against Domestic Violence
350 New Scotland Ave.
Albany, NY 12208
Phone: 518-482-5465
Fax: 518-482-3807
Toll-Free: 800-942-6906
(Hotline)
Toll-Free TTY: 800-942-6906
(Hotline)
Website: nyscadv.org
E-mail: nyscadv@nyscadv.org

New York State Office for the Prevention of Domestic Violence
Alfred E. Smith Bldg., 80 S. Swan St.
11th Fl., Rm. No. 1157
Albany, NY 12210
Phone: 518-457-5800
Fax: 518-457-5810
Website: www.opdv.ny.gov

Peaceful Families Project
P.O. Box 771
Great Falls, VA 22066
Phone: 703-474-6870
Website: www.peacefulfamilies.org
E-mail: info@peacefulfamilies.org

Rape, Abuse & Incest National Network (RAINN)
2000 L St. N.W.
Ste. 406
Washington, DC 20036
Phone: 202-544-1034
Fax: 202-544-3556
Toll-Free: 800-656-HOPE
(800-656-4673)
Website: www.rainn.org
E-mail: info@rainn.org

South Carolina Coalition Against Domestic Violence and Sexual Assault
P.O. Box 7776
Columbia, SC 29202
Phone: 803-256-2900
Website: www.sccadvasa.org

Stop Abuse For Everyone
10030 Scenic View Terr.
Vienna, VA 22182
Phone: 503-853-8686
Website: www.stopabuseforeveryone.org
E-mail: safe@safe4all.org

U.S. Department of Health and Human Services Office on Women's Health
200 Independence Ave., S.W.
Washington, DC 20201
Phone: 202-690-7650
Fax: 202-205-2631
Website: www.womenshealth.gov/index.php

Washington State Coalition Against Domestic Violence (WSCADV)
1402 Third Ave.
Ste. 406
Seattle, WA 98101
Phone: 206-389-2515
Fax: 206-389-2520
TTY: 206-389-2900
Website: www.wscadv.org
E-mail: wscadv@wscadv.org

Women's Justice Center
P.O. Box 7510
Santa Rosa, CA 95407
Phone: 707-575-3150
Website: www.justicewomen.com
E-mail: rdjustice@monitor.net

Child Abuse

Child Welfare Information Gateway
Children's Bureau/ACYF
1250 Maryland Ave.
S.W. Eighth Fl.
Washington, DC 20024
Toll-Free: 800-394-3366
Website: www.childwelfare.gov
E-mail: info@childwelfare.gov

Child Witness to Violence Project
Department of Pediatrics
Boston Medical Center
88 E. Newton St., Vose Hall
Boston, MA 02118
Phone: 617-414-4244
Website: www.
childwitnesstoviolence.org

National Children's Advocacy Center
210 Pratt Ave.
Huntsville, AL 35801
Phone: 256-533-KIDS
(256-533-5437)
Fax: 256-534-6883
Website: www.nationalcac.org

Elder Abuse

Clearinghouse on Abuse and Neglect of the Elderly (CANE)
University of Delaware
Department of Consumer Studies
Alison Hall W.
Rm. 211
Newark, DE 19716
Website: www.cane.udel.edu
E-mail: CANE-UD@udel.edu

National Center on Elder Abuse
National Association of State
Units on Aging
University of California—Irvine
Program in Geriatric Medicine
1000 S. Fremont Ave.
Ste. 22 Bldg. A-6
Alhambra, CA 91803
Fax: 626-457-4090
Toll-Free: 855-500-ELDR
(855-500-3537)
Website: www.ncea.aoa.gov
E-mail: ncea-info@aoa.hhs.gov

National Clearinghouse on Abuse in Later Life
307 S. Paterson St.
Ste. 1
Madison, WI 53703-3517
Phone: 608-255-0539
TTY/Fax: 608-255-3560
Website: www.ncall.us
E-mail: ncall@wcadv.org

National Committee for the Prevention of Elder Abuse (NCPEA)
1730 Rhode Island Ave.
N.W. Ste. 1200
Washington, DC 20036
Phone: 202-464-9481
Fax: 202-872-0057
Website: www.
preventelderabuse.org
E-mail: info@preventelderabuse.
org

Chapter 49

Domestic Violence Hotlines

National Domestic Abuse Hotlines

National Domestic Violence Hotline
Toll-Free: 800-799-SAFE (800-799-7233)
TTY: 800-787-3224

Rape, Abuse, and Incest National Network (RAINN)
National Hotline
Toll-Free: 800-656-HOPE (800-656-4673)

Safe Horizon Domestic Violence Hotline
Toll-Free: 800-621-HOPE (800-621-4673)

Domestic Violence Hotlines by State

If your state is not listed below, call the National Domestic Violence Hotline (listed above).

Alabama Coalition Against Domestic Violence
Toll-Free: 800-650-6522

Alaska Network on Domestic Violence and Sexual Assault
Phone: 907-586-3650

Information in this chapter was compiled from sources deemed accurate. All contact information was verified and updated in January 2016.

Arizona Coalition Against Domestic Violence
Toll-Free: 800-782-6400
TTY: 602-279-7270

Arkansas Coalition Against Domestic Violence
Toll-Free: 800-269-4668

California—Support Network for Battered Women
Toll-Free: 800-572-2782

Florida Coalition Against Domestic Violence
Toll-Free: 800-500-1119 (Florida callers only)
TTY: 800-621-4202

Hawaii State Coalition Against Domestic Violence
Toll-Free: 808-832-9316

Iowa Coalition Against Domestic Violence
Toll-Free: 800-942-0333

Idaho Coalition Against Sexual and Domestic Violence
Toll-Free: 800-669-3176

Kansas
Toll-Free: 888-END-ABUSE (888-363-2287) (Kansas callers only)

Maine Coalition to End Domestic Violence
Toll-Free: 866-834-HELP (866-834-4357) (Maine callers only)

Massachusetts
Toll-Free: 877-785-2020

Minnesota Day One Domestic Violence Crisis Line
Toll-Free: 866-223-1111

Mississippi State Coalition Against Domestic Violence
Toll-Free: 800-898-3234 (Mon-Fri 8 a.m.–5 p.m.) (Mississippi callers only)

New Hampshire Coalition Against Domestic and Sexual Violence
Toll-Free: 866-644-3574
Toll-Free: 800-277-5570 (Sexual Assault)

New York State Coalition Against Domestic Violence
Toll-Free (English): 800-942-6906
TTY (English): 800-818-0656
Toll-Free (Spanish): 800-942-6908
TTY (Spanish): 800-780-7660

North Dakota Council on Abused Women's Services
Toll-Free: 800-472-2911 (North Dakota callers only)

Ohio Domestic Violence Network
Toll-Free: 800-934-9840

Oregon Coalition Against Domestic Violence and Sexual Assault
Toll-Free: 888-235-5333 (Statewide Crisis Center)

Rhode Island Coalition Against Domestic Violence
Toll-Free: 800-494-8100

South Dakota Coalition Against Domestic Violence and Sexual Assault
Toll-Free: 800-572-9196

Utah LINK Line
Toll-Free: 800-897-LINK (800-897-5465)

Vermont Network Against Domestic and Sexual Violence
Toll-Free: 800-228-7395 (Domestic Violence)
Toll-Free: 800-489-7273 (Sexual Violence)

Virginia Family Violence and Sexual Assault Hotline
Toll-Free: 800-838-VADV (800-838-8238)

Washington State Domestic Violence Hotline
Toll-Free: 800-562-6025

Elder Abuse Resources

Eldercare Locator
Toll-Free: 800-677-1116
TTY: 800-677-1116
Website: http://www.eldercare.gov/ELDERCARE.NET/Public/About/
Services.aspx
E-mail: eldercarelocator@n4a.org

Elder Abuse Resources by State
For state reporting numbers, government agencies, state laws,
state-specific data and statistics, and other resources, visit
http://www.ncea.aoa.gov/Stop_Abuse/Get_Help/State/index.aspx.

Chapter 50

State Child Abuse Reporting Numbers

Alabama
Alabama Department of Human
Resources (DHR)
Phone: 334-242-9500
Website: dhr.alabama.gov/
services/Child_Protective_
Services/Abuse_Neglect_
Reporting.aspx

Alaska
Alaska Office of Children's
Services
Toll-Free: 800-478-4444
Website: dhss.alaska.gov/ocs/
Pages/default.aspx

Arizona
Arizona Department of
Economic Security
Phone: 602-252-4045
Toll-Free: 800-882-4151
Website: des.az.gov/services/
child-and-family/arizona-child-
support-services-home-page

Arkansas
Arkansas Department of Human
Services
Toll-Free: 800-482-5964
Website: access.arkansas.gov/
Voter.aspx

California
California Department of Social
Services
Toll-Free: 800-540-4000
Website: www.dss.cahwnet.gov/
cdssweb/PG20.htm

Information in this chapter was compiled from sources deemed accurate. All
contact information was verified and updated in January 2016.

Connecticut
Connecticut Department of Children and Families
Toll-Free: 800-842-2288
Toll-Free TDD: 800-624-5518
Website: www.ct.gov/dcf/site/default.asp

Delaware
Department of Services for Children, Youth and their Families
Toll-Free: 800-292-9582
Website: kids.delaware.gov/services/crisis.shtml

District of Columbia
Child and Family Services Agency
Phone: 202-442-6100
Fax: 202-727-6505
Website: cfsa.dc.gov/service/working-child-welfare

Georgia
Division of Family and Children Services (DFCS)
Toll-Free: 855-GACHILD (855-422-4453)
Website: dfcs.dhs.georgia.gov/child-abuse-neglect

Hawaii
Hawaii Department of Human Services
Phone: 808-832-5300
Toll-Free: 800-494-3991
Website: humanservices.hawaii.gov

Idaho
Idaho Department of Health and Welfare
Phone: 208-334-KIDS (208-334-5437)
Toll-Free: 855-552-KIDS (855-552-5437)
TDD: 208-332-7205
Website: healthandwelfare.idaho.gov/Children/AbuseNeglect/ChildProtection ContactPhoneNumbers/tabid/475/Default.aspx

Illinois
Illinois Department of Children and Family Services
Phone: 217-785-4020
Toll-Free: 800-25-ABUSE (800-252-2873)
Website: www.illinois.gov/dcfs/Pages/default.aspx

Indiana
Indiana Department of Child Services
Toll-Free: 800-800-5556
Website: www.in.gov/dcs/2372.htm

Iowa
Iowa Department of Human Services
Toll-Free: 800-362-2178
Website: dhs.iowa.gov/child-welfare/differential-response

Kansas
Kansas Department of Children and Families
Toll-Free: 800-922-5330
Website: www.dcf.ks.gov/Pages/Default.aspx

Kentucky
Cabinet for Health and Family
Services (CHFS)
Toll-Free: 877-KYSAFE1
(877-597-2331)
Website: chfs.ky.gov/dcbs/dpp/
childsafety.htm

Louisiana
Department of Children &
Family Services
Toll-Free: 855-4LA-KIDS
(855-452-5437)
Website: dss.louisiana.gov/
index.cfm?md=pagebuilder&
tmp=home&pid=109

Maine
Maine Department of Health
and Human Services
Toll-Free: 800-452-1999
Toll-Free TTY: 800-963-9490
Website: www.maine.gov/
dhhs/ocfs/hotlines.htm

Maryland
Maryland Department of
Human Resources (DHR)
Toll-Free: 800-332-6347
Toll-Free TTY: 800-925-4434
Website: www.dhr.state.md.us/
blog/?page_id=3957

Massachusetts
Massachusetts Bureau of Family
Health and Nutrition
Toll-Free: 800-332-2733
Website: www.mass.gov/eohhs/
gov/departments/dph/programs/
family-health/perinatal-early-
childhood-special-health-needs.
html

Michigan
Michigan Department of Health
& Human Service
Phone: 517-373-3740
Toll-Free: 855-444-3911
Website: www.michigan.
gov/mdhhs/0,5885,7-339-
73971_7119---,00.html

Minnesota
Minnesota Department of
Human Services
Phone: 651-431-2700
Toll-Free: 800-366-5411
Website: www.dhs.state.mn.us/
main/idcplg?IdcService=
GET_DYNAMIC_
CONVERSION
&RevisionSelection
Method=Latest
Released&dDocName=id_000152

Missouri
Missouri Department of Social
Services
Phone: 573-751-3448
Toll-Free: 800-392-3738
Website: dss.mo.gov/cd/can.htm

Montana
Montana Child and Family
Services Division (CFSD)
Toll-Free: 866-820-5437
Website: dphhs.mt.gov/cfsd/index

Nebraska
Nebraska Division of Children
and Family Services (DCFS)
Phone: 402-471-9272
Toll-Free: 800-652-1999
Website: dhhs.ne.gov/children_
family_services/Pages/children_
family_services.aspx

New Hampshire
New Hampshire Division for
Children, Youth & Families
Phone: 603-271-6562
Fax: 603-271-6565 (Report Child
Abuse Fax)
Toll-Free: 800-894-5533
Toll-Free TDD: 800-735-2964
Website: www.dhhs.state.nh.us/
dcyf/cps/contact.htm

New Jersey
New Jersey Department of
Children and Families
Toll-Free: 855-INFO-DCF
(855-463-6323)
Toll-Free TDD/TTY:
800-835-5510
Website: www.state.nj.us/dcf

New Mexico
New Mexico Children, Youth
and Families Department
Toll-Free: 855-333-SAFE
(855-333-7233)
Website: cyfd.org/
child-abuse-neglect

New York
New York Office of Children and
Family Services
Phone: 518-473-7793
Toll-Free: 800-342-3720
Toll-Free TDD/TTY:
800-638-5163
Website: ocfs.ny.gov/main/cps/
Default.asp

North Carolina
North Carolina Department of
Health & Human Services
Toll-Free: 877-362-8471
Website: www.ncdhhs.gov/dss/
cps/index.htm

North Dakota
North Dakota Department of
Human Services
Phone: 701-328-2310
Toll-Free: 800-472-2622
Website: www.nd.gov/
dhs/services/childfamily/
cps/#reporting

Ohio
Ohio's Public Children Services
Agencies (PCSAs)
Toll-Free: 855-OH-CHILD
(855-642-4453)
Website: jfs.ohio.gov/ocf/
childprotectiveservices.stm

Oklahoma
Oklahoma Department of
Human services
Toll-Free: 800-522-3511
Website: www.okdhs.org/Pages/
default.aspx

Oregon
Oregon Department of Human
Services
Toll-Free: 855-503-SAFE
(855-503-7233)
Website: www.oregon.gov/DHS/
children/abuse/cps/report.shtml

Pennsylvania
Pennsylvania Department of
Human Services
Phone: 717-783-1964
Toll-Free: 800-932-0313
Toll-Free TDD: 866-872-1677
Website: www.dhs.pa.gov

Rhode Island
Rhode Island Department of Children, Youth & Family
Phone: 401-528-3502
Toll-Free: 800-RI-CHILD (800-742-4453)
Website: www.dcyf.ri.gov/child_care.php

South Carolina
South Carolina Department of Social Services
Phone: 803-898-7601
Toll-Free: 800-422-4453
Website: dss.sc.gov

South Dakota
South Dakota Department of Social Services
Phone: 605-773-3165
Toll-Free: 800-227-3020
Website: dss.sd.gov/childcare

Tennessee
Department of Children's Services
Toll-Free: 877-237-0004 or 877-54ABUSE (877-542-2873)
Website: apps.tn.gov/carat

Utah
Utah Child & Family Services
Toll-Free: 855-323-DCFS (855-323-3237)
Website: dcfs.utah.gov

Vermont
Vermont Department for Children and Families
Toll-Free: 800-649-5285
Website: dcf.vermont.gov/protection

Virginia
Virginia Department of Social Services (VDSS)
Phone: 804-786-8536
Toll-Free: 800-552-7096
Website: www.dss.virginia.gov/family/cps/index.html

Washington
Washington Department of Social and Health Services
Toll-Free: 866-ENDHARM (866-363-4276) or 800-562-5624
Toll-Free TTY: 800-624-6186
Website: www.dshs.wa.gov/ca/child-safety-and-protection/how-report-child-abuse-or-neglect?2=

West Virginia
West Virginia Bureau for Children and Families
Toll-Free: 800-352-6513
Website: www.dhhr.wv.gov/bcf/Pages/default.aspx

Wisconsin
Wisconsin Department of Children and Families
Phone: 608-267-3905
Fax: 608-266-6836
Website: dcf.wisconsin.gov/children/CPS/cpswimap.HTM

Wyoming
Wyoming Department of Family Services
Phone: 307-777-5536
Fax: 307-777-3693
Website: dfsweb.wyo.gov/social-services/child-protective-services

Chapter 51

Programs Providing Shelter for Pets of Domestic Violence Victims

Alabama
Mobile County Animal Shelter
7665 Howells Ferry Rd.
Mobile, AL 36618
Phone: 251-574-3647
Fax: 251-574-6441
Website: www.mobilecountyal.
gov/animals/animal-services.html

Arizona
City of Mesa Animal Control
20 E. Main St., Ste. 250
Mesa, AZ 85201
Phone: 480-644-2268
Fax: 480-644-4994
Website: www.mesaaz.gov/
residents/animal-control
E-mail: animalcontrol.info@
mesaaz.gov

Pinal County Animal Control
1150 S. Eleven Mile Corner
Casa Grande, AZ 85194
Phone: 520-509-3555
Fax: 520-866-7610
Website: pinalcountyaz.gov/
animalcontrol/pages/home.aspx
E-mail: AnimalCare@
pinalcountyaz.gov

California
Assistance Dog Special
Allowance (ADSA)
744 P St.
Sacramento, CA 95814
Phone: 916-657-2628
Fax: 916-653-4001
Website: www.cdss.ca.gov
E-mail: ADSAUser@dss.ca.gov

Information in this chapter was compiled from sources deemed accurate. All contact information was verified and updated in January 2016.

Auburn Animal Shelter
11251 B Ave.
Auburn, CA 95603
Phone: 530-886-5500
Fax: 530-886-5538
Website: www.placer.ca.gov
E-mail: ANSInfo@placer.ca.gov

The County of Los Angeles
Department of Animal Care and
Control
5898 Cherry Ave.
Long Beach, CA 90805
Phone: 562-728-4882
Fax: 562-422-3408
Website: animalcare.lacounty.
gov

Eastern Placer County Animal
Shelter
10961 Stevens Ln.
Truckee, CA 96161
Phone: 530-546-1990
Website: www.placer.ca.gov
E-mail: ANSInfo@placer.ca.gov

Long Beach Animal Care
Services
7700 E. Spring St.
Long Beach, CA 90815
Phone: 562-570-7387
Website: www.longbeach.gov/acs

Riverside City/County Animal
Shelter
3900 Main St. – 4th Fl.
Riverside, CA 92522
Phone: 951-826-5341
Website: www.riversideca.gov

Victorville Animal Control
14206 Amargosa Rd.
Victorville, CA 92392
Phone: 760-955-5089
Website: www.victorvilleca.gov/
animalcontrol.aspx
E-mail: animalcontrol@
ci.victorville.ca.us

Colorado

Centennial Animal Services
7272 S. Eagle St.
Centennial, CO 80112
Phone: 303-325-8070
Fax: 303-325-8079
Website: www.centennialco.gov/
Animal-Services
E-mail: CAS@CentennialCO.gov

Firestone Animal Control
151 Grant Ave.
Firestone, CO 80520
Phone: 303-833-0811
Fax: 303-531-6271
Website: www.firestoneco.gov/
animalcontrol
E-mail: mpowers@firestoneco.
gov

Florida

Miami-Dade County Animal
Services
7401 N.W. 74 St.
Medley, FL 33166
Phone: 305-884-1101
Fax: 305-805-1619
Website: www.miamidade.gov/
animals
E-mail: asdlostandfound@
miamidade.gov

Seminole County Animal
Services
232 Bush Blvd.
Sanford, FL 32773
Phone: 407-665-5201
Website: www.seminolecountyfl.
gov/departments-services/
public-safety/animal-services
E-mail: bhunter@
seminolecountyfl.gov

Georgia

Augusta Animal Services
4164 Mack Ln.
Augusta, GA 30906
Phone: 706-790-6836
Fax: 706-798-8978
Website: www.augustaga.
gov/586/Animal-Services

Fayette County Animal Shelter
1262 Hwy 74 S.
Peachtree City, GA 30269
Phone: 770-631-7210
Website: www.fayettecountyga.
gov/animal_control/index.htm
E-mail: rrathburn@
fayettecountyga.gov

Gilmer County Animal Shelter
4152 Hwy 52 E.
Ellijay, GA 30540
Phone: 706-635-2166
Website: www.gilmercounty-ga.
gov/departments/animal-shelter.
aspx

Indiana

Bloomington Animal Shelter
3410 S. Walnut St.
Bloomington, IN 47401
Phone: 812-349-3492
Fax: 812-349-3440
Website: bloomington.in.gov/
documents/viewDocument.
php?document_id=70
E-mail: animal@bloomington.
in.gov

Columbus Animal Shelter
2730 Arnold Dr.
Columbus, IN 47203
Phone: 812-376-2505
Website: www.columbus.in.gov/
animal-care-services

South Bend Animal Care and
Control
521 Eclipse Pl.
South Bend, IN 46628
Phone: 574-235-9303
Website: southbendin.
gov/government/division/
animal-care-control

Kansas

Wichita Animal Shelter
3303 N. Hillside St.
Wichita, KS 67219
Phone: 316-350-3366
Website: www.wichita.gov/
Government/Departments/WPD/
Pages/AnimalControl.aspx
E-mail: AnimalControl@wichita.
gov

Maryland
Baltimore County Animal
Services
13800 Manor Rd.
Baldwin, MD 21013
Phone: 410-887-PAWS
(410-887-7297)
Fax: 410-817-4257
Website: www.
baltimorecountymd.gov/
Agencies/health/animalservices
E-mail: animalservices@
baltimorecountymd.gov

Frederick County Animal
Control
1832 Rosemont Ave.
Frederick, MD 21702
Phone: 301-600-1546
Fax: 301-600-1547
Website: frederickcountymd.
gov/15/Animal-Control

Montgomery County Animal
Services & Adoption Center
7315 Muncaster Mill Rd.
Derwood, MD 20855
Phone: 240-773-5900
Fax: 301-279-1063
Website: www.
montgomerycountymd.gov/
animalservices

Missouri
City of St. Louis Animal Care
and Control
2801 Clark Ave.
St. Louis, MO 63103
Phone: 314-657-1500
Fax: 314-612-5367
Website: www.stlouis-mo.gov/
government/departments/health/
animal-care-control

Jefferson City Animal Shelter
2308 Hyde Park Rd.
Jefferson City, MO 65109
Phone: 573-634-6429
Fax: 573-659-8209
Website: www.jeffersoncitymo.
gov/government/animal_control

Nebraska
City of Lincoln Animal Control
3140 N. St.
Lincoln, NE 68510
Phone: 402-441-7900
Fax: 402-441-8626
Website: lincoln.ne.gov/city/
health/animal
E-mail: animal@lincoln.ne.gov

New Jersey
Gloucester County Animal
Shelter
1200 N. Delsea Dr.
Clayton, NJ 08312
Phone: 856-881-2828
Fax: 856-881-0538
Website: www.
gloucestercountynj.gov/depts/a/
shelter
E-mail: gcas@co.gloucester.nj.us

New Mexico
City of Albuquerque Animal
Welfare
8920 Lomas N.E.
Albuquerque, NM 87112
Phone: 505-768-2000
Website: www.cabq.gov/pets

Ohio

Lake County Dog Shelter
2600 N. Ridge Rd.
Painesville, OH 44077
Phone: 440-350-2640
Fax: 440-350-2600
Website: www.lakecountyohio.
gov/dogs/dogshelterhome.aspx

Pennsylvania

City Of Pittsburgh Animal Care
and Control
3001 RailRoad St.
Pittsburgh, PA 15201
Phone: 412-255-2935
Website: pittsburghpa.gov/
animalcontrol
E-mail: ACC@pittsburghpa.gov

Texas

Arlington Animal Services
1000 S.E. Green Oaks Blvd.
Arlington, TX 76018
Phone: 817-459-5898
Fax: 817-459-5698
Website: www.arlington-tx.gov/
animals
E-mail: animalservices@
arlingtontx.gov

Austin Animal Center
7201 Levander Loop Bldg. A
Austin, TX 78702
Phone: 512-978-0500
Website: www.austintexas.gov/
department/animal-services

Collin County Animal Services
4750 Community Ave.
McKinney, TX 75071
Phone: 972-547-7292
Fax: 972-547-7290
Website: www.collincountytx.
gov/animal_services
E-mail: animalshelter@
collincountytx.gov

Fort Worth Animal Care and
Control Shelter
4900 Martin St.
Fort Worth, TX 76119
Phone: 817-392-1234
Website: fortworthtexas.gov/
animals

Midland Animal Shelter
1200 N. Fairgrounds Rd.
Midland, TX 79710
Phone: 432-685-7420
Website: www.midlandtexas.
gov/391/Animal-Services
E-mail: poneill@midlandtexas.
gov

Virginia

Fairfax County Animal Shelter
4500 W. Ox Rd.
Fairfax, VA 22030
Phone: 703-830-1100
Website: www.fairfaxcounty.gov/
animalshelter

Orange County Animal Shelter
11362 Porter Rd.
Orange, VA 22960
Phone: 540-672-1124
Fax: 540-672-7047
Website: orangecountyva.gov/
index.aspx?nid=158
E-mail: vstrong@
orangecountyva.gov

Washington

Clark County Animal and Pets
1300 Franklin St.
Vancouver, WA 98660
Phone: 360-397-2489
Website: www.clark.wa.gov/
community-development/
animals-and-pets
E-mail: animal@clark.wa.gov

King County Animal Control
21615 64th Ave. S.
Kent, WA 98032
Phone: 206-296-7387
Website: rentonwa.gov/living/
default.aspx?id=44

Index

Index

603